RUSSIAN ORIENTALISM

RUSSIAN ORIENTALISM

Asia in the
Russian Mind from
Peter the Great to the
Emigration

David
Schimmelpenninck
van der Oye

Yale UNIVERSITY PRESS
New Haven & London

Published with assistance from the foundation established in
memory of Calvin Chapin of the Class of 1788, Yale College.

Set in Galliard type by The Composing Room of Michigan, Inc.
Printed in the United States of America.

Library of Congress Cataloging-in-Publication Data
Schimmelpenninck van der Oye, David.
   Russian orientalism : Asia in the Russian mind from Peter the
Great to the emigration / David Schimmelpenninck van der Oye.
      p.   cm.
   Includes bibliographical references and index.

   ISBN 978-0-300-11063-0 (hardcover : alk. paper)   1. Orientalism
—Russia—History.   2. Asia—Study and teaching—Russia.
3. Russia—Intellectual life—18th century.   4. Russia—Intellectual
life—1801–1917.   5. Asia—Foreign public opinion, Russian.
6. Public opinion—Russia—History.   7. Russia—Relations—Asia.
8. Asia—Relations—Russia.   I. Title.
   DS32.9.R9S35   2010
   303.48'247050903—dc22

                                                    2009033262

A catalogue record for this book is available from the British Library.

This paper meets the requirements of ANSI/NISO Z39.48-1992
(Permanence of Paper).

10 9 8 7 6 5 4 3 2 1

Pour Marie

CONTENTS

PREFACE

This book resulted from conversations I had with Jonathan Brent, editorial director at Yale University Press, when I was a graduate student. I was trying to convince him of the merits of publishing my thesis about the origins of the Russo-Japanese War, which I was then writing. My suggestion fell on deaf, albeit polite, ears, and the book eventually appeared with another press. However, about two years later, Jonathan asked me if I would like to undertake a more general study about how Russians have thought about Asia. It was an offer I could not refuse.

As someone who grew up during the Cold War, I have long been intrigued by the nature of Russia's identity. Living in Rotterdam in the early 1960s, I found it easy to imagine another assault from the East twenty years after the previous one. And, as my grandmother once joked, Asia begins just past Venlo (a small town on the German border). As a boy I therefore readily believed that Napoleon was right about what scratching a Russian will reveal about the latter's true essence. I outgrew such stereotypes long ago. However, I remain fascinated by how they came about. More important, how do Russians themselves think about such matters? In a sense, this book is an exploration of these questions.

I am fortunate to have worked at a university that has encouraged my peculiar academic pursuits. In addition to being a most congenial environment for scholarship, Brock University also generously funded my research, including a munificent three-year Chancellor's Chair of Research

Excellence. I also benefited enormously from a Social Science and Humanities Research Council of Canada Standard Research Grant. Together, these awards enabled me to spend over half a year in Russia and Finland to carry out my research. A short-term grant from the Kennan Institute also funded work at the Library of Congress. I began writing this book in 2003 as a fellow at the National Humanities Center in Research Triangle Park, North Carolina, for which I am grateful as well.

A book like this could not have been undertaken without the hospitality many libraries extended to me. These included Sterling Memorial Library, the New York Public Library (its Slavic and Baltic Reading Room will be sorely missed), the Robarts Library, the Russian State Library (a.k.a. "Leninka"), the Russian National Library ("Publichka"), the library of the St. Petersburg Branch of the Oriental Institute, Kazan University's library, and, of course, the Slavonic Library in Helsinki—the most idyllic haven for studying Imperial Russia's past. Brock's remarkable Inter-Library Loan Department was able to track down much of what I neglected to read when I was abroad.

Portions of this book appeared originally in *Ab Imperio, Comparative Studies of South Asia, Africa and the Middle East,* and *The International Journal,* as well as in the following edited volumes: William Leatherbarrow and Derrek Offord, eds., *A History of Russian Thought;* Michael David-Fox et al., eds., *Orientalism and Empire in Russia;* Svetlana Gorshenina and Sergej Abashin, eds., *Le Turkestan russe colonial;* and I. Gerasimov et al., eds., *Novaia imperskaia istoriia postsovetskoro prostranstvo* (A New Imperial History of the post-Soviet space). They are republished here with the kind permission of their editors.

Although it has been years since I was a student, my teachers—in particular Paul Bushkovitch—continue to be generous with their help. I have also pestered many other scholars and friends and remain thankful that they did not flee when I asked for their advice: Oleg Airapetov, Volodya Alexandrov, Sasha Andreev, Wladimir Berelowitch, Nikos Chrissidis, Micha David-Fox, Laura Engelstein, Lee Farrow, Tatiana Filippova, Liudmilla Gatagova, Bernice Glatzer Rosenthal, Charles Halperin, Valerie Hansen, Leonid Heller, Nathan Hunt, Maija Jansson, Edward Kasinec, Aleksandr Kavtaradze, Micha Kemper, Nathaniel Knight, Marlène Laruelle, John LeDonne, Dominic Lieven, Ralph Locke, Tania Lorkovic, Irina

Lukka, Maureen Lux, Suzanne Marchand, Lorraine de Meaux, Bruce Menning, Irina Rybachenok, Mikhail Ryzhenkov, John Sainsbury, Elizabeth Sauer, Dany Savelli, Jennifer Siegel, Jonathan Spence, Jennifer Spock, John Steinberg, Mark Steinberg, Richard Stites, David Stone, Vera Tolz, Elizabeth Valkenier, Lynne Viola, Paul Werth, Cynthia Whittaker, and David Wolff.

I knew that it was time to complete this book when my daughter, Esmée, then aged five, innocently asked me on the eve of my departure for a conference: "Papa, will this help you to finish it?" She and her brother, Sacha, remain a source of loving encouragement, as is my bride, Marie. It is to her I dedicate this book.

NOTE ON DATES AND TRANSLITERATIONS

Dates are according to the Julian calendar, which was used in Imperial Russia. In the nineteenth century, this calendar was twelve days behind the Gregorian calendar commonly employed in the West, whereas in the twentieth century it followed by thirteen days. For example, when Russians in St. Petersburg celebrated the New Year on January 1, 1895, it was already January 13, 1895, in Paris and London.

Transliterations from the Cyrillic alphabet adhere to the Library of Congress system, except for names and words widely known in English by other spellings. Thus, for example, I use Alexander III and Nicholas II, rather than Aleksandr III and Nikolai II. Where Russian surnames were adapted from German or other Western languages, I generally use the original.

Unless otherwise indicated, translations from European languages are my own.

INTRODUCTION: WHAT IS
RUSSIAN ORIENTALISM?

I am Asian too.

—Joseph Stalin

The Age of Exploration some five hundred years ago was one of
European geography's most important epochs. Beginning in the late fifteenth century, captains, merchants, and other adventurers burst free from
their small continent and journeyed the globe, bringing back reports of entirely new worlds with fabled riches and wondrous inhabitants. The Portuguese navigator Bartolomeu Dias first rounded the Cape of Good Hope,
while his compatriots Vasco da Gama and Ferdinand Magellan did much
to chart the Pacific Ocean. Others, like Christopher Columbus and John
Cabot, found enormous realms across the Atlantic.

One of the lands Europe "discovered" in those years was Russia.
"Scythia" or "Sarmatia," as fifteenth-century geographers still often called
Muscovy, was not entirely alien to the medieval West.[1] Hanseatic merchants had long traded with Novgorod and other Russian cities. The Teutonic Order, Sweden, and Poland also had occasion to deal with their
eastern neighbor, while from the 1470s Moscow's tsars periodically invited
Italian artists and architects to their capital for important commissions.
However, none of these individuals seemed to tell their compatriots much
about Russia when they returned from their visits.[2] Muscovy truly entered
into the educated Europeans' consciousness only in the sixteenth century,

when more curious and perceptive men, such as the Habsburg diplomat Baron Sigismund von Herberstein and the Englishmen Sir Richard Chancellor and Giles Fletcher, began to write about it.[3]

While the Renaissance's scientific standards were a dramatic improvement over those of the Middle Ages, its ethnography left much to be desired. The preconceptions Europeans held about the people who inhabited alien lands could be nearly as fantastic and false as the bizarre portraits compiled by the fourteenth-century English knight Sir John Mandeville in his famous *Travels*. This was certainly true of the way they imagined Muscovites. It did not help matters that for much of the time Poles were at war with Russia. In their efforts to rally the other Catholic monarchies to their struggle, the Poles did their best to blacken their foe with the tar of the heathen Turk.[4]

One of the most common Renaissance perceptions of Russia involved its Asian identity. Because of Muscovy's location on the remote eastern edge of Europe, the exotic costumes worn by its emissaries, and the immense, despotic power its sovereign was reputed to wield over his subjects, it was easy to conclude that the eastern European realm was no less Oriental than Persia or Cathay. When the Flemish cartographer Abraham Ortelius published his 1570 atlas, *Theatrum Orbis Terrarum*, he depicted the Russian tsar in a Mongol yurt.[5] Some forty years later, Jacques Margeret, a French subaltern who had extensively traveled in Russia, complained that many Europeans still seemed unaware that Christendom extended east of Hungary.[6] In Shakespeare's England, "Muscovite strangers" and "Scythian monsters" became stock characters of the stage.[7] To others, Russia's Oriental nature had more sinister attributes. One German warned that the secretive eastern land presented a threat not unlike the Mongols in earlier centuries: "[The Tsar] is terribly powerful. Having already usurped a good part of Livonia, he stands poised to invade Germany. . . . We can only pray for the mercy of our God that we . . . never fall under his yoke, for his tyranny would be such that we would prefer to be dead, whether our conquerors be Turks, Tartars or Muscovites."[8]

The cliché stuck. Up to the present, Russia's exoticism, eastern geography, and frequently repressive rule have continued to encourage the Western view that it is essentially Asian. The characterization has come from various points on the political spectrum. When a French aristocrat, Astolphe Marquis de Custine, traveled to Russia in 1839, much reminded him of the Orient, from the eyes of the inhabitants, with "the deceitful, furtive glance of the Asiatics," to its autocratic government, a "despotism of the East."[9] In his opinion, "we are here on the confines of Asia."[10] Meanwhile, Karl Marx saw the tsar's empire as "semi-Asiatic" and an "Oriental despotism."[11] "The bloody mire of Mongol slavery . . . forms the cradle of Muscovy," he thundered, "and modern Russia is but a metamorphosis of Muscovy."[12] In the twentieth century, a distinguished Sinologist explained how the Soviet Union's political order betrayed its "Oriental root."[13] And shortly after the Soviet Union's collapse, *Time* magazine worried that "Russia Could Go the Asiatic Way."[14]

Certainly since their conversion to Christianity over ten centuries ago, most Russians would have denied being Oriental. In their frequent warfare with Inner Asian nomads, medieval Russians saw themselves as defenders of the Cross against the wicked pagans (*pogany*) of the steppes. From the eighteenth century, when Peter the Great and his heirs strove to impose Western ways on their empire, educated Russians would have tended to agree with Mikhail Gorbachev's assertion that "we are Europeans."[15]

Nevertheless, given that it straddles both of Eurasia's two continents, Russia's geography has instilled some ambiguity among the inhabitants about its continental allegiance. In its earliest incarnation, as the Kievan principalities that flourished during the eleventh and twelfth centuries, Russia had cultural and commercial links with both European and Asian lands. Conquest and occupation by the Mongols in the thirteenth century effectively severed Russia's links with the West. Even after Muscovy freed itself from the Golden Horde two hundred years later, it remained largely isolated from the rest of Europe.

When Peter the Great and his successors began returning Russia to the European fold in the eighteenth century, they encountered strong resistance from many of their subjects. At first this opposition came primarily from the clergy and other conservatives, who saw the West's Latin culture as anathema to their Orthodox faith. By the nineteenth century, however, some members of the educated elite, influenced by German Romanticism, also began to argue that Russia's place was not in the West. Earning the epithet of Slavophiles, they saw their society as fundamentally distinct from

Mongols were rulers ut the thirteenth cent.

the sterile materialism and rationalism of the Latin world. Nevertheless, the Slavophiles did not consider their nation to be Asian.[16] They believed that Russia's identity lay in a different Europe, whose past bound them to the traditions of Byzantium's Orthodox Church and the agrarian communalism of the ancient Slavs.

Yet there were Russians who imagined a kinship with Asia. The early nineteenth-century historian Nikolai Karamzin believed that "Moscow owes its greatness to the Khans," arguing that its tsars had adopted their autocratic ruling style from the Mongol political tradition.[17] Some began to detect a deeper affinity with the continent, like the fin-de-siècle poet Aleksandr Blok, who proclaimed: "We are Scythians and Asians too, with slanting eyes bespeaking greed!"[18] Others, such as the late nineteenth-century conservative newspaper publishers Prince Esper Ukhtomskii and Prince Vladimir Meshcherskii, identified with the East in their aversion to Western materialism and liberalism.[19] One offshoot of this line of thinking was the early twentieth-century idea that Russia forms a separate "Eurasian" continent, combining both Asian and European elements.

This confusion among Russians about their continental identity makes the question of how they have seen the Orient all the more intriguing. "What is Asia to us?" Dostoyevsky famously asked after General Mikhail Skobelev stormed the central Asian fortress of Geok Tepe in 1881. The answer was straightforward: It "provides the main outlet for our future destiny."[20] Asia was one place where Russians could be the Europeans' equals. To this cheerleader of General Skobelev's glorious exploits in the sands of Turkestan, the East was something to be conquered for the greater glory of tsar and fatherland. In this sense, Dostoyevsky neatly fits into the Orientalist template devised by the late literary scholar Edward Said. But the novelist was hardly speaking for all Russians when he saw the East as an arena for atavistic imperialist conquests for the sake of conquest. Many of his compatriots have had a less straightforward view of the East. And even if most Russians considered themselves to be European, this did not necessarily translate into an antipathy for Asia.

There is a rich literature about Russians' sense of their place in the world. However, much of it derives from the mid-nineteenth-century debate between the Westernizers (advocates of European kinship) and the

Slavophiles (those who believed that Russia must follow its own path).[21] Scholars therefore tend to focus on the relationship with Europe. To be sure, Russian perceptions of the East have not been entirely neglected. Sometimes such works consisted of anti-Soviet efforts to discover "Oriental" or even "Tartar" roots in the Russian national psyche.[22] More objective studies, including Mark Bassin's *Imperial Visions* and Robert Geraci's *Window on the East,* focus on specific aspects of ideas about Asia.[23]

Recent scholarship about European attitudes toward Asia has been largely shaped by Edward Said's ideas about Orientalism. Until the late 1970s, the noun "Orientalism" had two quite particular definitions. As an academic term, it referred to the study of the East, usually the Near East. Orientalism was a scholarly pursuit that involved mastering some rather difficult languages, and its practitioners were a rarefied and somewhat eccentric breed. Meanwhile, to art historians, Orientalism referred to a nineteenth-century school of painters such as Eugène Delacroix, Eugène Fromentin, and Jean-Léon Gérôme, who favored Near Eastern subjects. In both cases, the word was neutral and carried no negative connotations.[24]

With the appearance of Said's eponymous book in 1978, Orientalism assumed a pejorative sense. No longer the effete pursuit of some doddering dons or an artistic interest in the exotic, it began to be seen as an important weapon in the armory of Western imperialism, an intellectual tool for ensuring the West's dominion over the East. In a nutshell, Said's *Orientalism* argues that the scholarly apparatus whereby the West studies the East is a means to oppress it. Occidentals do this by thinking about the Orient as "the Other," a mysterious, feminized, malevolent, and dangerous "cultural contestant."

Said explains that Europeans often see the world in Manichaean terms. In Rudyard Kipling's words, "East is East and West is West, and never the twain shall meet." The legacy of the French philosopher Michel Foucault in Said is clear, especially in Foucault's notions of "discourse," the linguistic apparatus whereby the dissemination of knowledge becomes a way to conquer, subjugate, and repress. According to Said, Orientalism is "a scientific movement whose analogue in the world of empirical politics was the Orient's colonial accumulation and acquisition by Europe."[25]

When Said refers to the West, he means primarily nineteenth- and twentieth-century Britain and France, and he subsequently extended his argument to the United States. The scholar virtually ignores other European nations with a strong orientological tradition, such as Germany, the Netherlands, Hungary, and Russia. As for the Orient, Said is deliberately vague. He generally focuses on the Near East and North Africa, ignoring Inner and East Asia altogether.

Said's notion of Orientalism as the instrument of Western imperialism would have sounded very familiar to Soviet ears. In 1922 the editor of a Moscow-based journal, *Novyi Vostok* (The New East), argued that, for British, French, and German orientological societies, "scholarly study of the East is merely secondary," adding that, "their primary goal is to do whatever they can in to help their respective governments conquer . . . Asian lands."[26] Six years later Solomon Vel'tman suggested that "colonial *belles lettres* have become a weapon of the European ruling classes' political propaganda in their colonialist aggression."[27] Until the late 1930s, when such attitudes became unfashionable, some even detected a link between tsarist empire building and poetry. According to Nikolai Svirin, who wrote several studies about the Oriental theme in Romantic verse, "so-called Russian 'exotic' literature was basically colonialist."[28]

The entry for "Vostokovedenie" (Orientology) in the second edition of the authoritative *Bol'shaia sovetskaia entsiklopediia* (Great Soviet Encyclopedia), published in 1951, anticipated Said even more closely when it excoriated Western scholarship: "Reflecting the colonialist-racist worldview of the European and American bourgeoisie, from the very beginning bourgeois orientology diametrically opposed the civilizations of the so-called "West" with those of the "East," slanderously declaring that Asian peoples are racially inferior, somehow primordially backward, incapable of determining their own fates, and that they appeared only as history's object rather than its subject. Bourgeois orientology entirely subordinates the study of the East to the colonial politics of the imperialist powers."[29] Vera Tolz noted that, while Said did not read Russian, such attitudes nevertheless influenced him. As she points out, Said's critique of Western orientology was based on that of an Egyptian Marxist, Anwar Abdel-Malek, in an earlier article, "Orientalism in Crisis." The latter's first citation was for the Soviet encyclopedia entry.[30]

A profoundly influential book, *Orientalism* has come under intense criticism from many scholars. Some object that those who study the East are not ipso facto hostile to the object of their interest. Thus Robert Irwin denounced Said's book as "a work of malignant charlatanism."[31] Irwin's history of the European discipline of orientology argues that many of its practitioners were quite sympathetic to Asia. He questioned whether scholars would really sacrifice decades of arduous and solitary toil to something they detested. Indeed, it has not been unusual for Europeans who devoted their careers to the East, whether as academics or administrators, to yield to its charms. Colonial bureaucracies in the nineteenth century worried about their officials overseas "going native," while foreign ministries today often strictly limit the postings of its diplomats to guard against the affliction of "localitis." During the McCarthy era, several of the U.S. State Department's "old China hands" were charged with being apologists for Mao Zedong. Robert Kaplan took a similar tack in the 1990s in his book *The Arabists,* when he argued that, far from being hostile to the Near East, its specialists at Foggy Bottom were dangerously sympathetic to the region.[32]

Said was not alone in writing about Western attitudes toward the East. But earlier works explained that Europeans saw Asia in a much more positive light, as a source of wonder or wisdom. Among the former is Henri Baudet's *Het Paradijs op Aarde* (1959, Paradise on Earth). While he acknowledges that since antiquity the Orient had on occasion menaced the Occident, Baudet is more interested in the mythology of the unspoiled, premodern East.[33] The Age of Reason's fascination with chinoiserie and turquerie suggests that Europeans were entirely capable of imagining Asia as, at the very least, benign. They were also quite ready to admire the East for its sagacity, as Raymond Schwab explains in his classic *La Renaissance orientale* (1950).[34] However, Said's darker vision of Occidental contempt and fear of the Orient dominates thinking about the subject today.

Although Said did not discuss Europeans east of the Rhine, it was only a matter of time for Russianists to begin considering the relevance of the Orientalist thesis to their own field. The most obvious candidate for their scrutiny has been the rich literature about the mid-nineteenth century tsarist wars in the Caucasus Mountains. Leading Russian writers such as Aleksandr Pushkin, Aleksandr Griboedov, Mikhail Lermontov, Aleksandr

Bestuzhev (Marlinskii), and Leo Tolstoy all either served or traveled in the region, and their works bear a strong imprint of the exotic campaign. This genre has already produced several monographs, beginning with Susan Layton's *Russian Literature and Empire*.[35] The Indian scholar Kalpana Sahni broadened her inquiry geographically to central Asia, as well as chronologically to the Soviet period, in *Crucifying the Orient*.[36] As the title suggests, her approach is less than detached.

Yet how relevant is Edward Said's perspective to Russia? Not long after *Orientalism* saw the light of day, Bernard Lewis criticized the book for ignoring the German tradition of Oriental scholarship.[37] Said brushed off this criticism, but it remains an important one. Central to Said's argument is the idea that the academy and colonialism act in concert. Germany's colonial interests in the Near East, however, tended to be negligible during the golden age of the Orientalist school. For Germans, there was clearly no inherent link between knowledge and power as far as the Orient was concerned. This point is important for Russia as well, since its scholars, especially those interested in the East, have been strongly influenced by the German academy.

More generally, Russian views of Asia have always been complex. Even in the reign of Alexander II, as Generals Cherniaev, Kaufman, and Skobelev were subduing central Asian khanates, Russian thinking about the East ran the spectrum. At one end were such men as Skobelev, Dostoyevsky, and the bellicose explorer Nikolai Przheval'skii, who saw the East as backward and useful only as an arena for tsarist conquest. Yet there were many others who saw Asia in a more favorable light.

A forum on the pages of *Kritika* underscored this problem. The discussion took as its starting point an earlier article by Nathaniel Knight in *Slavic Review*.[38] In the latter, Knight had examined the posting of the nineteenth-century orientologist Vasilii Vasilevich Grigor'ev to Orenburg as an official for the Ministry of Internal Affairs. Knight argued that Grigor'ev, as a scholar whose interests very much clashed with those of his superiors, disproves Said's model of the hand-in-hand *politik* of science and the state. Another historian, Adeeb Khalid, began the *Kritika* debate by invoking the career of Nikolai Petrovich Ostroumov.[39] Unlike Grigor'ev, Ostroumov enthusiastically used his knowledge of Islam and Turkic languages to assist tsarist authorities in extending their sway over Asian lands and peoples. Ostroumov would seem to illustrate the Orientalist thesis. In a sense, both Knight and Khaleed are right: some Russian orientologists do not fit Said's mould, while others do. It is impossible to reduce Russian scholars of Asia to a single archetype.

The example of Grigor'ev is nevertheless useful. Many Russian orientologists—but by no means all—were sympathetic and respectful of the nations they studied. The leading figures in St. Petersburg, Kazan, Moscow, and other centers of scholarship about the East tended to be relatively nonjudgmental, especially when compared to their nineteenth-century Western European contemporaries. Military supremacy in central Asia did not necessarily translate into gloating within the academy about the East's backwardness.

An added wrinkle is the fact that many Russians have been conscious of their own Asian heritage. In her study of Russian literary depictions of the conquest of the Caucasus, Susan Layton remarked that "Both culturally and politically Russia has genuine roots in . . . Asia, which made the Orient both self and other."[40] Not a few orientologists of the Imperial Russian school, such as the Chuvash Father Hyacinth (Bichurin), the Iranian-born Aleksandr Kazem-Bek, and the Buriat Dorzhi Banzarov, were themselves Oriental in origin.[41]

And Russians know a very different East as well, for the compass point also refers to the Orthodox half of Christendom, in contrast to the Catholic West. The poet Vladimir Solov'ev alluded to the distinction between the Asiatic Orient that had menaced Europe ever since the Persian Wars and the Christian Orient when he asked, "Which East will [Russia] be: The East of Xerxes or of Christ?"[42] Nevertheless, they both share something in being the West's antithesis. Russians who opposed western European culture could imagine kinship with one or the other for similar reasons.

If Edward Said's work is not wholly relevant to Russian Orientalism, it does raise some interesting questions about the relationships between knowledge and power. Russian efforts to explore, study, and understand the East often have been directly linked to imperial aims.[43] A number of prominent nineteenth-century orientologists, including Father Hyacinth and Osip Senkovskii, had close ties to the Ministry of Foreign Affairs. And Nathaniel Knight reminds us about Grigor'ev's government service in Orenburg on the Asian steppe frontier. Russian orientology was not always the compliant handmaiden of the state, but there were intimate ties between the two.

Said's interest in cultural representations also highlights the importance of going beyond the polemics of the "thick journals," the nineteenth-century periodicals that played a major role in the nation's intellectual life, to understand Russia's perception of the world. According to Barbara Heldt, "the literary image of another country and its inhabitants . . . is often the image that most people hold."[44] Susan Layton, Katya Hokanson, Harsha Ram, and others have already demonstrated that the poetry and prose of the nineteenth-century campaign to "pacify" the Caucasus can tell us something about Russian views of the Orient. Paintings, prints, music, opera, and the decorative arts are also important sources for understanding how Russians saw the East.

Can we speak of a Russian Orientalism? This book endeavors to answer the question by examining attitudes to Asia during the Imperial era: the two centuries from Peter the Great's reign to the February Revolution of 1917. Russians looked at the East through many lenses. This book focuses on two of them, orientology (*vostokovedenie*) and culture. To keep the story clear, it highlights representative individuals rather than attempting to provide an encyclopedic account of everyone of importance. In this respect, I freely admit to borrowing the approach taken by one of my teachers, Jonathan Spence, in his history of Western views of China, *The Chan's Great Continent*.[45]

Just as those in the West are vague about where the East lies on the map, Russians are equally imprecise about their notions of *Vostok* (the East). This project is an exploration of imaginary geography. In the Russian mind, there are both one Orient and many Orients, from the ancient Tartar city of Kazan in Europe only 600 kilometers east of Moscow, to Asian lands such as Persia, India, China, Mongolia, and Japan. This book therefore considers the East broadly, extending the horizon to all Oriental regions that interested Russians, including Inner and East Asia. Because I am interested in exploring notions of a putative "other," I generally refer to what Solov'ev called "the East of Xerxes," rather than the "East of Christ." While I recognize the importance of Said's ideas, I do not share his distaste for the terms "Oriental," "orientology" and "Orientalist." I therefore use them in the neutral, pre-Saidian sense, much as Russians understand *Vostok, vostokovedenie,* and *vostokoved* (orientologist).

Russians have never been of one mind about Asia. Said's Orientalist schema assumes unanimity, a shared view both of Asia and about how to confront it that simply never existed. The Russian Empire's bicontinental geography, its ambivalent relationship with the rest of Europe, and the complicated nature of its encounters with Asia, have resulted in a fragmentary understanding of the East among its people. To paraphrase a cliché from Aleksandr Motyl's 1969 film *White Sun of the Desert,* Russian Orientalism is a complicated question.

1

THE FOREST AND THE STEPPE

By virtue of its geography, the Russian state came under the influence of both the West and the East from the very first centuries of its existence.

—Vasilii Barthold

Long before they thought of East and West, Europe and Asia, or Christian and pagan, for the people who eventually became the Russians, forest and steppe defined their notion of self and other. The East Slavs, from whom Russians derive their ancestry, first settled Europe's wooded northeastern periphery sometime in the latter half of our era's first millennium.[1] Precisely what enticed them to this dark, primeval land during the era of the great migrations that followed Rome's collapse remains obscure.

Some of these Slavs eventually came to pay tribute to the Khazars, a more powerful nation of nomadic Inner Asian origin that controlled the region around the lower Volga River from the seventh through the ninth centuries. As part of the Eurasian steppe's loose confederation of Turkic tribes, the Khazars profited from commerce with the great powers of the day, including the caliphate of Baghdad, Persia, and Byzantium. Culture came with coin, and their various trading partners influenced the nomads. The elite eventually adopted Judaism, while much of the general population converted to Christianity and Islam. It was by exchanging furs, wax, honey, and other products of the forest for Arab silver that various Slavic groups had first come into contact with the Khazars. The caches of Near Eastern coins dating from the eighth through the eleventh centuries that have been found throughout northwestern Russia testify to a lively Slav trade with the Orient at the time.

Sometime in the eighth century, this lucrative enterprise caught the attention of Scandinavia's aggressive Varangians (Vikings), and they began to insinuate themselves into the weaker realms of the East Slavs. The exact nature of the Norsemen's relationship with the Rus, as Russia's ancestors were known, continues to excite controversy. Nevertheless, it was under their leadership that the first state eventually emerged among these Slavs, with its capital in Kiev near the forest's boundary with the steppe. Despite having Scandinavian leaders, in its earliest days this young entity remained subject to the Khazars. Both ninth-century Byzantine and Carolingian sources refer to the Slavs' Varangian ruler by the Turkic title of *kagan* (khan), although he would subsequently come to be known as the grand prince (*velikii kniaz'*).[2] According to the Turkologist Vasilii Barthold, "From the very first centuries of its existence, the Russian state came under the influence of both the West and the East by virtue of its geography. . . . Russia's strongest cultural ties with the East appear to have been during its earliest, pre-Christian period."[3]

Kievan Rus soon developed into a strong independent nation that traded and warred with its various neighbors, including Byzantium, Khazaria, the Bulgars (an Islamic Turkic nation then along the middle Volga), a succession of Asian nomadic confederations on the southern steppe, and the Catholic kingdoms to the west. One of Kiev's most fateful steps was Grand Prince Vladimir's decision in 988 to adopt the Eastern Orthodox Christianity of Byzantium, which brought it within that empire's cultural orbit. While Vladimir's baptism definitively placed his realm within Christendom, adopting the faith's Greek rather than Latin variant sowed the seeds for future conflict with the West.

During most of its existence, for much of Rus the primary external threat came from the steppe. An immense prairie that stretched across Eurasia from Manchuria near the Pacific Ocean to Hungary in central Europe, this grassland acted like an inland sea, affording easy passage to the various pastoral tribes that ranged the featureless expanse. Over the centuries, wave after wave of Inner Asian groups swept westward, occupying the southern Russian steppe until being forced out in turn by a more powerful nomadic alliance. The first to enter recorded history in some detail were the Scythians, an Iranian people whom the fifth century B.C.E. Greek Herodotus famously described in his *History*.[4] In the time of the Kievan Rus, two Turkic confederations, the Pechenegs and the Polovtsy (a.k.a. Cumans or Qipchaks), successively controlled the lands on its southern frontier.

Kiev's monastic chronicles and the other written sources that have survived suggest an unrelenting contest between its settled farmers and the Asian nomads. [5] The *Primary Chronicle,* the earliest and most important of the former, contains frequent references to clashes with the Pechenegs, the main nomadic foe from the 960s to around 1040, and the Polovtsy, who eventually supplanted them after 1060. A closer look at the *Chronicle,* however, suggests that the relationship between the forest and the steppe was not invariably hostile. In fact, they were much more often at peace than on the march.[6]

When Pechenegs and Polovtsy first came into contact with Kiev, both of these encounters began on a cordial note. The Pechenegs were initially Rus's allies in a campaign against Byzantium in 944. There would be many other occasions for joint operations and, as Kiev began to weaken, it was not unusual for rival princes to enlist Polovtsian support in their frequent internecine struggles. Indeed, princes often cemented such alliances by marrying a son to a nomadic khan's daughter. By the 1100s, some Russian princes may have well been mostly Turkic by blood.[7] Meanwhile, Pechenegs and other refugee nomads often entered Kievan service by settling the vulnerable south to guard against incursions from the "wild field" beyond, much as Cossacks would do in later centuries. And, as on China's northern marches, Kiev engaged in a lively commerce with its nomadic neighbors, trading the forest's products for those of the steppe.

Although the Pechenegs and Polovtsy constituted a similar challenge to the Kievan Rus, the chronicles portray them in a strikingly different light.[8] The *Primary Chronicle*'s descriptions of the various confrontations with the Pechenegs are laconic and virtually free of epithets. By stark contrast, from the very beginning the Polovtsy were invariably seen as the equivalent of a biblical scourge. The chroniclers' negative portrayal of the Polovtsy reflects Kiev's conversion to Christianity. Before Vladimir's baptism, the East Slavs saw the steppe nomads as troublesome neighbors. By adopting Byzantium's faith at the turn of the tenth century, however, the Rus also assimilated its view of the world, which sharply distinguished between believers and nonbelievers. When the Polovtsy launched their earliest assault on the Kievan realm in 1061, the *Primary Chronicle* recorded that "This was the first evil the pagans and godless enemies inflicted." A raid seven years later was described as divine punishment: "For our sins God unleashed the pagans against us." And in the entry for 1096, the year the Polovtsy raided Kiev's Monastery of the Caves, they were "the godless sons of Ishmael."[9]

Judaic and Christian cosmography further endowed the Polovtsy with demonic and even apocalyptic associations. In one passage, the *Chronicle* suggests that they are among the "unclean" tribes linked to the land of Gog and Magog, the satanic forces whose appearance will presage the end of the world. According to the chronicler's interlocutor, this region consists of "certain mountains" to the northeast, the compass point traditionally associated with the realm of evil.[10] To the Orthodox monks who compiled the *Primary Chronicle,* the Polovtsy were wicked primarily because they were not Christian. Even if their beliefs at the time were shamanist, the chroniclers increasingly described them in the language of Byzantine anti-Islamic polemics. This was not surprising, since the Eastern Roman Empire first became acquainted with Islam during the great seventh-century Arab advance. As a nomadic "people of sheep and camels," the new foe had seemed much more like the Huns, Avars, and other barbarian hordes that had menaced Byzantium than such traditional Oriental enemies as Persia.[11]

When the *Primary Chronicle* referred to the Polovtsy and other Turkic nomads as "godless sons of Ishmael," it associated them with Muhammad's legendary ancestor. According to the book of Genesis, Ishmael, the son of the Biblical patriarch Abraham and his concubine Hagar, had been banished to the desert as a boy. By Jewish tradition, the "wild man" thereby became the forefather of various bedouin tribes. It therefore was all too easy for eleventh-century monastic scribes in Kiev to conflate Near Eastern and Inner Asian nomads.

> Might it not become us, brothers,
> To begin in the diction of yore
> the stern tale
> of the campaign of Igor,
> Igor son of Sviatoslav?
>
> . . .

> Imbued with the spirit of arms,
> he led his brave troops
> against the Kuman land
> in the name of the Russian land.[12]

So begins the twelfth-century *Song of Igor's Campaign,* the best-known literary monument of Rus's encounter with the steppe. Like the roughly contemporaneous French *Chanson de Roland,* it tells of an ill-fated clash with the godless other. And, just as in the *Chanson,* the Igor song is based on a relatively minor engagement that was poetically transformed into an event of epic importance. But whereas the *chanson de geste* depicts Roland's tragic end in the Pyrenees as part of the millennial struggle between Christianity and Islam, the Igor song's religious message is much more subdued.

Igor Sviatoslavich was a junior prince on the steppe frontier. Like a number of other highborn Russians at the time, Igor had family ties with the Asian nomads, and he fought together with them against his dynastic rivals.[13] Nevertheless, according to the chronicles, in spring 1185 the prince launched a campaign to the east against the Polovtsy.[14] Neglecting to confer with his cousin, Grand Prince Sviatoslav Vsevolodovich of Kiev, Igor impetuously set out on his own with his son Vladimir, his brother, and their *druzhina* (retinue).

As they marched into the steppe, some wavered when a solar eclipse, a traditional ill omen, darkened the skies. The prince rallied his troops, and they carried on. Fortune initially seemed to favor Igor, and he easily captured a Polovtsian camp. But his success proved to be short-lived when, the following dawn, with his men still groggy from their postvictory revels, the enemy launched a surprise attack. After three days of ferocious combat, Igor's druzhina found itself overwhelmed. Along with his son, the commander became a prisoner of the Polovtsian Khan Konchak. Unlike Roland's fate, Igor's misadventure had a happy ending. The prince escaped captivity, and his son married the khan's daughter before being allowed to return home as well.

Discovered in the late eighteenth century by an aristocratic collector of antiquities, the Igor song was hailed by no less than Aleksandr Pushkin as "an isolated monument in the desert of our literature."[15] The work's sophistication, which seems so out of place in late twelfth-century Rus, and the fact that its sixteenth-century manuscript copy perished in flames during Napoleon's occupation of Moscow in 1812, have led to persistent speculations that it is a much more recent forgery.[16] Most likely written by an educated layman who possibly had been a veteran of the prince's druzhina, it offers some valuable insights into Rus's view of the East.[17]

References in the Igor song to pre-Christian gods, magic, and other pagan elements suggest that the young Orthodox Church's hold on the popular imagination was not yet entirely secure. While the *Hypatian Chronicle's* account of Igor's fiasco attributes his defeat to God's punishment for his sins, the song tends to blame the prince's foolish hubris and insubordination. As many commentators have suggested, the latter text's message is distinctly secular in stressing the perils of political disunity in the face of foreign military threats. There is only one mention of defending the faith at the very end, and the emphasis is much more on fighting "for the Rus's land" (*za zemliu russkuiu*).

By the same token, the *Song* does not portray the Polovtsy as a diabolical force. Unlike the chronicles, it uses the terms "pagan" and "Polovtsian" synonymously; here both are more ethnic rather than religious designations. If, according to the *Hypatian Chronicle,* their chief is "the damned, godless and thrice-cursed [Khan] Konchak," the strongest epithet the *Song* musters is "pagan slave." Unlike the monks who kept the chronicles, the Igor song's anonymous author saw the Polovtsy as a dangerous adversary, but nothing more.

The *Song*'s warnings about the dangers of discord proved eerily prescient when, half a century later, a far more destructive foe appeared on the steppe. The chronicles tell of the arrival in 1223 of the "Tatars," a mysterious and unusually violent nomadic people on the steppe. Even the Polovtsy buckled before them, and their khans appealed to the Russian princes for help. "Today they took our lands; tomorrow they will take yours," one of the khans warned.[18] Accordingly, in April a joint expedition was organized to counter the new menace.

Poorly organized, fractious, and hobbled by confused lines of command, the allies proved to be no match for the Tatars. They were thoroughly routed when they joined battle later that spring on the banks of the Kalka River near the Sea of Azov in southeastern Russia. And then, just as suddenly as they had appeared, the "evil Tatars" reversed their course and vanished back into Inner Asia. "We know neither whence they came nor whither they went," wrote a chronicler. "Only God knows, since he inflicted them on us for our sins."[19] For the next fourteen years an uneasy calm reigned on the steppe.

These Tatars were of course the Mongols, the formidable nomadic confederation that Genghis Khan had crafted from the traditionally unruly horsemen of the eastern Inner Asian steppe at the turn of the thirteenth century. Having already routed armies in northern China, Persia, and many other lands in-between, their brief foray into southern Russia in 1223 was only a reconnaissance. In 1235, eight years after Genghis's death, his grandson, Batu Khan, renewed the westward advance. The Islamic Bulgar nation on the Volga fell the following year, and its entire population was massacred.

The northeastern Russian principalities were next. In the campaign of 1237–38, Riazan, Vladimir, and the relatively minor town of Moscow were all stormed, while the grand prince, Iurii Vsevolodich, was killed in battle before Batu's warriors withdrew. The next year they turned their attention on southern Russia, razing town after town until in December 1240 the ancient capital of Kiev was also sacked. Novgorod to the north was spared by the fortuitous intervention of a spring thaw, but its ruler, Prince Alexander Nevsky, wisely pledged submission to the khan to spare his domain from the onslaught.

For over two centuries, Russians would be subject to what they eventually came to call the "Mongol yoke" (*Tatarskaia iga*).[20] The first decades were the harshest, as punitive expeditions, disease, and economic dislocation reduced the population by over a quarter. Yet despite its initial toll, Batu's conquest proved not to be the Armageddon the chronicles make it out to be. Unlike other Mongol khans in China, Persia, and central Asia, Batu refrained from occupying his Russian possessions. The forest held little appeal to the steppe nomads, while the relative poverty and backwardness of the principalities further lessened their attraction. Instead, the Golden Horde, as the Russians subsequently called Batu's khanate, exercised indirect control from its capital, Sarai, on the Caspian steppe through *basqaqs*, or residents, who collected tribute and conscripts, as well as maintaining order. And by the end of the thirteenth century, much of this system was abolished in favor of even more autonomous Russian princely collaborators.

If the Golden Horde exacted a heavy tribute, Russia's economy not only recovered from the invasion but also in some cases even profited from alien rule. Since the khans were mostly interested in deriving income from their Slavic provinces, they hardly discouraged trade. As a result, northern towns like Novgorod and Moscow grew rich through their ties with the Mongols' far-flung commercial network. However, the main Russian beneficiary of the new order was the Orthodox Church. Despite its conversion to Islam in the early fourteenth century, the Golden Horde resolutely maintained the steppe tradition of religious tolerance. The Russian clergy was entirely free to minister to its believers and enjoyed fiscal exemptions as long as it offered prayers for the khan's well being. Indeed, it was under the Mongol yoke that the church became the great champion of Russian national identity. As Charles Halperin notes, Russian priests found themselves in the curious position of "praying simultaneously for the immediate perdition of all Mongols and (by agreement) for the good health of the khan."[21]

In the nomadic world, leadership was based more on personal charisma than on the accident of birth order. While bloodlines conferred legitimacy, being the firstborn did not carry the same importance it did in many settled societies. At the same time, since the khans practiced polygamy, they often had many potential heirs. Therefore, succession struggles among Genghis Khan's multitudinous descendants were frequent. The Golden Horde outlasted the other three states that had emerged from Genghis's great empire, but its cohesion also inevitably deteriorated over time, and by the fourteenth century it was periodically convulsed by internal strife.

That era also saw the increasing power of Moscow's princes, who proved unusually adept at increasing their authority over their Russian rivals while also winning a favored place at Sarai. In 1380, during one period of political turmoil in the Golden Horde, the Muscovite Prince Dmitrii even challenged it militarily at Kulikovo Field on the Don River (thereby earning his celebrated epithet "Donskoi"). Dmitrii Donskoi's victory proved short-lived, since his foe sacked Moscow two years later and exacted a higher tribute. Nevertheless, as Sarai's political order continued to disintegrate, it never succeeded in fully reasserting its authority. Dmitrii's grandson,

Grand Prince Vasilii II, was the last to receive the khan's patent of rule, and his heir, Grand Prince Ivan III (the Great), successfully renounced his submission to the Horde in 1480.

How did Russians see their Asian overlords at the time? The answer is surprisingly complicated. Muscovy's church-dominated literature about the two-and-a-half century Mongol yoke bequeathed one of the most durable images of the Oriental other to the Russian imagination. It is not a flattering portrait. *The Tale of the Destruction of Riazan* is typical of the genre. Located on northeastern Russia's frontier, Riazan was the first Russian principality to fall to the Mongols when they struck in 1237. The story tells of their depredations in gruesome detail as they invaded the princely capital, "Smashing into the Cathedral of the Assumption of the Blessed Virgin [the Tatars] put the Great Princess Agrippina, her daughters-in-law, and other princesses to the sword, slaughtered the bishops and the priests, torched the holy church, and cut down many others. And throughout the city, men, women, and children were also hacked to pieces. And others were drowned in the river. . . . And in the city not one remained among the living. . . . And this all happened because of our sins." Although they had not yet converted to Islam, the Mongols were labeled with the usual Byzantine invective for Muslims, such as "infidel," "godless," as well as "children of Hagar." Meanwhile, Khan Batu was "evil," a "godless, false, remorseless emperor."[22]

The Tale of the Destruction of Riazan was written long after the event it describes, most likely in the sixteenth century.[23] Scholars have pointed out that contemporary accounts of the Mongol period were much milder in tone, and often minimized or even ignored their Asian overlords' presence according to what Halperin has called an "ideology of silence."[24] This resulted in part because Russia's spiritual patron, Byzantium, generally enjoyed fairly good relations with the Golden Horde. (In 1273 Emperor Michael VIII even gave a daughter in marriage to Khan Nogai.)[25]

More intriguing, as Halperin convincingly argues, the monastic chroniclers of the time studiously ignored the very fact of Sarai's sovereignty. While they acknowledged that Batu Khan's hordes had ravaged the Russian land, they presented their depredations in the same light as the earlier raids by the Polovtsy. In a way, the monks were right. Aside from the *basqaqs* in the immediate decades after Batu's assault, the Mongols did not

THE FOREST AND THE STEPPE

physically occupy Russia. As Halperin adds, "The medieval writers' reti-
cence about the true nature of Russo-Tatar relations is a sign of neither ignorance nor timidity. Instead, it is itself a form of resistance to oppression.
It has, however, had the regrettable result of misleading historians."[26]

It was only after Muscovy had finally repudiated the Golden Horde and
begun a counteroffensive against its remnants that the Orthodox Church
took to adopting a harsher rhetoric about the Mongols. Comparisons of
different accounts over time of the same event, such as the Battle of Kulikovo, show that this was a relatively gradual process, which reached its
apogee in the sixteenth and seventeenth centuries. The invective continued to be couched in anachronistic anti-Islamic Byzantine language about
the Mongols' Polovtsian predecessors, but the stress on evil and perfidy
was much greater.[27]

Muscovite churchmen's use of the word "Tatar" further muddied the
waters. Ironically, the original Tatars had been the Mongols' tribal arch-
enemies on the eastern steppe. The Chinese had long dealt with the Tatars
and came to employ their name as a generic label for their pastoral neighbors across the Great Wall. While Genghis Khan largely obliterated the
tribe in the late twelfth century, the label stuck, and it would eventually
also be used by Arabs, Indians, and Europeans to describe all Mongolian
nomads. In the West the term had a particularly ominous connotation,
since it was easily confused with Tartarus, the infernal region of classical
mythology. "Tatar" now refers to the Turkic, Islamic descendants occupying the Golden Horde's former domains on the steppe.[28] Yet for all of
its sinister drama and longevity, the image of the wicked Tatar fashioned
by ecclesiastical polemics did not monopolize Muscovite views of the
Asian.[29] Moscow's princes had long not only been intimately acquainted
with the Golden Horde but also often acted as its leading Russian collab-
orator. As a result, if Byzantium shaped their view of God, Sarai helped influence their understanding of secular politics.[30]

Historians continue to speculate about the Mongol legacy in Russia
today, but its impact on Muscovy is undeniable. At least through the sixteenth century, Muscovite diplomacy with its Muslim neighbors followed
Mongolian practice.[31] The adoption of words with Tatar roots into the
Russian language, like *den'gi* (money), *kazna* (treasury), and *tamozhnia*
(customs house), also hint at influences on the bureaucracy.[32] Indeed, it

was partly by assimilating the ways of the steppe that Moscow successfully conquered the khanates of Kazan and Astrakhan, two of the Golden Horde's successor states on the Volga, in the 1550s.[33]

Muscovy also absorbed elements of the Golden Horde more directly in welcoming its khans and lesser notables into the aristocracy. [34] Already before its collapse, a number of the Horde's "white-boned" (upper class) entered into Russian service; as early as the Battle of Kulikovo some Tatars fought on the side of Prince Dmitrii.[35] Nearly two centuries later, when Tsar Ivan IV turned west to invade Livonia after vanquishing Kazan and Astrakhan, he appointed a Tatar khan, Shah Ali, at the head of his troops, and a number of other Tatar nobles also served as senior officers during the lengthy campaign.[36] Much as on the steppe, Moscow had no qualms about integrating conquered nations and according the elites a similar status in its own society, as long as they agreed to serve the ruler. And, as was certainly not the case in such Catholic kingdoms as Spain, in choosing marriage partners among the upper class, caste generally trumped race (provided one converted to Orthodoxy). As a result, a variety of ethnic elements have long flowed in the veins of Russia's blue bloods.

Many families in the official tsarist genealogy boasted a Tatar provenance. They included distinguished names such as Iusupov, Kurakin, Dashkov, Kochubei, Ushakov, and Karamzin, among a host of others. Some of these bloodlines are spurious, reflecting the Russian nobility's imaginative "genealogical xenophilia."[37] Whether invented or real, the eagerness of Slavic nobles to flaunt their Asian origins does not suggest a high degree of racial prejudice with regard to the Orient. When the young poetess Anna Gorenko adopted a pseudonym at the turn of the twentieth century, she readily took the name of one her Tatar maternal ancestors, Akhmatova.[38]

Russian familiarity with the Golden Horde thus did not inevitably breed contempt. While the church increasingly championed hostility toward the Tatars, secular views tended to be more benign. Writing in the context of European relations with another Islamic foe, one scholar remarked, "in the West something of a contradiction existed between the practical policies of governments *vis-à-vis* the Ottomans and the general tenor of published *turcica:* the former often reflected none of the hostility of the latter."[39] The same was true of Muscovy and the Mongols.

Until the seventeenth century at the earliest, the steppe nomads dominated Russian perceptions of the Orient. But there were glimpses of other
easts, including the Near East, India, and eventually China. Some of these
impressions came from the chronographs, or compilations of various histories of the world, that were based on similar Byzantine digests.[40] The
first Russian chronograph was produced in the fifteenth century, apparently by a learned Serb, and copies were made with updates of recent
events until the era of Peter the Great. Before increased contacts with the
West in the 1600, one of the few visual representations of the known world
in Muscovy also originated in Byzantium: the *Christian Topography* by the
sixth-century geographer Cosmas Indicopleustes (the "Indian navigator").[41] Meanwhile, the reports of the tsar's envoys to various Oriental
courts provided relatively more objective firsthand accounts of Asian
neighbors. However, these did not tend to have a wide readership at the
time.[42]

Better known to literate Muscovites was the *khozhenie,* an Orthodox
pilgrim's account of his voyage to the Holy Land or to Tsargrad (Constantinople).[43] The first khozhenie was by Igumen (Abbot) Daniil in the
early twelfth century.[44] Crusaders had occupied Palestine only a few years
earlier, and the igumen had the honor of attending the Easter midnight
mass at the Cathedral of the Holy Sepulcher as the guest of Jerusalem's
Frankish King Baldwin. Daniil wrote his khozhenie as a Baedeker for
Orthodox faithful and therefore quite naturally focused on sites important to Christians. At the same time, his descriptions of the long journey
also made it an exciting adventure story. Nevertheless, as one scholar
points out, the abbot's tone was relatively objective, even when he described the "pagan" Saracens.[45] Subsequent khozheniia could be more
critical of "impious" and "embittered, cursed, cruel" Muslims. After the
Fourth Crusade's sack of Christian Constantinople in 1204, however, other
Russian Orthodox pilgrims were no less restrained in their travelogues
about "impious" Catholic perfidy.[46]

The most popular medieval khozhenie is also the most intriguing. While
it followed many of the genre's conventions, including descriptions of religious monuments and ceremonies, the destination was the distinctly non-
Christian land of India.[47] In 1466 Tsar Ivan III sent a diplomatic mission
to the small Transcaucasian khanate of Shirvan in what is now Azerbaijan.

Among the party was a merchant from Tver, Afanasii Nikitin.[48] As the group neared the Caspian Sea port of Astrakhan, Tatars attacked it, dispersing the travelers. Some returned to Russia, while Nikitin went on to Persia and eventually crossed the Arabian Sea to India.

Fifteenth-century Muscovites were hardly ignorant about India, but they only knew it as a far-off fairy-tale wonderland from such Byzantine sources as *The Tale of the Indian Kingdom* and the *Christian Topography*.[49] Based on the legend of Prester John, the mythical Asian Christian monarch, *The Tale of the Indian Kingdom* describes a magical realm of great wealth inhabited by fabulous peoples and beasts. These stories left their mark on folklore. Thus one *bylina* (epic song) recounts the exploits of Diuk Stepanovich, an elegant foreign boyar's son who arrived at Prince Vladimir's court in Kiev from "opulent India."[50] Preceding Vasco da Gama by some twenty-five years, as Russians patriotically note, Nikitin was the first of their compatriots to have left a description of India from direct observation.[51]

The doughty merchant spent four years in the subcontinent's Muslim Bahmani Sultanate, which at the time was on the march against the Vijanagar Empire, its southern, Hindu rival. His account, *The Journey beyond Three Seas,* begins much like that of any devout Orthodox Christian: "By the prayers of our Holy Fathers, Lord Jesus Christ, Son of God, have mercy on me, your sinful servant Afanasii, son of Nikitin."[52] Having traversed two seas, the Caspian and the Arabian, in May 1469 Nikitin landed at the Indian port of Chaul, just south of modern Mumbai. He was immediately struck that "all people go about naked: [women] cover neither their heads nor their breasts," adding, "The men and women are all black. Wherever I went, many followed me, curious at seeing a white man."[53] Misfortune once again crossed Nikitin's path when, in the town of Juunar, a khan confiscated his stallion and held it hostage for a thousand gold pieces unless the Russian merchant converted to Islam. A miraculous intervention by a kindly Muslim notable saved him from apostasy, and he proceeded further inland to the Bahmani capital of Bidar.

Nikitin spent a year and a half in the city and its environs. Here he saw the Muslim court in all its splendor, with its seven-gated palace built of lavishly gilded carved stone. As Nikitin recorded, whenever the sultan left its confines, he traveled with an escort of 10,000 cavalry, 50,000 foot soldiers, and 200 elephants in gilt armor, as well as hundreds of trumpeters, dancers, monkeys, and young maidens. Meanwhile, nobles were conveyed in silver litters preceded by twenty horses in golden harnesses. But there was also much misery, for "the land is extremely crowded; in the country-side people are very poor."[54] After some time, Nikitin won the trust of the Hindus, who formed the bulk of the sultanate's population. He described their beliefs in some detail, including the many *buts* (Buddhas, i.e., statues of deities) to whom they prayed "in the Russian manner," as well as the caste system.

Like many travelers to the Orient, Nikitin considered the women to be highly promiscuous: "During the day wives lie with their husbands, but at night they go with foreigners and sleep with them. . . . They love to en-tertain white men."[55] Other details were similarly apocryphal, including the fire-spitting *gukuk* bird and the well-organized armies of apes that dwelt in the forest. But on the whole, the merchant's account is remark-able for its matter-of-fact objectivity in an age when Mandevillean mon-sters were more typical of Europeans' tales about distant overseas realms.

Even more striking is Nikitin's growing Islamicization during his years away from home. If he began his journey as a devout Christian, over time the *Journey*'s author increasingly adopted Muslim religious habits. As he lost track of the Orthodox calendar, Nikitin began to observe Islamic prac-tices, including the month-long Ramadan fast. Meanwhile, he also took to praying in a curious blend of Arabic, Turkic, and Slavonic, even conclud-ing his tale in this macaronic language: "By the grace of God I crossed three seas. . . . God is great [*Ollo akber'*]! God the blessed, the blessed Lord, Jesus Spirit of God! Peace be with you! God is great. There is no God but Allah the Creator. Praise be to God, Glory to God! In the name of God, merciful and gracious!"[56]

During Nikitin's years in the Muslim world, it eventually seemed that no great gulf separated the two monotheistic creeds. "Muhammad's faith re-mains true. And God alone knows the true faith," he remarked.[57] One American scholar has gone so far as to argue that Nikitin secretly con-verted to Islam, although it is more likely that he was merely adapting to his new environment. In any case, the merchant shared none of the Or-thodox clergy's aversion toward the Prophet. [58]

In April 1471, "on the fifth Easter Sunday [abroad] I decided to return

to Russia," Nikitin tells us.[59] Taking a long detour to diamond and car-
nelian mines, among other exotic sights, he reached the port of Dabhol
and set sail for Hormuz in February 1472. Nine months later, having traversed Persia and the Black Sea (the third of the *Journey*'s three), Nikitin
was back in his native land. The trip had been a commercial failure; prices
in Islamic India discriminated against the infidel and were simply too high
for Russian merchants to make a profit. Moreover, Nikitin died before
reaching his hometown. But the account that survived him was a literary
success. By century's end, copies were already being widely circulated, and
to this day Nikitin's *Journey beyond Three Seas* remains one of the most
beloved works of medieval Russian letters.

Muscovy's Islamic neighbors were the most familiar Oriental others.
After Ivan the Terrible conquered the khanates of Kazan and Astrakhan in
the 1550s, the tsar counted growing numbers of Tatars and other Turkic
subjects within the expanding borders of his realm. According to the 1897
census, the first undertaken in Imperial Russia, they constituted 11 percent
of the population, thereby forming the third largest ethnic group after the
Russians themselves and the Ukrainians.[60] Most Tatars lived in their own
regions, primarily around the middle and lower Volga River to the east, as
well as in the Crimea, although over time they established important communities in the major cities as well.

Afanasii Nikitin was not the only fifteenth-century Russian merchant to
venture eastward. Others also traveled to Asian lands, especially to Turkey
and Persia.[61] However, unlike Nikitin, they left few accounts of their journeys. Most of the Muscovite texts about the Orient that survive were written by the clergy. As we have discussed, these grew increasingly hostile as
the church supported the autocracy's expansive urges more militantly.
Nevertheless, this antagonism tended to be reflected in the chronicles and
historical tales of Russia's struggle with the *basurman* (Muslim infidel),
rather than polemical texts. Paul Bushkovitch explains that Muscovy's
church did not have a well-developed literature of polemics against
Muhammad's faith. He adds: "The knowledge about Islam in Russia before Peter [the Great] was not extensive and largely restricted to a short
and frequently inaccurate description of Islamic customs."[62]

Despite direct contact with Muslims since the Golden Horde's conversion to Islam in the early fourteenth century, most of what Muscovy's

clergy knew about their beliefs came from Byzantium. Tellingly, the longest relevant passage in the *Primary Chronicle* is by a "Greek philosopher," whom the mother church in Constantinople had sent to Kiev in 986 to help convince Prince Vladimir that he should adopt Eastern Christianity. The learned Greek begins his discussion by discrediting earlier missionaries from the Muslim Bulgars, whose religion "defiles both Heaven and Earth." Muhammad's followers are "cursed more than all other men," and await the same fate as Sodom and Gomorrah, "which God submerged with burning stones." Aside from explaining that they await eternal damnation, the Orthodox scholar does not use any particularly sophisticated theological arguments against the Muslims. Instead, he continues by disparaging their hygiene, explaining that they supposedly wet their excrement and drink the liquid. Vladimir agrees that this is a disgusting habit.[63]

Over the centuries a scattering of Byzantine texts dealing with Islam percolated northward. They include those of Saint John of Damascus, which appear to be the only relevant ones to have been translated into Russian before the seventeenth century.[64] Born into a prominent Syrian Christian family some fifty years after the Hegira (622), Saint John had begun his career as a tax collector for the Umayyad caliphs but eventually entered an Orthodox monastery near Jerusalem. A wide-ranging author on religious questions, the theologian was the first to develop the Christian argument against Islam in his "On Heresies," a description of over a hundred "false" beliefs. In essence, Saint John argued that Muhammad was not a real prophet and that he advocated sexual license. However, aside from ridiculing the Koran's *sura* about a miraculous camel, he did not directly address Islamic teachings.[65]

While other Eastern Christians, such as Nicetas of Byzantium and Emperor John IV, also wrote treatises against Islam, their invective tended to be less vitriolic than that of the Latin Church. Closer diplomatic and commercial contacts with the Abbasid Caliphate and other Muslim powers somewhat tempered Byzantine attitudes. More important, the Crusaders' sack of Constantinople in 1204 made Orthodox Christians increasingly distrustful of Rome. Thus, according to the French medievalist Alain Ducellier, Byzantines began "to compare [Catholics with] Muslims, favoring the latter more and more."[66]

One of the few to write about Islam in Muscovy was the monk Maksim the Greek, "the Russian Church's first true scholar," according to a Dutch historian.[67] Maksim entered the world around 1480 as Michael Trivolis in the Greek town of Arta. Educated in Renaissance Italy, he was living in the Orthodox monastic complex at Mount Athos when in 1518 Grand Prince Vasilii III sent for a learned man to help with Slavonic translations of liturgical works. Despite a lengthy banishment on charges of heresy during his years in Russia, the monk wrote prolifically about spirituality, including polemics against Catholicism, Judaism, and Islam. Among the latter were such treatises as "A Denunciation of the Hagarine Allure and the Foul Dog Muhammad's Designs" and "Answers of a Christian to the Hagarines," which adhered to the Byzantine polemical tradition established by Saint John of Damascus six centuries earlier.[68]

Aside from the writings of Maksim, who had been schooled in Catholic institutions, most of the serious literature about Islam that reached Muscovy after Constantinople's fall came from the West. One such work was Riccoldo da Monte Croce's *Contra legem sarracenorum* (Against the Law of the Saracens).[69] Written by a thirteenth-century Dominican missionary who had traveled to Baghdad, the polemic repeated traditional aspersions about the Prophet's character and the Koran's veracity.[70] Rome's attitudes to Islam were generally more hostile than those of the Eastern Church.[71] However, as Russian rule over newly conquered Tatar lands on the Volga after the 1550s would suggest, the circulation of such texts (in any case largely limited to Orthodox clergy) did not invariably translate into ruthless assimilation among Muslim subjects; Muscovite tsars did not follow Spain's example after the fall of Granada in 1492.

Traditional Russian secular attitudes toward the East are more elusive, but byliny and folktales (*skazki*) offer some clues.[72] Since the church frowned on such literature, they were transmitted orally until ethnographers like Vladimir Dal' began systematically recording them in the nineteenth century. While it is difficult to establish their origins, epics and folktales reflect the pre-Petrine worldview.

Among the byliny, the most popular is the "Kievan cycle," which tells of the exploits of *bogatyrs* (medieval warriors) at the court of Grand Prince Vladimir. A blend of history and fable, these byliny occupy a place in Russian culture somewhat akin to England's Arthurian legends. Dragons and bandits abound, but the bogatyr's perennial adversary is the Tatar, as the

Mongols who appeared on the scene in the thirteenth century came to be known. The valiant Il'ia Muromets invariably goes to battle on the steppe with these enemies, a vague amalgam of the "idolatrous" Pechenegs and Polovtsians and the Islamic Golden Horde. Even "the pagan serpent" (*Zmeia Poganaia*), the dragon with whom Il'ia's comrade-in-arms, Dobrynia Nikitich, battles, often has Turkic traits and hails from "the Saracen Mountains" to the east.[73]

In the folktales, as in the epics, the foreign enemy is invariably Asian. Some tell of valiant exploits against Saracens, and others of cruel Turkish sultans. India and China, however, are less menacing. In one skazka, Ivan-Bogatyr, "the Peasant's Son," ventures to the Middle Kingdom, where he wins the heart of the emperor's daughter, Laota; after killing a fearsome rival, he accedes to the throne as her husband. Intimacy with the East indirectly influenced folklore as well. According to the Slavist Roman Jakobson, "The intercourse and struggle of ancient Russia with the nomadic Turkish world bequeathed . . . many names and attributes to the Russian tales."[74] Even the word *bogatyr* came from Tatar.[75]

Some medieval folkloric views about the Orient persisted into the early twentieth century. "Kopek novels" and other inexpensive literature produced for the newly literate lower and lower-middle classes during tsarism's latter decades still often portrayed the Near East as menacing.[76] Tatars continued to be regarded as the most dangerous minority within the empire's borders, while Turks were the main foreign threat. Typical stories included *Slavery among the Asiatics, The Turkish Captive,* and *Turkish Amusements, or the Mohammedan Bestialities.* References to the past only reinforced such notions, as one history aimed at a mass readership published in 1898 suggested when describing the Mongol invasion over six hundred years earlier: "Out of the Asiatic steppe there surged into Russia the Tatars, the remnants of whom you have probably seen. These people were terrible; they were ferocious in appearance and pitied no one."[77]

Of course, the glimpses fairy tales show into the Muscovite mind do not provide the whole picture. As in Kievan times, frequent contact and intermarriage with neighbors on the southeastern frontier lessened the distinctions between self and other.[78] The Cossacks of the steppe, whom one scholar aptly described as a "Slavic-Oriental synthesis," are the most dramatic example of this phenomenon.[79] While Orthodox in belief, their ranks included a variety of nationalities, including Russians, Poles, Tatars, and others. And the Cossacks' celebrated style of warfare was largely derived from their Inner Asian antecedents on the Wild Field.

In the beginning, the steppe nomad was Russia's Oriental other. According to the chronicles the monastic scribes kept, encounters were invariably hostile, and the Slavic inhabitants of the forest suffered an unending succession of raids and wars. This grim literature is deceptive, since the relationship between the forest and the steppe was not inherently or always antagonistic. While there were clashes, trade and intermarriage also characterized the European Slavs' interaction with the Inner Asian nomads. Symbiosis rather than struggle was the order of the day. Even the two and a half centuries of Mongol rule were more benign than the histories compiled by churchmen in their wake would lead us to believe.

The written evidence about attitudes to the East in the Muscovite era, however sketchy, likewise suggests antagonism, particularly to Islam. Much of this literature was also produced under the aegis of the Orthodox Church, which increasingly provided ideological support for the tsars' campaigns against Muslim foes. Meanwhile, what little Russians knew about Asia tended to come from Byzantium until the West exposed them to a more secular outlook. But this would have to wait until Peter the Great's reign at the turn of the eighteenth century.

If the church did not portray the Muslim East in a favorable light, neither did it monopolize Russian attitudes. Afanasii Nikitin's fifteenth-century account of his trip to India makes this abundantly clear. More important, Russians were relatively late in developing a sense of national identity. In consequence, their sense of race tended to be much weaker than among western Europeans. Until the modern age, the peasant's primary allegiance was to his Eastern Christian faith. It is no coincidence that the Russian noun for peasant, *krestianin,* comes from *khristianin* (Christian). But this loyalty was to the triple-armed Orthodox version, not the simpler Latin one. The Catholic *nemets* (western foreigner) was just as alien as the Muslim basurman. According to a well-known saying, "Much woe has been wrought on us by the Crimean khan and the Roman pope."[80]

2

THE PETRINE DAWN

Russia's destiny is to become the link that joins two worlds, the western and the eastern.

—Gottfried Wilhelm von Leibniz

The story of orientology as an academic discipline in Russia begins with Tsar Peter the Great's reign at the turn of the eighteenth century. Motivated by his commercial and political ambitions in Asia, as well as by a genuine desire to learn about the world around him, the tsar laid the foundations for the systematic and scientific study of the Orient among his subjects.[1] As with many of his efforts to drag his empire into European modernity, Peter acted on the advice of a foreigner. The German philosopher and mathematician Gottfried Wilhelm von Leibniz had long been fascinated with China.[2] One of the leading figures of the early Enlightenment, Leibniz fully shared his age's infatuation with the Middle Kingdom. Like many of his contemporaries, he had read the favorable accounts of Jesuits who portrayed the Qing dynasty as the apotheosis of reason and toleration, and he came to see its civilization as the equivalent of his own. According to Leibniz, "human cultivation and refinement [are] today . . . concentrated, as it were, in Europe and in Tschina, which adorns the Orient as Europe does the opposite edge of the earth."[3]

There was much the Middle Kingdom could teach the West. While it might be less accomplished in technology and warfare, China's political order was far superior to Europe's. "It is difficult to describe," Leibniz argued, "how beautifully all the laws of the Chinese, in contrast to those of other peoples, are directed to the achievement of public tranquility and the establishment of social order."[4] Equally important to someone who had grown up in the aftermath of the Thirty Years' War, the early seventeenth-century conflict largely driven by confessional hatreds that ravaged much of Germany, was the relative absence of religious persecution by the Qing. The Kangxi Emperor's decree granting religious toleration to Catholic missionaries in 1692 stood in stark contrast to King Louis XIV's decision seven years earlier to revoke the Edict of Nantes, thereby depriving French Protestants of their freedom to worship.[5]

Russia also intrigued the German polymath's omnivorous intellect. If civilization was concentrated at Eurasia's two extremes, the lands that lay in between were not necessarily doomed to barbarism.[6] With a ruler eager to bring enlightenment to his subjects, "the Muscovites" had been uniquely blessed by geography, since their "vast realm connects Europe with China."[7] By learning the best from both, eventually Peter's young nation might well reach a higher level of development.[8] Therefore, to Leibniz Russia was both the logical intermediary as well as the geographical link between East and West.

The basic idea of the latter was hardly original. In the sixteenth century, when English merchants sought shortcuts to fabled Cathay's riches, intrepid adventurers such as Anthony Jenkinson traveled overland through Russia and central Asia to find a suitable approach. But if these Elizabethan explorers saw Muscovy as a potential commercial conduit, Leibniz envisaged it as the channel for knowledge and wisdom. In his words, the nation's "destiny was to become the link that joins two worlds, the western and the eastern."[9] What was more, under its energetic Tsar Peter, Russia would be much more than a passive thoroughfare.

There was another reason for the German philosopher's interest in Peter's dominion. Leibniz had long been a proponent of associations of learned men that, with the patronage of a monarch, would gather and disseminate knowledge for the betterment of humanity, like the Royal Society in London.[10] He had already advised the Elector of Brandenburg, Frederick III, in establishing what would become the Prussian Academy of Sciences in 1700. Peter, who ruled over an infinitely larger realm, offered intriguing possibilities for such a "Gelehrt Collegium" as well. Upon learning that the tsar was planning his Great Embassy to the West in 1697, the philosopher did his best to secure an audience to champion his project.[11] While he proved unsuccessful this time, Leibniz had more luck in arranging a meeting fourteen years later, when Peter traveled to Saxony to marry his eldest son, Aleksei, to a German princess.[12]

The tsar did not betray great enthusiasm during the encounter, but he corresponded with Leibniz over the next few years and solicited more concrete proposals for scholarly institutions.[13] The notion was attractive to Peter, since he had been favorably impressed by his visit to the Royal Society in 1698. In 1717, on his second major European tour, Peter had extensive discussions with members of the Académie des Sciences in Paris, who made him a member *hors de tout rang*.[14] Eight years later, on December 27, 1725, the Russian Academy of Sciences held its first formal session.

Leibniz, who died in 1716, did not live to see the establishment of the academy (nor did Peter, who succumbed to illness in January 1725). Leibniz's demise may have been a blessing in disguise, since it saved him from the possible disappointment of learning that the institution that arose on the banks of the Neva River departed from his vision in several important respects. Most glaring was the absence of much pedagogy. Passionate about education, Leibniz had always stressed that Peter's academic institutions should be as actively involved in teaching as in research.[15] His advice, as well as that of others, was reflected in the Senate's proposal of January 1724 for the *sotsietet* (society), which also called for a university and gymnasium (secondary school).[16] However, when the academy opened its doors the next year, there was not much mention of the university. While there would be a secondary school, it was always a poor relation of the more illustrious research institution.[17]

Leibniz's various proposals for learned societies had invariably mentioned the need to study Asia.[18] His advocacy for a Russian *Gelehrt Collegium* was no exception. Already in 1712, in a letter following up his meeting with the tsar at Torgau, he expressed his hope that "your highness might unite China with Europe," through scholarship.[19] Yet the Senate's proposal of 1724 only specified three general fields—mathematics, the natural sciences, and the humanities—without going into specifics.[20]

That the Academy of Sciences did involve itself in orientology came about as much by chance as by design. When Peter's officials set about recruiting foreign scholars for the young institution, they identified a schoolmaster in the East Prussian town of Königsberg, Gottlieb-Siegfried Bayer.[21] A man of wide-ranging linguistic abilities, Bayer had studied Arabic and Chinese on his own, in addition to the ancient Greek and Hebrew he had mastered at university. Eager to attract the Prussian polyglot, the academy offered him three possible chairs: classics, Russian history, or Oriental letters. Bayer chose the latter, and he would remain in Russia until his death in 1738.

Vasilii Barthold suggests that the opportunity to study Asian civilizations in a land closer to the continent may have influenced Bayer's decision.[22] The scholar's future research would appear to confirm this supposition. The academy's first orientologist did publish the *Monumentum Sinicum*, a compilation of European works about China, albeit to mixed reviews.[23] However, Bayer's most important contributions to scholarship involved his interest in the foreign sources of Russia's history, both eastern and western. Taking full advantage of Peter's Kunstkamer (chamber of curiosities) and other collections, he studied documents in a wide range of languages, from Mongolian, Chinese, Norse, and even Sanskrit (but not Russian).

In writing about the Scythians, Bayer became one of the first to study Russia's Asian origins. Many subsequent orientologists would follow in his steps, thereby contributing to an intellectual current whose ultimate outcome would be Eurasianism some two hundred years later. But when the academician interpreted the Nordic sagas to conclude that Vikings had first founded the Russian state, he sparked an acrimonious debate.[24] By initiating the notorious Normanist controversy, Bayer earned much opprobrium from his new compatriots. As recently as 1950, the Arabist Ignatii Krachkovskii denounced the "false Norman theory" Bayer had first formulated. Krachkovskii's overall assessment of Bayer's accomplishments was not much more positive, and he described him as "a scholar of broad but not always deep knowledge of Oriental languages. [Bayer] devoted a fair bit of time, albeit in dilettantish fashion, to sinology, bestowing upon it many grandiose works, part translation and part compilation."[25]

Georg-Jacob Kehr, the academy's other orientologist in the eighteenth century, joined the group in a more roundabout way.[26] Educated in Near

Eastern languages at Halle's Collegium Orientale Theologicum, where he had studied with the renowned Damascene Salomo Negri, Kehr had been recruited by the Russian College of Foreign Affairs in 1732 as a translator and language instructor. In 1735 the Academy of Sciences asked him to sort out the Kunstkamer's collection of some four thousand "Tatar" coins.

Peter had set up the Kunstkamer in 1714 in his Summer Palace, according to the custom of every self-respecting German prince of his day. "A typical manifestation of Baroque culture," it housed an eclectic collection of pickled natural specimens (with an emphasis on the freakish), mathematical instruments, and diplomatic gifts.[27] Because of Russia's eastern geography, there was also a wide assortment of archaeological and ethnographic rarities from Siberia, China, and other Asian lands.[28] Within a few years the mass of exotica grew too large for the Summer Palace, and in 1718 a new building was begun across the Neva River on Vassil'evskii Island, where it eventually became the Museum of Anthropology and Ethnography. Peter continued to add to his various collections. One of the more valuable additions toward the end of his life was a group of manuscripts he looted during his Persian expedition in 1722.[29] With the establishment of the Academy of Sciences three years later, the Kunstkamer came under that institution's aegis.

As for Kehr, Russians have regarded his scholarly accomplishments somewhat more highly than those of Bayer. One biographer described him as "the first orientologist in Russia."[30] Among the works he bequeathed to his extensive archive are translations of manuscripts in the academy's holdings, such as Persian astronomical tables as well as an important central Asian history, *The Family Tree of the Turkmen,* by the seventeenth-century khan of Khiva, Abu al-Ghazi Bahadur. None of these were published during his lifetime, although they would prove invaluable to scholars in the nineteenth century.

Neither Bayer nor Kehr left a particularly deep imprint on Russian orientology. Aside from a handful of young interpreters whom Kehr taught at the College of Foreign Affairs, they had no students.[31] At the same time, the Germans did not make much of an effort to disseminate their works in their adoptive homelands. Despite his remarkable talent for languages, Bayer never even deigned to learn Russian.[32] Indeed, during its early years, the academy was a thoroughly alien institution. Its proceedings were in Latin, while the first four presidents and the vast majority of its members were German (the first Russian academicians would be the scientist Mikhail Lomonosov and the poet Vasilii Trediakovskii, both appointed in 1745).[33]

In 1747 Empress Elizabeth signed a new statute for the Academy of Sciences, which not only freed its members from any teaching duties but also gave it a much more practical orientation by abolishing all chairs in the humanities. Although the university the tsarina would found in Moscow seven years later did have faculties of letters and history, during the first fifty-odd years of its existence there would be virtually no instruction in Asian languages. The discipline of orientology would have to wait until the nineteenth century for more propitious circumstances.

Outside of the Academy of Sciences, most of Peter the Great's efforts to create an apparatus for studying the East were equally slow to take root. The tsar's expansive commercial and political plans for Asia required officials competent in its languages, and he made many attempts to establish schools to train them accordingly. The first was a decree of June 18, 1700, to the new metropolitan of Siberia to find "two or three good and learned young monks who might learn Chinese and Mongolian," presumably to prepare them as missionaries. While the Soviet Turkologist Andrei Kononov grandly calls the order's date "the birthday of Russian orientology," there is no record of its ever being carried out.[34]

Peter's next try came quite by chance, as the result of a maritime mishap.[35] In winter 1695 a Japanese commercial transport sailing along Honshu's coast from Osaka to Edo (now Tokyo) was blown off course by a typhoon. After drifting about the Pacific's open waters for over half a year, the vessel finally made landfall well to the north, on the eastern Siberian peninsula of Kamchatka. The unfortunate crew now faced a new peril as native Koriaks, who had only recently come under Russian rule, promptly took them prisoner. Some perished, others fled, and by the following year the only remaining survivor was an Osaka merchant's clerk, Dembei.

When news of the mysterious castaway eventually reached the local administrator, Vladimir Atlasov, he ordered Dembei to be brought to his garrison in what would prove to be the first recorded encounter between a Russian and a Japanese. Since Dembei had already learned Koriak from his captors, the pair managed to converse with the help of an interpreter. Atlasov listened with great interest to tales of a fertile land rich in silver and gold, which he took to be India. His report to the Siberian Office, the government department responsible for the Asian territory, likewise intrigued his superiors, who summoned the "Indian" to Moscow. Dembei arrived there in 1701, and when more learned officials determined his true nationality, they hastened to present him to the tsar.

Japan had already piqued Peter the Great's curiosity. During his first trip to Europe a few years earlier, he had learned about the island nation and seen its exotic artifacts in the Netherlands, which then enjoyed a monopoly on all trade with the Tokugawa shogunate. The recent conquest of Kamchatka had brought Russia temptingly close to the archipelago, and the time seemed ripe to test the Dutch commercial stranglehold. However, the tsar had no subjects who could speak Japanese. Dembei's presence provided the perfect opportunity to teach some of them.

Peter met the castaway in January 1702, and he immediately made plans to put his involuntary guest to work. On the same day the tsar decreed that Dembei would remain in Moscow and learn Russian. Once Dembei had acquired a basic command of the language, he would in turn take on three or four Russian boys and instruct them in his native tongue for the generous wage of five kopeks a day. The Japanese clerk may not have had much choice in the matter, but he did secure the tsar's promise of an eventual return to his homeland.

Once again, scholars are unsure whether any lessons were actually given. It is known that, when in 1710 Dembei reminded Peter of his pledge to send him back to Osaka, the latter promptly had him converted to Orthodox Christianity and assigned to the staff of Siberia's new governor in Tobolsk. Twenty-five years later, Empress Anna had somewhat greater luck with two other Japanese likewise shipwrecked on Kamchatka: Sozo and Gonzo.[36] Eventually baptized into the Orthodox Church as Kuzma Schulz and Demian Pomortsev ("from the seashore"), respectively, the duo began teaching their language at the Academy of Sciences in 1736. But with the death of Demian Pomortsev three years later in 1739, the courses came to an end, and it would take until the late nineteenth century for Japanese instruction to be resumed at any academic institution in the capital.[37]

One of Peter the Great's most lasting contributions to Russian orientology was the first Russian ecclesiastical mission in Beijing. In the nineteenth century some of the institution's alumni would go on to become leading Sinologists. During its earlier decades, however, the mission's language school suffered from neglect in St. Petersburg. Its only scholars of note were Ilarion Rossokhin and Aleksei Leont'ev, who both held modest positions as translators at the Academy of Sciences. In his history of the Beijing mission, Eric Widmer suggests that the school's principal accomplishment during the first hundred years of its existence was its mere survival. This was already much better than nearly all of the eighteenth century's other attempts in Russia to teach Asian languages.[38]

Peter felt little need to organize instruction in Near Eastern languages, since he had no shortage of subjects who already knew them well. [39] These included Islamic minorities such as Kazan's Tatars, who spoke a Turkic tongue related to that of the Ottomans and whose elite was often schooled in Arabic. There were also foreigners who offered their services to the tsar. One of the best sources abroad for Near East experts consisted of the Greeks, Serbs, Romanians, and other Orthodox nations then under Turkish rule. Constantinople's sultans often drew on the abilities of their more learned men for their own administration. While many were willing to do so, others found the vigorous young monarchy of their Muscovite coreligionists more appealing. Chief among the latter was the Moldavian Prince Dimitrie Cantemir.

Most Russians today associate the surname "Kantemir" (according to its transliteration from the Cyrillic) with Dimitrie's son Antiokh, an important figure of eighteenth-century literature. Poet, satirist, and diplomat, Prince Antiokh Dmitrievich Kantemir was one of the leading lights of the Petrine Enlightenment. Yet Antiokh's father was no less prominent in his day. Dimitrie Cantemir's birth in 1673 also places him in the early Enlightenment, but he can best be described as a Renaissance man. His considerable talents ranged from the natural sciences, philosophy, and history to architecture and literature. And Turks still hold his musical compositions in high regard.[40]

As the son of the Moldavian *hospodar*, the ruler of one of the two Romanian principalities then under the sultan's vassalage, Dimitrie was sent to Constantinople in 1688. The Ottomans typically kept a close male relative of their governors in the capital to ensure the latter's loyalty. It was not a harsh sentence. Many a provincial grandee's offspring happily succumbed to a life of indolent luxury in the fabled metropolis. Initially housed in the Moldavian princely palace, young Dimitrie took a distinctly different path by devoting his enforced idleness to more cerebral pursuits.

Dimitrie's formal education was at the Academy of the Orthodox Patriarchate, in the Greek district of Phanar. Despite its ties to the highly traditional Byzantine Church, the school's faculty was strongly influenced by more liberal humanist and neo-Aristotelian currents. At the same time, he also learned Turkish, Arabic, and Islamic theology from leading Ottoman scholars, such as the philosopher Sadi Effendi and the Koran specialist Nefioglu. During the two decades Cantemir spent on the Bosporus as a young man assiduously pursuing his studies, his outlook was accordingly shaped by the three great intellectual legacies of Byzantium, the Italian Renaissance, and Islam.

About a hundred years later, in another Oriental dynasty then at the height of its splendor, China's Qianlong Emperor mused about being like "the sun at midday." As the commentary on this saying pointed out, "When the sun stands at midday, it begins to set; when the moon is full it begins to wane. The fullness and emptiness of heaven and earth wane and wax in the course of time. How much truer is this of men."[41] The same could have been said about the Ottoman sultans at the turn of the seventeenth century. Stretching like a giant crescent from central Europe through the Near East and into northern Africa, their realm was one of the most formidable of its day. Meanwhile, the capital of Constantinople was a city of great wealth then at the cusp of a cultural and intellectual rebirth known as the "tulip age." Yet despite all its outward brilliance, the Ottoman dynasty had already entered into decadence. Generations of ineffectual rule and growing corruption began to undermine the ruling house's political authority. At the same time, a recent military campaign into central Europe that had taken Janissaries to the very gates of Vienna in 1683 ended disastrously with the Treaty of Karlowitz sixteen years later, effectively ending the Turkish military threat to Christendom.

Dimitrie Cantemir's relatively privileged position afforded him an excellent opportunity to witness the Ottomans' incipient decline. His erudition made him a favorite guest of Constantinople's luminaries, and he was well acquainted with European diplomats, such as Russia's Count Petr Tolstoi. Cantemir also spent some time in the field, witnessing firsthand the Turks' decisive defeat by the Austrians at the Battle of Zenta in 1697. This military background may have been one of the reasons for his appointment as Moldavia's hospodar in 1710, on the eve of a war with Russia.

Although Turkey opened the hostilities, Russia went on the offensive. Hoping to rely on the sympathies of their two Orthodox hospodars, Peter the Great marched his forces south into the Romanian principalities. While the other temporized, Cantemir threw his lot in with the tsar. In April 1711 he signed a treaty that offered military support and fealty to the Romanovs in exchange for refuge, should the fighting go badly. It did. Despite the Moldavian's summons, only about 5,000 of his compatriots joined the 38,000-man Russian army. When he confronted vastly larger Turkish forces on the Prut River three months later, Peter met with defeat and was forced to sue for peace.[42]

The tsar kept his promise to Cantemir. Despite the Ottomans' insistence on their errant hospodar's return, he was allowed to join the retreat and begin a comfortable exile in Russia. As in Constantinople, Cantemir devoted much of his energy to scholarship. Some of his efforts focused on his homeland. The Berlin Academy of Sciences, which elected him to membership in 1714, asked him to write a *Description of Moldavia,* and he began a *Chronicle of Romanian Wallachians and Moldovans.*[43] These works also carried a clear political message in emphasizing his nation's link to Roman civilization. Another treatise, *A Study of the Nature of Monarchy,* called on Peter the Great to carry on his struggle with Turkey to assume his rightful place as the universal sovereign uniting East and West.[44]

In 1720, apparently at the tsar's request, Cantemir completed *The System of the Religion and Condition of the Turkish Empire.* Published in Russian two years later, it repeated many traditional Christian arguments against Islam: Muhammad was a false prophet, the Koran was full of lies, and the faith was brutishly fanatical in "advocating the murder of unbelievers."[45] But *The System*'s author did not slavishly follow the medieval church's polemics against the infidel. He represented Islamic texts without too much editorializing and reminded his reader that "Eastern peoples are in no way inferior to Westerners."[46] Cantemir's relatively objective tone drew the ire of the Holy Synod, Peter the Great's newly established secular administration of the Russian Orthodox Church. On the pretext of deeming his sources to have been inadequately cited, it refused to print the book. Only after the emperor's direct intervention did the synod relent, and the volume came off the presses.[47]

Cantemir's most significant work was the *History of the Growth and Decay of the Othman Empire*, which he completed in 1716.[48] While the Latin original remained unpublished, during his appointment as the tsarina's ambassador in London his son Antiokh dutifully arranged for an English translation to be printed in 1734, and French and German versions soon followed. Encyclopedic in scope, with extensive biographical, geographical, religious, and ethnographic notes, the *History* chronicled the Ottoman dynasty from its fourteenth-century origins until the early 1700s. The first volume, which deals with the period until 1696, was largely based on the survey of the author's friend Sadi Effendi. The more detailed second part, "Being the History of the Author's Own Times," gave a firsthand account of the fifteen years until the hospodar's flight in 1711.

There had been earlier European studies of Ottoman history, beginning with *De la république des Turcs* in 1559 by the Collège de France's eccentric first Arabist, Guillaume Postel. What set Cantemir apart was his extensive and evenhanded reliance on Turkish chronicles, to the point of repeating their interpretation of confrontations with the Christian powers. He objectively presented events such as the Byzantine capital's fall to Sultan Mehmed II in 1453, and stressed the Ottomans' many cultural accomplishments. Remarkably, the *History* even adhered to the Islamic calendar, whose years are counted from the Hegira (Muhammad's emigration from Mecca to Medina in 622 C.E.) rather than from the birth of Jesus Christ.

Cantemir's basic message was hardly edifying: great powers, like living beings, are born, enjoy youthful vigor, a civilized maturity, and ultimately die—the same organic view of history that would subsequently be adopted by Montesquieu and Gibbon in their histories of Rome. Of course, unlike the latter, in the eighteenth century the Ottoman Empire was still very much alive. However, as the prince stressed, it was already well into its dotage, and the end was utterly inescapable.

Cantemir's book remained the standard reference on the Ottoman Empire for European scholars until it was supplanted a hundred years later by the Austrian orientologist Josef Freiherr von Hammer-Purgstall's massive 10-volume *Geschichte des osmanischen Reiches*. The baron cattily dismissed the earlier work, "which has until now enjoyed such unjustified renown," for ignoring many important Turkish sources and fabricating etymologies.[49] Whether deserved or not, Cantemir's *History* still garnered the praise of the British scholar Sir William "Oriental" Jones. Edward Gibbon and Voltaire both relied on it for their works, and Byron mentioned the prince twice in his verse tale, *Don Juan*.[50] Its impact in Russia was virtually nonexistent, however, since it remained unpublished there.

Peter the Great valued his Moldavian guest's intellectual accomplishments. When the tsar began to set up the Academy of Sciences, he seriously considered appointing the prince as its first president.[51] Cantemir also found time for less scholarly activities. The estates and the generous pension Peter had granted him enabled the exile to continue the life of a grandee. With his noble title confirmed by his new sovereign, Cantemir was easily accepted into Russia's higher circles. In 1719, five years after the death of his first wife, he took the hand of the eighteen-year-old daughter of Field Marshal Prince Ivan Trubetskoi, Anastasia, with the tsar acting as best man. Reputedly "the foremost beauty of her day," the young woman boasted one of the most distinguished lineages.[52]

Having already been appointed to the Senate in 1718, Cantemir also remained involved in Russian affairs of state. Above all, Peter relied on him for his knowledge of the Near East. In 1722, as the tsar began a campaign of conquest against Persia in the Caucasus, the prince joined him as a leading counselor. During the operations his duties included printing proclamations to the local population in Persian and Turkish on the first Russian press with an Arabic font.[53] Unfortunately, when he developed diabetes, the rigors of the march proved too taxing on the prince, and he died shortly after retiring to his estate the following year.

Like many subsequent leading figures in Russian orientology, Dimitrie Cantemir occupied an ambiguous position between East and West. A portrait at the Musée de Rouen nicely captures this duality. Erroneously titled *Le hospodar de Valachie*, the oil depicts a slender young man with delicate, almost feminine features in a European silk brocade jacket, a linen cravat at the neck, and a luxuriant Louis XIV–style wig topped by a blue-and-white turban *à la turque*.[54] Even after he had become the loyal subject of a Christian tsar, Cantemir rarely hid his Oriental connection. A German traveler recounts one of Peter the Great's lavish masquerades, where the prince appeared on a float in his Ottoman guise, wearing the costume of a vizier and surrounded by attendants in Turkish dress bearing a banner with the Islamic crescent.[55] With a surname supposedly derived from "Khan" and "Timur" (Tamerlane), Cantemir proudly, if spuriously, claimed aristocratic Tatar roots—much like some Russian princely houses.[56]

Russians already knew about Asia before Peter's day. By virtue of their geography they had long had direct contact with the East. Peter's achievement was to sow the seeds of orientology in his young empire. Many failed to flower, and it would take until the nineteenth century for Russia to develop a proper native tradition. Nevertheless, as Barthold rightly points out, "despite long-standing ties between Russia and the East, Russian orientology traces its origins to Peter the Great and it became the same kind of 'Western' discipline as other academic fields."[57]

The Promethean tsar's westernizing reforms have typically been portrayed as entirely utilitarian. Historians of orientology in Russia therefore often attribute his initiatives in this regard as motivated by political and commercial aims.[58] While this may have been the case, such explanations do not tell the whole story. Yuri Slezkine once remarked that seventeenth-century Muscovites had not shown much curiosity about the outside world. Influenced by the European Enlightenment, however, Peter and his contemporaries began to see curiosity as a virtue. [59] The tsar's Asian coin collection and his order to loot Persian manuscripts were clearly not entirely motivated by *raison d'état*.[60] As in the West, Russian orientology was also driven by a distinctly unpractical thirst for pure knowledge. This was an equally important legacy of the Petrine dawn.

3

CATHERINIAN CHINOISERIE

I lay here in the summer-house of the khan,
Amidst the infidel and the faith Mohammedan.
'Cross from the house there stood a mosque most tall,
Whither five times a day an imam the people did call.
I thought to sleep, my eyes barely shut for the night,
When, with ears stopped, he did roar with all his might . . .
Oh, miracles of God! Who amongst my kin of yore
Slept calmly, free from the khans and the hordes?
And disturbed from my sleep amidst Bakhchisarai
By tobacco smoke and cries . . . Is this not paradise?

—Catherine the Great

Few sovereigns have celebrated their silver jubilee more extrava-
gantly than did Empress Catherine II of Russia. In 1787, to mark the
twenty-fifth anniversary of her accession to the throne, the German-born
monarch invited a select group of diplomats and courtiers on a seven-
month journey to admire her latest acquisition, the Crimean Peninsula on
the Black Sea. Organized by her erstwhile lover and current viceroy of the
region, Prince Grigorii Potemkin, at a cost roughly equivalent to a quarter of the imperial government's annual revenues, the southern excursion
fully confirmed Catherine's reputation among European contemporaries
as one of their richest and mightiest monarchs.[1]

The 3,000-kilometer trip began shortly after the New Year's celebrations. On the morning of January 7, a train of fourteen gilded carriages on
runners accompanied by 184 loaded sleighs and forty spares left the palace

at Tsarskoe Selo near St. Petersburg. Among the more important guests of the tsarina and her current favorite, Count Aleksandr Dmitriev-Mamonov, were the French, British, and Austrian ministers to her court. For some three weeks the lavish suite sped over central Russia's snowy expanses into Ukraine, reaching Kiev on January 29. Here the group halted for three months to await the spring thaw so that it could proceed downriver on the Dnieper.

Despite their still being some 500 kilometers from the former khanate, to some the Orient already seemed very much in evidence. The French diplomat Louis-Philippe Count de Ségur was struck by the variety of Eastern delegations paying homage to the "*impératrice conquérante*," from Don Cossacks "richly dressed *à l'asiatique*," Tatars, Georgians, and Kirghiz, to "savage Kalmoucks, who bear a true resemblance to the Huns."[2] And he described meetings with Prince Potemkin, who had just linked up with the party, like "the audience of the vizier of Constantinople, Bagdad, or Cairo."[3]

On April 22 the Dnieper was sufficiently clear of ice for the august assembly to board the flotilla that would take it further south. No less sumptuous than their winter transport, seven gold and scarlet galleys unobtrusively crewed by some three thousand oarsmen, guards, and attendants cruised majestically until the cataracts at Kaidak made further travel by river impossible. Here Austria's Emperor Joseph II, travelling as "le Comte de Falkenstein," also joined the tsarina.

As the imperial procession trundled across the seemingly endless grasslands, Ségur tactlessly muttered about "*l'ennui des déserts*."[4] But Potemkin had thoughtfully provided some diversion, for shortly after leaving Kherson the group found itself surrounded by thousands of Don Cossacks who had seemingly appeared out of nowhere. Accompanied by Kalmyk horsemen "resembling Chinese," the warriors staged a mock battle for the entertainment of Catherine's guests. Now forming the empress's guard, the Cossacks would eventually be joined by 1,200 Crimean Tatar cavalry and, with a nod to Herodotus, even a regiment of "Amazons" (actually the wives of Greek settlers) clad in crimson skirts, neoclassical breastplates, green tunics, and white ostrich plumes. These spectacular displays of exotic militaria were more than a theatrical caprice. By confidently placing her party under the protection of an assortment of

nationalities who in centuries past had menaced Muscovy's southern frontier, Russia's tsarina was unambiguously demonstrating her dominion
over her Asian subjects.[5]

Potemkin's choreography successfully evoked the Oriental atmosphere
of Catherine's new conquests. The French ambassador recalled a conversation he had had with the Austrian emperor on the eve of their entry into
the Crimea. Encamped just north of Perekop, the narrow isthmus that
joins the peninsula to the mainland, the pair took a leisurely stroll in the
warm twilight. Some camels passed in the distance. Joseph mused, "What
a singular journey, and who would have dreamt of seeing me with Catherine the Second and the ministers of France and England wandering in the
desert of the Tatars! It is altogether a new page of history." To which
Ségur replied, "It appears to me rather like a page from the Arabian
Nights' Entertainments." The Asian exotic manifested itself again a little
later during the duo's promenade, when a group of Kalmyk nomads drove
an enormous wheeled tent across their path.[6]

While Catherine's tour would end with a twenty-fifth anniversary gala
in Moscow, its highlight was the Bakhchisarai sojourn in late May. Signi-
fying "the palace of gardens" in Persian, Bakhchisarai had formerly been
the capital of the Crimean khanate, the last political remnant of the Golden
Horde. As recently as the seventeenth century, Crimean Tatars had staged
destructive raids deep into the Russian heartland. Vassals of the Ottoman
Empire, they had remained a threat to the rich farmlands of the southern
frontier until Catherine annexed their peninsula in 1783.[7] But within four
years Prince Potemkin had transformed the erstwhile foe's homeland into
a peaceful garden of vineyards, orchards, and picturesque mountains, dot-
ted with quaint tows and villages whose architectural turquerie had been
carefully preserved.[8]

The verse Catherine presented to her viceroy, "I lay here in the summer-
house of the khan," had been composed in the residence of the former ruling Girey dynasty.[9] An Oriental pastiche that combined Moorish, Persian,
Arabian, Chinese, and Turkish styles—with the occasional Gothic touch
—the palace now hosted the empress and her guests. For many of the visitors, the compound's marble fountains, airy galleries, and peaceful court-
yards evoked an Eastern fairyland. As well as waxing poetic about a paradise of mosques and tobacco smoke, Catherine described Bakhchisarai as

"a Chinese village" when she wrote to her daughter-in-law.[10] The Count de Ségur, who lodged in the harem, was given to more elaborate fantasies: "We might have supposed ourselves to be really in the midst of a town in Turkey or Persia. . . . I remember that having lain down on my sofa, over-come by the extreme heat, and enjoying the murmuring of the water, the freshness of the shade and the fragrance of the flowers, I gave myself up to oriental luxury, and was enjoying all the inactivity of a true Pacha."[11]

The Russian scholar Andrei Zorin argues that the Crimea held "tremen-dous symbolic capital" for its new ruler.[12] Nearby is the town of Kherson, where according to the *Primary Chronicle* Prince Vladimir had been bap-tized into the Christian faith in 988. As Catherine's poem implies, the peninsula's proximity to the birthplace of the Russian Church and its lush orchards suggested paradise.[13]

There were also many links to classical Greece, which long ago had col-onized the Crimean shores. During latter decades of the eighteenth cen-tury, Russian culture had taken a distinctly Grecophile turn.[14] Catherine even dreamt of a "Greek project" to restore Byzantium, albeit under her younger grandson, whom she had optimistically named Constantine. Her subjects stressed the peninsula's Hellenic past by restoring the area's Greek name, "Taurus," and christening the nearby Black Sea port Odessa after Homer's hero Odysseus.[15] When Catherine's guests on her Tauric tour described their cruise in Ukraine, they wrote not about the Dnieper but the Borysthenes, as the river had been known in antiquity.[16] And as her party entered Kherson, a ceremonial archway emblazoned with the words "The Way to Byzantium" greeted it.[17]

Yet despite its Hellenic associations, or partly because of them, it was the Orient that the Crimea most often evoked in Catherine's day, both in Rus-sia and abroad.[18] Even if geographers placed it within Europe, the Scythian and Tatar heritage, as well as centuries of Ottoman cultural influence, had made the peninsula seem much more of the East than of the West. The em-press and her travel companions all employed Asian tropes in their many letters and reminiscences of the trip.[19] In the early nineteenth century, poets such as Aleksandr Pushkin and his Polish contemporary Adam Mickiewicz likewise rhapsodized about the former khanate's Oriental nature. Military humiliation in the 1850s would, of course, give the Crimea a distinctly dif-ferent connotation in the minds of subsequent generations of Russians.

The most striking thing about Catherine the Great's Crimean Orient is its playful quality.[20] Like Mozart's Rondo alla turca or Meissen porcelain figurines of Chinese sages, the Bakhchisarai she and her companions visited was perceived as a realm of fairy tales, dreams, and reveries—"*un tableau magique*," according to Ségur.[21] Even when the empress referred to the "khans and hordes" of bygone days in her poem to Potemkin, the allusion only heightens the contrast with the verse's picturesque, thoroughly harmless mosques and imams. And it is in this sense, as an object of whimsical curiosity, that Russians came to see the East more generally during the century of their rapid Westernization.

Catherine could imagine traveling from her capital on the Neva to the Crimea as a journey from Europe into Asia. However, like all eighteenth-century Romanov sovereigns, beginning with Peter the Great, she had no doubts about her empire's continental identity. In the first chapter of her *Nakaz*, the instruction she issued in 1767 to solicit opinions from her subjects about a new law code, Catherine confidently proclaimed that "Russia is a European state."[22] Visitors from the West, however, were not always so sure. Already when he crossed the border between Prussia and Poland on his way to Russia, Ségur felt that he had "gone altogether beyond the bounds of Europe." And even St. Petersburg, despite its distinctly Western architecture, struck him as quasi-Oriental. According to the French count, the city "unites . . . the manners of Asia and those of Europe."[23]

Nevertheless, by Catherine's day European cartographers had begun to draw the border with Asia with greater precision. As Larry Wolff has pointed out, Enlightenment mapmakers were much more scientific and consistent than their predecessors in delineating the globe's features. Continental boundaries were a case in point. Thus, from antiquity until the eighteenth century, Asia was variously believed to begin at the Don or Volga rivers, or even farther west. By placing the border at the Ural Mountains, Vasilii Tatishchev, one of Petrine Russia's most learned officials, ultimately settled the question—at least for dispassionate geographers.[24]

Largely marked by water, Asia's other contours were less controversial. What comprised "the Orient" remained a little more ambiguous. Most Russians would have agreed with Antoine Galland's definition in the preface of his early eighteenth-century compilation of Near Eastern tales, *The*

Thousand and One Nights: "I take the noun Oriental to include not only the Arabs and the Persians, but also the Turks and Tatars, and virtually all other Asian peoples, right up to China, Muslims or pagans and idolaters [i.e., Buddhists]."[25] But even to Russians the division between Orient and Occident in their own realm was not necessarily clear, as Catherine's Crimean reveries suggest. While Siberia was clearly both Asian and Oriental, the empire's population also included Muslim, pagan, and Buddhist nationalities well to the west of the Ural Mountains.

Despite Bayer, Kehr, Cantemir, and a handful of others, the Russia of Peter and his heirs had not shared much of eighteenth-century Europe's fascination with the Orient. This would begin to change when Catherine the Great seized the throne in a palace coup in 1762. Over the course of her thirty-four-year reign, Asia, and especially China, became fashionable among the elite in Russia's two capitals. The aristocratic circles that were seized by the Enlightenment's passion for all things Oriental were rarefied and comparatively small, and they drew their inspiration from the West. Nevertheless, the Catherinian age marked the beginnings of a more sophisticated understanding of the East. Paradoxically, it was at a time when Russians identified with Europe most strongly that they regarded Asia with the least self-doubt.

Russia's growing interest in the East after midcentury was shaped by the personality of its energetic ruler, who was intimately involved in her empire's intellectual and cultural life. According to the nineteenth-century historian Vasilii Kliuchevskii, "only [Catherine the Great] always joined power and thought. After her reign, as before, the two never met, or they failed to recognize each other."[26] As Isabel de Madariaga points out, the nature of Russia's court-centered culture under Elizabeth and Catherine II magnified the empresses' influence.[27]

Born to a minor German princely household as Sophie von Anhalt-Zerbst in 1729, Catherine was a woman of unusual intellect, energy, and ambition. Summoned to St. Petersburg at the age of fourteen to marry Empress Elizabeth's nephew and heir, Peter, the match proved unfulfilling. As she later recalled, "eighteen years of tediousness and solitude [from her arrival in Russia until she took power in 1762] caused her to read many books."[28] These included such classics as Plutarch and Tacitus, as well as many of the leading authors of the Enlightenment, from Voltaire, Pierre

Bayle, and Montesquieu to d'Alembert and Diderot.[29] As a result, when Catherine acceded to the throne she was one of Europe's best-read monarchs, fully conversant with the intellectual currents of her era.

Catherine's love affair with books did not end when she seized the throne, but now she also became a prolific author in her own right. Her self-professed "writing mania" touched on a wide range of subjects, from law and history to prose, theater, and even opera librettos. The tsarina's output fills no less than eleven published volumes, not to mention various collections of her extensive correspondence.[30] Guilty by association with the institution of serfdom, not to mention her notorious penchant for guards' officers, Catherine has been dismissed by many as a shallow thinker.[31] But the French historian Albert Sorel was being a bit harsh when he quipped, "The ideas of the century passed over her like a beam of light on the surface of a pool, without warming the depths below."[32] While Catherine was not beyond manipulating the truth to advance her and her empire's interests, her writings demonstrate an intelligent understanding and engagement with the European Enlightenment. This was particularly true with respect to her predilection for chinoiserie, as the eighteenth-century's cultural infatuation with East Asia came to be known.

Without question the man most responsible for shaping the attitudes of Catherinian St. Petersburg about the East was the French philosophe Voltaire.[33] Already close to seventy years old in 1762 and living in exile in the Swiss village of Ferney, Voltaire was well known to Russian readers. Leading writers, beginning with Prince Antiokh Kantemir in the 1730s, had translated his texts, and many devoured Voltaire's works in the original.[34] According to the Venetian libertine Giovanni Giacomo Casanova, whose colorful exploits included a visit to Russia in 1765, "In those days Russian literati and officers knew, read, and celebrated only the philosopher of Ferney, and when they had read everything Voltaire had published thought themselves even more learned than their apostle."[35]

Voltaire's most prominent Russian admirer was the empress herself. During the unhappy leisure of her years as the tsarevich's neglected consort, Catherine had become well acquainted with his writings, and upon deposing her hapless spouse she immediately began a lengthy correspondence with the celebrated exile.[36] Their epistolary friendship was not without tangible benefits to both parties. Despite his biting critiques of the Bourbons, the bourgeois philosophe craved the company of kings, and after having fallen out with Prussia's Frederick the Great he was eager to cultivate another august patron. Meanwhile, Catherine gained an enthusiastic propagandist who helped burnish her reputation in Europe as the model enlightened despot. Nevertheless, the relationship was more than a cynical partnership, and the pair did share a similar outlook on many questions, such as the need for firm rule in backward nations and religious toleration, as well as a dislike of the Roman Catholic Church.[37]

Like Leibniz, Voltaire idealized China.[38] While the Jesuit fathers of the Parisian *collège* he attended had failed to impart the Catechism, they did instill in him a deep respect for the Middle Kingdom—or at least for the roseate portrait of the land of Cathay painted by their missionaries. Disillusioned with the politics and culture of his native France, Voltaire saw in the Chinese many of the virtues that seemed to be lacking in his compatriots. As he put it, the former "are the first, as well as the most ancient, people in the world in morals and policy."[39] Even when Paris's salons began to tire of the Orient in the latter half of the eighteenth century, Voltaire still confessed to being "a sort of Don Quixote" in his passion for China.[40]

There are several recurring themes in the philosophe's voluminous writings about the Middle Kingdom. First, he profoundly respected the Confucian ethic. "What they best know, cultivate the most, and have brought to the greatest perfection, is morality," he enthused.[41] Voltaire was also impressed by the sagacity of the political order, with its emperor as the "chief philosopher," ruling his domain with the stern benevolence of a father yet always acting in harmony with his subjects' laws and traditions. And he shared Leibniz's admiration for the Celestial Empire's tolerance of alien creeds. The state where Confucianism had coexisted for centuries with Taoism, Buddhism, Islam, and even Judaism was often invoked in his censure of the ancien régime's intolerance.

The positive qualities Voltaire detected in the Chinese—Confucius' rational morality, enlightened despotism, and religious tolerance—also appealed to Catherine. She noted that "To do nothing without principle or without reason, not to allow oneself to be led by prejudice, to respect religion, but not to give it any power in State matters, to banish everything that reeks of fanaticism and to draw the best of every situation for the public good, is the basis of the Chinese empire, the most durable of all those known on this earth."[42] But Catherine did not always ape her French correspondent's laudatory view of China.[43] Her own experience with the Qing government was distinctly rocky. At times commercial disputes, border clashes, and competition for the loyalty of nomadic Kalmyks and Zungars severely strained relations between St. Petersburg and Beijing. Early in her reign, Catherine even contemplated war with her Eastern neighbor.[44] In one letter she complained to Voltaire that "the Chinese are so quarrelsome."[45] On another occasion he was chided for being unrealistic: "Sir, you have lavished so much praise on China . . . yet my own dealings with this state would go a long way toward destroying any notions about their *savoir-vivre*." The empress diplomatically added that she was dealing with the Manchu, "the Tartar nation that conquered China, and not the Chinese themselves."[46] Catherine could also be more whimsical. To another friend, the Habsburg courtier Charles-Joseph Prince de Ligne, she jested about her "good neighbor," the Qianlong Emperor:

> Le Roi de la Chi, i, i, i, i, i, ne
> Quand il a bien bu, u, u, u, u, u, u,
> Fait une plaisante mi, i, i, i, i, ne![47]

Still, regardless of any difficulties with the Qing government, Catherine's literary works fully adhered to Enlightenment tropes about the Middle Kingdom as a land of virtue and wisdom. Thus her comic opera *Fevei*, originally written as a didactic story for her grandsons Alexander and Constantine in 1783, described a good ruler of Chinese ancestry.[48] At the same time, her works about other Eastern regions could be less flattering. In her fairy tale "Tsarevich Khlor," the hero is kidnapped by a Kirghiz khan,[49] and her anti-Masonic play *The Siberian Shaman* portrays the main character as a charlatan.[50] Nevertheless, in all these texts the Orient is an allegorical land, an exotic fairytale realm.

Catherine was not alone in playing with Eastern motifs in their prose and poetry.[51] When Maria Sushkova, the wife of a Siberian governor, likened the tsarina to Confucius in a fictitious "Letter of a Chinese to a Tatar noble in St. Petersburg on business," she was hardly committing lèse-majesté:

In Peking, o Nobleman, we read your verses,
And loving truth, we say in agreement:
On the Northern throne, we see Confucius.[52]

Other writers used Oriental themes in Aesopian fashion when commenting about politics. The Russian publisher Nikolai Novikov, who was given to poking fun at Catherine's efforts to portray herself as a Voltairian enlightened despot, embroidered a translation of a Chinese text to draw an unfavorable comparison with the empress. "The Testament of Yongzhen, Khan of China, to His Son," which appeared in his short-lived satirical journal *Pustomelia* (The Tattler) in 1770, presents the typical wise Chinese philosopher-king in quoting the late emperor: "[From the start of my reign] I worried day and night about the well being of my subjects; I strove to ensure that they would find me neither lazy, nor ignorant, nor unworthy of being their ruler. . . . I assiduously endeavored to ensure that all justice throughout my realm was fair, that all people were contented and tranquil, and that the state grew stronger."[53] The point was made, not with great subtlety, by printing immediately below this piece Denis Fonvizin's "Letter to My Servants," a scathing indictment of social injustice in Catherine's own empire. The tsarina may not have been amused; literary scholars have debated whether this unflattering juxtaposition of the Chinese ideal with Russia's sad reality had anything to do with the fact that no more issues of *Pustomelia* appeared thereafter.[54]

Fonvizin, an official in the College of Foreign Affairs and the foremost dramatist of his day, also engaged in allegorical chinoiserie. In 1779 he published a translation of *Da Xue*, a Confucian text that stresses the obligations of the ruler toward his subjects.[55] The subtext was clear: govern benevolently, or you may find your throne in great peril. According to a historian, the following phrase was understood as a reference to the Cossack Emilian Pugachev's great revolt five years earlier: "A sovereign forbids in vain that which he allows himself; [for then] no one will obey him . . . [and the ruler's] throne will fall under the burden of arrogance, and its ruins will be your grave."[56]

By using Asian motifs to discuss the shortcomings of one's own land, Russian authors were following a well-established European literary practice. *The Spectator*, an influential early eighteenth-century British periodical, occasionally carried Chinese tales that indirectly alluded to contemporary society.[57] However, the best-known example of this genre was Montesquieu's *Lettres persanes*. First published in 1721, this fictional correspondence between two Oriental travelers, whose seemingly naive observations witheringly mocked French politics and habits, won a wide readership throughout Europe.[58]

Catherinian culture's flirtation with the Orient extended well beyond the written word and was applied particularly to architecture and the decorative arts. Again, the emphasis lay on China and entirely reflected Western fashion. *Kitaishchina,* as chinoiserie was known in Russian, had already made its appearance at the turn of the eighteenth century. During his journeys to the West, Peter the Great had been particularly struck by the Chinese and Japanese porcelain he saw everywhere in Holland, as well as in the Prussian king's Porzellankammer at Schloß Charlottenburg and in the lacquer room at Rosenborg Slot in Copenhagen.

The latter two formed the model for the "Chinese room" the tsar commissioned for his wife, Catherine I, at Peterhof's Monplaisir Palace.[59] The modest Dutch-style house's interior, with its dark oak-paneled walls, Netherlandish oil paintings, black-and-white chessboard floors, and Delft-tiled kitchen, evoked Amsterdam's canals rather than the Gulf of Finland, on whose shore it stood. At first glance, the Chinese room, a dazzling little enclave of gilt and deep red frames holding ninety-four lacquer panels with traditional Middle Kingdom motifs, would have seemed a bizarre aberration, a jarring contrast to the sober Calvinist patrician ambience that pervaded the rest of Monplaisir. Yet it was entirely in keeping with the northern European taste at the time for the Baroque exotic.

The start of regular caravan trade with China gave Peter more direct access to precious Eastern objets d'art, which began to decorate his palaces and those of his intimates. The statesman Count Jacob Bruce, for one, amassed an impressive collection of over two hundred Chinese pieces.[60] According to one contemporary, when the tsar married off his niece Ekaterina Ioannovna to a German prince, "the nuptial bed was placed in a room decorated in the Japanese style and filled with Japanese lacquered articles, such as are often to be found in Russian houses."[61] Meanwhile, under Peter's daughter, Empress Elizabeth, the mining engineer Dmitri

Vinogradov opened what would eventually become the Imperial Porcelain Factory, thereby providing an important domestic source for fine ceramics.[62] These material forms of kitaishchina reached their apogee during Catherine the Great's long and prosperous reign. Porcelain production boomed as entrepreneurs like Francis Gardner opened private factories to help meet growing demand.[63] While there were various styles, the material's Asian origins naturally lent itself to Oriental themes.

The empress was an avid aficionada of both porcelain and architecture, and the latter reflected her interest in the East.[64] Already in the first year of her reign, she commissioned the Neapolitan architect Antonio Rinaldi to build a new summer residence at Oranienbaum, also on the Gulf of Finland. While its Baroque pink-and-white exterior is entirely Occidental, inside an entire suite of rooms is decorated with silk walls, inlaid wood floors, and painted ceilings.[65] All in the most flamboyant rococo chinoiserie, they would eventually earn the structure its current name of "the Chinese Palace."

Particularly remarkable is a delicate drawing room whose walls are hung in panels of embroidered silk backed by some two million glass beads to re-create shimmering azure, mauve, and rose Oriental landscapes. Its floor was originally set with glass mosaic, but the fragile surface proved impractical and was eventually replaced by parquet.[66] Symbolizing Russia's destiny, in another room the ceiling featured an allegory by the Bolognese painter Serafino Barozzi of *The Union of Europe and Asia.*

Catherine's most ambitious project was the Chinese Village at Tsarskoe Selo, another imperial retreat near the capital.[67] Originally designed by Rinaldi in the 1770s, the project was turned over to her new Scottish architect, Charles Cameron, in 1780 and remained incomplete at the time of Catherine's death sixteen years later. The inspiration came from even farther west than that for her namesake's Monplaisir. Both Rinaldi and Cameron were largely following the conventions of the *jardin anglo-chinois,* a style of landscape design that had been developed in England in the mid-eighteenth century as a reaction against the strict geometric formalism of French parks. Championed by such treatises as William Halfpenny's *Rural Architecture in the Chinese Taste* (1751) and Sir William Chambers's *Dissertation on Oriental Gardening* (1771), the Anglo-Chinese garden favored quaint temples and pagodas seemingly casually scattered amid man-made waterfalls, ponds, woods, and glades.

The ensemble at Tsarskoe Selo included bridges decorated with dragons and Chinese figures holding lanterns, a Large Caprice (summer house) topped by a tiny pavilion in the style of Fujian Province, and the Chinese Theater. The village itself comprised a series of small houses arranged octagonally around a larger pagoda, resembling the more famous structure Sir William had built at London's Kew Gardens a few decades earlier. Combined with Cameron's neoclassical structures, the park at Tsarskoe Selo was a strange blend of Oriental and European antiquity, as the poet Gavrila Derzhavin suggested:

> Here is a theatre, there a swing,
> Beyond, an Eastern pleasure-dome.
> Hark how the Muses on Parnassus sing
> While creatures fated for the hunt do roam.[68]

The Middle Kingdom dominated the imagined Orient of the Catherinian Enlightenment, but the Islamic world also had a place. While attitudes toward the Near East were more ambivalent, even then the images it evoked in St. Petersburg and Moscow's literary circles were largely playful and benign. As with China, Russian views of the Near East almost entirely reflected those of Western thinkers. While some Europeans regarded Turkey and Persia as incorrigibly decadent and tyrannical, others, like the British diplomat's wife Lady Mary Wortley Montague, found much to praise in Ottoman culture. Intriguingly, her letters first popularized the Turkish habit of inoculating against smallpox, a practice eagerly taken up by Catherine.[69]

The age's spirit of tolerance helped many Russians to consider Islam in a more objective light. Meanwhile, traditional hostility toward the faith tended to fade in light of the diminished threat posed by the Ottomans and other Muslim foes on the imperial frontier. As Mark Batunskii points out, whereas in an earlier age the noun *musul'manin* had distinctly negative connotations, by the eighteenth century it was largely perceived as a neutral term.[70]

Of course Catherine herself had actually gone to war with Turkey on several occasions. Nevertheless, the empress carefully distinguished between the Ottomans, who ruled despotically and had destroyed Byzantium, and their religion.[71] Thoroughly infused with her age's cosmopolitanism and respect for other faiths, she prominently declared her protection for the beliefs of her Islamic subjects in her Decree of Toleration of 1785 and other legislation.[72] Voltaire, whose own opinions about the Near East were decidedly mixed, sycophantically cheered her victories over her Ottoman foe.[73] Yet even then he cursed Catholic adversaries, such as the Poles and Jesuits, in the same breath. In one letter of 1769, the philosophe reminded Catherine, "It is true that you have two great enemies, the Pope and the Padisha of the Turks."[74]

The translation into French of *The Thousand and One Nights* in the early eighteenth century also had an impact on Enlightenment views of Islam. According to the French orientologist Maxime Rodinson, "Thereafter, the Muslim world no longer appeared the province of the Antichrist, but rather as an essentially exotic, picturesque world where fantastic genies could, at their whim, do good or evil."[75] Russian authors in the late eighteenth century likewise tempered their distaste for the Oriental despotic with a thirst for the exotic. Most patriotically supported their country's frequent campaigns against the Porte. Even Novikov, as he subtly criticized Catherine's rule through Chinese allusions, poked fun at the Ottomans in the same issues of his journals.[76] But when writers put the Near East in a more distant or allegorical setting, it often became more like the wondrous land of *The Thousand and One Nights*.[77]

The most famous eighteenth-century Russian literary example of the Islamic world as a fairy-tale realm was Gavrila Derzhavin's "Ode to the Wise Princess Felitsa."[78] The poet, who took great pride in his family's Tatar ancestry, based his panegyric to Catherine on her children's story, "Tsarevich Khlor." Composed in 1782, supposedly in Arabic by "a certain murza," Derzhavin's ode lavishes praise on the "Godlike queen of the Kirghiz-Kaisak Horde" and her "incomparable wisdom," all the while portraying the noblemen in her entourage rather less favorably. Catherine thanked the author, then a retired lieutenant-colonel, for his exquisitely crafted flattery with a diamond-encrusted gold presentation snuffbox, promotion to the civil-service rank equivalent of army general, and a provincial governorship.[79]

If Derzhavin's verse technically dealt with a Turkic nomadic people in central Asia, in 1792 the fabulist Ivan Krylov wrote about the Near East more specifically in his "Kaib: An Oriental Tale."[80] This allegory was hardly an ambitious courtier's hosanna to his monarch. Praised by the early nineteenth-century literary critic Vissarion Belinskii for "its satirical mood," Krylov's Oriental tale instead attacked Catherine and her court with the same searing wit as Montesquieu had taken on Louis XIV in his *Lettres persanes* seven decades earlier.[81]

"Kaib" tells the story of the eponymous caliph's search for truth. There is a happy ending, as the hero ultimately succeeds in his quest. What is more interesting is Krylov's description of the ruler and his entourage. Kaib is a sovereign of great wealth who builds lavish palaces, generously supports the arts, and is constantly showered with extravagant praise for his wisdom and beneficence. His counselors are all corrupt nonentities, and, of course, he has a seraglio filled with young beauties—"none more than seventeen years old"—to satisfy his king-size sensual urges. If these parallels with his own empress were not particularly subtle, Krylov's malicious pen also alluded to Catherine's disingenuous patronage of freethinking in one of Kaib's proclamations: "Gentlemen! This is my wish: That he who has any objection may express it freely. At the very instance he will be granted five hundred ox-hide whip strokes on the soles of his feet, whereupon we shall be pleased to consider his opinion."[82]

In the eighteenth century, Russia learned to look at the East through Western eyes. At first, even the initiative to study Asia had come from Europe rather than from within. Astute observers such as Leibniz understood that Russia's geography made it unusually well suited to act as an intermediary for the passage of knowledge between the Orient and Occident, and that the nation had much to gain in the bargain. It would take some time for Russians to grasp this truth. However, as educated Russian society became more thoroughly westernized, its interest in the East began to be aroused. Under Catherine, the European Enlightenment's fascination for the Orient, especially for China, also captured the imagination of St. Petersburg and Moscow.

Like all Romanov sovereigns, Catherine had military, diplomatic, and commercial dealings with the Asian powers on her borders, such as the Ottomans, Persians, and Chinese. This intercourse yielded considerable direct knowledge about the East, and such firsthand information was often at variance with the more benign portrait painted by the West's philosophes. Indeed, one skeptical Russian diplomat, Vasilii Bratishchev, even took advantage of an assignment to Beijing in 1757 to compile an "Inquiry, or Some Verifications of the Voltairians' Remarks about China." Published thirty years later and little read by his compatriots, the account took issue with a number of claims made by Voltaire and others about the Middle Kingdom.[83]

In her study of eighteenth-century Russian literary perceptions of China, Barbara Widenor Maggs notes: "Symbolic, perhaps of Russia's position [vis-à-vis] China is the attitude of Catherine the Great. Like the intellectuals of the West she could praise the Chinese for their adherence to reason and their banishment of fanaticism, and for establishing the most durable empire in history. At the same time, as a political head of state, she could declare her aggressive ambition to have one day broken the insolence of China."[84] Yet despite her empire's difficulties with its Oriental neighbors, the leading authors of Catherine's court-centered culture much preferred the optimistic views of western European literature. According to Eric Widmer, "Whenever Montesquieu or Voltaire, or Jesuit letters had something to say on China, it would be infinitely more interesting to the salons of St. Petersburg than anything Ilarion Rossokhin could ever expect to write."[85] By the same token, *The Thousand and One Nights* was probably the most popular source about the Islamic world among Russian readers.

As Widmer suggests, academic study of Asia hardly made an impact on Catherinian thought. Throughout the eighteenth century, the discipline, such as it was, remained a foreign import, largely alien to intellectual life in St. Petersburg and Moscow. Its leading practitioners came from abroad, their writings were often more widely read in the West than in their new homeland, and the very notion that Russians should study the Orient was first proposed by foreigners such as Leibniz.

The Catherinian intellectual encounter with the East occurred precisely at the time when Russians most identified with the West.[86] Confident about their place in the world, Russia's elite saw the Orient as an object of wonder, amusement, and beauty. At the same time, they had no doubt that Russia was fundamentally distinct from Asia. It was only in the next century, as many began to question the relationship with Europe, that attitudes toward Asia likewise became more ambivalent.

4

THE ORIENTAL MUSE

Go to the Caucasus and you will return a poet.
—Mikhail Lermontov

On 30 Floréal, year VI, or May 19, 1798, according to the French revolutionary calendar, a distinguished group of 167 scientists, engineers, scholars, and artists sailed from the Mediterranean port of Toulon. These learned men were joining a flotilla under the ambitious Corsican general Napoleon Bonaparte, whose aim was to wrest Egypt from Ottoman control. While the venture was primarily motivated by the Directoire's desire to cut Britain's links with India, Napoleon also had more intellectual aims. Along with dealing a severe blow to the colonial prosperity of France's hated maritime rival, possession of the lower Nile would enable his brain trust to systematically study, catalogue, and describe a great ancient civilization, in the best tradition of the Enlightenment's *encyclopédistes*.[1]

At first Napoleon seemed set to repeat the brilliant success of his Italian campaign the previous year. Within three weeks of landing at Alexandria, his troops routed Mamluk forces at the Battle of the Pyramids and were soon in possession of Cairo. But the Corsican's glory was short-lived. No more than ten days after he had vanquished Egypt's defenders on land, the Royal Navy sank his fleet in Aboukir Bay, cutting the French expeditionary army off from the homeland and ultimately dooming the operation.

Nevertheless, the setback did not deter Napoleon's cultural efforts. Before its inevitable return home three years later, his corps of savants carried out an unprecedented inventory of Egyptian antiquities, whose crowning achievement was the twenty-volume *Déscription d'Egypte*. According to Edward Said, the invasion was the defining moment in modern scholarship of the East, "the first in a long series of European encounters with the Orient in which the Orientalist's specialized expertise was put to functional colonial use."[2] The ill-fated Egyptian expedition also left an important legacy to art, as over the coming decade painters produced over seventy canvases glorifying the future emperor's military exploits.[3] And when French generals began their conquest of Algeria in the 1830s, many artists joined them in the Napoleonic fashion, thereby helping to launch a vogue in Europe's salons for Near Eastern themes.[4]

The literary impact of Napoleon's campaign on the Nile was more subtle but no less profound.[5] French efforts to strike at Britain's most valuable colony via Egypt now brought the Ottoman Empire to the forefront of great-power politics. Although the Porte's grip on its vast possessions had already been loosening for at least a hundred years, during the previous century only its more immediate European neighbors, Austria and Russia, had paid its troubles much heed. But the events of 1798 made the eastern Mediterranean a vital geopolitical concern for the continent's other leading chancelleries as well. Right up to 1914, the "Eastern Question"— the European rivalries to benefit from Ottoman infirmity—would be one of the most incendiary elements of Western diplomacy.

Turkey's travails also raised its profile in European drawing rooms and salons. As Victor Hugo observed in 1829, "Whether as image or thought, the Orient has become a general preoccupation for both the intellect and the imagination. . . . The whole continent inclines to the East."[6] At the same time, the Ottomans' decline made their picturesque empire much more accessible to foreign tourists. Many of them published colorful travel accounts that were greedily devoured back home by a public eager to escape vicariously from their more humdrum bourgeois existence, thereby feeding a literary fashion for the Near East much more intense than the eighteenth century's playful turquerie. The most influential works by far were Lord Byron's phenomenally popular Orientalist verse. Informed by the flamboyant poet's own grand tour of the eastern Mediterranean in 1809–11, the fictional *Childe Harold's Pilgrimage* that he began publishing soon after his return to London, as well as *The Giaour, The Bride of*

Abydos, and his other "Oriental tales" of the time, virtually dominated European letters for about a decade after their publication in the early 1810s.

The age's Romantic sensibilities made the European public particularly receptive to this eastward turn. Essentially a reaction against eighteenth-century classicism, Romanticism rejected the former's emphasis on reason, order, restraint, and decorum, not to mention its idolization of the Greco-Roman past.[7] Although it was initiated by a 1761 French novel, Jean-Jacques Rousseau's *La nouvelle Héloïse,* a tale championing passion and the imagination over society's conventions, the movement's deepest roots lay in German philosophical and literary trends during the eighteenth century's closing decades. Pioneered by a Lutheran pastor from East Prussia, Johann-Gottfried Herder, the leading advocates included Friedrich Schlegel, Friedrich Schelling, and Johann Wolfgang von Goethe in his younger years. Along with others, these writers stressed the primacy of emotion, intuition, spontaneity, and the mystical. They firmly believed that poetry was the most direct means to the sublime.

In rebelling against Hellenism, the German Romantics also looked to alternative sources of wisdom, especially to their own medieval past and the East. The Orient was particularly appealing. Theories about European languages' origins in India heightened interest in Asian antiquity. At the same time, the Near East's exoticism and sensuality appealed strongly to contemporary aesthetic tastes. According to Schlegel, "We must seek the most sublime Romanticism in the Orient."[8]

Increasingly receptive to broader European literary trends, early nineteenth-century Russian authors could not fail to be influenced by Romanticism. The movement's Orientalist proclivities were no exception. But if Lord Byron and other Western poets helped spark Russians' interest in the East, there were also sources of inspiration much closer to home.[9] Not only did Russia repeatedly clash with Turkey and Persia on the southern frontier, but it was also becoming increasingly involved in a lengthy struggle to "pacify" insurgent Islamic minorities in the Caucasian highlands within its own borders. Indeed, many leading writers of the day had direct knowledge of Russia's Orient through travel or service in the Caucasus. This familiarity made Russian Romantic poets conscious of a special affinity with Asia. Meanwhile, their nation's eastern geography made them particularly susceptible to Herderian notions about Oriental roots, which the presence of various Islamic minorities on the empire's territory only reinforced. As the Ukrainian-born writer Orest Somov pointed out in his influential essay of 1823, "On Romantic Poetry": "No nation on earth is as rich in various popular beliefs, legends, and mythologies as Russia. . . . Without crossing the border, Russian poets can roam freely from the North's austere and gloomy folklore to the luxuriant and brilliant fantasies of the East."[10]

The nineteenth-century literary critic Vissarion Belinskii asserted that "Pushkin discovered the Caucasus."[11] By the same token, the bard also introduced Russians to the literary Orient. He did have antecedents, such as Gavrila Derzhavin, Nikolai Novikov, and Empress Catherine II, who had already invoked the East with their quills in the late eighteenth century. But nothing did more to popularize Asian themes in the Russian reader's imagination than Pushkin's "southern poems" of the early 1820s.

For his compatriots, Pushkin's literary role resembled that of Byron in European letters. Indeed, many have seen him as the English lord's Russian double. For one thing, their biographies bore many resemblances. Both proudly boasted their blue-blooded pedigrees yet felt themselves at odds with society's conventions and politics. Marked by passionate affairs, clashes with authority, exile, and tragic, early deaths, their tempestuous lives personified the spirit of the Romantic age in strikingly similar ways. Slavists often cringe at comparing their verse too closely, and Pushkin would eventually come to disown the Englishman as a model.[12] However, when it came to literary Orientalism, in his younger years he was unquestionably Russia's Byron.

Generally acclaimed as his nation's greatest poet, Aleksandr Sergeevich Pushkin was born in 1799 to a somewhat dissolute but cultured retired guards officer in the old capital of Moscow.[13] His family had a distinguished past—the name appears no less than twenty-eight times in Nikolai Karamzin's *History of the Russian State*—but its prominence had faded since the ascent of the Romanovs some two hundred years earlier. In the poet's own words,

> A fragment of decrepit stock
> (And not the only one, alas),
> I hail from ancient boyars . . .[14]

Aleksandr's mother, Nadezhda Osipovna, née Gannibal (Hannibal), had a less conventional background, for her grandfather had come to Russia as an African slave boy in the early eighteenth century.[15] Presented to Peter the Great by his Turkish ambassador, the lad had been christened Abraham Petrovich and raised under the former's care. The tsar took a shine to little Abraham. Blessed with a quick intellect and an aptitude for geometry, Peter's favorite rose to the rank of general as a military engineer in the army. Proudly highlighting his black identity, Abraham styled his surname after Rome's great Carthaginian adversary.

Aleksandr Pushkin flaunted both of his lineages. He tirelessly alluded to his father's illustrious bloodline, which apparently originated with a thirteenth-century Prussian warrior who had entered Prince Alexander Nevsky's service.[16] A friend once chided him for his aristocratic airs: "Are you proud of your five-hundred-year-old nobility? . . . For God's sake, be Pushkin! You are a clever enough fellow in your own right." Pushkin indignantly corrected him: "You are angry that I praise my *six*-hundred-year nobility."[17]

As for his mother's black roots, these were a source of great pride as well. When Pushkin referred to himself as "the wild descendant of negroes," he did not do so disparagingly.[18] In the cosmopolitan atmosphere of Imperial Russia's urban haut monde, mixed racial origins carried far fewer negative connotations than in the Anglo Saxon world. Catherine O'Neil notes that literate St. Petersburg readily associated ebony skin with Shakespeare's jealous but noble Moor Othello and shared in European "stereotypes about Africa and black men as wild, fiery, sensual, threatening, and at the same time fascinating in their sexual prowess."[19] To a young man with a ravenous carnal appetite, these were all positive attributes.

According to the imprecise geography of the day, Africa was almost as Oriental as Asia. Because the former's northern third lay within the orbit of Islamic civilization and was still nominally under Ottoman authority, it was easy for Europeans to conflate the Sahara with the Levant. Meanwhile, many of the characteristics the Romantic imagination considered to be typically Oriental—unbridled passion, savagery, indolence, and despotism—were both southern and eastern.[20] Victor Hugo made this point when he emphatically included Spain, which technically lies at Europe's western extremity, in the poetic East of *Les Orientales*.[21] And when in 1830 French troops embarked at Toulon for the Algerian campaign, they knew they were going to the Orient.

This imprecise demarcation between east and south was doubly true in the Russian mind. A glance at the map showed that Constantinople lay west of St. Petersburg, while the Caucasus Mountains were well within the empire's European borders, as defined in the early eighteenth century by the father of Russian geography, Vasilii Tatishchev. To Pushkin, therefore, his African blood was quasi-Oriental—as the noun he used to label his great-grandfather, *arap,* suggests. [22] A cognate of "Arab," this archaic Russian word for a black from Islamic Africa simultaneously conveyed both the South and the East, as did "Moor" in English. By the same token, Pushkin's southern poems, a series inspired by a journey to the Caucasus and the Crimea, were just as "Eastern" as Lord Byron's Oriental tales.

Pushkin received the best education possible in Alexander I's realm. In 1811 the emperor founded a special college to train boys of good breeding for high government posts, the Tsarskoe Selo Lycée. Later renamed the Imperial Alexander Lycée and transferred to the capital, the institution was initially housed in a wing of the Catherine Palace at the tsar's summer residence. With its intimate ties to the court, the new school promised able graduates a brilliant career in the army and the more prestigious branches of officialdom (the first year's intake included the future foreign minister, Prince Aleksandr Gorchakov). Despite striking his examiner as "empty-headed and thoughtless," Pushkin demonstrated a good aptitude for French and drawing, and he won admission to the inaugural class.[23]

The lycée's progressive six-year course of study stressed the "moral sciences" and was not overly taxing. As a result, the lad could also indulge in his own pursuits, such as writing verse, in which he proved to be remarkably gifted. Pushkin actively participated in his school's rich literary life and was soon corresponding with leading poets in nearby St. Petersburg. By the age of fourteen he had published his first composition in the capital's biweekly *Vestnik Evropy* (Messenger of Europe) and would see three more poems in print before graduation. Pushkin's facility with the pen did not always do him service, especially when he wrote malicious epigrams of men in authority, including his headmaster. The most celebrated indication of Aleksandr's precocious talent came when the aging court poet

Derzhavin was invited to examine the lycée's students in 1815 and famously proclaimed the fourteen-year-old to be his successor upon hearing him recite a nostalgic rhyme about Tsarskoe Selo.

During his final year in school, Pushkin spent many a late night happily carousing with guards officers stationed in the imperial residence. His dreams of joining them when he completed his studies in 1817 were dashed when his father pointed out that he could not afford the expense of supporting a cavalry subaltern and proposed a distinctly less glamorous career in the infantry instead. There were alternatives. While the couture was not as dashing as a hussar's tunic, diplomacy was a perfectly respectable career for a young blueblood. It also offered the important perquisite of beginning work in the imperial capital. Securing an appointment in the foreign office, Pushkin moved to St. Petersburg in June 1817 at the ripe age of eighteen.

Pushkin's professional obligations as a junior tsarist official were even less onerous than his studies at the lycée. While he was perennially short of cash, his charm, school connections, and talent quickly won him entrée into fashionable social and literary circles. He also indulged in less respectable pursuits. A verse he penned on the spot during an evening out with some friends nicely conveys his days as a young man-about-town in St. Petersburg:

> In the glass goblet champagne's
> Cold stream hissed.
> We drank—and Venus with us
> Sat sweating at the table.
> When shall we four sit again
> With whores, wine and pipes?[24]

Pushkin's debauchery did not diminish the output of his pen. In 1819 he completed his first major work, *Ruslan and Ludmilla*. A fairy tale in verse set in ancient Rus, this fantasy playfully combined many exotic elements in the French classical manner. *Ruslan and Ludmilla* was inspired in part by *The Thousand and One Nights*, the French collection of Arabic stories that had first acquainted Pushkin with the East as a child. Scheherezade, malicious genies, Persian opulence, and harems all blended with elements of *byliny* to create what one scholar described as "a harmonic fusion of national and Oriental traditions."[25]

Published in 1820, *Ruslan and Ludmilla* made Pushkin's reputation as a poet. Before the author could savor his success, however, the manuscript of a more political poem he had circulated among friends, "Ode to Liberty," caught the emperor's attention. It was only through the intercession of influential friends that Pushkin avoided exile to Siberia. Instead, he was punished with a transfer to the southwestern frontier in May 1820.

Although Pushkin chafed at the provincialism of his new environs, the banishment came as a blessing to his nascent literary career. He also had the good fortune of being assigned initially to an indulgent superior who was not overly alarmed at having a disgraced poet on his staff. During his four years away from the capital's distractions, Pushkin composed most of his southern poems and began work on his great novel in verse, *Eugene Onegin*.

Pushkin's southern poems were the result of a reunion shortly after arriving at his new posting with a friend from Tsarskoe Selo, the young guards officer Nikolai Raevskii. Raevskii's father, a general who had distinguished himself in the recent war against Napoleon, was en route with his family to the Caucasian spa town of Piatigorsk. When he learned that his son's chum happened to be in town, the general magnanimously invited him along for the summer. The next few months were an idyllic time as Pushkin enjoyed the company of the Raevskii clan, which included four charming daughters. The latter took it upon themselves to teach their new guest English with Byron's works, which were then all the rage. Fired by the lord's verse, as his travels with the Raevskiis took him from the dramatic alpine scenery of the Caucasus to the Crimea's subtropical verdure, Pushkin picked up his "exiled lyre."

Pushkin's stay at Piatigorsk inspired the first of his narrative southern poems, *Kavkazskii plennik* (*The Captive of the Caucasus*). Completed in 1821, it tells of a disillusioned Russian youth who is seized by Circassian highlanders as he roams the mountains in flight from society's falsehoods and duplicity. Held in their camp, the prisoner wins the love of a Circassian maiden. While he is too jaded to return her passion, she nevertheless helps him flee. Brokenhearted, the girl drowns herself as her beloved returns to the safety of the Russian lines.

Since the twelfth-century *Song of Igor's Campaign*, captivity narratives had been a recurring feature of Russian literature, as they were in the

West.[26] What was new here was Pushkin's relatively positive portrayal of the captors. Like earlier authors of the genre, the poet initially describes the foe as savage:

> The idle Circassians sit . . .
> They recall the former days
> Of raids that could not be repulsed
> Of the treachery of sly leaders,
> Of the blows of their cruel sabers,
> And of the accuracy of their arrows that could not be outrun,
> And of the ash of destroyed villages . . .

Yet as the prisoner watches the highlanders behead slaves for their amusement at a feast, his thoughts take him back to the equally violent pastime of dueling back home. Perhaps his own kind is no less barbarous than the Caucasian "other." To be sure, his homeland does not have much to commend itself. The prisoner recalls its

> Despised vanity,
> And double-tongued hostility,
> And simple-hearted slander . . .

Meanwhile, the longer the Russian is their involuntary guest, the more he comes to admire his captors:

> Among the mountain people the prisoner observed
> Their faith, customs, upbringing,
> Loved the simplicity of their life,
> Their hospitality, their thirst for battle,
> The swiftness of their movements,
> And the lightness of their feet, the strength of their fists.[27]

If Pushkin ultimately does not malign the Circassians, his poem's attitude toward the tsarist effort to subdue them is more complicated. Some scholars have detected in the body of the work a veiled critique of the pacification campaign.[28] Yet two months after he had completed it, Pushkin added an epilogue that lauded Russia's Caucasian mission much as Derzhavin's odes had sung hosannas to Catherine's earlier campaigns in Asia. Pushkin's close friend Prince Petr Viazemskii privately complained about the jingoist postscript, which struck him as highly discordant, adding that "poetry is not the executioner's ally."[29]

Although Pushkin's attitudes to the autocracy were highly ambiguous, he was not categorically opposed to Eastern conquest. Shortly after his holiday with the Raevskii family, he wrote to his brother that "The Caucasus, this sultry Asian frontier, is interesting in all respects. Ermolov [the general who first commanded the counterinsurgency] has filled it with his name and his benevolent genius. . . . We must hope that this conquered land . . . will not be a hindrance to future wars—and, perhaps, will help us carry out Napoleon's chimerical plan to conquer India."[30] And in the unfinished history of Peter the Great that he undertook after his return to the capital, Pushkin lauded the tsar's wars against "predatory" Turkish and Persian neighbors.[31] Regardless of Pushkin's political views, there was no contradiction between opposition to the emperor and enthusiasm for extending Russia's Asian dominions. Many of Pushkin's radical friends, such as the conspiratorial leader Pavel Pestel', strongly supported a vigorous expansionist policy in the East.[32]

Lord Byron's *Childe Harold*, which established the trope of the gentleman rebel who flees to the untamed Orient in search of freedom, clearly influenced Pushkin's *Captive*. There are similarities as well with the novels of François-René de Chateaubriand, such as *Atala*, the story of a young American Indian woman who falls in love with a captive from another tribe but commits suicide to preserve her vow of chastity. Rousseau's noble savage and his glorification of alpine splendor left their mark too.

The Captive of the Caucasus, in turn, was a seminal work in Russian letters. It initiated a number of important nineteenth-century literary conventions, including the "superfluous man," the Caucasus as an exotic sanctuary from society's oppression, and the honest, brave highlander. At the same time, Pushkin blurred the boundaries between European and Asian. Susan Layton suggests: "Despite the poet's ambivalence about the matter, this catalogue of savage virtues in 'The Prisoner of the Caucasus' launched the Muslim mountaineers on a long literary career as the Asian 'others' whom the nineteenth-century Russians proved eager to embrace as surrogate 'selves.'"[33] This symbiosis of self and other would become an intriguing feature of Orientalism in Russian culture.

Pushkin's *Captive* was prescient in likening Beshtu, one of the range's more prominent peaks, to Mount Parnassus, sacred to the Muses of Greek mythology, for his poem launched a Caucasian vogue among Russian Romantic writers.[34] Many of them also had involuntary firsthand knowledge of the region. Aleksandr Bestuzhev, who penned a number of popular tales about the mountains under the pseudonym Marlinskii in the 1830s, had been exiled there as a common soldier for his participation in the abortive coup of December 1825.

Mikhail Lermontov, a Life Guard hussar subaltern of Scottish descent who dabbled in Romantic poetry, was also banished to the campaign against the Islamic insurgents. An avid admirer of Pushkin, Lermontov had incurred the tsar's displeasure in 1837 for circulating a verse that suggested that the great poet's death was the result of a high-level conspiracy. His Oriental exile inspired Lermontov's most important work, *A Hero of Our Time*, which is considered a masterpiece of Russian Romantic prose. Described as "a *Childe Harold* in Russian cloak," the novel about a world-weary officer's erotic and military exploits in the Caucasus betrays Byron's strong imprint, while also bearing many traces of Pushkin's work, including *The Captive*.[35]

Together with Pushkin, Lermontov and Bestuzhev (Marlinskii) were among the better-known Russian writers to find inspiration in the mountains. The 1830s saw a host of what Layton calls "little Orientalizers," whose often sensational and patriotic exotica appealed to a less discriminating audience.[36] The last major prerevolutionary writer to turn to Caucasian themes was Count Leo Tolstoy. In addition to his own "A Prisoner of the Caucasus," a children's story whose plot resembled Pushkin's poem, Tolstoy also published a distinctly un-Romantic novella about the region in 1863, *The Cossacks*. Much later in life the increasingly rebellious aristocrat penned a savage indictment of the tsarist small war against the Muslim highlanders with his novel of 1904, *Hadji Murad*.

Pushkin's *The Captive* also struck a chord with the literate public more broadly. According to Belinskii, it was so popular that, twenty years after its publication, most educated Russians could still recite its description of the Circassians from memory. Indeed, many read *The Captive* not just for its aesthetic merits but also as a source of information about a little-known region.[37] Belinskii was not exaggerating when he claimed that it "first acquainted Russian society with the majestic image of the Caucasus and its bellicose natives."[38] The poem would inspire a number of creative works, including a ballet, songs, César Cui's most popular opera, and more recently a film.

After their stay in Piatigorsk, the Raevskii family and Pushkin sailed to the Crimea, where the poet spent what he later described as the happiest period of his life. One of their excursions on the peninsula took them to the old Tatar palace at Bakhchisarai. Like Catherine the Great during her jubilee tour of 1787, Pushkin was enchanted, and the occasion moved him to write another well-known narrative poem, *The Fountain of Bakhchisarai*. Initially titled *The Harem, The Fountain* was based on an old legend about a Crimean khan's frustrated love for Maria, a virginal blonde Polish princess he had seized in a raid, and the violent jealousy this aroused in another female slave, the dark-haired Georgian Zarema.[39] Much more than *The Captive,* this poem incorporated various Near Eastern literary elements, from an epigraph by the thirteenth-century Persian poet Sa'di to the evocation of roses, nightingales, the moon, and other typical Oriental metaphors.[40]

Starting with Belinskii, many critics have read a clear opposition between West and East in Pushkin's depiction of the Madonna-like Maria on one hand and the sultry Zarema, as well as the despotic khan, on the other.[41] However, as one Soviet scholar pointed out, the poet shows no preference for either the pure Occidental maiden or her passionate Oriental rival. Instead Pushkin portrays them as two sides of the same feminine coin.[42] As for the khan, while he is described as "the scourge of peoples, the savage Tatar," his yearning for the unattainable princess humanizes him. The reader ultimately feels sympathy for the lovesick Crimean chieftain.

While under Sa'di's spell, Pushkin also wrote shorter poems after his fashion, including "The Grape," "The Rose Maiden," and the briefer "Fountain of Bakhchisarai Court." He was hardly unique. Translations of Near Eastern verse were a favorite of Romantic authors, and they inspired a number of simulations. Although there is no evidence that Pushkin ever read it, the best-known example of this genre was Goethe's *West-Eastern Divan,* the German poet's 1819 celebration of love that blended Arabic, Persian, Turkish, and even Indian styles with his own. Like Goethe,

Pushkin saw such efforts as a synthesis of Orient and Occident; he never aspired to adopt an entirely Asian literary persona. Pushkin explained his approach in a letter to Prince Viazemskii: "The Oriental manner was my model, inasmuch it is possible for us rational, cold Europeans to adopt it. . . . Even when enraptured by Eastern splendor, the European must retain the taste and perspective of the European."[43]

The Fountain of Bakhchisarai was published in March 1824 to great public acclaim and earned its author a generous honorarium. Pushkin was less fortunate in his nominal career with the foreign office. Now assigned to Count Mikhail Vorontsov, the governor-general of New Russia (southern Ukraine) in Odessa, he intemperately flirted with his new superior's coquettish younger wife. Making matters worse, authorities intercepted a letter that appeared to espouse atheism. Fired from his post, Pushkin was banished to his family's estate at Mikhailovskoe that summer.

Although he was now deep in the Russian countryside, the Orient continued to be Pushkin's muse. Already in Odessa he had begun to read the Koran, and he now deepened his study of the Islamic text. Pushkin was particularly fascinated by Muhammad, whose persecution and exile seemed to parallel his own recent travails. At the same time, the bard was struck by the Prophet's ability to move people with the power of his words alone.[44] He was soon busy with a new cycle, *Imitations of the Koran*. Its nine poems, which retell the story of the Muhammad's life, are both a summons to resist oppression as well as a semiautobiographical vision of the poet's prophetic mission.[45]

Pushkin hardly appreciated it at the time, but his confinement at Mikhailovskoe came as a blessing in disguise, since it cut him off from the political turmoil surrounding Nicholas I's accession to the throne after Alexander's death toward the end of 1825. A number of Pushkin's friends were Decembrists, members of a conspiracy to seize the throne and establish a constitutional monarchy. They wisely avoided involving their hotheaded companion in their scheme. Their fondness for his verse was well known to the authorities, however, and he might well have been implicated in the plot had he not been languishing in rural solitude.

In September 1826 Nicholas summoned Pushkin to a remarkable meeting at the Moscow Kremlin, where the new tsar had been staying for his coronation. In a lengthy interview Nicholas questioned the poet about his sympathies for the Decembrist plot. Although Pushkin freely admitted that he would have participated had he been given the opportunity, the tsar magnanimously forgave him and offered his protection and patronage. It proved to be a Faustian bargain. The new arrangement bound Pushkin tightly to his sovereign, restricting his freedom to express himself even more than under the previous reign. While he was allowed to return to the capital and continued to write, he felt increasingly trapped.

In 1829, frustrated at the rejection of his marriage proposal to a young beauty, Natalia Goncharova, Pushkin took an unauthorized journey back to the south. Russia was once again at war with Turkey, and the poet wanted to visit his old friend Nikolai Raevskii at the front. The trip resulted in a travelogue, *Journey to Arzrum,* whose prosaic and often cynical tone entirely nullified the poet's earlier Romantic passion for the East: the Caucasian scenery was banal, a pretty but decidedly unfeminine Kalmyk lass alarms him with her flirtation, a Persian court poet he encounters somewhat later speaks plainly rather than issuing the anticipated stream of florid "Oriental bombast," while the Ottoman foe is hardly courageous or menacing.[46] As he walked about the newly captured eastern Turkish city of Arzrum (Erzurum), Pushkin reflected, "I know of no expression that makes less sense than the words: Asian opulence. . . . Now we can say: Asian poverty, Asian swinishness, etc."

When Byron had died in 1824, Pushkin had remarked that English lord's "genius paled with his youth . . . [later on] he was no longer the fiery demon who created 'The Giaour' or *Childe Harold.*"[47] He also unknowingly predicted the course of his own career. As tastes changed, by 1830 Pushkin was no longer at the forefront of Russian literary life. According to D. S. Mirsky, he "was venerated by the younger generation rather as a relic of the past than as a living force."[48]

Along with these professional frustrations, Pushkin's private life also had its disappointments. Although Natalia Goncharova finally agreed to become his wife, married life proved unhappy. The young woman's renowned beauty made her the object of increasingly unwelcome masculine attention. One suitor, Baron Georges-Charles d'Anthès, a dashing French émigré serving as an Imperial Russian Guards officer, was particularly persistent. When in late 1836 the poet began to be openly ridiculed as a cuckold, the inevitable duel followed. It proved to be Pushkin's last. Mortally wounded, he died in great pain two days after the confrontation, on January 29, 1837.

Published in 1835, two years before his death, Pushkin's *Journey* proved the epitaph for the Romantic flirtation with the East in Russian letters. Although it would take over two more decades to subdue the Islamic highlanders, and tsarist troops would be involved in various other Asian wars from the Crimea to Korea for much of the empire's remaining existence, none of these campaigns excited the same literary response as had the Caucasus in Pushkin's day. By the 1840s realism had replaced Romanticism, and writers turned their attention closer to home as the Russian peasant replaced the Circassian as the exotic other of their creative imaginations.[49] Only at the turn of the twentieth century would Russian poets again become enchanted with the Orient. But Asia remained very much alive in other artistic domains.

As in literature, interest in the East among Russian painters in the modern age came initially from the West. The Islamic Orient had intrigued European artists since at least the Renaissance. At the turn of the sixteenth century, intimate contact with the Turks inspired Venetian artists such as Gentile Bellini to record Near Eastern scenes and statesmen. The seventeenth-century Dutch master Rembrandt drew on his extensive collection of imported props to execute portraits of individuals clad in sumptuous Eastern silken robes and turbans. And following more playful eighteenth-century turquerie, a rococo fad for all things Ottoman, French artists such as Charles-André van Loo painted canvases featuring pashas, sultanas, eunuchs, and odalisques in fantasy seraglios, while English aristocrats commissioned Sir Joshua Reynolds to portray them in Oriental settings.[50] But the Near East's artistic appeal reached its zenith in the nineteenth century with the rise of Orientalism as a distinct style of European painting.

Political developments clearly played a role. If Napoleon's Egyptian expedition began to revive interest in the region, Greece's struggle for independence in the 1820s and France's North African campaigns during the following decade helped to sustain it. At the same time, the West's growing dominion over the Mediterranean greatly simplified travel to the lands on the sea's eastern and southern shores.[51] With their vivid sunlight, languid sensuality, and picturesque ruins, they became a popular destination among painters, much as Italy had been in earlier centuries.[52]

Like its literary counterpart, Orientalist painting was an offshoot of Romanticism. Predominantly French, the artistic style featured scenes supposedly taken from daily life in the Islamic world. Some were indeed faithful genre paintings and ethnographic portraits, striking largely because of their exotic locale. At the same time, Orientalist artists often imagined scenes of excess sexuality, violence, cruelty, sloth, and other sins proscribed by Christian morality. Luxurious harems, murderous tyrants, and somnolent hashish addicts were favorite motifs.

The Death of Sardanapalus (1827) by the French Romantic Eugène Delacroix is typical of the genre.[53] Based on Lord Byron's tragedy of 1821, the canvas depicts the legendary last Assyrian king reclining on a magnificent bed, calmly contemplating the execution of his concubines and horses before his own inevitable doom. Red and white silks mingle chaotically with peacock feathers, gold vessels, jeweled swords, pale female flesh, and a terror-stricken horse against a backdrop of fire and smoke. Perhaps to remind the viewer of the cliché that Eastern license came in many forms, a muscular African slave, naked save for a strategically placed black cloth, provides a homoerotic accent.

Historians of art traditionally have explained that Orientalism's popularity was driven primarily by escapism. By portraying in lush and arresting colors Asia's supposed boundless carnality, savagery, indolence, and luxury—all traits alien to the age's sober bourgeois sensibilities—Orientalist paintings provided a refuge for repressed fantasies. In his 1977 book on the subject, Philippe Julian suggested that "In the century of coal, whole cities lay under a mantle of drabness. An Orientalist picture in a Victorian drawing room was a kind of escape. To our great-grandparents, these canvases were not only a reminder of a different world, of something picturesque and heroic, but they hinted at pleasures that were often taboo in Europe and titillated a secret taste for cruelty and oppression."[54]

Despite such possible Freudian connotations, academic attitudes to Orientalism remained fairly benign until the 1970s.[55] However, not long ago an American writer remarked, "[Orientalism is] arguably the most politically incorrect artwork going today."[56] What first gave the style a more sinister air was the publication in 1978 of Edward Said's *Orientalism*.[57]

While Said paid little attention to painting, some art historians were quick to appropriate his argument about the link between representation and repression.[58] The most sophisticated study along these lines is Linda Nochlin's article, "The Imaginary Orient."[59] A feminist academic, Nochlin examines the style from a gendered perspective. Thus Delacroix's Orientalism was motivated not by lust for imperial power, but lust pure and simple.[60] More intriguing is her interpretation of the hyperrealistic approach of later Orientalists such as Jean-Léon Gérôme, which she sees as deliberately deceptive. Far from being, as one contemporary put it, "one of the most studious and conscientiously accurate painters in our time," Gérôme pursued a calculated strategy of "realist mystification" by presenting an imaginary Orient with seemingly photographic precision.[61]

Nochlin's observations about Gérôme could arguably also be applied to his Russian student, Vasilii Vereshchagin, Russia's Orientalist painter par excellence. Vereshchagin's path to Gérôme's atelier in Paris was hardly predictable or direct.[62] Born in 1842 to a landowner of moderate means in the northwestern Government of Novgorod, he was given a typical upbringing for a future officer in the tsar's armed forces: tutors at home, three years at a junior military school, and another six at the Naval Cadet Corps in the capital.

The latter may well have inspired Vereshchagin's indefatigable wanderlust.[63] As in all navy schools, the cadets were encouraged to learn about the world beyond their homeland's shores, an effort strongly supported by directors that had included such maritime explorers as the illustrious circumnavigator Admiral Ivan Fedorovich Krusenstern. Geography proved to be among Vereshchagin's favorite subjects, and during his spare time he repeatedly reread *The Frigate Pallada* (1858), the novelist Ivan Goncharov's recent travel account. Vereshchagin's high grades earned him cruises to western Europe along with the other better students during his last two summers in school. It was during these journeys abroad that he became acquainted with the writings of the radical émigré Aleksandr Herzen, which helped shape his progressive political views.

When Vasilii graduated at the top of his class in 1860, there was every expectation that he would join his classmates in a career with the imperial fleet. But already at school there had been factors that set him apart from the others. Although industrious and intelligent, the cadet proved to be sickly. More alarming, his sensitive stomach could not withstand seafaring. He was also subject to a nervous and excitable temperament, which, according to his close friend the prominent art critic Vladimir Stasov, he had inherited from his half-Tatar mother.[64] And Vereshchagin liked to draw.

As a boy Vasilii had shown a remarkable aptitude in making sketches, a talent his more dedicated art teachers at school recognized and encouraged. When in his penultimate year at the corps the curriculum no longer included drawing classes, the cadet enrolled in the Society for the Encouragement of the Arts, which functioned as a preparatory school for the Imperial Academy of Arts. The instructors initially regarded him as something of a dilettante. However, Vasilii's stubborn insistence that he saw his future at an easel rather than aboard ship convinced them to take him seriously.

Vereshchagin's parents humored their son's interest for the time being. According to the conventions of the day, sketching was a perfectly acceptable parlor amusement for a member of his class. But as a living, the arts were considered a trade fit only for serfs and other rabble.[65] When, shortly before receiving his diploma, Vasilii announced that he had decided to forsake the navy for further study at the Academy of Arts, his parents were appalled. He later recalled their reaction: "For the son of distinguished gentry . . . to become an artist—the shame!"[66] Unable to dissuade their son through either the mother's anguished tears or the father's stern warnings of future privation, they reluctantly gave in.

Vereshchagin enrolled in the Imperial Academy of Arts at a time of considerable turmoil for the venerable establishment. Founded nearly a century earlier by Empress Catherine the Great, and from 1850 a subsidiary of the Ministry of the Court, its function was to promote the arts along European lines. As an institution of imperial patronage, the academy loyally reflected the neoclassical tastes of its Romanov masters. But when Emperor Nicholas I died in 1855 as his armies faced defeat against the Western powers in the Crimea, the autocracy's grip on society and culture became less confident.[67]

Within the academy, the first to challenge the status quo were its students. Like many educated youth in the turbulent years that followed the "Iron Tsar's" death, they sought to cast off the shackles of the past and adopt a more socially conscious ethos. One of the guiding lights of the *shestidesiatniki,* the generation of the 1860s, was Nikolai Chernyshevskii, a radical son of a priest from the provinces. His novel of 1863, *What Is to Be Done?*—with its strident advocacy of socialist egalitarianism, sexual emancipation, and sacrificial self-denial—became gospel to progressive Russian youth. More directly relevant to those enrolled at the academy, ten years earlier Chernyshevskii had written a master's thesis on "The Aesthetic Relation of Art to Reality."[68] Arguing that art must replicate the real world, especially that of the common people, the author called on it to condemn the iniquities of the existing order. He famously called for art to be "a textbook for life," rather than to decorate the palaces of the ruling class.[69]

Chernyshevskii's angry rejection of "art for art's sake" found a receptive audience among the academy's students. In 1863—the same year the Salon des Refusés defied Paris's artistic establishment—fourteen of them walked out of the institution's gold medal competition, having refused to paint its obligatory theme from Scandinavian mythology. Led by Ivan Kramskoi, they struck out on their own by forming a cooperative workshop, following the model in *What Is to Be Done?* Although the venture eventually foundered, another effort at artistic emancipation in 1870 proved to be much more successful. Known as the Wanderers (*Peredvizhniki*) after their formal name, the Society of Traveling Art Exhibitions, the new group would transform Russian painting into a truly national school that obeyed Chernyshevskii's dual summons to represent reality and criticize its ills with "morally indignant" canvases.[70]

Vereshchagin also heeded Chernyshevskii. As he would later write in his extensive musings about his craft, "The notion of art as obedient to absolute beauty . . . is outdated. Instead of pure, absolute beauty, modern art . . . is linked to everyday life in all its aspects."[71] But unlike some of his schoolmates, Vereshchagin's rebellion against the academy took a more solitary path. He had begun his new schooling well enough and soon became particularly close to a young liberal professor, Aleksandr Beidemann, who took him along on a commission to decorate the new Russian cathedral of Saint Alexander Nevsky in Paris.

In his third year at the academy Vasilii won a silver medal for his sketch based on Homer's *Odyssey.* However, a few months later—and half a year before the revolt of the fourteen—he shocked the faculty by impetuously burning a larger sepia drawing of the same theme, "to avoid any more of such nonsense," he explained.[72] Although he would not formally withdraw from the academy until 1865, Vereshchagin spent the summer of 1863 in the Caucasus, supporting himself through art lessons to Russian officers' children. Following the example of Pushkin and Lermontov, he roamed the mountains in his spare time, filling three sketchbooks during his stay.

Vereshchagin's life took a lucky turn early in 1864, when he inherited 1,000 rubles from his uncle. Abandoning the relative poverty of his Caucasian existence, the aspiring young artist traveled to Paris and talked himself into an apprenticeship with a new professor at the prestigious Ecole des Beaux-Arts, Jean-Léon Gérôme. When the latter asked who had recommended him, Vereshchagin cockily replied, "Your paintings," adding, "I will study only with you and with no one else."[73] Gérôme had begun his career two decades earlier specializing in classical themes, but he added the Near East to his repertoire after several journeys there in the 1850s. His Oriental canvases were characterized by dramatic light and color, as well as highly realistic brushwork, all reminiscent of the Dutch Golden Age.[74] Because of the artist's scientific attention to local detail, some contemporaries classified him a *peintre ethnographe*.[75]

Vereshchagin's sojourns in Gérôme's atelier left their mark both in technique and choice of subject. Yet, although the men would remain on cordial terms, Vereshchagin's relationship with his new school was little better than with the academy back in St. Petersburg. Chafing at Gérôme's insistence that he copy neoclassical paintings at the Louvre Museum, after about a year he again decamped for the Caucasus.

Vereshchagin's second voyage to the Russian highlands set the pattern for many of his future travels. Over the course of six months, he produced numerous sketches of the region and its people, encyclopedically recording the various national types of the latter with photographic accuracy. The artist's interest in exotic local customs led to a characteristically macabre drawing of self-flagellants during a Shiite festival in Nagorno-Karabakh, *A Religious Procession of the Moharrem Celebration at Shusha*. Vereshchagin also wrote a detailed account that was soon published in the popular French monthly *Le tour du monde* (Around the World).[76] Extensively illustrated, the travelogue was full of clichés about the barbarous, menacing Orient, from the filthy, drink-addled Kalmyk nomads and thieving gypsies to the "audacious, coarse and vengeful" Kabardians.[77] Despite having been pacified by Russian arms, the threat of violence was ever present in the mountains, driven by "religious fanaticism, and the hate common to tribes subjugated by their conquerors."[78]

Vereshchagin left the Caucasus in the autumn of 1865 with high hopes of publishing a journal dedicated to the region, but he could not raise the necessary start-up capital. He therefore returned to Paris, where he proudly showed his drawings to Gérôme. While full of praise, his teacher suggested that he should now master the more difficult skill of painting in oils. This time Vereshchagin took the advice, and he began to work hard to acquire the new craft.

During a conversation with his former academy professor in summer 1867, Vereshchagin learned that General Konstantin Petrovich von Kaufman, the tsar's new governor-general of Turkestan, wanted to hire a young artist for his headquarters in Tashkent. There would be considerable hardship and danger, since Russian troops were still actively campaigning in the central Asian province. Nevertheless, Vereshchagin rushed to offer his services to the general. "I had no *passionate love for the East,* God forbid!" he later told a friend. "*I studied* in the East because I was *freer* there . . . than in the West. Instead of a Parisian garret or some room . . . on Vasil'evskii Island [in St. Petersburg], I would have a Kirghiz yurt."[79] Satisfied with Vereshchagin's educational credentials and the quality of his sketches, Kaufman took him on.

After some hurried preparations, Vereshchagin set out in August from Orenburg, a major trading center in southwestern Siberia on the central Asian steppe frontier.[80] He proceeded on the post road to Tashkent by *tarantass,* a basketlike wooden chariot uninhibited by springs; one French account described it as "an instrument of torture."[81] The 2,000-kilometer journey took him south to the Aral Sea and then southeast along the Syr Darya, reaching the colonial capital in six weeks. Aside from the typical discomforts of traveling in a largely untamed land, it was an uneventful journey. Vereshchagin's first impression of his new hometown was hardly favorable. He recalled: "For those acquainted with the Levant, Tashkent offers nothing new: One sees mostly mud houses, oil-paper windows, grayish walls, and torturous narrow streets where the rains dig muddy pits that swallow horses right up to their knees."[82] Taking an apartment in a local quarter, he busied himself over the next few months by capturing the architecture and the remarkable ethnic diversity of the population in his sketchbooks.

The artist was particularly interested in Tashkent's less wholesome aspects, including its opium dens, beggar guilds, prisons, and *bachas* (dancing boys). He did point out that things had been even worse before tsarist troops had captured the city a dozen years earlier, as there had also been thousands of slaves then. While he occasionally detected undercurrents of hostility, Vereshchagin was convinced, like many of his compatriots, that most of the new Russian subjects were becoming reconciled to their new rulers. As the inhabitants of a suburb greeted him warmly, he mused: "Were they sincere? Allah alone, who knows their hearts, can say. Perhaps they were, since we know that in central Asia the Infidels govern with greater firmness and justice than the indigenous potentates."[83]

Next spring the general sent his artist on an ethnographic survey of the provincial countryside. Accompanied by two Cossacks and a Tatar translator who claimed princely blood, Vereshchagin made his way southward along the upper Syr Darya to study the local Kirghiz and Sart communities. About thirty kilometers from Tashkent, there were reports that Kaufman was marching on the emir of Bukhara. Vereshchagin's thoughts raced: "War! And so close to me, right here in central Asia!"[84] This was so much more interesting than folklore.

The object of Kaufman's assault was Samarkand, Tamerlane's ancient capital. Vereshchagin hastened to the fabled city, but much to his disappointment it had already fallen the day before his arrival. Nevertheless, there were magnificent medieval monuments to be drawn, and he put his pencil to work. The young artist's wish to see combat close up was soon realized when, shortly after Kaufman left Samarkand with the bulk of his troops to pursue the emir, the local population rose against the Russian garrison.[85] For a week in early June 1868, the 500-man force the general had left behind held out against overwhelming odds. Seizing a rifle from a fallen soldier, Vereshchagin played a major role in the defense. At one point, when some troops wavered during a counterattack, he rallied them by storming ahead with the shout "Brothers, after me!" He also joined two sorties out of the citadel into the labyrinthine city streets beyond, narrowly escaping death on both occasions when his comrades rescued him from encounters with the foe.

Vereshchagin displayed fearlessness off the battlefield as well. After the siege had been lifted, he criticized Kaufman in front of his staff for not having done more to secure the fortress. Although one officer indignantly suggested that the artist be shot for insubordination, the general did not take offense and even nominated him for the Saint George Cross, Russia's highest decoration for military bravery.[86] At the time, Vereshchagin objected to the distinction, but he relented when the order's council voted to award the medal. He proudly wore it on his civilian jacket for the rest of his days. Fiercely jealous of his independence, the painter would refuse all other honors during his career, even a professorship at the Imperial Academy of Arts.[87]

The events in Samarkand exacted their toll on Vereshchagin's fragile health. Succumbing to a fever, he decided to travel to Paris to continue work on his paintings. Hopes of organizing a show in the French capital did not materialize, although *Le tour du monde* once again printed his travel account. Early in the following year, the artist got word that Kaufman was back in St. Petersburg. Might he be convinced to sponsor an exhibition? The general, who was eager to show off his central Asian domain to the Russian public, readily gave his consent when Vereshchagin broached the question.

Occupying three rooms at the Ministry of State Domains on the Moika Canal for a month in spring 1869, the Turkestan exhibition displayed stuffed animals, mineral specimens, costumes, and artifacts, as well as Vereshchagin's sketches and paintings. With free admission and its central location just south of Saint Isaac's Cathedral, it attracted large crowds. Emperor Alexander II paid a visit on the opening day with Kaufman as his guide, and expressed his satisfaction. When the tsar asked for the painter to be presented to him, however, the latter made himself scarce. "I do not like to do the bidding of important men," he later explained to his brother.[88]

The highlight was the room with Vereshchagin's canvases, which featured two battle scenes, *After Victory* and *After Defeat,* as well as a genre painting, *The Opium Eaters.* There was also a photo of another oil, *The Bacha and His Admirers.* Portraying an anxious young dancing boy in a girl's dress surrounded by a group of well-fed, middle-aged central Asian men as they greedily eye their quarry, the painting had been destroyed earlier by the artist on the advice that it might offend.[89]

The Opium Eaters particularly struck viewers.[90] Narcotics were a favorite theme of Orientalist art, which often included a narghile or hashish pipe in its harems and souks.[91] What made this particular work unusual was its objective approach, utterly devoid of moralizing disapproval or clichéd exoticism. Although clearly in an Eastern setting, it struck the critic Andrei Somov as offering a more general comment about human degradation.[92] Vereshchagin hinted that Asians were no more predisposed to the vice than others when he mused, "Is the day far off when opium will become widespread in Europe, as if Europe doesn't already consume enough Western opium, that is to say tobacco?"[93]

The two other paintings rebut the notion of Oriental and Occidental as polar opposites. One featured two Uzbeks contemplating their trophy of a dead Russian soldier's severed head, while in the other a tsarist colonial rifleman casually smokes his pipe as many central Asian corpses litter the ground around his feet. In displaying these two scenes of humanity's indifference to the savagery of war, the artist suggested that East and West were actually not far apart. As if to stress this point, he ironically titled the first canvas *After Victory* and the second *After Defeat,* that is, from the enemy's perspective.

Encouraged by the success of his first exhibition, Vereshchagin headed back to central Asia as soon as the show closed in April 1869. Kaufman now arranged an appointment for him at the civilian rank of collegiate registrar on the staff of Major General Gerasim Kolpakovskii, his deputy as governor of the Semireche district in eastern Turkestan. Based in Tashkent, over the next year the artist traveled extensively throughout the province. He did not hesitate to seek out danger once again. On one occasion Vereshchagin joined a Cossack raid deep into Chinese territory to discipline Islamic insurgents, earning more laurels by saving the life of the unit's commander.

Kaufman was clearly pleased with his painter. When Vereshchagin returned to St. Petersburg in 1870, the general awarded him a three-year stay abroad to translate his central Asian experiences into art. The official goal would be to "acquaint the civilized world with the life of a little-known people and to enrich learning with materials important for the study of the region." Left unsaid was the equally important motive of allaying European suspicions about tsarist colonial expansion.[94]

This time the destination was Munich. Because of the Franco-Prussian War, Paris was not an attractive option that year. The Bavarian capital also happened to be the home of a friend, the young Elisabeth Marie Fischer, whose hand he soon took. To simulate Turkestan's bright desert light, Vereshchagin designed a special open studio that rotated on rails to keep his models fully in the rays of the sun as it rose and set during the day. Working with a frantic energy, by 1873 he had completed an impressive thirty-five canvases. They would be sensations.

Vereshchagin's Turkestan series consisted of genre paintings and battle scenes, in addition to a few ethnographic studies. While some were imaginary, many were based on personal experience and observation. Together they justified Russia's mission in central Asia by invoking Orientalist tropes about despotism, cruelty, fallen glory, and vice. Yet some canvases also raised disturbing questions about the conquerors themselves.

A major theme in Western perceptions of the East at the time was the notion of stagnation and barbarism amid traces of greatness rooted in centuries long past. Vereshchagin captured the idea in two paintings that contrast the Timurid Empire at its apogee with the miserable reality of the present. *At Tamerlane's Doors* (1872–73) imagines a fourteenth-century view of the conqueror's palace in Samarkand. Possibly inspired by Gérôme's *The Seraglio's Guard* (1859), it features a pair of sentries armed to the teeth as they stand watch in perfect symmetry over its entrance. Some critics have pointed out that the men in their finely decorated robes are purely ornamental, for the main subject is the pair of massive wooden doors at the center. To emphasize their master's despotic power, the guards face inward rather than toward the viewer, while the intricately carved doors, half hidden in shadow, heighten the air of mystery.

No such awesome majesty attends *At the Mosque's Gate's* (1873), the previous painting's contemporary companion. Rather than two formidable guards, here a sad duo of mendicants with begging bowls await the worshippers' alms at the entrance of a central Asian mosque in Vereshchagin's own day. Gone too is the symmetry of the men; one of the paupers leans on his staff, while his companion is hunched in quiet sleep. And these doors, now in the full glare of the sun instead of shadowy darkness, clearly show signs of age.

Vereshchagin must have had a change of heart about the propriety of certain themes when he painted *The Sale of the Child Slave* (1872). Much like Gérôme's well-known *The Snake Charmer* (1870), it is a commentary on two evils Europeans at the time commonly associated with the East: slavery and pederasty. In his tiny shop, a merchant slyly extols the quality of his ware to a wealthy, aged client, who lustfully eyes a nude boy while hypocritically counting his prayer beads. The painter again effectively manipulates light and shadow, heightening the contrast between the child's innocent nakedness and the old man's luxuriant bright yellow silk robe and white turban.

Vereshchagin paid little attention to heterosexual motifs. Whereas harems and odalisques abounded in Western Orientalist art, they are entirely absent from his Turkestan series. Indeed, women almost never made an appearance in any guise whatsoever.[95] This lacuna was hardly an expression of misogyny. Like Chernyshevskii, the artist advocated female emancipation, and his travelogues waxed indignant about sexual inequality in central Asia: "From the cradle, sold to a man; as a child taken by that man, when she is neither psychologically nor physically mature, she never lives a real life, for childbirth ages her [and she will spend the rest of her days] exploited and withered by a beast of burden's toil."[96] The only exception was a relatively little-known work, *Uzbek Woman in Tashkent* (1873), which portrayed a female passerby entirely hidden by her burqa and face mesh. The only glimpse of skin is a small flash of wrist, accidentally exposed amid the sexless garment's folds. The painter underscores his protest against the confined segregation of women in central Asia by placing the subject next to a tall, prisonlike wall that entirely cuts her off from the blue sky and green trees beyond.

Turkestanis' cruelty to their fellow men featured more prominently in Vereshchagin's art. One canvas, *The Samarkand Zindan* (1873), imagined the citadel's notorious subterranean prison with its doomed inmates, which the painter saw before Kaufman ordered it destroyed.[97] Much more dramatic was a reconstruction of another scene before the Russian capture, *They Rejoice* (1872). On Samarkand's market square, with the decaying turquoise facade of the great seventeenth-century Shir-Dar mosque as backdrop, a mullah exhorts the faithful to wage jihad against the infidel. In the foreground a variety of spectators, from the emir and merchants on camel-back to beggars and feral dogs, watch the scene. Separating the onlookers from the rest of the crowd is a straight line of ten tall poles with darkened tops, which on closer scrutiny prove to be the heads of Russian casualties. An epigraph on the frame with the following words from the Koran re-minds the European viewer of Islam's proverbial fanaticism: "Thus God commands, that all infidels die! There is no god but God . . ."[98]

If the genre paintings in his Turkestan series repeated many common Orientalist motifs, Vereshchagin's battle scenes were much less stereotyp-ical. Some effectively conveyed the excitement of combat. Based on the artist's own experience during the siege of Samarkand, *At the Fortress Wall: "Hush. Let Them Enter!"* (1872) pictures a group of desert troops prepar-ing to meet an anticipated enemy strike through a break in the crumbling defenses.[99] The title refers to the reply the commanding officer gave Vereshchagin when the latter suggested rushing out to attack the foe. The men's anxious expressions, their erect bayonets, and the composition—a broadening white line pushing against the gray of the shaded barrier—all convey the tension moments before the clash.

Likewise inspired by an episode the artist had witnessed, *Mortally Wounded* (1873) presents war in a distinctly minor key.[100] Shot in the chest, a dying soldier staggers ahead as red blood begins to stain his white tunic. An enveloping cloud of thick dust and smoke suggests his immi-nent departure from the living. According to a Russian specialist of the genre, "All war artists have pictured casualties as an inevitable accessory of crowded battle scenes, but until Vereshchagin no one ever made a wounded soldier the main subject of a virtually solitary scene."[101]

Their combination of exotic vistas, thrilling action, and macabre realism made the Turkestan series an instant success with the public. Since Russia was still very much on the margins of the European art world, Vereshcha-gin arranged his debut in a more cosmopolitan setting at London's Crys-tal Palace. The reviews for the exhibition, which opened in April 1873, were almost universally positive. The *Pall Mall Gazette* praised the paint-ings as "very luminous and spirited pieces . . . giving us the acquaintance of an original and considerable artist," while *The Spectator*'s critic gushed, "They are not like anything that has ever before been seen in England;

they stand alone in their beauty and barbarism. The color of them, the cruelty of them!"[102]

The choice of London as his venue was intriguing. At the time Britons were particularly anxious about Russia's central Asian ambitions, which they regarded as a threat to India. The artist portrayed his empire's advance much like Prince Aleksandr Gorchakov's famous circular of 1864, which had justified the conquest of Tashkent as an action perfectly normal for "all civilized states that come into contact with half-savage, wandering tribes."[103] In the preface to his exhibition's catalogue, Vereshchagin drew an even more explicit parallel with British colonial expansion: "The Central Asian population's barbarism is so glaring, its economic and social condition so degraded, that the sooner European civilization penetrates into the land, whether from one side or the other, the better."[104] He added that he hoped his paintings would "assist in dispelling the distrust of the English public towards their natural friends and neighbors in Central Asia."[105]

Vereshchagin brought his Turkestan series to St. Petersburg the following year. Exhibited at the Ministry of Internal Affairs, the show attracted "countless multitudes."[106] Despite—or perhaps because of—murmurs of official disapproval, the show garnered generally good reviews in the press, as well as the enthusiastic praise of other artists.[107] The writer Vsevolod Garshin was moved to pen a verse "At Vereshchagin's First Show," Modest Mussorgsky composed a ballad based on *Forgotten,* while Ivan Kramskoi, a leading member of the Wanderers, wrote that "it is a milestone, a conquest of Russia, far greater than Kaufman's victory."[108] Although Vereshchagin was unable to interest the tsar in buying the paintings, the Moscow-based industrialist Pavel Tretiakov soon acquired them for his collection.

To paraphrase Dostoyevsky, what was central Asia to Vereshchagin? When he learned that Stasov was writing an article about his exhibition for the prominent St. Petersburg daily *Novoe Vremia* (New Times), he dashed off a letter explaining his thinking behind the Turkestan series. The artist suggested that he could have focused on colorful Oriental costumes. But he really had a more serious aim in mind. "My main purpose," he continued, was "to describe the barbarism with which until now the *entire way of life and order* of central Asia has been saturated."[109]

Vereshchagin had titled a group of seven paintings in the series *Poèmes barbares*. Based partly on episodes in Kaufman's ongoing small wars, he intended them to be "chapters" within a narrative about a successful raid on a tsarist unit by the emir of Bukhara's forces. Beginning with *They Observe* (1873), which pictured Uzbek and Kirghiz scouts as they spy on their foe, the canvases took the viewer through the assault, the Russians' last stand, the tribute of their severed heads to the emir back in Tashkent, celebrations on the market square (*They Rejoice*), and a prayer of thanksgiving at Tamerlane's grave.

The final "chapter" of these "barbaric poems" was also Vereshchagin's best-known work, *Apotheosis of War* (1871–72). On a light brown post-apocalyptic desert plain against a backdrop of an ancient city's ruins and Daliesque, desiccated trees, an enormous pyramid of white human skulls rises into the cloudless blue sky. The only sign of life is a flock of black ravens, searching in vain for remnants of carrion on the fleshless heads. The artist had initially planned to title the work *Apotheosis of Tamerlane*, since it had been inspired by accounts of the medieval khan's custom of leaving such monuments. However, Prussia's recent clash with France had reminded him that war's cruel violence remained as much a feature of his own century as it had been of the fourteenth. To stress this point, he inscribed the frame with the ironic epigraph, "Dedicated to all great conquerors, past, present and future."[110]

The subtext is obvious. If the Oriental was barbarous, the Occidental could be just as uncivilized. There was no fundamental difference between East and West. War was the clearest proof. In his letter to Stasov about the Turkestan series, he concluded with this point: "I must remind you of the fact that both warring sides appeal *to a single God* . . . a truth that is just as valid in Asia as it is in enlightened Europe."[111] Whether a soldier took to arms with the cry "Allahu Akbar!" "S nami Bog!" or "Gott mit uns!" the tragic outcome was the same. The implication for a generation of Russians who flaunted their atheism was that religious zeal led to fanaticism and violence among all nations, regardless of race or creed.

A firm believer in progress and the perfectibility of mankind, Vereshchagin did not think that Turkestan was eternally condemned to barbarism. Given the proper circumstances, the East could reach the same level of development as the West. What was necessary was the fatherly guidance of the latter. Europeans, including his own compatriots, had a duty to bring civilization to their Asian brethren, a task best accomplished by conquest and rule. According to Vereshchagin, "Whatever the cost, and with all due respect to the law and justice, the question [of colonizing Turkestan] must be settled, and with the least possible delay. It concerns not just Russia's future in Asia, but above all the well-being of those under our rule. In truth, they have more to gain from seeing our authority definitively established than to return to their former tyranny."[112]

The artist's conception of Russia's mission in central Asia was the colonial equivalent of "going to the people," the vast agrarian populist migration to the Russian countryside in the summers of 1873 and 1874 to bring enlightenment to the peasantry. There was no inherent contradiction between such left-leaning sentiments and championing General Kaufman's small wars. Friedrich Engels once explained to Karl Marx that "Russia in truth performs a progressive task in the East. . . . Russian rule is a civilizing force for the Black and Caspian Seas, as well as for Central Asia."[113]

While the tsar's attitude to Vereshchagin's Turkestan series remains unclear, some of the paintings did offend a number of his senior officials. Many of the battle scenes portrayed Russia's central Asian campaign in a distinctly inglorious light. The artist's own political views—some labeled him a nihilist—did not help. Yet contrary to his reputation in later years, Vereshchagin was not dogmatically pacifist. He never questioned tsarist ambitions in Turkestan. During Russia's war with Turkey in 1877–78, he fully supported its war aims, even if his brush produced a scathing critique of the way they were executed. Indeed, when his brother Aleksandr considered leaving the military after being wounded on the Balkan front during that conflict, he urged him to stay on and fulfill his duty to fatherland and family.[114] And when Japan went to war with Russia in 1904, he bombarded Nicholas II with letters urging the tsar to take a firm line against the "yellow faces." He also offered his help: "If my saber isn't strong, permit my pencil to serve you."[115] What Vereshchagin did oppose were the excesses of war and the incompetence of the generals who waged it.

At the same time, as an artist who firmly believed in his obligation to portray reality, Vereshchagin considered himself honor bound to avoid glorifying or sentimentalizing an inherently cruel enterprise. To him, the way painters traditionally had portrayed war was fraudulent. In a discussion of the more established German military artist August-Alexander von Kotzebue, he explained, "He was a battle painter of the old school. . . . On his canvases it was obvious that [soldiers] attacked, charged, maneuvered, took prisoners and died as the academy taught, and entirely according to the official accounts of the commanders, in other words, as they wanted it to be known and not as it really happened."[116]

Not one to rest on his laurels, Vereshchagin left St. Petersburg even before his show at the interior ministry had ended. In April 1874 he sailed with his wife to India, where he spent the next two years traveling throughout the immense colony. Although at times his progress was hampered by British suspicions that the former navy officer was a tsarist spy, Vereshchagin's canvases of the journey were entirely apolitical, focusing on the subcontinent's exotic architecture, people, and scenery in rich, bright colors.

Vereshchagin never completed all the Indian paintings he had planned, since rising tensions in the Balkans between the Orthodox populations and their Ottoman overlords soon drew his attention. By the time war had broken out between Russia and Turkey in April 1877, he had secured himself a posting to the staff of a senior tsarist general to see the action firsthand. Even more than his Turkestan battle scenes, the works that resulted from his year at the Balkan front captured the difficult campaign in all its inglorious misery. While he again fully supported St. Petersburg's military aims, his brush highlighted the grim toll on the troops and the callous indifference of their commanders.

In the following three decades Vereshchagin took extensive sojourns in Palestine, the Philippines, North America, and Japan, all of which yielded more paintings. It was during a second voyage to northeast Asia as Japan took up arms against Russia that the artist met his end on March 31, 1904, aboard Admiral Stepan Makarov's flagship *Petropavlovsk* when it struck a mine in Manchurian waters off Port Arthur.

Neither Vereshchagin's brush nor his pen had shied away from expressing strong opinions. When it came to central Asia, these included a strong faith in Russia's *mission civilisatrice,* the duty of all modern nations to bring the benefits of more enlightened ways to their less advanced brethren. In this way, General Kaufman's campaign in Turkestan happened to coincide with the artist's progressive political leanings. At the same time, his commitment to Chernyshevskii's credo of critical realism obligated him to present war's brutal cost to Russian conscripts in searing honesty.

As a student of one of Paris's foremost teachers, Vereshchagin naturally adopted the tropes of Orientalist art about the East's cruelty, fanaticism, and vice. Nevertheless, as his writings make clear, he made no fundamental Saidian distinction between European "self" and Asian "other." In an oft-quoted remark he made in later years, Vereshchagin repeated his firm belief that the two were not really quite so far apart: "We often hear claims that our century is highly civilized, and that it is hard to imagine how mankind could possibly develop even further. Is not the opposite really true? Wouldn't it be better to accept that mankind has only made the most tentative steps in all directions, and that we still live in the age of barbarism?"[117]

When early nineteenth-century Russian poets found their muse in the Orient, they were following a European trend. But they took a different course. If, like the great Romantic Lord Byron, the Russians also traveled to the East, they rarely did so by going abroad. For Pushkin, Lermontov, Bestuzhev (Marlinskii), and the others, the Caucasus was well within their own country's borders. At the same time, their attitudes were not just shaped by the peculiarities of political geography. Although Russia's Romantic poets considered themselves to be European, they were also aware of a special affinity with Asia. Pastor Herder's ideas about Eastern roots seemed much more concrete to them than to his own compatriots to the west.

Bestuzhev put it well: "The two-faced Janus, Russia simultaneously looked both to Asia and to Europe."[118] And when gazing East, Romantic Russia also saw some reflections of itself. Whether consciously or not, this recognition that the boundaries between Orient and Occident were much less distinct than for Germans, French, or English made Pushkin and his contemporaries more empathetic with the East. In Said's terms, there was much less difference between self and other. While the Orient was less important to Russian painters, Vasilii Vereshchagin's canvases and prolific writings show that artists could have very similar thoughts about the East's alterity.

Pushkin's era would come to be known as the Golden Age, when Russian letters first reached their full florescence. As a result, while Asia faded into the literary background during the rest of the nineteenth century, the Oriental theme would remain inextricably linked to this time of poetic greatness. And it did not stay entirely dormant, particularly as Russians entered the twentieth century.

5

THE KAZAN SCHOOL

If, as Peter the Great prophesied, Russia was summoned to bear the West to Asia and to acquaint Europe with the East, then Kazan is unquestionably the main caravanserai on the path of European ideas to Asia and Asian character to Europe.

—Aleksandr Herzen

After flowing eastward from near Moscow toward Asia for some 800 kilometers, the Volga River sharply veers southward, eventually emptying into the Caspian Sea, which washes onto the shores of Iran. At this bend it is joined by the Kama, whose headwaters originate in the Ural Mountains, thereby continuing the riparian path to Siberia. The strategic and economic importance of this juncture is clear: in an age when much long-distance travel was by water, the confluence of the Volga and Kama rivers provided a three-way maritime link between Europe, the Near East, and East Asia.

The Turkic Bulgars were among the first to benefit from the region's commercial advantages by settling it in the fifth century C.E. and founding the city of Bolgar there. Much like the Kievan Slavs to their west, who profited from trade along the rivers "from the Varangians to the Greeks," the Bulgars grew rich by shipping furs and other valuable commodities between the Kievan principalities and the great civilizations to the south, including the Byzantine Empire and the Caliphate of Baghdad. But whereas Kiev adopted the faith and culture of Christian Byzantium, during the tenth century the Bulgars converted to Islam. From then on, the fates of many in the middle Volga region would be closely linked to the Muslim world.

In 1236 Batu Khan swept the Bulgar khanate into the dustbin of history. While its capital succumbed to the Mongol onslaught, some survivors migrated north and founded a town on a promontory overlooking the Volga and a tributary that joins it there. Legend has it that, as a meal was being prepared on this spot following one of Batu Khan's hunts, the large pot that contained the repast accidentally tumbled into the latter stream. Accordingly, the smaller river and the new settlement were named Kazanka and Kazan, respectively, after the Arabic noun for "cauldron." Kazan flourished, and after the Golden Horde disintegrated in the mid-fifteenth century, it became the capital of one of its Tatar successor khanates. As the Eurasian balance of power began to shift from Islam to Christendom, and European gunpowder started to prevail over central Asian nomadic archery, Kazan came under increasing pressure from the expanding Muscovite principality. In 1552 Tsar Ivan the Terrible forcibly joined the khanate to his dominions. As a result of various waves of conversion, expulsion, and migration, the city's population eventually became largely Russian. By the early 1800s, according to one count, of Kazan's 25,000 inhabitants only a fifth was still Tatar.[1]

Over the many years since Ivan's conquest, the fires that periodically devastated the largely wooden city had purged it of most its Islamic elements, and much of Kazan acquired a distinctly Russian air, complete with an imposing stone kremlin, onion-domed churches, and neoclassical noble mansions. Nevertheless, the surviving Tatars maintained their own community in the "lower town." Prospering as intermediaries for Russia's Oriental trade, they built new mosques, whose minarets also adorned Kazan's skies. Many nineteenth-century travelers were struck by the sharp contrasts between the elements of provincial Russia and the Islamic Orient that coexisted peacefully in what was now a major regional capital. One visitor who stopped in Kazan on his way to Beijing recalled "this strange blend of Russian sophistication and Asian simplicity, Islam and Christianity, Russian and Tatar, the vista of churches and mosques, the sound of pealing bells mingling with the savage, penetrating howls of the muezzins. . . . In short, [the city] is an astonishing panorama of paradoxes."[2]

Although the city had by now been largely Russified, the majority of the surrounding countryside's population still consisted of Tatars and other Turkic and Finnic minorities. Consequently, Kazan became one of the Russian autocracy's first laboratories for dealing with Eastern nationalities. At the same time, until the railway age the city retained its role as a major entrepôt for commerce with the East. As the Romanovs' bureaucracy grew more sophisticated, it also became the leading administrative center for their Asian possessions.[3] As a result, well into the nineteenth century Kazan served as the empire's principal observation post for the Orient. Much like St. Petersburg's traditional function with regard to the West, Kazan, in the words of one American scholar, was Imperial Russia's "window on the East."[4]

When in 1804 Emperor Alexander I decreed the founding of three new universities for his empire, Kazan was chosen as one of their sites. Given the city's location, its new campus not surprisingly developed an expertise in scholarship about Asia. Alexander's statute had also provided for chairs of Oriental letters at some of his other universities, but most of them were slow to develop. Only in Kazan's Eastern soil did the seed quickly take root. With its manifold Eastern nationalities, administrative responsibilities for Siberia, and educators who had a fascination for Asia, the city's young university had all the right conditions for orientology to flourish and flower.

During the eighteenth century there had already been sporadic Russian initiatives to study Asia in St. Petersburg and elsewhere. None of these, however, were systematic or sustained. By the same token, just as it had been the tsar's pleasure to grant Kazan an institution of higher learning in 1804, fifty years later orientology there abruptly halted when the curriculum was concentrated in St. Petersburg by imperial fiat. Meanwhile, other important centers for the study of the East arose elsewhere in the empire, such as the Lazarev Institute in Moscow (after 1919, the capital's Oriental Institute) and Vladivostok's short-lived Eastern Institute. Nevertheless, during the decades of its primacy, the Kazan school pioneered orientology in the Russian academy.

With its sizable community of Tatars and its proximity to the Near East, Kazan, more than any other major center of orientology in late Imperial Russia, complicated the Saidian distinction between self and other. At the same time, the link between scholarship and the state was particularly strong in Kazan. Asian languages were taught at the university explicitly to train officials for government service in Asia, both within the empire's borders and abroad. And, when the Kazan Theological Academy began to offer courses in Turkish, Arabic, and Mongolian, its goal was to teach missionaries to take the Gospel to Russia's non-Christian minorities.[5]

The foundations for orientology in Kazan were laid well before the university opened its doors in 1805. Already half a century earlier, when in 1758 Empress Elizabeth decreed the establishment of a gymnasium (grammar school) for the city, its first director began to press for Tatar classes to be added to the curriculum. Catherine the Great, no doubt influenced by her celebrated visit of 1767, finally granted the request in 1769. Her decree specified that Sagit Halfin, a Tatar interpreter employed by the admiralty, would be transferred to the gymnasium to teach the language beginning in the fall of that year. Halfin's pedagogy was practical and purely aimed at producing competent government translators.[6] His courses had already proved their worth within five years, when, in the aftermath of Emilian Pugachev's violent rebellion along the Volga River, imperial authorities called on graduates to study the causes of discontent among minorities who had joined the rising.[7]

Catherine had also considered adding some universities to the one founded at Moscow under Elizabeth in 1755, but her grandson, Alexander I, ultimately carried out the task with his regulations of 1802 and 1804 establishing (and reestablishing) campuses at Vilnius, Kazan, and Kharkov.[8] Coming during the earlier, more liberal phase of his reign, Alexander's initiative was thoroughly in keeping with the best traditions of the Enlightenment, and it granted considerable autonomy to the institutions' faculties. At the same time, his decrees stressed the utilitarian imperative of producing bureaucrats, teachers, and physicians for the empire.[9] The universities also were given a supervisory mandate over all regional lower schools in the educational districts in which they were based. As the empire's easternmost campus, Kazan thereby became responsible for all secular teaching in an enormous region stretching from the governments of Nizhnyi-Novgorod, Penza, and Saratov in central Russia to all of Siberia and the Caucasus.[10]

Alexander's university statute of 1804 provided for chairs in Oriental letters (i.e., Arabic and Persian) at Moscow and the two new universities of Kharkov and Kazan.[11] Kharkov was the first to fill the post, hiring a resident Lutheran pastor, Johann-Gottfried Bärendt, in 1805 to teach Hebrew and other Oriental languages. Although the cleric can rightly be considered to have been the first professor of orientology in a Russian university, the appointment does not appear to have been a great success, since it was not renewed the following year. The chair remained dormant for some two decades until a Leipzig graduate, Bernhard Dorn, was recruited in 1829. His affiliation with Kharkov was somewhat lengthier, and he read Arabic and Persian there for seven years. However, when in 1835 the foreign ministry lured him to its own Asian language school in St. Petersburg, no successor was named.[12]

Moscow University had a little more luck, and it would prove to be the only institution in these early years able to attract a native Russian orientologist, Aleksei Boldyrev, to its campus. Educated at Göttingen and Paris, where he had studied with the distinguished Antoine Isaac Silvestre de Sacy, Boldyrev arrived in Moscow in 1811 and enjoyed a successful career that culminated with the post of rector. Although he trained several scholars and published some Arabic and Persian readers, Boldyrev did not leave a great legacy, and upon his forcible retirement due to a political indiscretion in 1836 the university did not replace him for some fifteen years.[13]

As for Kazan, its rector solicited the advice of Oluf-Gerhard Tychsen, a specialist in Arabic numismatics at the eastern German university of Rostock. Tychsen naturally recommended one of his own students, Christian-Martin Frähn, for the job. Fully sharing his teacher's passion for Near Eastern material culture, Frähn was thrilled at the prospect of living near the ruins of ancient Bolgar and the Golden Horde settlements, and he readily accepted the post of professor of Oriental letters when it was offered to him in 1807. At Kazan the young German scholar enthusiastically busied himself with cataloguing coins and other antiquities from the region and began a lifelong effort to compile an Arabic dictionary. His scholarly achievements eventually attracted the attention of St. Petersburg's Imperial Academy of Sciences, which hired him in 1817 to organize its collection of Asian artifacts.[14]

Frähn did not prove to be a particularly effective teacher. Like many of his colleagues among Kazan's predominantly German faculty, he did not speak Russian. Frähn therefore conducted his classes in Latin, a language almost as alien to provincial undergraduates as the Arabic and Persian he offered. During his first year he did manage to attract five students, most of whom had already taken Tatar at the gymnasium. But, discouraged by their poor command of Latin, the absence of textbooks, and their instructor's relative inexperience, three of them soon transferred to other departments; another eventually succumbed to an illness. Ultimately, Frähn only produced one student, Ianuarii Iartsov, who went on to pursue a career at the foreign ministry's Asian Department.

When Frähn left for St. Petersburg, he suggested that the university appoint another Rostock graduate, Franz Erdmann, as his successor. The choice proved unwise. Like his compatriot, Erdmann had no command of Russian and was entirely unwilling to make the effort to learn it. Meanwhile, by most accounts his teaching was stultifying and uninspiring. By 1822 the professor did not have even a single student, and only the arrival two years later of a few Polish exiles who did know Latin replenished his enrollments. Although Erdmann remained at Kazan for twenty-six years, neither his scholarly nor his pedagogical accomplishments were noteworthy. Even Frähn eventually came to regard him as "thoroughly incompetent."[15]

Russian orientologists tend to minimize the contributions of Frähn and Erdmann to the Kazan school. Nevertheless, along with their compatriots at other Russian institutions, these early German scholars left an imprint in two important ways. First, they were students of an academic approach that emphasized philology, the secular study of ancient texts.[16] As Suzanne Marchand has noted, this preference of early nineteenth-century German *Orientalistik* for languages of the past rather than the present came in part because there were relatively few practical needs at the time to master modern Asian tongues. More important, philology was strongly rooted in German Romanticism, with its fascination for the primeval and its dislike of the Greco-Roman rationalist heritage.[17]

In this context, German orientologists were particularly intrigued by the theories of the eighteenth-century British Indian colonial official, Sir William "Oriental" Jones, about Sanskrit as the Indo-European *Ursprache*. Russian orientologists often shared the interest of their German colleagues in Asian influences on their own culture. However, if their Teutonic counterparts looked to ancient India of the distant past for traces of their origins, Russians could detect much more tangible traces of the Eastern inheritance in the cultural, political, and racial imprint of the relatively recent Mongol yoke. As the century progressed, the question of "Genghis Khan's legacy" became a matter of considerable controversy among *vostokovedy* in the pages of Russia's thick journals.

Orientology did not exactly prosper at Kazan during the first two decades of the university's existence. To be fair, the fault lay not entirely with Frähn and Erdmann, for the young campus also suffered from some teething pains. The writer Sergei Aksakov, who was among Kazan's first matriculants, recalled the excitement with which many had greeted its establishment in 1804: "Those were proud and happy days, days of pure love for knowledge and praiseworthy enthusiasm!"[18] Such high spirits soon dissipated, however, in the face of a slow start. For the first ten years the university did not even have its own separate facilities or administration. It existed, in the words of the historian Aleksandr Kizevetter, as "some amorphous auxiliary of the local gymnasium."[19] When classes began in 1805, it was hard at first to find both competent faculty and students to fill them. At the time of its second, "formal" inauguration in 1814, the university had an enrolment of only forty-two undergraduates. As for its modest staff, most professors were Germans who, like Frähn and Erdmann, taught primarily in Latin.[20]

Matters became even worse during the reaction that set in during the later years of Alexander I's reign in the wake of the Napoleonic Wars. As the emperor's sentiments increasingly shifted from his earlier Enlightenment liberalism to a darker, highly conservative mysticism, he began to see education primarily as a way of instilling Christian ideals into his subjects. In the words of one of his more prominent servants, schooling had to be "in accordance with the principle of the Holy Alliance" (Alexander's idealistic appeal to all God-fearing monarchs to live in peace and harmony).[21] Kazan's superintendent of education at this time, Mikhail Magnitskii, was particularly hostile to any deviation from Orthodox piety in all courses. Indeed, the official even had his doubts about the importance of higher education per se. Before being appointed to Kazan in 1819, Magnitskii had actually advocated the university's dissolution.

Declaring his goal to be "purifying and pacifying [Kazan University] as a Russian and a Christian," Magnitskii issued detailed guidelines for every subject on the curriculum, each of which had to demonstrate the superiority of the Orthodox faith, monarchical government, and the Russian nation. Thus lectures in world history were obligated to stress the backwardness and inadequacy of all heathen cultures.[22] Meanwhile, he commanded Professor Erdmann to minimize the achievements of Islamic civilization while teaching that it was mostly derivative from ancient Greek thought. Arabic and Persian literature were to be largely ignored, and the orientologist had to restrict himself to teaching the languages "only insofar as they may serve Russian commerce and diplomacy."[23] And when an instructor produced a Tatar reader at the university's request, the rector censored passages about Genghis Khan and Tamerlane because of their potentially subversive connotations among the empire's Tartar minorities.[24]

Magnitskii was even more hostile to Western influences. The conservative superintendent detected the specter of godless revolution in much of the contemporary European academy, especially in the wake of student unrest in Germany in the late 1810s. Similar stirrings of political activity among Russian undergraduates only seemed to confirm Magnitskii's worst fears: "The education, the books, and the men we have imported from Germany have caused the whole mischief that has been observed in our universities. There the infection of unbelief and revolutionary principles, which started in England and gained additional strength in pre-revolutionary France, has been erected into a complete . . . system."[25] Among the concrete steps he took to inoculate his charges at Kazan against such dangerous pathologies, Magnitskii weeded out suspect foreign textbooks, appointed a director of morality, and sacked seven German professors from the forty-two-man faculty.[26]

Yet despite his antagonism to other cultures, Magnitskii did recognize the practical value of orientology. Significantly, he spared Erdmann from his purge of the university's German professoriate. And when in 1826 a gifted young Persian scholar happened to be passing through town, he did not oppose the rector's request to hire him. On another occasion, Magnitskii even proposed that the university set up a branch in western Siberia to focus on Sinology.[27]

When Magnitskii was fired from his post as superintendent in 1826, ori-entology at Kazan had been injured, but not fatally so. The views of his successor, Mikhail Musin-Pushkin, about the discipline's importance were radically different, and under his enthusiastic tutelage the Kazan school would truly come into its own. But the central figure in this development would be the Persian visitor: Mirza Aleksandr Kasimovich Kazem-Bek.

In February 1842, sometime after his betrothal, Kazem-Bek wrote a letter to his fiancée's aunt to introduce himself. "Who am I?" he asked, going on to answer that he was "Of Persian ancestry, faithful to the Protestant Church, a subject of the Russian Empire and Professor of Turco-Tatar Letters at the Imperial Kazan University."[28] This response accurately de-scribes the various elements that shaped the orientologist's worldview and helps explain how his opinions about Islam and the East evolved over the years.

Although his academic and political outlook was cautiously progressive, the professor proudly flaunted his Persian origins. He enjoyed the atten-tion of passersby as he promenaded the city streets sporting a silk turban and colorful, flowing robes. (When during the Crimean War his Oriental attire drew negative comments in the St. Petersburg press as being an un-patriotic provocation, Kazem-Bek remained utterly unrepentant.)[29] And the academic's preferred form of address, Mirza Aleksandr Kasimovich, combined his Persian title of scribe with the traditional given name and patronymic that Russian etiquette requires.

Born in 1802 in the Persian city of Rasht, not far from the Russian bor-der, Muhammad Ali Kazem-Bek (as he was known before his conversion to Christianity) was the eldest son of an important official, Mirza Hadji Kasim Kazem-Bek. The family had long been prominent in the Caucasian port of Derbent, a former possession of the shah whose recent annexation by the Russians had led to Hadji Kasim's exile. Nevertheless, Muhammad Ali's father eventually reconciled himself to tsarist rule, and in 1808 he re-turned to his hometown to accept an appointment as chief *qadi,* or judge, for its largely Muslim community. Hadji Kasim provided his firstborn with a thorough education. Hoping that the boy would follow in his footsteps, the judge employed leading mullahs to train him in Arabic, logic, rheto-ric, and jurisprudence. Muhammad Ali soon proved to have strong inclinations toward scholarship. At the age of seventeen he had already mastered Arabic so thoroughly that he precociously wrote a grammar, and the following year he circulated other compositions in the language to his friends.

At around this time misfortune struck. Together with a number of other local notables, Hadji Kasim was convicted by a military tribunal of conspiring against Russian rule, and he found himself stripped of his property and banished to Astrakhan on the northern shore of the Caspian Sea. Lonely and old, Hadji Kasim was eventually allowed to summon his son, who joined him there in 1822. Among the exile's acquaintances in the Russian port was a group of Presbyterian missionaries who had been granted permission by Alexander I to proselytize among Muslims and other non-Christian inhabitants of the area. The learned judge liked the Scottish clerics, and he often invited them to his home to debate the relative merits of their faiths. Eager to defend his beliefs, his son soon joined these discussions as well. Although the younger Kazem-Bek was particularly zealous, going so far as to pen an Arabic tract, "About the Truth of Islam and the Errors of the Christians and Jews," he also took to the Scots.[30] When the latter inquired whether he might teach them Arabic and Turkish, Muhammad Ali accepted the job without demur.

The young man's daily visits to the missionaries invariably led to more conversations about God, and he soon began to have doubts about his devotion to Islam. As he explained: "My secret reason for studying Christianity so as to fight it all the better (or so I thought at the time) gradually opened me to a hitherto unknown consciousness. . . . My faith began to succumb, my misgivings gave me no peace, and my fascination drew me further and further."[31] Despite his father's fury, in the summer of 1823 Mohammed Ali was baptized into the Presbyterian Church, taking the Christian name of Aleksandr.[32] Echoing a cliché about Islam of the time, he later recalled, "I decided to leave the Muslim world. This way of life and thinking now seemed to me to be too fanatical."[33]

Aleksandr's apostasy predictably estranged him from the elderly Hadji Kasim, and the new convert moved in with his new coreligionists. He spent several years with them, immersing himself in writing religious tracts and learning English and Hebrew in the bargain. The Scots had hopes that their promising pupil would make a good missionary himself, but these were dashed when Russia's commander for the Caucasus, General Aleksei Ermolov, intervened. On the officer's orders, Kazem-Bek was informed that, as a Christian subject of the emperor with noble status, he was now legally obligated to state service.[34] While he was technically acting according to tsarist law, in fact Ermolov was motivated by the worry that the gifted young scholar might come to serve British imperial ambitions in the Caucasus during the early years of the Great Game with Russia for Asian influence.[35] Forbidden to have any more dealings with the Calvinist clerics, Aleksandr was told to choose an appropriate government appointment. The young Persian ventured that he might like to be an interpreter at the foreign ministry in St. Petersburg. Much to his chagrin, he was ordered instead to report to the dreary Siberian garrison of Omsk to teach Oriental languages at its local cadet corps (military school).

In the words of his official biographer, as Kazem-Bek made his way to his new job, a "lucky star" blessed him.[36] The path from Astrakhan to Omsk passed through Kazan, and it was here that, in January 1826, Aleksandr was forced to interrupt his journey for a while to convalesce from an illness. Armed with a letter of introduction, he found refuge with the university's rector, Karl Fuchs. As luck would have it, at the time Kazan happened to be looking for a new Tatar instructor. Kazem-Bek's erudition and charm quickly made him the ideal candidate for the opening. Fuchs successfully appealed to Foreign Minister Count Karl Nesselrode to release him from his obligations in Omsk, and in October 1826 the Persian was formally appointed to the university's faculty.

Kazem-Bek's new career coincided with the replacement of Magnitskii by a superintendent more sympathetic to orientology, Mikhail Musin-Pushkin.[37] A decorated veteran of the Napoleonic Wars boasting an illustrious lineage, Musin-Pushkin tirelessly promoted the field throughout his long affiliation with the Ministry of Education. As early as 1827 he proposed setting up a separate faculty for Oriental letters at Kazan, and fourteen years later he suggested that the university establish an Asian language institute. While both of these ideas fell on deaf ears among his superiors, after Musin-Pushkin's transfer in 1846 to St. Petersburg to become its superintendent of education, he would preside over the centralization of all orientology within that city's university in 1854.

Although Musin-Pushkin eventually became the main force behind the decision that ended the Kazan school's primacy, during the prior twenty years of his appointment to the eastern educational district the discipline of orientology expanded far beyond its modest beginnings. In 1828, within two years of his appointment as superintendent of Kazan, the subject of Turkish was promoted to its own chair, joining Persian and Arabic letters. Then in 1833 the university became the first in Europe to name a professor for Mongolian, followed by chairs for Mandarin Chinese in 1837 and two more in Armenian and Sanskrit in 1842. Musin-Pushkin even had plans to add Tibetan, Hebrew, and Kalmyk to the curriculum, but these remained unrealized when he left for St. Petersburg in 1846. Nevertheless, by 1841 he could justly boast to the minister that Kazan University taught Oriental languages in a "depth and variety unsurpassed by any other institution of higher learning in all of Europe."[38]

Two other leading officials of the day shared Musin-Pushkin's appreciation for the value of orientology. Having already penned his own plan for an *académie asiatique* back in 1810, Nicholas I's education minister, Count Sergei Uvarov, had long championed the discipline as well.[39] And the celebrated mathematician Nikolai Lobachevskii, whose nineteen-year rectorship of Kazan coincided with Musin-Pushkin's superintendence, also actively supported the expansion of Asian languages there.[40] In the charismatic Mirza Kazem-Bek, these three men found a scholar with the energy and the enthusiasm to implement their ambitions for developing orientology at the university.

Kazan's decision to take on an Asian native speaker to teach languages was hardly unprecedented. Kazem-Bek's predecessor as Tatar instructor had been Ibrahim Halfin, a grandson of the gymnasium master appointed by Catherine the Great, and the university subsequently hired other Tatars, Persians (including Kazem-Bek's brother), and even a Buriat for its faculty.[41] Meanwhile, St. Petersburg University likewise appointed an Egyptian and a Persian during the early nineteenth century. Whereas in later years, under the more assimilationist regimes of Alexander III and Nicholas II, some Asians may have faced discrimination in the Russian academy, these earlier appointments generally suffered no such handicaps during their careers.[42]

Kazem-Bek's own progress through the academic ranks was fairly

smooth. In 1830, within four years of joining Kazan's faculty, he was promoted from instructor of Turkish and Tatar to adjunct (*ad'iunkt*) professor and by 1837 to full (*ordinarnyi*) professor. When in 1845 Franz Erdmann was eased out of his post as professor of Arabic and Persian letters,
Kazem-Bek was transferred to the more prestigious chair. That year his
colleagues also voted him dean of his faculty. At the same time, Aleksandr
Kasimovich's scholarship quickly won the esteem of his colleagues in the
field. The Royal British Asiatic Society elected him a corresponding member in 1829, an honor the Russian Academy of Sciences would also be-
stow upon him in 1835. Other leading orientological groups in Paris,
Berlin, and Boston followed.

Kazem-Bek's early intellectual pursuits at Kazan focused on Oriental
texts.[43] He first attracted the notice of the profession in 1832 with an edition of the Turkish-language *The Seven Planets, or the History of the Khans
of the Crimea.* In 1839 the mirza published his Turkish grammar, which
earned him the first of four Demidov Prizes, the Academy of Science's
prestigious award for scholarly distinction.[44] The German edition, which
was completed in 1848, remained a leading textbook in European universities into the twentieth century.[45]

Having been schooled in law, Kazem-Bek naturally turned his attention
to Islamic jurisprudence. In addition to publishing scholarly works on the
matter, he also published important legal texts from Arabic to assist government officials in dealing with minorities who still administered their
traditional laws. In 1841 he edited an Arabic edition of the *Mukhtasar al-
wiqaya,* an important manual of jurisprudence used by Tatars and other
Turkic nationalities in Russia. At the same time, he was well aware that
more conservative bureaucrats might object to his relatively positive assessment of Islamic law. When in 1842 he completed an article about the
subject, the professor decided to send it to the Parisian *Journal asiatique*
rather than risk submitting it to the Russian Ministry of Education's
monthly.[46]

Upon moving to St. Petersburg in 1849, Kazem-Bek assumed increasing administrative responsibilities that distracted him from scholarship.
Shortly after his arrival, he was tapped by a government committee overseeing the translation of liturgical texts into Tatar, as well as by another
body that reviewed Islamic legal codes. It was as a reward for the latter that

in 1863 the mirza was promoted to the high *chin* (civil service rank) of confidential councillor.[47] Although he sought to maintain his scholarly detachment, Kazem-Bek's work inevitably aroused controversy. Tatar scholars distrusted the involvement of an apostate into what they considered to be their own affairs, while conservative Russians found him to be too sympathetic to Islam.[48] Despite his increasing involvement in affairs of state, the mirza nevertheless eventually completed a major concordance of the Koran, a project he had begun in Kazan.[49] His residence in the imperial capital interested him in more recent events in the Muslim world as well. Thus he wrote about the resistance to Russian rule in Dagestan, as well as concerning the Babis, a reformist sect in Persia.[50]

In addition to being an accomplished scholar, Kazem-Bek also proved to be an effective teacher. Unlike his German predecessors at Kazan, he took the trouble to master Russian, which boosted his popularity as a lecturer.[51] One alumnus remembered: "I wasn't so much interested in the Tatar language as in Prof. Aleksandr Kasimovich Kazem-Bek. When I occasionally encountered him on the street, I very much enjoyed seeing the lively figure in his unusual garb and listening to his speech."[52] Kazem-Bek trained a number of young men who went on to have their own distinguished careers as orientologists, including Il'ia Berezin and Nikolai Il'minskii. The mirza's best-known student was Count Leo Tolstoy, who enrolled in Kazan's orientology department in hopes of becoming a diplomat. Despite his linguistic talents, however, the undergraduate was much more interested in the card table and the bordello than his coursework, and after failing his first year he transferred to the university's less rigorous law faculty.[53]

Kazem-Bek was well liked outside of the classroom as well. While he claims to have been lonely and withdrawn during his early years at the university, his colleagues enjoyed his company. He was much sought after as a dinner guest, especially when prominent visitors came to town.[54] In 1836, during a tour of the city, Nicholas I took particular note of the Persian, pausing at length for a chat.[55] And his exotic, dark features found considerable favor among the opposite sex. One lady remarked, "His look was like lightning, and could not possibly be withstood."[56] She was apparently not alone. According to a French biographer of his great-grandson, the professor fathered four children out of wedlock in Russia.[57]

Despite his conversion to Christianity, Kazem-Bek was not implacably hostile to Islam. Although he detected some failings in his former faith, the
mirza did not deem it to be inherently flawed. His series of articles about
Islam's early history in the liberal journal *Russkoe slovo* (The Russian Word)
provided a comparatively objective account of the belief's origins and the
rise of the Prophet Muhammad.[58] He began by echoing many contemporaries who found the Muslim world of the nineteenth century to be
stagnant, corrupt, and despotic. But, he quickly pointed out, the Orient
did not have a monopoly on decadence, as the histories of Rome and
Byzantium had amply proven. Indeed, it was latter's very apathy and in-
sularity in the seventh century that had provided the right conditions for
the rise of a new religion to challenge Christianity on its southeastern
marches.

Kazem-Bek portrayed Islam's founder in a relatively favorable light.
While he dismissed the accounts of various miracles associated with the
future Prophet's youth as manifestations of popular ignorance and gulli-
bility, the mirza clearly saw Muhammad as an exceptional man, "blessed
with a strong memory, a powerful intellect, reserved and thoughtful."[59]
The Prophet had found his new belief after being thoroughly disillusioned
by "the sad state of the faith into which he had been born."[60] During his
travels as a young man, he had had many encounters with Christians and
Jews, which profoundly shaped his spiritual outlook. Given the "de-
plorable condition in Arabia and even Syria" of Christianity in his day—
riven as it was then by various heresies—it was inevitable that Muhammad
would find the Truth in a form influenced by but also very different from
the teachings of Jesus Christ.[61]

Islam, Kazem-Bek argued, was neither a conscious deception nor a
malevolent heresy. Rather, Muhammad's new faith was the result of a difficult, decades-long, agonizing spiritual quest.[62] Its initial achievement
was largely attributable to the Prophet's outstanding poetic gifts. Muhammad's eloquence was so remarkable that his many followers considered it
nothing less than "*a supernatural wonder.*"[63] But Islam's ultimate tri-
umph, Kazem-Bek believed, had more to do with the Prophet's ability to
harness the martial talents of his countrymen.[64] Thus Muhammad and his
followers inspired the nomadic Arabs, a people traditionally given to brig-
andage, to a campaign of conquest that soon spread the young belief far

beyond their desert homeland. As Kazem-Bek observed elsewhere, jihad (the struggle for the faith) served as "the primary weapon, which Muhammad employed so reliably, so accurately, to establish his religion. It served all the caliphs in their conquests of various nations."[65]

The key to Islam's remarkable vigor during its early centuries was the tremendous fanaticism it inspired among its followers. In stressing "fanaticism" as a central element of the Muslim belief, Kazem-Bek was hardly alone; many European Christians invoked the same epithet to slight the rival faith.[66] Yet if he often described Islam as "fanatical," the mirza was quick to point out that Gentiles could also be responsible for violent excesses. In one article he asked, "Was it not Christianity that unleashed rivers of blood on Saint Bartholomew's Night? Was not the name of Christ [invoked to purge] millions of heretics from the Church?"[67] "Fanaticism," he added, "characterizes all revolutions, especially those motivated by religion."[68]

Invoking another widespread notion of his day, Kazem-Bek often stressed the West's Eastern ancestry: "The very name [of] Asia alone should evoke respectful memories among all members of the Christian world, for it is the cradle of the human race . . . in its lands are the wellsprings of civilization. . . . We are the Orient's heirs."[69] In fact, he pointed out, the Islamic world claimed direct parentage over modern Europe, for "the Enlightenment . . . began to cast its rays from two sources—Florence and Andalusia."[70]

Ultimately, Kazem-Bek often argued, all nations were essentially alike. He saw no fundamental divide between Orient and Occident. If the Persian and Ottoman empires were despotic, this was the result of their current stage of historical development. By implication, their people were just as capable of enlightenment as Europeans of the modern age. Although the more advanced Christian West had a duty to promote progress in the Muslim East, true emancipation could only be achieved from within: "The Orient and Asia comprise the greatest part of the intelligent world. There the spirit of civilization flows and there an unseen force sows the seeds of truth. . . . The West cannot restore enlightenment to the East. . . . Only those born in the Orient's own lands can achieve their reform."[71] Kazem-Bek went on to explain that the Muslim faith was not necessarily an obstacle: "By itself, Islam is incapable of opposing enlightenment. That is the result of the clerical caste and of ignorance, the universal foes of civilization."[72] In his study of the Babis, a mid-nineteenth-century reformist movement in Persia, Kazem-Bek saw the harbingers of his compatriots' emancipation from the harsh rule of the shah and the mullahs.[73]

Central to Kazem-Bek's beliefs was a faith in progress. Some Russian conservative editorialists of the day angrily suggested that his study of the Babis was a veiled critique of the Romanov autocracy, and in the following century Soviet authors more approvingly also detected a hidden hostility to tsarism. However, Kazem-Bek was anything but a revolutionary. Although he approved of reform, he abhorred any violent radicalism, whether in the guise of Muhammad's jihad or the recent overthrow of the French monarchy. When in 1861 Russian student unrest led to the temporary closure of St. Petersburg University, Kazem-Bek was among the faculty's minority that supported the authorities.[74] The many decorations, generous pensions, and the high *chin* the imperial government bestowed on the professor during his career clearly indicate that it saw in him a loyal servitor.[75]

Kazan's recruitment of Mirza Kazem-Bek in 1826 had been the result of circumstance and good fortune rather than careful planning by the university. At the time Russian higher education was still in its infancy, and adequately trained professors were scarce. And with a more nationalist wind blowing through the academy, it was becoming increasing difficult to hire new faculty from Germany's respected institutions. The new tsar, Nicholas I, addressed this shortage by setting up a "professors' institute" at the University of Dorpat in his western province of Livonia. Now known as Tartu (in Estonia), the Baltic campus's proximity to Germany made it the logical home for such a venture. According to Nicholas's plan, the most promising Russian graduates would be sent to the institute to earn their doctorates and then spend a few years in Paris or Berlin for postdoctoral work to familiarize themselves more thoroughly with the most advanced scholarship in their disciplines.[76]

This approach worked reasonably well for such established fields as medicine and classical Greek. However, when in 1827 Kazan's superintendent, Mikhail Musin-Pushkin, wanted to add Mongolian to his institution's growing orientological curriculum, he was beginning with a blank slate.

Whereas the languages of the great Eastern civilizations of China, India, and Persia had already been taught in European universities for some time, there were no chairs for Mongolian. Even in Russia, which directly bordered on the Inner Asian realm, the discipline had barely been recognized. Beginning in the eighteenth century, courses for missionaries and interpreters were sporadically organized in the eastern Siberian city of Irkutsk, and the Academy of Sciences appointed its first full-time specialist for the subject in 1829.[77]

Musin-Pushkin's motives for setting up a chair in Mongolian were largely practical. As with Tartar, languages closely related to the tongue were spoken by significant minority populations in the empire, most prominently the Kalmyks on the lower Volga and the Buriats around Lake Baikal. In addition to equipping officials to deal with these subjects of the tsar, the new discipline would also prove useful for customs officials and diplomats assigned to Russia's eastern outposts. But, according to its first professor, the university's administration also had scholarly reasons for adding the subject, given the Mongol nation's "vast literature, which might shed much light on . . . ancient India and the peoples of Central Asia."[78]

The tsar's education minister, Count Uvarov, enthusiastically approved Musin-Pushkin's request, and the search was on for a suitable candidate. There was no embarrassment of riches. The only two reputable scholars in Russia with any knowledge of the language were Father Hyacinth (the former head of the Russian Ecclesiastical Mission in Beijing) and Isaac Schmidt. The latter was the son of an Amsterdam merchant who had immigrated with his family to flee French occupation of his homeland in 1795. Isaac had developed an interest in Mongolian while working for a trading firm among the Volga Kalmyks for three years at the turn of the nineteenth century. Eventually settling in the capital, he became involved with the St. Petersburg Bible Society, translating liturgical texts into Mongolian and Kalmyk, its close linguistic relative. By 1819 he had abandoned his father's profession to devote himself fully to scholarship.

Although he was elected to membership in the Academy of Sciences ten years later, Isaac Schmidt does not occupy a prominent place in the pantheon of tsarist orientologists. His accomplishments were respectable, including some important pioneering works in Mongolian and Tibetan philology. However, the irascible Dutchman did not take kindly to criticism, and he is best remembered for his quarrels with more illustrious Russian colleagues.[79]

Franz Erdmann, Kazan's senior scholar of Eastern letters, suggested that his university train its own Mongolian professor by recruiting a promising philologist in Germany and sending him to St. Petersburg to learn the language from Isaac Schmidt. While agreeing to the idea in principle, Musin-Pushkin and Lobachevskii devised an alternative more in keeping with the patriotic tenor of the times. Why look abroad, they wondered, when Kazan had perfectly good young scholars of its own? And didn't it make more sense for them to acquire the tongue among the empire's own Mongolian Buriat subjects in eastern Siberia rather than from a European scholar in the westernized capital?[80]

The choice fell on Erdmann's best student, Osip Mikhailovich Kovalevskii. Born Józef Kowalewski in 1800, the man who would become Kazan's most prominent Mongolian specialist was, like his future colleague Kazem-Bek, a non-Russian subject of the tsar. Osip Mikhailovich's ancestors were minor Polish gentry from near the city of Grodno, in today's Belarus, and his father officiated as a priest in the Uniate Church, the branch of Orthodoxy that is loyal to Rome. Young Józef had already developed a strong interest in the classics at his gymnasium, which led him to pursue the subject at the University of Wilno (Vilnius).

Now Lithuania's leading institution of higher learning, in the early nineteenth century Wilno was a hotbed of Polish nationalism.[81] Along with many other undergraduates of his generation, Kovalevskii strongly sympathized with the movement. Acquaintance with the patriotic historian Joachim Lelewel and friendship with another Wilno student, the Romantic poet Adam Mickiewicz, only confirmed these sentiments. In his first year Kovalevskii became an early member of Mickiewicz's secret society, the Filomaci, or "friends of science." Three years later he took an even more active role in a related organization, the Filareci.

These clubs were among many underground groups with oppositionist political aims that formed in the Russian Empire during the restive last decade of Emperor Alexander I's reign. Upon Alexander's death in 1825, two such societies in Russia proper and in Ukraine would attempt a coup d'état, the Decembrist revolt. As for the Filareci and Filomaci, their activities had already come under tsarist scrutiny two years earlier during a crackdown on Polish nationalism.[82] While authorities were unable to prove conclusively that the two clubs had any overt political goals, they nevertheless banished twenty of the leading members, including Kovalevskii and Mickiewicz, to other parts of the empire. Six were sent to Kazan, where Kovalevskii and two of his comrades were ordered to study Eastern languages at the university.[83] It was a heavy-handed way of boosting Erdmann's meager enrolments, but at least the German professor now had three students who could understand his lectures in Latin.

Although he had little choice in the matter, Kovalevskii made the best of his new curriculum. He proved equally adept at mastering Arabic and Tatar as he had Greek. With his passion for antiquity, the Pole also shared the interest of other scholars in Kazan for the region's Turkic and Mongol origins. He was fascinated by the anthology of tales about Genghis Khan and Tamerlane that his Tatar instructor, Ibrahim Halfin, assigned him, and he eagerly made the outing to the nearby Bolgar ruins. As Kovalevskii would later recall, "the Kazan khanate's history became the purpose of my work" during his first three years at the university.[84]

When Lobachevskii asked Kovalevskii if he might like to spend a few years in Siberia to learn Mongolian and then perhaps get a chair in the subject, he did not jump at the offer. Then as now, the empire's eastern marches evoked the end of the world: a distant, desolate, icy prison for criminals and political undesirables. He wrote many for advice, including his compatriots Mickiewicz and Osip Senkovskii. Everyone urged him to take on the challenge. As a result, in the spring of 1828 the former classicist set off on the lengthy journey with a younger fellow student, Aleksandr Popov. Again, Kovalevskii looked at the bright side. Upon crossing the Urals in early June, he exulted in a letter that "the passage . . . gives me an surprising sensation. At the highest peak I shook off the European dust with a fond farewell. I am in Asia! . . . An entirely new air rushed pass my face."[85]

Irkutsk was the duo's destination. There, a government official well versed in the language, Aleksandr Igumnov, was assigned to teach them the basics of literary Mongolian. Formal instruction would be supplemented by extensive stays in the surrounding area and beyond for practice among the local population. Erdmann and a colleague had also given the students detailed instructions for learning about the little-known lands

that were to be their home for the next three years, including history, geography, beliefs, ethnography, statistics, popular medicine, and economy,
among others. In short, they were to report on "everything, important or
unimportant" that caught their eyes.[86] At the same time there was also a
generous budget to buy books and manuscripts for the university's library.

Kovalevskii and Popov conscientiously obeyed their teachers, quickly
mastering Mongolian and its more colloquial Buriat variant. Meanwhile,
Kovalevskii also traveled to the Mongolian capital of Urga (today known
as Ulan Bator), and he met the chief hierarch of Buriat's Yellow Hat sect
Buddhists, the Khambo Lama, who invited him to spend some time at his
datsan (monastery) at Goose Lake. The latter sojourn, which included
permission to observe rituals, talk to the monks, and study the extensive
collection of religious texts, sparked a lifelong interest in Buddhism. Osip
Mikhailovich also had the good fortune of being in Irkutsk when members
of the Russian Orthodox Church's eleventh mission to Beijing were passing through on their way to take up their ten-year residency there. He
seized this rare opportunity to travel to the Chinese capital, where he spent
a year perfecting his Mongolian and picking up some Manchu, Chinese,
and Tibetan in the bargain.[87] Back in eastern Siberia, the industrious student even found time to set up a local Russian-Mongolian school in the
border town of Troitskosavsk for the sons of Buriat Cossacks and officials.

The tour, which had initially been planned for four years, stretched out
to five. Kovalevskii and Popov returned to Kazan in early 1833 and were
immediately ordered to St. Petersburg to be examined by the Academy of
Sciences. Isaac Schmidt was duly impressed by the pair's knowledge of
Mongolian. On the basis of his highly favorable report to Education Minister Uvarov, Kovalevskii was appointed to head Kazan's newly established
Mongolian department, its third in Eastern letters, while Popov was given
a job as a teacher of Mongolian at the First Kazan Gymnasium.

Lobachevskii's experiment had clearly been a success. In the coming
years, his university would periodically send its brightest orientology graduates abroad to Asia to complete their training as faculty for Kazan's growing department. Some of the beneficiaries would go on to become among
the nineteenth century's most prominent scholars of the East, including
the Turkologists Il'ia Berezin and Nikolai Il'minskii as well as the Sinologist Vladimir Vasil'ev.[88]

As Kazan's first Mongolian specialist, Kovalevskii's most pressing task was to produce proper study aids for his classes. Whereas his colleagues who taught Turkish, Arabic, and Persian could at least rely on the work of Western orientologists, the new professor's field was essentially virgin linguistic soil. Within two years of taking up his post, he published a grammar. By 1837 he had completed a two-volume Mongolian reader, which garnered him his first Demidov Prize and promotion to full professor.

Kovalevskii's crowning achievement was his Mongolian-Russian-French dictionary. On the advice of Father Hyacinth, whom he had befriended in Irkutsk, the Pole had already begun compiling Mongolian words and expressions during his Siberian sojourn. Upon returning to European Russia he presented a 40,000-word vocabulary to the Academy of Sciences, which formed the basis of his subsequent lexicon. Published in three volumes between 1844 and 1849, the work remains a standard reference to this day.[89] Kovalevskii had wisely acceded to the repeated urgings of the distinguished French Sinologist Stanislas Julien to make his dictionary trilingual, thereby rendering it useful for Western scholars as well. Along with earning him a second Demidov Prize, Kovalevskii's accomplishment also helped convince the Academy of Sciences to elect him to full membership in 1847. However, the post of Academician would have entailed a move to St. Petersburg, and Nicholas I was apparently not prepared to release the politically unreliable Pole from his banishment. The tsar blackballed the honor.[90]

Nicholas's suspicions may also have been the reason for preventing the professor from accompanying most of his colleagues to the capital upon the dissolution of Kazan's orientology program in 1854. Nevertheless, the autocracy did recognize his abilities, appointing him rector of the university that year. Kovalevskii held the post for five years until he was dismissed after a wave of student unrest—a frequent occupational hazard among tsarist university administrators in the turbulent decades before 1917. Two years later, in 1862, Kovalevskii secured appointments as professor of general history and dean of the Faculty of History and Letters at Warsaw's Main School (from 1869 its university).

Kovalevskii's life continued to be marred by political turmoil. Within a year of his arrival in Warsaw, Poles rose for a second time that century against their Russian masters. Kovalevskii remained aloof from the insur-

gency, but he suffered an incalculable loss when in September 1863 someone lobbed several bombs at the tsar's viceroy from another apartment in
the building where he lived. The entire structure was torched in reprisal,
claiming the professor's library. Among the valuables that perished in the
conflagration were a wide range of unpublished works Kovalevskii had
written over the previous decades, including multivolume histories of Asia
and of Mongolian literature, a study of Buddhism, and biographies of
Tibet's Dalai Lamas, not to mention a six-part account of his Asian travels. The disaster effectively ended Kovalevskii's scholarly output. Aside
from a lesson plan for his history survey at Warsaw, he published no more
works during his lifetime.[91]

Kovalevskii's outlook strongly resembled that of his Kazan colleague,
Mirza Kazem-Bek. A firm believer in progress and the importance of education, the Pole never doubted that Asians had the potential of being
Europeans' cultural equals under the right circumstances. After all, "people basically think alike, and the fundamental oneness of all mankind unites
us much more powerfully than any superficial differences in development."[92] As Kovalevskii saw it, no civilization, no matter how exotic or ancient, was "ahistorical." Although they might now be on different places
of the road, all nations followed the same path toward enlightened modernity. "Eastern Asia remains in many ways little known," he reasoned.
"Nevertheless, while to us its advance might seem slow, their people are
moving along an identical course as those in other parts of the world."
He strongly opposed the notion that Orient and Occident were antipodes,
stressing that both were subject to the same "general [laws] of history."[93]
  China was a case in point. By the late eighteenth century, many Europeans had come to regard the Middle Kingdom as corrupt, petrified, and
utterly incapable of redemption. In his *Outline of a Philosophy of the History of Man,* written in the 1780s, Johann Gottfried Herder had famously
dismissed the Chinese as "an embalmed mummy, wrapped in silk, and
painted with hieroglyphics." The very idea that this antique Oriental relic
might enter the modern age struck Herder as utterly ridiculous. "[They]
could never become Greeks or Romans," he declared. "Chinese they were
and will always remain."[94] Kovalevskii disagreed. He vigorously dismissed
Herder's notion of "China as the foe of innovation, entirely trapped in

old forms."[95] This did not mean that Osip Mikhailovich idealized the Middle Kingdom. Unlike Voltaire, he had traveled to the Asian empire and witnessed firsthand the cruelty, corruption, and vast disparities in wealth under the Qing. According to Kovalevskii, "this most ancient and populous realm, having developed long ago, isn't moving ahead. All around is decay." However, he implied that this decrepitude was more the result of its rulers' failings rather than some inherent Oriental incapacity for progress. "Only a major political upheaval," he concluded, "can put China on a new course."[96]

The clearest statement of Kovalevskii's ideas about East and West was his 1837 inaugural lecture as full professor to Kazan University, "On the Acquaintance of Europeans with Asia."[97] Surveying the contacts between the two continents since the dawn of time, Osip Mikhailovich noted that the earliest encounters had invariably been characterized by mutual ignorance and hostility: "just as Jews used the word *goy*, Muslims *giaour* and Greeks *barbarian* for all aliens, likewise the Chinese soiled page after page of their chronicles with derogatory terms for their neighbors." Such suspicions were naturally compounded by periodic confrontations. "Europeans had from time to time been subjected to invasions by Asian people," Kovalevskii noted, quickly adding that the West had also at least twice assaulted the East, under Alexander the Great and during the Crusades.

Like the more peaceful intercourse between the two continents through trade and travel, these clashes were not entirely destructive, since "the upheavals left rich legacies [by] bringing new ideas." Thus even war promoted the transmission of learning and progress between Orient and Occident. Much like Kazem-Bek, Kovalevskii saw the Crusades as a good example of this phenomenon:

> There was a time when the haughty European looked down on Asia as a sanctuary of idleness and voluptuousness, populated by savage barbarians, a land of immense luxury and servility. . . . Remember how, under the banner of the Faith, innumerable masses of Christians rushed to the shores of Asia Minor, to extirpate their sworn enemies . . . but, to their utter surprise and embarrassment, encountered an enlightened way of life. . . . I could go on about the mutual benefits that resulted from this violent struggle be-

tween West and East, but will only repeat the words of one of our writers, "that at the walls of Jerusalem, near the Savior's tomb (naturally unwittingly) was lain the first stone of the future political structure of Europe. The knights of the Cross . . . at an immense cost [inadvertently] carried back to Europe the spark of freedom and enlightenment."

The East, of course, was the source of much learning and wisdom, from the Chinese invention of gunpowder, printing, and paper money to India's religious and moral ideas. "How much there is to discover [in Asia] for the linguist, the poet, the philosopher, the archaeologist, the historian! How many secrets its rich lands conceal!" he marveled. By the same token, the West also had a great deal to teach the East. It was through the "electrical power" of enlightenment, Kovalevskii stressed, that the gap separating the nations of Asia and Europe could be closed.

In the spring of 1878, at the ripe old age of seventy-seven, Kovalevskii was honored with a jubilee to mark the fiftieth anniversary of his distinguished career.[98] Colleagues lauded his numerous accomplishments. In addition to his pioneering works in Mongolian language and the history of Buddhism, Osip Mikhailovich had also taught some of the leading scholars of the next generation, including St. Petersburg University's distinguished Sinologist Vladimir Vasil'ev and the Kazan Theological Seminary's Aleksei Bobrovnikov. Perhaps his most gifted student was the young Buriat Dorzhi Banzarov. Although poor health and professional disappointments frustrated his relatively short career, Banzarov published, among other works, the first study of Inner Asian shamanism in the European academy.[99] As for Kovalevskii, he ended his days not long after his jubilee, when death quietly claimed him in October 1878 as he worked in one of Warsaw University's reading rooms.[100]

In 1852 Karl Voigt, a comparative literature professor at Kazan, reviewed the progress of his university's orientological faculty over the previous ten years.[101] He found much cause for satisfaction. Voigt proudly listed the section's five chairs of Arabic-Persian, Turkish, Mongolian, Sanskrit, and Chinese letters (Armenian had been closed in 1851 due to poor enrollments). Together, these fields employed six professors, along with several lecturers as well as an instructor in Arabic calligraphy. Voigt also boasted about the faculty's scholarly accomplishments over the past decade, which had garnered their authors no less than three Demidov prizes, decorations, and two presentation diamond rings from the tsar himself.

Orientology had flourished at Kazan in other ways as well. The university's library justly took pride in its extensive holdings of Orientalia, much of which had been gathered by Kovalevskii, Berezin, Vasil'ev, and others on their study tours. When he visited the city in 1843, a Westphalian nobleman, Baron August von Haxthausen, noted without exaggeration that "no [other] library in the world possesses such a rich collection of Asian manuscripts."[102] The strong interest in numismatics among German faculty, such as Bernhard Dorn, Franz Erdmann, and the former rector Klaus Fuchs, had also left the university with the most extensive collection of Asian coins in Europe at the time, while Kovalevskii and other acquisitive travelers had given their institution enough artifacts to set up a renowned chamber of Oriental curiosities.[103] Meanwhile, in 1829 Kazan's university press had assumed responsibility for the gymnasium's *Aziatskaia tipografiia* (Asian printing house). Founded in 1800 at the request of Tatar merchants, the latter possessed rare fonts in, among others, Arabic, Turkish, Tatar, Mongolian, Tibetan, and Sanskrit scripts. As the empire's primary publisher of Islamic religious texts, the Aziatskaia tipografiia was a lucrative enterprise, and profits from its sales to Muslims both in Russia and abroad were the university press's most important source of revenues.[104]

The only important challenge Voigt detected was the recent decline in enrollments. Having reached a high of forty-two students in 1848, or 14 percent of the university's total of about 300, by 1852 only sixteen were still taking its courses.[105] Along with the usual aversion to the tremendous toil required to master exotic tongues, undergraduates were also deterred by bleak employment prospects. Despite reasonable expectations for strong demand from the state for officials competent in Asian languages, few alumni managed to find jobs that made use of their special skills. According to one calculation, less than a third of Kazan's orientology graduates had landed appropriate positions.[106] But even here Voigt saw grounds for optimism. Already in 1851 the emperor had ordered his education minister to consider how Asian language training for future bureaucrats could be improved. Voigt had every reason to believe that Nicholas's concern would translate into better possibilities for his university's graduates as he predicted that "Kazan's young orientologists face a bright future."

Voigt's confidence was sadly misplaced. At the sovereign's command to reexamine Asian language instruction, Education Minister Prince Platon Shirinskii-Shikhmatov had assembled a committee in 1851 of senior bureaucrats and academics chaired by Mikhail Musin-Pushkin.[107] Although Musin-Pushkin had been transferred from Kazan to the capital to become superintendent of its educational district in 1845, he remained a strong champion of his former university's orientology faculty. He had long advocated setting up an Asian institute to centralize all teaching of Eastern languages in the empire. With its distinguished faculty, its many Asian minorities, and its proximity to the Orient, Kazan seemed to him to be the most logical home for such an entity.[108] Musin-Pushkin's superiors agreed with him about the need to concentrate Asian language instruction under one roof, but they had an entirely different location in mind. Given the subjects' importance to the state, it struck them as more logical to base it in the imperial capital. While it would take some time for the news to reach Kazan, by 1851 the decision to make St. Petersburg the new center for tsarist orientology had already been made.[109]

Three years later, on October 22, 1854, Tsar Nicholas I signed a Senate decree drafted by his new education minister, Avraam Norov, to establish a Faculty of Oriental Languages at St. Petersburg University, entirely dissolving the discipline at Kazan.[110] Kazan's First Gymnasium suffered the same fate, although the latter would be allowed to continue offering Tatar courses, "out of consideration for local needs."

In an obituary of his former mentor, Il'ia Berezin observed, "Mirza Kazem-Bek is a rare phenomenon in the academy. . . .Thanks to the unusual circumstances of his Asian upbringing and his subsequent European maturation, he combined broad Oriental knowledge with Occidental scholarship."[111] Berezin's assessment can also be applied to the Kazan school more generally. Based in the erstwhile Tatar stronghold "on the confines of Asia," but at the same time part of an archetypal institution of the Western Enlightenment, Kazan University joined Oriental "other" with Occidental "self" more than any other school in Europe.

The most significant achievement of Mirza Aleksandr Kazem-Bek, Osip

Kovalevskii, and their Kazan contemporaries in the nineteenth century's second quarter was to develop orientology as a proper academic discipline. The support of superiors such as Musin-Pushkin and Lobachevskii was crucial, and they were fortunate to have as their education minister Count Uvarov, a man strongly convinced of the field's importance. But the central figure was Kazem-Bek, who is rightly considered by many to be the father of the Kazan school.[112] Both as educator and as administrator, the Persian mirza shaped Kazan's approach to orientology in a number of important ways.

Above all, Kazem-Bek championed a practical approach to the study of languages. Responding to the imperial bureaucracy's need for competent translators and interpreters, he advocated a thorough study of Turkish, Arabic, and Persian not only in the classroom, but also through conversations with mullahs, merchants, and other residents of Kazan fluent in these tongues. And his more promising graduates were given further opportunities for practice through carefully scripted study tours in the East.[113] By the same token, Kazem-Bek strenuously objected to burdening his students with prerequisites he considered to be needless distractions, such as the traditional requirement for proficiency in Latin.[114] After his transfer to St. Petersburg, he would continue to stress the primacy of the practical in the face of considerable opposition from others on its faculty, who favored a more theoretical approach grounded in the traditions of German philology.[115] He met with much less success, however, among his colleagues in the capital.

While Kazem-Bek considered the study of language important in its own right, he also saw a wider application. Agreeing with the German philologists on this point, he stressed that "there is no better guide to understanding the past of nations than by considering their tongue. This is the sole path to true knowledge, hidden in the labyrinth of ignorance."[116] Conversely, to master a language effectively, Kazem-Bek considered it crucial to be knowledgeable in the relevant culture, history, and politics. The minister of education concurred, and Uvarov's university statute of 1835 accordingly commanded that Kazan's three professors of Oriental letters (Erdmann, Kazem-Bek, and Kovalevskii) also teach their students about the literature and politics of their areas of specialization.[117] The same was also true of orientology at the Kazan Theological Academy, although beyond languages the emphasis there naturally lay more on religion.

The Kazan school's practical orientation was intimately linked to the needs of the state. In 1769 Catherine the Great had ordered Tatar to be taught at the First Gymnasium to train translators for government service. Likewise, the university was expected to produce personnel for government service in Asia, although in practice few graduates found positions that properly used their rarefied skills.[118] As we shall see in the next chapter, Kazan's involvement in missionary activity, especially among Russia's own Asian minorities, also motivated the stress on the practical study of languages.

Another important characteristic of the Kazan school was its emphasis on the Islamic East. Although Kazan initiated the study of Mongolian and also established the first Russian university chair in Mandarin, scholarship of Inner and East Asia remained decidedly secondary to the interests of most of the faculty, both at the university and subsequently at the theological academy. This was partly the result of a similar emphasis in Western institutions, on whose curricula Russian universities had been modeled according to Alexander I's statute of 1804.[119] At the same time, Kazan's own population and geography did much to encourage the study of Turkish, Arabic, and Persian, not to mention Tatar.

Intimacy with Asia did not inevitably translate into respect for its civilizations. Particularly toward the end of the nineteenth century, when it largely focused on missionary work within a climate of growing Great Russian nationalism, the Kazan school's successors at the theological academy could be particularly hostile to the Islamic world. However, during the century's more tolerant first half, scholarship at the university was marked by a profound esteem for the Orient. Even Kazan's mandate to produce translators, interpreters, and other specialists to serve the autocracy did not distract from scholarship that implicitly valued the East as a source of wisdom and learning. In this way, the Kazan school bequeathed an important legacy, for it reminded Russians that they could learn from Asians just as they might from other Europeans.

6

MISSIONARY ORIENTOLOGY

To take on any belief system one must know it inside out, including all of
the logic and all of the facts on which it is based. Without such an intimate
acquaintance any confrontation with its more able advocates is bound to
lose much of its effect.

—Mikhail Mashanov

Kazan University's primacy over Russian orientology effectively
ended with the transfer of its faculty to the imperial capital. There was a
brief revival of instruction in Turkish, Arabic, and Persian during the
1860s, but it soon foundered in the face of student apathy.[1] Nevertheless,
the discipline did not entirely vanish from the city. In 1854, the very year
Nicholas I officially shut down the university's chairs in orientology, the
Most Holy Synod in St. Petersburg authorized the Missionary Division at
the Kazan Theological Academy, with sections devoted to the languages
and religions of the empire's Eastern minorities. The new department had
endured an agonizingly long gestation period, and its fate over the academy's remaining six decades would always be tested by indifference, if not
outright hostility, from leading clergy. In many ways, the Missionary Division's travails reflected both the Russian Orthodox Church's distrust of
other faiths and its ambivalence toward spreading the Gospel to nonbelievers.

Unlike its Western cousins, the Russian Church had long ago lost much
of its missionary vocation. During the first centuries after Kievan Rus's

conversion to Orthodox Christianity in 988, most minorities among the Eastern Slavs who took the Cross did so in tandem with their assimilation into the dominant culture of the region. On occasion, however, pious monks had evangelized the various Finnic tribes in the wilderness beyond Novgorod.

Ironically, this effort witnessed a remarkable revival under Mongol rule, in the fourteenth and early fifteenth centuries. Inspired by the charismatic Saint Sergius of Radonezh, founder of the Holy Trinity Monastery near Moscow, scores of monks established their own communities and hermitages in the remotest reaches of northeastern Russia. Some consciously sought to emulate the hardships of the early church's Desert Fathers in terrain as inhospitable as the Sinai, such as the Solovetskii Islands in the White Sea. Others renewed the campaign to take the Gospel to unbelievers among the various peoples that inhabited the endless taiga.

Among the latter, the most celebrated was one of Saint Sergius's friends, Saint Stefan of Perm. Born around 1340 to a sexton in the northern town of Ustiug, Stefan became fascinated as a boy with the language of the Komi, a Finnic minority living in the region.[2] One day a holy fool told the lad that he would grow up to become the apostle to the Komi. Inspired by this prophecy, Stefan moved to a monastery, where he studied to become a missionary. At the time, spreading the word of God to the heathen involved a thorough knowledge of Greek, then the language of Orthodox theology. While Stefan soon mastered it, he also knew that the Komi would only listen to him if he preached in their tongue. Accordingly, the monk set about translating the liturgy into Komi, a task that first entailed devising an alphabet for the illiterate nationality.

With Saint Sergei's blessing, in 1379 Stefan ventured even deeper into the land of the Komi and built a small church at Perm, in the foothills of the Ural Mountains. Despite initial resistance, his zeal and his sensitivity to native ways attracted many followers. Within five years Stefan was named bishop of Perm, and over time the Komi were largely brought into the Christian fold. By preaching in the vernacular, Saint Stefan was following in the hallowed tradition of Saints Cyril and Methodius, the ninth-century Macedonian brothers who had evangelized the Slavs by devising a written language for the liturgy in Slavonic.

Others shared Saint Stefan's apostolic fervor during this golden age of

Russian monasticism. However, as the power of Muscovy's autocracy waxed in the fifteenth and sixteenth centuries, the Orthodox Church's missionary drive waned. Ivan IV's capture of Kazan in 1552 effectively made conversion an enterprise of the state. The tsar's promotion of evangelization was partly driven by ideology; leading clerics had characterized the campaign against the khanate as a holy war against "godless Saracens."[3] But Ivan was also motivated by a pragmatic desire to bind the alien lands closer to his realm.[4] Pacifying the Tatars in the countryside proved to be nearly as difficult as the arduous campaign to seize the fortified city itself. It would take another five years to crush the most determined resistance, and even then many Tatars were not reconciled to Muscovite rule, as a major revolt in 1589 would confirm.[5] Baptism therefore became a means to eradicate the religious roots of opposition to the Christian conquerors.

Upon Kazan's fall, the tsar commanded that its population "know the true God and together with us praise the Holy Trinity forever."[6] He did not tarry. On the day of his triumphal entry into the vanquished capital, Ivan ordered all Muslims expelled and laid the foundations for a cathedral as well as several monasteries. [7] Three years later, he appointed one of his most talented churchmen, Gurii (Rugatin), as the newly established Kazan diocese's first archbishop. Along with enjoying supervisory authority over secular authorities, the cleric was also encouraged to convert nonbelievers, albeit "through love and not through fear." Eventually canonized as "the Enlightener of the *inorodtsy* [non-Slavs]," Saint Gurii proved to be a zealous apostle. He built schools open to children of all faiths and scrupulously obeyed the tsar's wishes to act "gently, quietly, and sweetly." He was also effective. During his eight years as archbishop, an estimated 20,000 Muslims in Kazan accepted the sacrament of baptism.[8]

Saint Gurii's tenure marked the high point of Russian attempts to bring the erstwhile khanate's Tatars into the Christian fold. Over the next three hundred years, missionary efforts in the mid-Volga region followed an inconsistent course, sometimes aggressive, on other occasions hesitant and discreet. And they were never motivated by any particularly great evangelical fervor within the Orthodox Church itself. Instead, the periodic campaigns to convert nonbelievers invariably reflected the autocracy's desire to assimilate minorities through spiritual Russification.[9]

Until the late seventeenth century, Saint Gurii's successors did not follow a particularly aggressive course in bringing the Gospel to the tsar's Muslim and animist subjects. In part, they were hampered by the lack of qualified priests. Diplomacy also constrained them, since Moscow was reluctant to anger the Turkish sultan by forcibly converting his coreligionists.[10] More important, Russian Orthodox churchmen still held to Byzantine attitudes toward other faiths, which was somewhat less hostile than that of the Catholic West. If Rome insisted on complete confessional homogeneity, Christian Constantinople's emperors had been able to live with a variety of creeds (as did its Ottoman rulers after they conquered the city in 1453).[11]

According to Valerie Kivelson, pious Muscovite tsars certainly saw their conquests in the East as victories for the Cross. However, building churches and monasteries, along with settling newly acquired lands with Russian Christians, sufficed to make them Orthodox. She suggests that "the conversion of natives, while a pleasant and even desirable by-product [of colonization], was far from essential. . . . Submission [to the tsar] rather than conversion fulfil[led] the agenda set forth for Muscovy's imperial, Christian march across the continent."[12]

The clearest indication of the contrasting policies toward other faiths between Latin and Greek Christendom is demographic. Half a century before Ivan took Kazan, King Ferdinand and Queen Isabella completed Spain's *reconquista* by forcibly expelling all Muslims and Jews who refused baptism.[13] Louis XIV's revocation of the Edict of Nantes in 1685 similarly led to a flight of France's Huguenots. As a result, until the twentieth century, such countries had overwhelmingly Catholic populations. But toward the end of the nineteenth century, according to one reliable calculation, over one-tenth of the Russian Empire's population was Muslim.[14] At the time, Russia's tsar had more Islamic subjects than the Ottoman sultan.[15]

More systematic efforts at conversion came in the eighteenth century's first half, at the order of such Western-oriented monarchs as Peter the Great, Anna Ivanovna, and Elizabeth.[16] The campaign reached its height in the 1740s and early 1750s, when most of the mid-Volga's Chuvash, Cheremis, and other animist peoples were baptized into the Orthodox faith, although results among Tatars were less successful.[17] While these sovereigns were primarily motivated by a desire to make their empire more uniform, the missionaries' provenance also played a role. Among the latter, many came from the Kievan Academy, which had been strongly influenced by Polish Jesuit colleges before Left-Bank Ukraine's absorption by Muscovy some ninety years earlier. Their attitudes about conversion and spiritual conformity were therefore closer to the Catholic ideal.[18]

The autocracy changed tack once again during the century's latter decades. Swayed by Enlightenment ideals of religious toleration, Catherine II largely dissolved the missionary apparatus her predecessors had established at Kazan. The empress even supported Islamic conversions of animists elsewhere in her realm, on the grounds that the monotheistic faith would help pacify them. Moreover, as Robert Crews has pointed out, Catherine did much to legitimize Islam's status in the Russian Empire by establishing a state-run Muslim hierarchy to parallel the Orthodox Church's Holy Synod.[19]

The results of this lackluster and capricious enterprise among Muslims were predictable: the census of 1796 counted 27,306 baptized souls among the Government of Kazan's 211,340 Tatars, only slightly more than Saint Gurii's tally 250 years earlier.[20] Furthermore, by all accounts the vast majority of the former were Potemkin Christians. A visitor to their villages in the late 1840s found them to be largely "inclined to Islam in spirit." While they might go to church on Sundays, Orthodox Tatars often knew little of their adopted faith and tended to respect mullahs more than priests.[21] Matters were not helped by the fact that the *Kriashen,* as they called themselves, were marginalized both by Russian Christians as well as by Kazan's more prosperous and better-educated Muslim Tatars.[22]

In retrospect it is not surprising that some Kriashen periodically sought to return to the belief of their ethnic brothers. In 1827 a group of 138 Orthodox Tatars formally petitioned Nicholas I for permission to be reclassified as Muslim. Still inclined to follow his grandmother's tolerant line toward other religions, the newly crowned tsar was not unduly concerned by the request, although he did turn it down. Over the coming decade, however, the rising tide of Kriashen apostasy began to worry the increasingly nationalist autocracy. Even more alarming, in the 1840s some of the Kazan diocese's non-Tatar nationalities began to forsake the Bible for the Koran as well.

Developments elsewhere further fueled anxieties about Islam. Imam

Shamyl's lengthy resistance against tsarist rule in the Caucasus convinced many about the faith's innate "fanaticism," while growing tensions with Ottoman Turkey gave rise to concerns about a Muslim fifth column within the empire's borders.[23] It was against this backdrop of rising Kriashen apostasy as well as hardening attitudes toward Islam in some circles that the Holy Synod eventually inaugurated the Missionary Division at the Kazan Theological Academy in 1854.

Neither the Missionary Division nor the Theological Academy itself had enjoyed an easy birth. The latter began its existence in 1723 as the archbishop's Slavic-Latin School (*arkhiereiskaia slaviano-latinskaia shkola*) for priests' sons. Within a decade, it was transformed into a proper seminary, making it one of Russia's oldest.[24] Already in this incarnation the institution was seen to have a special duty for the East. Thus in 1737 Empress Anna, who was particularly keen to assimilate her Asian minorities, expressed her wish that the seminary train priests to tend to inorodtsy, although it is uncertain whether this desire actually materialized into language classes or other specialized instruction during the eighteenth century.[25]

In 1797 Paul I upgraded the seminary's status to that of an academy. As one of the empire's four such establishments (along with the others in Kiev, Moscow, and St. Petersburg), the Kazan Theological Academy was responsible both for training seminary faculty as well as for supervising all education by the Orthodox Church in the sees under its jurisdiction. Like Kazan University in the secular realm, the academy's pedagogical purview extended over Russia's European east as well as Siberia and the Caucasus. In the words of one church historian, it was to be "the outpost of Russian belief, Russian nationality and Russian rule *in partibus infidelium*."[26] Despite these grandiose ambitions, inadequate resources led to the academy's demotion in 1818 back to a seminary, under the aegis of the Moscow Theological Academy. But overseeing both central Russia and the east proved entirely beyond Moscow's capacities, and within less than twenty-five years the Holy Synod upgraded Kazan once again.

The new academy's missionary mandate was now explicit. At the ceremony on November 8, 1842, marking the institution's reopening, its secretary proclaimed, "The beginning of the Kazan Academy marks the dawn of a crusade."[27] The most pressing need was for language instruction. In

May 1842 the synod's resolution outlining the academy's mandate had already directed its administration to determine which tongues would be most appropriate for its special task. No fewer than nine were identified, ranging from Tatar and Kalmyk to Yakut, Tungus, and Ostiak. After two years of further deliberation, it was decided to focus on the languages of the region's two predominant non-Christian faiths: Islam (i.e., Tatar and Arabic) and Buddhism (Mongolian and Kalmyk). Ideally, these courses would be taught by the academy's own faculty. Since none were yet competent to do so, however, two instructors, Mirza Aleksandr Kazem-Bek and Aleksandr Popov, were brought in from the outside for the time being. Within a year and a half, their two most promising students, Nikolai Il'minskii and Aleksei Bobrovnikov, were ready to replace them in their respective specialties.[28]

The academy did not go out of its way to make its new instructors feel welcome. Since no chairs had officially been budgeted in their fields, the pair was assigned to other departments with full teaching loads there as well. Even here the administration bungled. In light of their respective abilities, Il'minskii was to join mathematics, while Bobrovnikov would be in biblical history. Due to a bureaucratic lapse, however, Bobrovnikov ended up in the mathematics department, and Il'minskii was placed in natural science. Unwilling to admit this mistake to their superiors in St. Petersburg, officials let matters stand.[29] Meanwhile, enrollments in the language classes proved hard to maintain. Of the thirty-five who enrolled in the two subjects when first offered by the new pair in 1846, only fifteen managed to complete them.[30]

A new wave of apostasy in 1847 gave added urgency to the academy's special mandate.[31] It was glaringly apparent that, by themselves, language courses were not enough to train clergy to take the Gospel to Russia's Eastern inorodtsy; priests also needed to be thoroughly familiar with their beliefs. According to Kazan's new archbishop, Grigorii (Postnikov), the most effective solution would be to set up a separate division exclusively devoted to missionary studies. While the synod quickly gave its consent, the academy's own administration was loath to act with similar alacrity.[32]

Once again there were interminable rounds of consultations and other delays. It ultimately took until 1854, or twelve years after the Kazan Academy's rebirth, for the Missionary Division to be established. The new unit was to have four separate sections: the anti-Islam, anti-Buddhism, anti–Old Believer, and the Chuvash-Cheremis sections (to convert animists among those nationalities). Yet, if the impetus for setting up the Missionary Division had been growing concerns about Islam, most of its resources were soon deployed to prepare for campaigns against the Old Believers, the descendants of dissident Russian Orthodox who had refused to adopt the liturgical reforms of the seventeenth century.

No name is more closely linked to Kazan's nineteenth-century missionary efforts than that of Nikolai Ivanovich Il'minskii. Successively a seminarian, an orientologist, and the leading educator of Kazan's Kriashen, Il'minskii left an ambiguous legacy. At the height of his career, in the 1870s and 1880s, he was influential if controversial. Enjoying strong support in the autocracy's highest circles, including the steadfast loyalty of the powerful chief procurator of the Holy Synod, Konstantin Pobedonostsev, Il'minskii was condemned by others as inimical to Russian nationalism. Twentieth-century assessments were equally mixed. To many—but certainly not all —Western scholars, Il'minskii cut an attractive, even somewhat saintly figure. Igor Smolitsch, a leading German specialist of the Russian Orthodox Church, wrote that "N. I. Il'minskii (1821–1891) holds a place of honor in the history of the Russian Mission," lauding his "energy, profound knowledge and idealism."[33]

Soviet views are particularly intriguing. Without denying his abilities in Near Eastern languages and Islamology, there was distinct unease with Il'minskii's conservative politics. Any friend of the reviled Pobedonostsev could only be an "inveterate reactionary," as one Soviet orientologist characterized him in the 1960s.[34] However, in championing minority language rights, Il'minskii had a distinct influence on Leninist nationalities policy.[35] Isabelle Kreindler, an American biographer, even hints that the Orthodox missionary should occupy a minor place in the hagiography of the founder of the Russian Communist Party. When in 1887 Vladimir Lenin's older brother, Aleksandr, was condemned to be executed for his role in a regicide plot, Il'minskii tried to seek an imperial pardon via the education minister.[36]

Il'minskii did not begin his academic career with any particular interest in the East. A priest's son from Penza, a central Russian city about 400 kilometers southwest of Kazan, he graduated from the local seminary in

1841 with top marks. Although Penza's seminary offered Tatar courses, the youth focused on a more typical curriculum. When the Kazan Academy reopened its doors the following year, Il'minskii enrolled in its first class, where he specialized in mathematics. By all accounts he was popular and gifted. His Russian biographer, who had known him personally, described him as, "short of stature, lively as quicksilver, endowed with an attractive dark complexion, chestnut hair, and a sparkling, honest mien, as well as talkative, clever, ever cheerful, and well-disposed to all. . . . He immediately won the place of every classmate's best friend and the most able student in the eyes of his instructors and the administration."[37]

It was only by chance that orientology attracted Il'minskii's attention. In his third year at the academy, he learned that the university's distinguished Turkologist, Mirza Kazem-Bek, would also be coming there to offer Tatar and Arabic courses. Having already mastered Latin, Greek, Hebrew, French and German, Il'minskii was confident of his linguistic abilities, and the challenge of studying with the exotic Persian mirza piqued his curiosity. Beginning in January 1845, Nikolai Ivanovich accordingly joined ten others in Kazem-Bek's classes twice a week.

The encounter marked the start of a fruitful collaboration. As Kazem-Bek's best student at the academy, Il'minskii was the obvious choice to become the institution's own Near Eastern language instructor upon graduating in 1846. Despite his new responsibilities, which included teaching mathematics and Hebrew in addition to Arabic and Turco-Tatar, Nikolai Ivanovich enthusiastically obeyed the rector's orders to pursue his studies with the university professor for another year. Since Kazem-Bek focused on Arabic, Il'minskii took the unusual step of taking lodgings in Kazan's Tatar quarter, the better to hone his knowledge of their tongue as well.

As apostasy to Islam again began to surge among the mid-Volga's minorities within a year of his appointment, Il'minskii's specialized skills quickly found themselves in demand. In early 1847 he was asked to join Kazem-Bek in supervising a committee at the academy to commission translations of Orthodox texts into Tatar on order of the tsar. The following year Archbishop Grigorii asked Il'minskii to visit Kriashen villages in the countryside to study their faith firsthand. Two extensive tours during the summer recesses of 1847 and 1848 convinced Il'minskii that the allegiance of the Tatar converts to Orthodoxy was tenuous at best.[38] As he reported, many had already secretly returned to the Islamic beliefs of their ancestors, and only a few related to Christianity as piously as did Russians themselves. The young professor also found that earlier efforts by missionaries to shore up the Orthodox faith among the Kriashen were entirely ineffective. Largely ignorant of Islam or even the Tatar language, most of the monks sent to combat apostasy had been content merely to baptize as many willing souls as possible without staying behind to tend to their new flocks.

Il'minskii advised the archbishop that the only way to combat Islam among the Kriashen was to launch a new mission with clergy "thoroughly conscious of the importance of their great and holy task."[39] And the best way to instill this awareness would be through a special four-year program at the Kazan Academy to train priests in the language and mores of the Tatars. Such a curriculum would also have to include a strong grounding in the tenets of Islam, all the better to fight it. Il'minskii was convinced that the mullahs who strove to reclaim Kriashen souls could only be countered on their own terms. Adopting the motto "know thine enemy," he would describe his approach most succinctly in a speech to the academy some years later: "To make our arguments accessible to the Tatars we cannot clothe them in the garb of our own Christian concepts and history. On the contrary, we must adopt a Muslim perspective, accepting its religious worldview and conception of the past."[40] With Grigorii's strong support, Il'minskii's proposal became the guiding principle of the Missionary Division when it was finally launched in 1854.

Given Nikolai Ivanovich's expertise, he was the obvious candidate to head up the division's anti-Islam section. However, as had been the custom at Kazan University, he would first be sent to the Near East for a deeper grounding in the beliefs, culture, and languages of his spiritual adversaries. Also well in line with the university's tradition, Archbishop Grigorii wrote up an impossibly extensive set of instructions for the journey.[41] During a two-and-a-half-year tour of the Ottoman Empire, including Egypt, Palestine, Syria, and Asia Minor, Il'minskii was to perfect his Arabic, Turkish, and Hebrew, as well as picking up some Persian. He was also to study history and Islamic theology, both by reading classical texts as well as by visiting ancient temples and archaeological sites. There were some more practical aims too, as Grigorii added requests for a detailed study of Catholic and Protestant Near Eastern missions, to learn from their example. Meanwhile, Grand Duke Konstantin Nikolaevich, who was something of an amateur Turkologist, asked that Il'minskii personally send him periodic reports, a request that thoroughly rattled the academy's cautious clerics.

Il'minskii began his Near Eastern tour in November 1851 with a fourteen-month stay in Cairo. A major center of Islamic learning, the ancient city had the added advantage of being in Egypt, which was by then only nominally subject to the Porte. This would prove particularly useful for the Russian visitor at a time of growing Ottoman-Romanov tensions on the eve of the Crimean War. Il'minskii applied himself conscientiously to his task. Moving in with a scholar, Sheikh Ali El-Barrani, he devoted his days to reading literary works and grammars, while receiving personal instruction from his host every evening in Arabic, as well as in Muslim theology and law.

In addition to being a diligent student, Il'minskii was a conscientious tourist. He took long walks throughout Cairo, visiting its many mosques, monuments, bazaars, and schools, and indulged himself in a cruise on the Nile River to the ruins at Wadi Halfa in upper Nubia. In February 1853 Nikolai Ivanovich left the Egyptian capital and ambled his way through the Sinai Desert and the Levant, stopping in Jerusalem in time for Orthodox Easter. The ultimate destination was the great Ottoman metropolis of Constantinople, where Il'minskii was to devote another eight months to learning. However, by the time he reached Beirut he received word that Russian talks with the sultan's government to head off conflict had failed. At the tsarist consul's suggestion, Il'minskii decided to spend some months visiting Orthodox monasteries and other sites in the Lebanon Mountains, in the hope that diplomacy might take a calmer course. Much to his chagrin, all such expectations were dashed when in early October Turkey declared war on Russia, forcing a hasty return home. Yet despite its premature conclusion, the trip had been useful. According to the Soviet orientologist Ignatii Krachkovskii, "When [Il'minskii] returned to Kazan in February 1854, no other Russian Arabist could match his training in the field nor equal his knowledge of the living Arab East."[42]

At the end of his first year in Egypt, Il'minskii had submitted a paper to the Kazan Theological Academy summarizing what he had learned about

Islam so far. Without being unduly sympathetic, the account nevertheless provided a relatively dispassionate account of the Prophet and his faith's principal tenets.[43] Thus, while he pointed out various historical inaccuracies in the Koran, Il'minskii characterized it as a text of great literary beauty, filled with many edifying thoughts. Like many of his earlier writings, Nikolai Ivanovich's essay did not seethe with fear and loathing of the infidel.

Il'minskii's final report of his study tour painted a similarly objective portrait of the Near East.[44] In common with many other Europeans of the day, he repeatedly noted Islam's fanaticism and its constant summons to *jihad*. At the same time, the scholar in him was impressed by the faith's devotion to learning. Indeed, Il'minskii went out of his way to refute the notion that Islam was anti-intellectual. If the Muslim academy had any shortcomings, it was the fact that it had not yet progressed to a more modern level, remaining instead "mired in awkward scholastic hair-splitting from which Europe freed itself long ago."[45] But there were signs of hope. Contact with more cosmopolitan Cairenes had convinced him that exposure to the West would temper Islam's severity, suggesting that "the Muslim's fanaticism and religious pride slowly but surely vanishes upon more intimate acquaintance with the Europeans."[46]

If there was an undercurrent of hostility in Il'minskii's final report, it was primarily directed at Western Christendom. As he saw it, Catholic and Protestant missionaries, who had been flocking to the Near East as Ottoman power declined, were the greatest threat to its vulnerable Orthodox communities. According to Il'minskii, Christians in Palestine, Lebanon, and Syria had not suffered unduly over the centuries of relatively tolerant Turkish administration. More recently, however, zealous Western interlopers were proving increasingly successful in their attempts to attract the Orthodox to their versions of the Christian faith. Il'minskii believed that Catholics and Protestants were particularly keen to proselytize among Christians in the Near East because Muslims had proven largely resistant to their efforts. Not without a hint of schadenfreude, he noted that "the Protestants' successes are remarkably modest in comparison to the money and resources their missions exhaust."[47] As Nikolai Ivanovich had already discovered during his earlier forays among Kazan's Islamic Tatars, the Muslims under Ottoman rule retained an unshakable devotion to their beliefs. No amount of spiritual or material effort could possibly loosen Islam's iron grip on its faithful.

This realization had far-reaching consequences on Il'minskii's thinking about evangelization. For one thing, the Orthodox Church's traditional approach, which relied on debates with Tatar mullahs and other educated elites, struck him as entirely ineffective. No matter how convincing or correct, Christian logic was incapable of countering the fanatical ardor Muhammad's teachings inspired in his followers. As Nikolai Ivanovich once remarked, "arguing with people like that is obviously hopeless."[48] More important, Il'minskii began to believe that the very notion of converting Muslims was utterly futile.[49] His own inability to make any headway among Islamic Tatars had convinced him that their minds were in the thrall of some occult force that rendered them impervious to doubt.[50] Only among the Kriashen and Russia's animist minorities did the church still have any hope. Thus, to Il'minskii, rather than being an enemy to be attacked head-on, Islam became the archrival in a desperate contest for the souls of the empire's non-Muslim inorodtsy.

Il'minskii's new convictions were already evident when he took the helm of the academy's new anti-Islam department in 1854. With the help of a Tatar instructor, he initially focused on language training. He also made an effort to introduce his students to Islam through reading assignments and lively tales about his own travels. Within two years, Il'minskii was able to devote himself to religion more systematically when Gordii Sablukov, another faculty member conversant in Tatar, took over primary responsibility for language. Although technically his appointment now was as professor in anti-Muslim polemics, Nikolai Ivanovich did not pay any attention to this subject, having already deemed it irrelevant. Indeed, when at the start of the new post his rector asked him to deliver a talk about how best to engage Islam, Il'minskii obstinately reiterated his logic: "Muslims venerate their Prophet with a passion that borders on ecstatic. . . . When combined with the Tatars' utter ignorance about science and history, the refusal to confirm their beliefs through independent study, not to mention the singular bias of Tatar scholars toward scholastic superficialities and a contempt for proper historical methodology, it becomes clear that even the most obvious objections to Mohammed will never penetrate the Tatar mind."[51]

While Il'minskii proved to be a popular teacher, his section's enrollments were never oversubscribed. Compared to the twenty-nine who matriculated in the anti–Old Believer curriculum in September 1854, only twelve entered his anti-Islam department (another three enrolled in the anti-Buddhist department and twelve in Chuvash-Cheremis).[52] As had been the case at Kazan University, the difficulty of learning non-European languages discouraged many, while uncertain employment prospects were an added disincentive. In 1867, three years before the synod shut down the Missionary Division, only ten of the anti-Islam section's thirty-six graduates had managed to find jobs that made proper use of their skills.[53] At any rate, Orthodox seminarians were rarely fired by any strong missionary zeal. When in 1865 Kazan's archbishop, Afanasii (Sokolov), appealed for students at the academy to combat yet another regional upsurge of apostasy, only five volunteered. Even then, the aspiring clerics did so on the condition that they receive a regular salary and not be forced to become monks.[54]

The most serious impediment for the anti-Islam section was the distinct lack of enthusiasm from Il'minskii's superiors. Archimandrite Agafangel (Solov'ev), the academy's rector at the time, was much more interested in combating the Old Believers. Not only did he teach in that department himself, but he was also not above diverting funds from the Missionary Division's other sections or even poaching their better students.[55] To Agafangel's suspicious imagination there was also something questionable about paying so much attention to the infidel in a Christian institution of higher learning, and he began to suspect Il'minskii of being a "propagandist for Islam."[56]

If Agafangel at least supported missions in principle, Archimandrite Ioann (Sokolov), who succeeded him in 1857, was altogether opposed to such endeavors. Deriding the division's sections as "henhouses," Ioann declared that studying Tatars was nothing more than "silliness" that distracted the academy's students from more pertinent subjects.[57] In the summer of 1858 the new rector proposed a major reform. Ostensibly to make generalists out of all of its students, he combined the anti–Old Believer and anti-Islam sections and trimmed the latter's faculty by transferring Il'minskii to mathematics.

Although the synod eventually rescinded this rebuff to its ablest missionary teacher, by then it was too late. Tiring of the academy's shenanigans, Il'minskii leapt at an offer to join the government's Orenburg Borderlands Commission, on the southern steppe frontier. Under the direction of Vasilii Grigor'ev, a rising scholar of central Asian history, this agency was responsible for administering the Kazakh Lesser Horde, a Turkic group of nomads then being absorbed into the Russian Empire. It was a move that would have profound implications for Il'minskii's future as well as for the fate of orientology at the Kazan Theological Academy.

During his three years in Orenburg as an "official for special assignments," Nikolai Il'minskii began the transformation from academic to activist. Much of his attention focused on assimilating Kazakhs through conversion to Orthodoxy. As in the mid-Volga region, Il'minskii discovered that his principal competitors in the contest for Kazakh souls were Muslim Tatars, who had been actively proselytizing beyond Orenburg for some time. Grigor'ev's strategy to combat this "tartarization of the Steppe" was to give Kazakhs a Christian education in their own language but using the Cyrillic alphabet. The latter was to discourage the use of Arabic, whose script would make Muhammad's teachings more accessible to them. After spending considerable time living among Kazakhs as they migrated with their herds to new pastures, Il'minskii eventually became convinced that this technique—sending young inorodtsy to Orthodox schools where they would learn the Gospel in their native tongue—would also be the best means to combat apostasy among the Kriashen back home.

Il'minskii's scholarship in Orenburg, which included the first Kazakh-Russian dictionary, did not remain unnoticed. When Kazan University managed to reestablish a chair in Turkic letters in 1861, it invited him to take up the post, which he would hold until 1872. While he tirelessly, if unsuccessfully, campaigned for a proper restoration of orientology there, his teaching duties remained light; the professor rarely attracted more than a handful of students, and on occasion none dared to take his grueling subject. Meanwhile, two years after he joined the university, the Kazan Theological Academy invited Il'minskii back as a full professor to replace Sablukov, who had just retired. Still reluctant to have anything to do with anti-Muslim polemics, he accepted the offer on the condition that he return on half pay at a junior rank and only teach language. According to his arrangement with the rector, the other half of Il'minskii's salary would be used to hire a recent graduate, Evfimii Malov, as instructor in polemics.

Despite now holding appointments both at Kazan's university and its theological academy, Il'minskii's career began to take a more practical turn. In 1864 Vasilii Timofeev, a devout Kriashen who had helped him translate Christian texts into Tatar, took in a few boys from his village and began to teach them at home. Il'minskii now found his true life's calling and began to devote himself directly to Timofeev's enterprise. From these humble beginnings would grow an extensive network of village primary schools for Kriashen and other Eastern minorities that by century's end numbered over three hundred.[58] Largely funded by charity, they all followed the approach Il'minskii had come to develop on the basis of his three years in Orenburg.

More commonly known as the Il'minskii system (although Nikolai Ivanovich himself modestly named it the "Saint Gurii system," after Kazan's first archbishop), the schools taught inorodets children a basic Orthodox curriculum in their native vernacular. The Il'minskii system was not without its detractors, including some education officials, who resented this intrusion on their pedagogical territory, and Russian nationalists, who were eager to impose their language on all minorities. At the same time, it also had some powerful champions among conservatives in the autocracy's higher reaches, including two successive chief procurators of the Holy Synod, Count Dmitrii Tolstoi and Konstantin Pobedonostsev. Such support was all the more remarkable within a climate of increasing Russification. When in 1864, following a second major Polish rebellion against tsarist rule, the Ministry of Education declared that all instruction throughout the empire be solely in Russian, the Il'minskii schools were exempted.[59] Il'minskii devoted the remaining three decades of his life to schooling the empire's minorities in the Orthodox faith according to his method. Although his earlier contributions to orientology won him election to the Imperial Academy of Sciences in 1884, he declined the honor to avoid having to leave Kazan.

The increasingly practical nature of Il'minskii's pursuits was paired with a deepening hostility to Islam. As he grew older (Il'minskii died in 1891), Nikolai Ivanovich found less and less to admire in the faith to which he had devoted so much of his intellectual energy in earlier years. In 1871 a former colleague remarked that he "lately relates with too much antipathy towards everything Muslim, [and] listens with reluctance to anything concerning Muslims."[60] Whether out of exasperation at the strength of their beliefs, elderly cantankerousness, or a combination of both, by the 1880s Il'minskii's views had hardened into open antagonism.[61] He frequently urged officials to take an uncompromising stance against the faith, reasoning that "any concession to Islam injures Orthodoxy."[62] In contrast to his more youthful enthusiasm about the taming power of modernity, Il'minskii now began to invoke the specter of pan-Islamism as the inevitable result of European-style education: "A dreadful storm-cloud is approaching the Mohammedans, a new civilisation, not Mongolian this time but Muslim, not by the barbarians of Asia but by civilised barbarians who have gone to universities, gymnasia and military schools."[63] With their portrayal of Islamic Tatars as sly, cunning, predatory, and dangerous to Christianity, Il'minskii's many letters to Pobedonostsev during the last decade of his life betray a disturbing similarity to the more odious anti-Semitic clichés of his some of his contemporaries.

As for the study of Islam at the Theological Academy, Il'minskii's first departure in 1858 was a setback from which it never fully recovered. According to its chronicler, the brief period from 1856 to 1858, when Il'minskii and Sablukov had joined forces, "can be considered the best years of [the anti-Islam department's] existence."[64] Upon replacing Il'minskii, Sablukov and those who followed him returned to the more traditional technique of polemicizing directly with Islam, an approach that never led to spectacular results. Nevertheless, the academy did boast a few accomplished Islamists among its ranks, most notably Sablukov and his student Evfimii Malov, who taught from 1862 through 1870. Sablukov would go on to publish the first Russian-language Koran directly translated from Arabic, whereas Malov wrote innovative studies of the Koran's pre-Islamic roots.

As discussed in chapter 5, orientology at Russian universities tended to focus on the East's major cultures to the detriment of Russia's own Asian minorities. The emphasis shifted at the Kazan Theological Academy, where proselytizing among the empire's inorodtsy increasingly attracted the attention of its professors. Yet if the academy now stressed such indigenous languages as Tatar, Kalmyk, and Buriat, the more established

Asian religions still merited greater attention than the animist beliefs of Russia's many unlettered Eastern "small peoples." Thus, only two years after its establishment in 1854, the Chuvash-Cheremis section of the Missionary Department was scrapped, while the chairs for anti-Muslim and anti-Buddhist polemics were irregularly staffed.

Given the ultimate aim of their efforts—combating Islam and converting its followers to Christianity—the men who held the anti-Muslim chair rarely approached their subject with scrupulous objectivity. With the significant exception of Nikolai Il'minskii in his earlier years, their views were often hostile, defensive, or a combination of both. To the academy's faculty, Islam was often characterized as fatalistic, morally flawed, and, of course, fanatical, while they described its founder as despotic yet weak and epileptic. In the words of Mikhail Mashanov, who taught at the academy from 1878 to 1911, Islam was nothing more than "an inconsistent compilation of various Jewish and Christian teachings . . . [combined] with Arab paganism."[65]

After decades of lackluster backing from the clerical establishment, orientology at the Kazan Academy enjoyed a modest rebirth under the aegis of Pobedonostsev. As chief procurator of the Most Holy Synod from 1880 to 1905, and Nikolai Il'minskii's patron, Pobedonostsev enthusiastically supported spreading the Gospel among the empire's minorities. In 1884 he boosted the Missionary Department by doubling the faculty devoted to its anti-Islamic and anti-Buddhist sections to four.[66] However, compared to better-supported secular establishments, such as St. Petersburg University, the academy remained a backwater for scholarship of the East until the new Bolshevik government shut it down in 1919.

Although a graduate of its seminary rather than the academy, the man who is generally regarded as the founder of Russian Sinology, Father Hyacinth (Iakinf), né Nikita Bichurin, was another product of the church's institutions of higher education in Kazan. Aleksandr Pushkin's friend, a foreign ministry official, and a habitué of early nineteenth-century St. Petersburg intellectual and literary circles, the exotic monk left his imprint outside of academe as well, even inspiring several novels and a play.[67] At the same time, Father Hyacinth was a perennial nuisance to his superiors, and the story of his life provides a good example of the troubled relationship between orientology and the church in Imperial Russia.

Father Hyacinth's career is closely linked to one of the more remarkable institutions in the early history of tsarist Sinology, the Ecclesiastical Mission in Beijing.[68] That organization's story begins with Russia's first clash with China, at the fortress of Albazin on the Amur River in East Asia.[69] Occupied in 1650 by a Cossack adventurer, Erofei Khabarov, the Siberian outpost increasingly came to be seen as a challenge to the Qing dynasty's northern marches. In 1685 the Kangxi Emperor's forces captured Albazin, effectively halting the Russian advance. Four years later the two empires signed the Treaty of Nerchinsk, which still marks much of the boundary between eastern Siberia and Manchuria.[70]

When Kangxi's troops seized Albazin, their commander offered the defeated Russians a choice between returning home or entering into Chinese service. While most rejoined their compatriots, about forty-five Cossacks opted for the latter and were enrolled in a guard company of the Yellow Bordered Banner in Beijing. One involuntary companion of this group was Father Maksim (Leont'ev), Albazin's chaplain, whom the Qing's new recruits forcibly took along to the Chinese capital to serve as their priest.

Kangxi hospitably treated the *Albazintsy,* as his Cossacks came to be known. He personally welcomed them when they arrived in Beijing, paid them the same wage as his own bannermen, and allowed them to take Chinese wives. As for Father Maksim, the emperor assigned him a Buddhist temple in the northeastern corner of Beijing's "Tatar City," which was consecrated as the Saint Nicholas Chapel. The hapless priest had his work cut out for him, since the small Russian community was bound eventually to be absorbed into the Middle Kingdom's "heathen millions." Indeed, a little over a century later, one Russian traveler reported that only twenty-two descendants of the Albazintsy had been baptized, and most of them were thoroughly Sinified.[71]

Russian officials nevertheless took a lively interest in Beijing's Orthodox enclave. When Andrei Vinius, in his capacity as head of the Sibirskii Prikaz (Siberian office) reported to Peter I about Father Maksim's activities, the tsar issued a decree in 1700 "for the consolidation of the Orthodox faith and the propagation of the Holy Gospel among the idolatrous population of China." The idea was to send two or three clergy to Beijing to study Chinese and preach among the Albazintsy. The metropolitan of

Kiev was ordered to supply the candidates, since his priests had the greatest expertise in proselytization.

The tsar's desire to establish a more permanent Orthodox foothold in Beijing was hardly inspired by missionary zeal; Peter was primarily interested in improving trade with the fabled China market. In the absence of regular diplomatic links, which the Middle Kingdom's rulers were not prepared to grant the "red-bearded barbarians," a colony of priests might serve as a good alternative. The Kangxi Emperor rebuffed Peter's initial attempts to secure Chinese permission for an Orthodox mission in Beijing. But in 1712, eager to secure Russian permission for his embassy to the Kalmyks, an Inner Asian people who had migrated to the steppes around the lower Volga, Kangxi relented and agreed to a mission, headed by Archimandrite Illarion (Lezhaiskii).

This first Ecclesiastical Mission arrived in 1715, although it would take another twelve years to secure permission for the Russian Orthodox Church to send regular missions to the Chinese capital, according to the Treaty of Kiakhta.[72] There would be twenty missions in all, including two under the aegis of the émigré Russian Orthodox Church Outside of Russia after 1917. The missions were primarily charged with saving the souls of the Albazintsy. Unlike their Catholic or Protestant counterparts, the Orthodox fathers tended not to seek new converts among the Chinese. According to one of the mission's historians, Archimandrite Nikolai (Adoratskii), "the activities of the Orthodox Mission in Peking were entirely consistent with Russian government policy, which always refrained from trying to weaken China or attempting to entice its populace with the benefits of Christian civilization, unlike the other European [Church] Missions." Father Nikolai implied a distinct contrast with the more sinister aims of the Jesuits: "Our Mission always limited itself to the moral-religious sphere. It refrained from proselytizing, interfering in politics, intriguing at the court, or promoting commercial goals." According to the archimandrite, the Orthodox Church's mission to Beijing helped to keep Sino-Russian relations cordial.[73]

Father Nikolai's thesis of a "special relationship" between the Romanov and Qing dynasties was a common theme in tsarist thinking about the world. Diplomats, as well as conservative writers such as Prince Esper Ukhtomskii, often argued that Russian policy in East Asia differed fundamentally from that of the more ignoble aims of capitalist powers such as France and Great Britain.[74] While such views might have been prevalent among official circles in St. Petersburg, few Chinese had any illusions about Russian motives. During the Boxer uprising of 1900, a violent anti-European popular reaction in northern China, neither Orthodox converts nor establishments were exempt from the xenophobic fury. According to one calculation, the Boxers murdered some two hundred Chinese Orthodox Christians and destroyed the Russian mission's compound.[75]

The Ecclesiastical Mission had a pedagogical function as well, for it also included some students. Typically schoolboys who had shown an aptitude for foreign languages, the lads were sent to Beijing to learn Chinese and Manchu, so that they might serve as dragomans for Russia's foreign office. They were an unruly lot, and a fair number perished from drink or disease. The clergy did not always set the best example. The head of the third mission, Archimandrite Illarion, was given to drunkenly parading about the Beijing compound in drag.

By the 1850s, the Ecclesiastical Mission's academic role was being supplanted by institutions back in Russia. The University of Kazan had already established a chair in Chinese philology in 1837, and the University of St. Petersburg soon followed suit. Meanwhile, the establishment of formal diplomatic relations between China and Russia in 1861 freed the fathers in Beijing from any diplomatic responsibilities. Nevertheless, the fact that today the Russian Federation's embassy to China occupies the former mission's grounds is a daily reminder of the Orthodox Church's pioneering role as intermediary between the two Asian powers.

The Beijing mission's most famous member entered the world in 1777 as Nikita Iakovlevich Bichurin, the son of a Chuvash village deacon in the government of Kazan.[76] The Chuvash, a people of mixed Finno-Ugric and Turkic blood living upriver from Kazan, had only recently begun to be converted to the Orthodox faith. Many had resisted Catherine II's efforts at spiritual Russification, and not a few Chuvash participated in Pugachev's great uprising just a few years before Bichurin's birth.

As the promising son of a cleric, Nikita was enrolled in the Kazan Seminary. He proved to be an excellent student. Finishing first in his class in 1799, the graduate was asked to stay on to teach grammar at the new

Kazan Theological Academy. Within a year he was tonsured as a monk, taking the name Hyacinth. Two years later he found himself appointed archimandrite of a monastery in Irkutsk and rector of the local seminary. It was too rapid an ascent. At the tender age of twenty-four, Father Hyacinth proved incapable of maintaining discipline among the rowdy seminarians. Within a few years a student revolt, which had to be put down by Cossacks, resulted in his demotion and exile to Tobolsk (harboring a serf girl as his "servant" did not help).

Although in disgrace, Father Hyacinth got a lucky break. Shortly after his arrival at the western Siberian city, he met Count Iurii Golovkin, a diplomat who was on his way to Beijing to negotiate better trade links with the Middle Kingdom. The count was traveling along with the new ninth mission, which was about to begin its term in the Chinese capital. When he became acquainted with the cleric, Golovkin thought him the perfect candidate to head the mission. Father Hyacinth's linguistic talents, intellectual abilities, and apparent administrative skills all impressed the count, who quickly arranged for him to be put in charge.

The archimandrite arrived at his new posting in January 1808 and would spend the next fourteen years in China. At first he immersed himself in his pastoral duties among the Albazintsy. Yet it must have seemed that keeping the Orthodox faith alive among these assimilated descendants of seventeenth-century Cossacks was a hopeless task. Among the thirty-five males in his flock, only a few even still had Russian given names. As his predecessor, Archimandrite Sofronii of the eighth mission, had reported back to the Holy Synod in St. Petersburg, "They don't go to church, for the Albazintsy have not only long ago forgotten their faith, but their language as well." Father Hyacinth later cynically remarked that their only motive in attending the liturgy at all was "ne dlia Isusa, a dlia khleba kusa" (not for Christ but for a morsel of bread).[77]

The archimandrite's first priority was to begin translating various Orthodox texts into Chinese, to make the service more comprehensible. As he labored over this work, he was troubled by the absence of a proper Chinese-Russian dictionary. The best reference was a Chinese-Latin dictionary that Catholic priests at the Portuguese mission had lent him. Within four years, Father Hyacinth had compiled his own lexicon, which he continued to supplement over the course of his stay. Meanwhile, to improve his knowledge of the living language, he frequently wandered about the city streets in Chinese gowns and chatted with passersby. The gregarious monk easily befriended many among the local population, including officials at the Lifan Yuan, the Qing foreign office, where he made himself popular by readily translating European diplomatic correspondence. At the same time, Father Hyacinth paid close attention to political developments. When Lin Qing, the son of a humble clerk, led his abortive Eight Trigram rebellion against the dynasty in 1813, the archimandrite sent an eyewitness account of the unrest back to St. Petersburg, yielding his first publication.[78]

Over time, Father Hyacinth became increasingly absorbed in learning about China, at the cost of his religious and administrative obligations. Two of the mission's language students died of drink, and another of his charges began to sell off church property. Meanwhile, Napoleon's invasion in 1812 cut off the already modest flow of funds from Russia, putting the mission in severe financial straits. As in Irkutsk, there was grumbling within the ranks, and disquieting reports began to reach the synod about the archimandrite's alleged improprieties. According to Egor Timkovskii, an official in the foreign ministry's Asian Department who met him in Beijing toward the end of his stay, these accusations were not entirely off the mark. In later years Timkovskii recalled spending many an evening back in Russia with the monk, who "over a glass of punch loved to regale me with tales of various Pekingese scandals, never denying his involvement in these antics."[79]

When in 1816 Father Hyacinth asked whether he might be able to renew his posting for another term, his request was quickly turned down. Upon returning to St. Petersburg in 1822, the archimandrite was charged with a variety of offenses, including "going to public places in improper garb, attending theaters and taverns . . . drinking, not performing church services, and generally not carrying out your . . . missionary responsibilities."[80] There were even allegations of vandalism, embezzlement, fornication, and pederasty. But Father Hyacinth's gravest transgression was that his real vocation was academic rather than spiritual. In Timkovskii's words, he "was a very gifted, intelligent, and even cheerful man, but also an ardent epicure and bon vivant. The religious calling was contrary to his character, and he had answered it quite by accident."[81] Stripping him of his clerical rank, the synod sentenced Father Hyacinth to exile at the Solovetskii

Monastery (near the Arctic Circle) "under strict surveillance" as a simple monk, although the tsar softened the punishment by having him sent to the slightly less austere surroundings of Valaam Island on Lake Ladoga.

If Father Hyacinth thoroughly managed to alienate his superiors in the Holy Synod, he also had some important patrons. The foreign office was particularly impressed with the monk's knowledge of the empire's eastern neighbor. Baron Pavel Schilling von Canstatt, the head of the ministry's Asian Department, eventually arranged for his return to St. Petersburg from Valaam in 1826 as an official in the department's pay. Despite several efforts to be freed from his vows, however, Father Hyacinth remained a monk. Assigned a comfortable two-room cell in the Saint Alexander Nevsky Lavra, he did most of his work in his quarters, rarely making his way to the ministry's buildings at the Choristers' Bridge.

Father Hyacinth now began to produce a remarkably prolific series of works about China and Inner Asia.[82] Within three years of arriving in the Russian capital, he published six books, beginning with his *Description of Tibet* in 1828, which was based on the 1792 account of a Qing official. Lauded by critic and orientologist Osip Senkovskii, among others, it was quickly translated into French.[83] Before the year was out, the monk also produced his *Notes on Mongolia*. Combining the travel diaries he had compiled during his return trip from Beijing in 1821 with discussions about the region's history, law code, and statistics, it appeared in French as well as German. Father Hyacinth's first books favorably impressed both Foreign Minister Count Karl Nesselrode as well as Education Minister Prince Karl Lieven, and in December 1828 he was elected a corresponding member of the Academy of Sciences. The following year saw the appearance of four more works: *The History of the First Four Khans of the House of Genghis, Description of Zungharia and Eastern Turkestan, San Zi Jing or the Three-Character Classic* (a children's primer of Confucian thought), and his *Description of Peking*. Although the first three were basically Russian translations of Chinese texts, he had personally compiled the latter on foot over the course of an entire year.

Father Hyacinth's prodigious output did not keep him from making many new friends in St. Petersburg.[84] Even before his exile to Valaam, he had earned a reputation as an unusually gifted scholar who had interesting things to say about China. The monk was close to such figures as Pushkin,

Karamzin, and Belinskii, as well as to the Imperial Public Library's director, Aleksandr Olenin. The latter supplemented his income by engaging
him to catalogue Chinese and Manchu holdings and appointed him an
honorary librarian, a distinction likewise bestowed on such other orientologists as Senkovskii and Christian Frähn. Shortly after returning from
China, Father Hyacinth had also made the acquaintance of the future Decembrist conspirator Nikolai Bestuzhev. In later years, Father Hyacinth visited the rebel in exile at Petrovskii Zavod in eastern Siberia, and Bestuzhev's
portrait of the cleric is now preserved in a Kiakhta museum.

Fond of high society, champagne, and cigars, Father Hyacinth was more
boulevardier than ascetic. With pale, Asian features, a tall, slender frame
garbed in black cassock, fluent French, and an inexhaustible supply of
amusing, often risqué anecdotes about the Middle Kingdom, he was a
popular guest in St. Petersburg's salons. The historian Mikhail Pogodin
once reminisced about Prince Vladimir Odoevskii's soirées: "Here went
jolly Pushkin and Father Hyacinth with his Oriental mien. The stout and
stern German traveler—Baron Schilling . . . Glinka . . . Lermontov . . .
Krylov, Zhukovskii, and Viazemskii were always there too."[85]

There has been much speculation about Father Hyacinth's friendship
with Aleksandr Pushkin.[86] The poet and the Sinologist first met in the late
1820s, possibly at Karamzin's house, and Pushkin read Father Hyacinth's
books, using his work for a history of the Pugachev rebellion.[87] Meanwhile, *Literaturnaia Gazeta,* the newspaper with which Pushkin was
closely affiliated, regularly published Father Hyacinth's articles. The monk
likely stirred the bard's imagination. In 1830 Pushkin applied to the Third
Section (the tsar's secret police) for permission to accompany Father Hyacinth on an expedition to Kiakhta and from thence on to China. Its chief,
Count Aleksandr Benckendorff, did not approve the request on the
grounds that, "this would excessively damage your pecuniary affairs, and
at the same time distract you from your occupations."[88]

Father Hyacinth traveled to Kiahkta on this journey along with Baron
Schilling to accompany the eleventh Ecclesiastical Mission on the Russian
leg of its journey to Beijing. The foreign ministry had ordered Schilling to
study the local population as well as the China trade. In addition to his official duties, the baron's companion had a characteristically ambitious
scholarly agenda of his own, which included revising his Chinese diction-

ary and grammar and verifying the accuracy of Russian and Qing maps, not to mention studying Mongolian. He also taught Mandarin, both to the mission's members during the journey and to local merchants' sons. The latter goal was particularly important. As the traditional centre of tsarist commerce with its Asian neighbor, Kiakhta had long played a major role in eastern Siberia's economy. However, as Father Hyacinth noted, its residents were woefully ignorant of their trading partner's tongue.[89] The monk's courses soon convinced a leading merchant to petition the foreign office to set up a more permanent establishment. Sanctioned by imperial decree in 1832, the result was the Kiakhta Chinese Language School, the first such institution in Russia.[90]

After some eighteen months in the border town, Father Hyacinth went back to St. Petersburg along with the previous Beijing mission personnel. Three more books soon followed: *The History of Tibet and Kokonor from 2282 B.C. to A.D. 1227,* the first edition of his Chinese grammar, and *A Historical Review of the Oirats or Kalmyks from the Fifteenth Century to Our Day.* While the first two were edited translations of Chinese works, the *Historical Review* was more than a compilation and won the author his first Demidov Prize. Based on both Russian and Chinese sources, the work told the story of the last major westward Inner Asian nomadic migration, whose descendants settled the steppes around the lower Volga. Father Hyacinth's stay in the Russian capital was interrupted within three years when he was ordered back to Kiakhta to help organize its new Chinese school. He took his duties seriously and also found time to write articles about such subjects as Chinese statistics, astronomy, education, and regional government, among others. Nevertheless, life in a frontier town held little appeal for the cosmopolitan cleric, and after repeated appeals to the foreign ministry he was allowed to return to St. Petersburg in 1838.

During the following decade, Father Hyacinth increasingly turned his attention to China proper. The Royal Navy's successful effort to blast the Middle Kingdom open to more British trade during the First Opium War of 1839–42 heightened interest among Russians in their East Asian neighbor, and the monk was only too happy to oblige. By 1848 he had published four more books, covering such topics as Chinese government, law, education, agriculture, and commerce, among a host of others. Closer to compilations of facts directly translated from Qing publications rather than coherent narratives, these works nevertheless found a wide readership.

Reviewers almost invariably praised the author for his undeniable erudition. Yet some also chided him for being overly uncritical about his subject. As Senkovskii put it in his inimitable prose, "Our honored Sinologist so ardently loves everything Chinese . . . that his Russian phrases often seem as if they had emanated from a stern mandarin's pursed, laconic lips."[91] In his comments about an earlier work published during the First Opium War, Senkovskii wondered how a tiny British force could possibly overwhelm the magnificent civilization Father Hyacinth evoked. "China must be some sort of fairy tale," he speculated, "the Chinese a hoax . . . [and] their illustrious empire some sort of painted and lacquered realm that can be consumed by the flame of a single, stearic candle." At the other end of the ideological spectrum, Vissarion Belinskii complained that the monk "mostly shows us the official side of China, in uniform and with its ceremonies."[92]

These assessments were on the mark. As a seminarian, Father Hyacinth had admired Voltaire's writings, even translating the latter's ode to religious toleration, the *Henriade*.[93] Much like the philosophe, he tended to idealize the Middle Kingdom as the apotheosis of reason. Its four-thousand-year-old history had created a realm whose laws were just, its ruler fair, and his subjects well educated and orderly. According to Father Hyacinth, "There is both much good and bad in the Chinese people, but the good outweighs the bad. This is because sound morals, instilled in children by their schools, sustained by their upbringing as well as the authorities' supervision, are confirmed by laws that encourage good deeds rather than forbidding bad ones."[94] Indeed, the Qing law code was "so close to the true foundations of government that it can teach something to even the most well-developed states."[95]

Senkovskii and Father Hyacinth also sparred over language. The former expressed his irritation that the monk did not publish in French or English. "Until now Russian has been beyond the notice of European academic discussion about matters Oriental," he argued, adding that "so it will remain for a long time."[96] Father Hyacinth disagreed. While he knew French, German, and Latin, he invariably published in his native tongue. Perhaps sensitive to his Chuvash heritage, the Sinologist ardently cham-

pioned Russian scholarship. In a letter to his friend Pogodin, he complained that "like children [Russian academics] prefer French falsehoods
to Russian truth."[97] On another occasion, Father Hyacinth dismissed
Western books about the East: "When we read the learned contributions
of foreign writers, it becomes evident that they often, as the Chinese
proverb has it, call an ass a horse, a goat a cow; their judgment about matters, especially those concerning . . . Central and East Asia, is no more reliable than that of a blind man about colors."[98]

Possibly motivated by stirrings of tsarist military interest in the region,
in 1846 the Academy of Sciences commissioned Father Hyacinth to compile a major study about ancient central Asian history.[99] By now close to
seventy years old and in failing health, he nevertheless plunged headfirst
into the task. The monk once again relied entirely on Chinese sources, beginning with the Han dynasty historian Sima Qian's *Historical Records* of
around 100 B.C.E. Published in three volumes in 1851, the *Collection of
Facts about the Peoples Inhabiting Central Asia in Ancient Times* covered
a vast region stretching from Turkestan to Japan. While the book earned
Father Hyacinth his fourth Demidov Prize, Mirza Kazem-Bek wrote a
scathing review, excoriating the author for uncritically replicating Chinese
accounts and ignoring Western sources.[100]

Not long after he began this book, Father Hyacinth had confessed to
Pogodin, "Time flies. What will be next—I have no idea."[101] The septua-
genarian monk clearly understood that the *Collection of Facts* would be
his last important work; after he completed it, he donated much of his library to the Kazan Academy. There would be a few more articles. Illness,
however, increasingly sapped his energy, and he died in his cell in 1853.

Father Hyacinth's contemporaries esteemed his works highly. Despite
his usual deluge of barbs, even the hypercritical Senkovskii was moved to
declare that "from the chaos of Asian texts, none of our contemporary orientologists have brought to light so many new facts, so many interesting
and important details about East Asia's past, as our indefatigable Sinologist, Father Hyacinth."[102] The Academy of Sciences awarded him its prestigious Demidov Prize no less than four times, while the monk's many articles in such periodicals as *Literaturnaia Gazeta, Severnyi Arkhiv, Teleskop,*
and *Moskovskii Telegraf* also brought him to the attention of the broader
educated public. At the same time, he made many valuable linguistic con-

tributions, including his famous twelve-thousand-character Chinese-Russian dictionary, a Chinese grammar, and a Manchu-Russian dictionary. Although Father Hyacinth is now largely unknown abroad, his work did catch the attention of European orientologists of his day. In 1831 the Paris Asian Society awarded him an honorary membership, and several of his books appeared in translation.

To appreciate properly Father Hyacinth's contributions to Russian Sinology, it is important to remember that the field basically did not exist before him. Eighteenth-century Russians were certainly interested in China. Yet aside from the relatively neglected works of such earlier alumni of the Beijing mission as Ilarion Rossokhin and Aleksei Leont'ev, before the nineteenth century the main source of knowledge about the Qing Empire was the West. Father Hyacinth was the first to produce a significant native body of work. While subsequent generations of orientologists found fault with his scholarship, few denied the value of his pioneering achievement.[103] According to Vasilii Barthold, thanks to the monk "already by 1851 . . . Russian study of China surpassed Western Europe."[104]

As well as being a trailblazer, Father Hyacinth left his imprint on the Russian Sinological tradition in two other ways. The first was the relative sympathy and objectivity with which he studied his subject. In an age when many Western specialists often disparaged the Middle Kingdom, Father Hyacinth tended to avoid judgment. Many subsequent Russian orientologists shared his unbiased approach. The other significant characteristic of the Russian school Father Hyacinth initiated was the relative importance accorded to Inner Asia. In addition to his studies of Han China, the monk also devoted much effort to the Qing's western periphery, including Mongolia, Xinjiang, and Tibet—regions that had only recently come under Beijing's domination. This was only natural. Whereas most Western Europeans approached China from the sea, Russians typically traveled to the Middle Kingdom via Mongolia. Indeed, when Father Hyacinth first arrived in Beijing, he initially studied Mongolian and Manchu, only later realizing that Mandarin was China's more important tongue.

The Kazan Theological Academy was the only one of the Russian Orthodox Church's four senior institutions of higher learning to teach Asian languages and beliefs.[105] Like the city's university, the academy developed this expertise largely because of its pedagogical mandate for the empire's east. Thus, as had been the case at the university, its orientology had a largely practical aim. But its ultimate objective was different. Instead of training government officials to deal with Asians both within and beyond the Russian Empire's borders, the academy prepared missionaries to convert unbaptized minorities to Orthodox Christianity (as well as to return Old Believers to the official church). Therefore, its faculty's perspective on the East was different from that of their secular colleagues at the university.

While the implications of this "missionary orientologist" worldview would seem to be evident, the reality proved to be more complicated. Many of those involved in anti-Islam and anti-Buddhist studies at the Kazan Theological Academy naturally held a strong antipathy to the objects of their scholarship. However, such hostility was by no means inevitable. As the earlier writings of its most prominent orientologist, Nikolai Il'minskii, suggest, even devout Christians could study a rival faith with relative detachment. Il'minskii's opinions about Islam hardened in his later years, but it is perhaps no coincidence that this enmity only developed when he had largely abandoned the ivory tower for practical missionary work.

If anything, Russia's best-known missionary orientologist, Father Hyacinth, was perhaps too sympathetic to those he studied. To be sure, he was hardly a faithful member of the church. Often described as "a freethinker in cassock," he had remained a monk against his will by order of the tsar, and his perspective was distinctly secular. Despite having been praised by subsequent generations of church leaders, his clerical contemporaries hardly encouraged his academic pursuits.

If the contributions of Kazan University to orientology are well known, those of the Theological Academy are considerably more obscure. Surveys of the discipline's history in Imperial Russia often suggest that serious scholarship of the East in Kazan ended in 1854, while those that do acknowledge its survival at the academy tend to criticize it as overly subjective and reactionary.[106] Given both the church's traditional apathy for proselytization and the low esteem held by many secular academics for Orthodox clergy in the nineteenth century, Kazan's missionary orientologists faced an uphill battle for intellectual respectability. But it would be going too far to dismiss the academy's place in Russian orientology altogether. As Mark Batunsky points out, the faculty of its anti-Muslim department "were the first professional Islamologists in the history of the Russian missionary endeavor who sought enthusiastically to substitute scientific methods and stereotypes characteristic of the nineteenth century for widespread, intuitively vague notions about the Muslim religion."[107]

7

THE RISE OF THE ST. PETERSBURG SCHOOL

An academy should be founded to mediate between the civilization of the West and the light of the East . . . where we might see the European critic beside the Asian Lama.

—Sergei Uvarov

Compared to its cousin on the Volga River, the St. Petersburg school was a late bloomer. Russian orientology's birth as an academic discipline had roughly coincided with the founding of the city on the Neva by Peter the Great at the turn of the eighteenth century. But, as we have seen, the groundwork Peter laid for studying the East did not prove particularly fertile in the decades after his death. Aside from a few other false starts, the autocracy made no more attempts to teach Asian languages until Catherine the Great's time. As for the Academy of Sciences, it played a subsidiary role until tsarism's twilight decades.

After a long slumber, orientology in the imperial capital reawoke in the early nineteenth century under Alexander I when he set up a system of universities. As with Peter's Academy of Sciences, these institutions had a utilitarian mandate. According to Alexander Vucinich, "The training of government officials for various positions emerged as a factor of primary importance in the establishment of Russian universities; in the eyes of the government, university professors were not independent representatives of free sciences, but officials [of the state]."[1]

There was an inherent paradox in Alexander I's approach toward higher education. When contemplating his new universities, the tsar had looked to two European models. There were France's vocational *grandes écoles,* the specialized colleges under strict state control that Napoleon had established to train his bureaucrats. Closer to home was the freer German archetype. Exemplified by the University of Berlin, which the Prussian education minister Wilhelm Baron von Humboldt had founded in 1810, these were autonomous institutions where the acquisition of knowledge was an end in itself (Oxbridge's entirely independent course was clearly out of the question).[2]

Although the autocracy's goals were more in line with the Gallic variant, it chose the Teutonic.[3] As a result, Russian universities were subject to alternating currents of liberalism and militarization, not to mention the contradictory imperatives of practical training and pure scholarship. The latter would prove particularly vexing for professors of orientology, especially those who happened to teach in the imperial capital, where the autocracy's organs of power were most immediate.

Along with the new campuses at Kharkov and Kazan, Alexander's 1804 statute had also provided for a university in St. Petersburg, but that would take another fifteen years to materialize. For the time being, aside from various military and other specialized schools, the capital's only institution of postsecondary education was its Pedagogicheskii institut (teachers' college). Renamed the Glavnyi (main) pedagogicheskii institut in 1816, its purpose was to train faculty for the empire's gymnasia and universities. Four years later, on February 8, 1819, Alexander I approved upgrading the teachers' college into a proper university.

Both the beginnings of St. Petersburg University and the rebirth of orientology in the Russian capital are intimately linked to the district's superintendent of education at the time, Count Sergei Semenovich Uvarov.[4] History has not been kind to him, since his name is linked to the century's most repressive tsar, Nicholas I. As Nicholas's education minister, Uvarov devised the ideological formula for his reign, Official Nationality, a doctrine based on the trinity of "Orthodoxy, Autocracy, and Nationality." As a result, Soviet historians have excoriated him as the reactionary lackey of "the gendarme of Europe," a sentiment shared by Nicholas Riasanovsky in his study of the ideology Uvarov devised.[5] In truth, Uvarov was more moderate politically than many other officials of the day, who often intrigued against him.[6] But the count also struck contemporaries as greedy, vain, and sycophantic. The Moscow University historian Sergei Solov'ev recalled: "Although Uvarov acted like a great landowner, there was nothing aristocratic about him. Quite the contrary, he was a good servant who happened to acquire decent manners in the household of a decent master (Alexander I)."[7]

Few denied Uvarov's considerable intellectual abilities. He had been schooled in the best principles of the European Enlightenment by an émigré French abbé. Like many of his caste, Uvarov was perfectly fluent in French, and he easily mastered German (the poet Goethe was one of his correspondents), English, and Italian as well. As a child of the late eighteenth century, Uvarov also shared his age's passion for Greek and Latin; throughout his career with the education ministry, he relentlessly supported the classics. If his pedagogical orientation was thoroughly Western, Uvarov's lineage claimed Eastern roots, which may have influenced his attitudes. According to the official tsarist genealogical reference, his family's origins lay with one Minchak Kosaev, a Tatar chief who had transferred his allegiance from the Golden Horde to Muscovy's Grand Prince Vasilii Dmitrievich in the fifteenth century.[8]

As a youth, Uvarov impressed Alexander I with his precocious intelligence, and he entered the foreign service in 1801 at the tender age of sixteen. His duties were not onerous. In 1802–3, Uvarov even found the time to spend a year at Göttingen's renowned university, then a leading center of early German Romanticism and, not coincidentally, orientology. Three years later, the young diplomat was appointed a secretary at the Russian embassy in Vienna. His aristocratic good looks and charm made him a favorite guest in the city's salons, and he easily befriended such leading intellectual lights as Madame de Staël and Charles-Joseph, Prince de Ligne.

Toward the end of his Austrian posting, Uvarov also got to know Friedrich von Schlegel. Fascinated by Johann Gottfried Herder's ideas about civilization's Indian origins, Schlegel had spent several years in Paris studying Sanskrit before moving to Vienna in 1809 when he became disillusioned with Napoleon. While still in Paris, Schlegel published his influential *Über die Sprache und Weisheit der Indier* (On the Language and Wisdom of the

Indians). Reiterating the ideas of such writers as William Jones and Herder, its author argued that European and Near Eastern learning, literature, and religion could all be traced back to ancient India. Schlegel then went on to make a startling prediction about an "Oriental Renaissance." According to his logic, much as several centuries earlier the rediscovery of Greek and Latin texts had taken the West out of the Dark Ages, translations of Sanskrit literature would entirely rejuvenate modern thought by reuniting the Occidental world with its Oriental wellsprings. Schlegel therefore urged his contemporaries to turn their attention eastward: "If approached with the same dedication . . . the study of India will have an effect on Europe no less profound and wide-ranging [as the Renaissance]."[9]

Raymond Schwab reminds us that the *Renaissance orientale* intrigued the German Romantic imagination.[10] Sergei Uvarov was similarly captivated. Returning to Russia later in 1809, he quickly set to writing about a "projet d'une académie asiatique" to be set up in St. Petersburg.[11] The proposed Asian academy's goals were grandiose, involving nothing less than revitalizing a Europe ravaged by revolution and war. Echoing Schlegel's recent tract, Uvarov suggested that this could only be achieved by relearning the primordial wisdom of India, "humanity's cradle." Eastern antiquity, he believed, was the best antidote to the contemporary West's odious ideologies: "Here we can find the knowledge most capable of destroying modern philosophies."[12] Underscoring his conservative rationale, Uvarov proclaimed: "Exhausted by the sanguinary excesses committed in the name of the human spirit, we yearn for one of those shocks that might renew it. We are called upon to preserve the enormous debris [of European civilization], to rebuild it, and not to construct some new edifice." At the very least, he added, the academy "would wisely employ restless minds."[13]

The northern capital was the most logical site for an Asian academy. After all, "Russia, so to speak, reclines on Asia. An immense land frontier puts it in direct contact with nearly all of the Orient's peoples." Uvarov confidently asserted that "among all European nations, Russia is best qualified to study Asia."[14] He also appealed to patriotic sentiments: "The time has come for the august protection His Majesty Emperor Alexander I has accorded to enlightenment to be extended to Asia, and, by raising it the level of the other nations, Russia might surpass them with the means at its disposal."[15] Uvarov stressed that his academy was not solely to be devoted to esoteric pursuits, since it would also provide "a very practical benefit [by] training the interpreters we need for our relations with Turkey, Persia, Georgia and China." Indeed, "never has *raison d'état* conformed so closely to the sublime exigencies of moral civilization."[16]

The academy's provisional structure reflected the current German obsession with philology. With the advice of Heinrich-Julius Klaproth, a Prussian orientologist at the Imperial Academy of Sciences, Uvarov proposed courses in Asia's major languages and literatures, with four separate sections for Chinese and Manchu; Arabic, Persian, Turkish, and Tatar; Hebrew; and, of course, those of India, "the most ancient, interesting, yet least known of all."[17] The author hastened to add that all of the proposed school's students would also be taught Greek and Latin, "the two foundations on which all possible knowledge rests."[18]

Had Uvarov's project been approved, it would certainly have been Europe's most comprehensive establishment for studying Asia. In 1810, the year he published his brochure, the only European institutions dedicated to teaching Eastern languages were the Ecole spéciale des langues vivantes orientales, which had been founded in Paris fifteen years earlier, and the Orientalische Akademie, a Viennese college for training dragomans (diplomatic interpreters). Elsewhere, individual chairs in Oriental letters were scattered among various universities.

Stripped of its lofty rhetoric, the basic idea of an institute devoted to orientology in the Russian capital was hardly original. After meeting Peter the Great, Gottfried Leibniz had recognized Russia's unique potential as a scholarly intermediary between East and West. In the eighteenth century, Georg-Jacob Kehr, Mikhail Lomonosov, and the Serbian educational reformer Theodor Jankovich de Mirjevo had penned proposals for Asian language schools in St. Petersburg. They had all likewise stressed Russia's proximity to the East. Kehr specifically cited the need to train specialists to help "extend the empire's southern reaches," meaning in the direction of Ottoman Turkey and the central Asian khanates.[19] And in 1802, Count Jan Potocki, a Polish diplomatic advisor to Alexander I, had composed a memorandum for an "académie asiatique."[20] (Given the similarities with his own project, Uvarov had almost certainly read it.)

Uvarov's invocation of the timeless Orient as a talisman to guard against subversive Occidental radicalism and revolution was more original. The nineteenth century would see a great debate in Russia between the Slavophiles, those who sought a return to their nation's Byzantine and Orthodox roots, and the Westernizers, who advocated European modernity. Uvarov was one of the first to look even further east, beyond Christendom, to buttress the traditional order. He would not be the last.

Uvarov's proposal shared the same fate as the earlier plans and remained unrealized. It was simply too premature for a nation whose educational system was still in its infancy.[21] Anyway, the autocracy soon had far more pressing concerns when Napoleon marched his Grande Armée into Russia. Nevertheless, unlike its predecessors, the proposal did not languish in the archives. Ambitious and endowed with a flair for self-promotion, Uvarov arranged for a hundred copies to be printed in the autumn of 1810 and circulated them widely, both in Russia and abroad. According to Cynthia Whittaker, they caught the attention of Napoleon, Schlegel, the tsar's influential sister Grand Duchess Ekaterina Pavlovna, and a number of prominent European orientologists, while Goethe wrote its author an enthusiastic reply.[22]

The generally favorable response did much to help Uvarov's career—not to mention his marriage to the education minister's daughter, also in 1810. Within a year his new father-in-law appointed him superintendent of the St. Petersburg Educational District, and he also soon won election to the Academy of Sciences. The catty comments of contemporaries notwithstanding, Uvarov proved to be an able administrator. By 1818 he was made president of the Academy of Sciences, a post he held until his death in 1855. Meanwhile, as St. Petersburg's superintendent, he played the leading role in transforming its teachers' college into a proper university.[23]

Throughout his career with the education ministry, Uvarov enthusiastically championed the development of orientology in Russia. In 1818, a year before the capital's university was founded, he established chairs in Persian and Arabic at its predecessor. On Sylvestre de Sacy's advice, Uvarov recruited two of the French scholar's students, Jean-François Demange and François Bernard Charmoy, offering them lavish wages to teach Arabic and Persian, respectively. The following year he also engaged Mirza Jafar Topchibaev, a Georgian-born subject of the tsar fluent in Persian and Turkish, as an instructor for conversational practice.[24]

At a special ceremony on March 22, 1818, to inaugurate orientology along with a chair in world history at St. Petersburg's future university, Uvarov delivered a lengthy speech reaffirming many of the views he had set out in his *projet* eight years earlier about Asia as civilization's progenitor. Russians must study Eastern languages, he stressed, to "stay close to the riches of this inexhaustible source of human wisdom."[25] Yet if Uvarov invoked a more sublime purpose, his superiors regarded Oriental letters purely in terms of the autocracy's practical need for qualified diplomats.[26] It would take another half century for his beloved Sanskrit to be taught in the capital. The languages first offered, Arabic and Persian, were directly linked to Alexander I's strategic interests (his reign saw campaigns against both Turkey and Persia).

The year 1818 also saw Uvarov establish the Asian Museum in St. Petersburg.[27] The previous year, Kazan's former professor of Oriental letters, Christian-Martin Frähn, had temporarily been hired to organize the many Eastern artifacts held by the Academy of Sciences. Since its beginnings as part of Peter the Great's Kunstkamer, the collection had grown tremendously over the past century. By now it comprised some twenty thousand coins, rare Islamic manuscripts, Buddhist xylographs, and an impressive library of European Orientalia, as well as East Asian objets d'art. Immediately upon his election as the academy's new president, Uvarov, recognizing their great importance to scholarship, began organizing a separate institution to house them. Officially founded in December 1818, with Frähn as its first director, the Asian Museum was the first institution at the academy devoted specifically to the East.

Although its holdings continued to grow, for much of the nineteenth century the museum was modestly staffed. Frähn, who headed it until 1842, was assisted only by a single deputy, and his successor, Bernhard Dorn, repeatedly appealed to the academy for more help during his forty-year tenure, with little success. Both reclusive antiquarians by temperament, neither Frähn nor—even more so—Dorn were overly enthusiastic about working with students or other scholars, and they devoted their considerable energies to cataloguing and studying the collection under their care. As a result, the Asian Museum played second fiddle to St. Petersburg University for most of its existence.

Uvarov's promotion of orientology was not without its setbacks. At St.

Petersburg University, the careers of the French duo he had hired were soon jeopardized when the dark clouds of obscurantist mystical piety that had enveloped Kazan's campus began to smother intellectual life there as well. The new education minister, Prince Aleksandr Golitsyn, was of the same mind about the dangers of alien Western secular ideas as his superintendent in Kazan, Mikhail Magnitskii. The writer and historian Nikolai Karamzin—no liberal himself—quipped that, under Golitsyn, the prince's department became the "Ministry of the Eclipse" (rather than "Enlightenment," as Russians call education).[28]

In 1821, on the pretext of a minor disturbance by some teenaged students at St. Petersburg University's preparatory school, Golitsyn engineered Uvarov's ouster as superintendent and replaced him with Dmitrii Runich, a former head of the Russian postal system. Aping Magnitskii's recent assault on Kazan's faculty, Runich now began to root out professors in St. Petersburg that he deemed politically unreliable. When the new superintendent convened a secret university assembly in midsummer and called upon instructors to condemn their colleagues publicly, Demange and Charmoy indignantly tendered their resignations.[29]

The "professors' affair," as Runich's purge came to be known, cost St. Petersburg's nascent university dearly. Of the twenty on the faculty, eleven were either fired or left of their own accord, while half of the students were expelled. Runich had also wanted to liquidate Oriental letters at the institution altogether, on the grounds that the Ministry of Foreign Affairs was also now teaching the subject. However, a faculty committee rejected his proposal. Indeed, because of that department's urgent demand for diplomats proficient in Near Eastern languages, none of the students enrolled in Arabic and Persian had been among those sent packing.[30]

As with Mirza Kazem-Bek at Kazan, the unhappy turn of events on St. Petersburg's campus came as a blessing for an ambitious outsider with the right abilities. Better known (and reviled) as the acid-tongued editor of a popular journal, over the next decade the university's leading scholar would be a flamboyant Pole, Osip Senkovskii. A man of multiple identities, he had entered the world in 1800 as Józef-Julian Sękowski, the son of an impoverished aristocrat living near Vilnius, and subsequently Russified his name upon settling in the imperial capital. Further muddying the waters,

Senkovskii also published under a variety of pseudonyms, including Baron Brambeus, Tutundju-Oglu-Mustafa-Aga, and Bitterwasser.[31]

Like his contemporary, the Kazan Mongolian specialist Osip Kovalevskii, Senkovskii had studied at Vilnius University with such prominent professors as the historian Joachim Lelewel and the classicist Gottfried Groddeck. Yet if he moved in similar circles, and also befriended the poet Adam Mickiewicz, Senkovskii had remained entirely unmoved by the university's nationalist fervor. His compatriots eventually reviled him for not sharing their ardent desire to free themselves from tsarist rule, particularly in the wake of the failed revolt of 1830 (which Senkovskii repudiated with typically venomous satire).[32] But Aleksandr Herzen had been wrong to label him a *polonais russifié*.[33] In truth, Senkovskii was far too cynical to be loyal to any flag.[34]

It was as a student at Vilnius that Senkovskii had come under the East's spell. Although the university did not have a chair in Oriental letters, both Groddeck and Lelewel had studied Arabic because of their respective interests in philology and history, and they encouraged some of their brighter charges to learn the language too.[35] According to Senkovskii, Groddeck lectured that: "the East explains Greece and Greece explains the East. They rose, flourished, and fell together," going on to urge, "Rummage through their ruins . . . there you will find treasures still hidden from the modern mind."[36] Senkovskii heeded the advice and mastered Arabic so thoroughly that in 1818, a year before his graduation, he published a Polish translation from the Arabic of the pre-Islamic sage Luqmān's fables. He also made good progress in Turkish, Persian, and Hebrew during his undergraduate years.

Impressed by Senkovskii's preternatural linguistic skills, and hoping that he might become Vilnius's first orientologist, his professors encouraged him to continue his language study in the Near East. Eager to escape a disastrous recent marriage, Senkovskii needed little urging. The only obstacle was his family's parlous financial state. The university's librarian, Kazimierz Kontrym, hit on a novel solution: he circulated an appeal asking thirty persons to each buy a thirty-ruble share to pay for the trip. In return, subscribers would receive an account of the journey as well as a revised, Polish version of a recent French work, Mouradja d'Ohsson's *Tableau général de l'Empire othoman*.

Kontrym's scheme was a success, and with 900 rubles in his pocket Senkovskii left Vilnius for Constantinople on September 1, 1819.[37] After an unpleasant overland journey through Ukraine to the Black Sea port of Odessa (there were the typical complaints about the bad roads, the squalor, the filth, and the mess), the young traveler reached the Turkish metropolis by January. Life here was more to his liking. Not only was the climate quite pleasant, but Senkovskii also soon met the wealthy Polish amateur orientologist, Count Wacław Rzewuski. The count took an instant liking to his countryman and introduced him to the tsar's envoy to the Porte, Baron Grigorii Stroganov. The latter clearly shared Rzewuski's favorable opinion, since he promptly offered Senkovskii a position as a dragoman at the Russian mission.

The job did not hinder the youth's peregrinations. Baron Stroganov wanted his new interpreter to continue working on his languages, and sent him on a tour of the Levant. Senkovskii's first stop was a Maronite college near Beirut, where he spent half a year learning under its rector, el-Khuri Antun Arida, a distinguished retired University of Vienna professor.[38] The Pole left a colorful description of his stay: "By the sweat of my brow, I hauled my books from one peak to the next—they were my sole possession. I shredded my throat in the wilderness, trying to perfect the purity of my Arabic pronunciation. . . . With the same desperation, when I returned to my cell in some Maronite monastery, I poured all my strength into toiling over Syrian and Arabic manuscripts from a learned monk's humble library. . . . Two, at most, three hours of sleep on a bare slab, with a dictionary as my pillow, were enough to reinvigorate me for my renewed labors."[39] While this account should be read with a grain of salt, Senkovskii's studies did take their toll on his health, and he had to cut his stay short in November 1820.

Senkovskii continued traveling south, via Acre and Jerusalem, to Cairo. Here he ingratiated himself with Suleiman Pasha, the French-born chief of the Egyptian army's general staff, and he was soon moving in the highest circles. The wave of Egyptomania that had swept Europe in the wake of Napoleon's ill-fated expedition left the young Pole entirely cold. He found the pyramids at Giza overrated, and scorned the "caravans of collectors," who paid exorbitant prices for dusty fragments of the past.[40] Nevertheless, Senkovskii was put out when the Greek revolt resulted in a diplomatic breach between Turkey and Russia, forcing him to leave Cairo in the summer of 1821. While he sympathized with the Greek cause, he shared none of his contemporaries' Byronic passion for the rebels. Rather than seeing them as romantic freedom fighters, the Hellenic insurgents he encountered during his homeward cruise through the Aegean Sea struck him as a rabble of cocky pirates.[41]

One explicit goal of Senkovskii's journey had been to gather Turkish sources about Poland's past. Kontrym's call for sponsors would have had a familiar ring to Russian ears a few decades later: "If we think about our origins and the relations our forefathers had with Eastern peoples in ages past, we readily see that many of our customs and institutions, and even some of our language and history, can only be understood by studying the Orient."[42] Senkovskii eagerly obliged, and early during his trip he wrote an article "On the Origins of the Polish *Szlachta* [Gentry]." The essay, which did not endear him to his teachers in Vilnius, argued that the upper classes were descended from remnants of the Mongol hordes that had swept into Poland six hundred years earlier and were therefore entirely alien to the nation's Slavic masses.

Senkovskii raised more Polish hackles in 1824 with the first volume of his *Collectanea* (Miscellany) of Turkish documents relevant to the former kingdom's history. Since they quite naturally explained relations between the two powers from the Ottoman perspective, patriots were outraged. Mickiewicz angrily condemned the work as "a grievous sin" and "a profanation."[43] Senkovskii was no more respectful of Russian shibboleths. After moving to St. Petersburg, he published articles that questioned the authenticity of the twelfth-century *Song of Igor's Campaign*, argued that Scandinavian sagas were a better source for Russian history than the *Primary Chronicle*, and likened the balls at the Assembly of the Nobility to the mating rituals of fireflies (earning a stern rebuke from Nicholas I's security chief, Count Benckendorff).[44]

Because of the rupture in relations with Turkey, Senkovskii's status with the foreign office was unclear when he reached St. Petersburg in the autumn of 1821. Once again, his patron Count Rzewuski intervened, recommending him to the foreign minister as a translator. The northern capital initially held little charm for Senkovskii. In a letter to Lelewel he likened it to "a beautiful woman, secluded in dark, dank, and insalubrious cave."[45] He began to see it in a better light when Runich's purge at the university unexpectedly opened new doors to him. With Charmoy and Demanges on their way out, both chairs for Oriental letters would soon be vacant. Senkovskii applied for the position in Arabic, but some administrators objected on the grounds that, at twenty-two years of age, he was far too young. A few months later, however, when Vilnius University extended him an offer, the education minister immediately matched it on the grounds of diplomatic exigency. As for the objections to Senkovskii's youth, they were handily overcome by subtracting two years from the birth date on his service record.[46]

Senkovskii set out his teaching philosophy in his inaugural lecture at St. Petersburg University on August 18, 1822.[47] He duly paid homage to Sylvestre de Sacy, "the father of all orientologists," whose textbook he would assign. At the same time, the newly minted professor explained that Arabic grammars approached the subject better than the European ones, adding that the language could only really be mastered by studying the former. He also criticized the assumption that there was a distinction between classical and modern (or "vulgar") Arabic. These were no more different than the literary and spoken versions of any Western language. In short, those who wanted to read and write modern Arabic had to learn it from the classics, "the way it is done in the East."

Senkovskii occupied his university chair for twenty-five years. During the first decade he was a dedicated teacher and a productive scholar. In addition to offering courses in Arabic, he also unofficially taught Turkish. Nor did he limit himself to language; he was the first to lecture about Near Eastern literature and geography. To one student, Senkovskii was "a living encyclopedia of the Orient," while another enthused, "He dealt with the dry subject of linguistics in such an interesting way that, before you knew it, the two-hour lesson was over."[48] Although his enrollments were modest, Senkovskii did train several successful orientologists, most notably the university's first historian of Asia, Vasilii Grigor'ev. Meanwhile, in addition to his two-volume *Collectanea,* Senkovskii also published a French translation of an early eighteenth-century history of Bukhara that won Sacy's praise.[49]

Senkovskii's best-known contribution to the field was also his most notorious. In 1827 an odd letter appeared in Faddei Bulgarin's new daily,

Severnaia Pchela (The Northern Bee). It purported to be from Tutundju-Oglu-Mustafa-Aga, "veritable Turkish philosopher" from Jaffa, who had been reduced to selling soap in the Gostinnyi Dvor, the St. Petersburg arcade.[50] One day, while sorting through scraps of paper to wrap his wares, the merchant happened to glance at a discarded copy of *Sur les origines russes* (On the Origins of the Russians) by the Austrian Arabist Joseph Freiherr von Hammer-Purgstall. Curiosity got the better of him, and Tutundju-Oglu began to read the piece, growing indignant at its many errors and mistranslations. In fact, the "letter" was a blistering attack on Hammer-Purgstall's study of Near Eastern sources about ancient Russia. Subsequently translated into French and English, Senkovskii's pseudonymous review was widely read. According to one of his students, the numismatist Pavel Savel'ev, orientologists tended to agree with the assessment but found its scathing tone impolitic.[51]

As a scholar, Senkovskii viewed the East through a relatively objective lens. "History is not fiction," he insisted. Its practitioners must study events from all sources, including "the stories of enemies." Senkovskii commanded: "Audi alteram partem!" (Listen to the other side).[52] He did not doubt that the Orient was an other.[53] Asians saw the world "according to different principles and an alternative logic." Indeed, East and West were "separate planets."[54] At various times the professor described the former as immoral, despotic, and unchanging. Sharing little of the enchantment with China of his contemporary, the Sinologist Father Hyacinth, he regarded its government as "the most cowardly in Asia." The Middle Kingdom's ideology, Confucianism, was nothing more than a "Machiavellian masquerade of patriarchal benevolence" used by the Qing dynasty to brainwash its 362 million subjects into submission.[55] As for Sanskrit (whose Russian champion, Count Uvarov, was no friend), the language was vastly overrated.[56]

Senkovskii's attitudes toward the Near East were more ambivalent. While he viewed Islam as fanatical and destructive to culture, he nevertheless considered it the most advanced religion in the East.[57] Meanwhile, he believed that the Ottoman political order was "not as stupid" as many Europeans made it out to be. In fact, Turks had "a profound understanding of civic freedom." As a conservative, Senkovskii saw their hostility to "dreamy Western theories" as a virtue, since it safeguarded them from unrest. He also commended the reforms of Turkey's current sultan Mahmud II (r. 1808–39), which, with a rare absence of irony, he approvingly implied paralleled those of his own sovereign, Nicholas I.[58] This did not mean, however, that Russia was Asian. "Paris resembles St. Petersburg," he wrote. "By contrast, St. Petersburg and Constantinople, Europeans [including Russians] and Turks are entirely irreconcilable opposites."[59]

Sometime in the early 1830s Senkovskii's academic ardor began to cool. Scholarship has a long gestation period, and its rewards require great patience. For an ambitious and talented young man with a quick pen, they did not come fast enough at the university. And, as the cultural center of a great empire, St. Petersburg offered other, more immediate outlets for those with a knack for writing well.

Soon after arriving in the capital, Senkovskii had looked up an acquaintance from his student days in Vilnius, Faddei Bulgarin (Tadeusz Bułharyn). Because of Bulgarin's association with Nicholaevan literary repression in the wake of the abortive Decembrist revolt of 1825, the transplanted Pole has generally come to be regarded as, in D. S. Mirsky's words, "a vile sycophant whom all honest men abhorred."[60] What made him all the more reprehensible to many was that, before 1825, Bulgarin had moved within the same liberal milieu as a number of future Decembrists. Together with Nikolai Grech, another commercial author of dubious politics, Senkovskii and Bulgarin have often been lumped together as a venal triumvirate of reactionary Russian letters in Nicholas I's early reign (a.k.a. the "reptile press"). This may be unfair to Senkovskii. His American biographer points out that he was never particularly close to Bulgarin, and their relationship grew distinctly frosty over the years.[61] Distasteful as his cruel wit may have seemed to many in those gloomy days, Senkovskii certainly was no toady. He was far too irreverent to be an autocrat's literary lapdog.

In any case, it was the earlier, more progressive Bulgarin whom Senkovskii first had befriended in 1821. Bulgarin, who was eleven years older, saw himself as a mentor to his compatriot. When Bulgarin launched his journal *Severnyi Arkhiv* (The Northern Archive) the next year, he included one of the young professor's travel accounts, and he also introduced him to a number of other writers. More reminiscences of Senkovskii's recent trip as well as his Oriental tales now began to appear in various periodicals.

St. Petersburg's readers shared the European fascination for the Near East, providing the prolific Pole with a ready audience. They eagerly devoured his stories, such as "The Bedouin," "A Lesson for Ingrates," and "The Thief." One of them, "Antar" inspired a symphonic suite by Nikolai Rimsky-Korsakov in 1868. Pushkin was "enchanted" with "The Knight of the Dun-Colored Steed," while the poet's friend Wilhelm Küchelbecker ranked Senkovskii among the top four writers in Russia.[62] The professor-turned-author would continue to write Orientalist prose until his retirement. Much more than in his scholarship, the East of Senkovskii's literary imagination abounds with Orientalist clichés of immobility, violence, beauty, and unbridled sexuality. He also played the part, as a visitor noted in 1839: "The study was furnished in an Oriental style, and in its depths, amidst a multitude of motley cushions, reclined [Senkovskii]. . . . He was usually dressed in a blue Albanian jacket and red Turkish trousers. A red fez adorned his head. On the carpet stood a crystal hookah, through which [he] emitted a stream of aromatic smoke."[63]

If Senkovskii capitalized on his age's romantic fashion for the exotic East, he could not help ridiculing it at the same time.[64] His most popular work, *The Fantastic Journeys of Baron Brambeus,* poked fun at both Orientalist prose and scholarship.[65] Published in 1833, the novel is a picaresque tale about the travels of a civil servant of the tenth *chin* whose outlandish adventures recall those of Rudolf Raspe's fictionalized Baron von Münchausen.[66] Like the protagonists of Pushkin's *The Prisoner of the Caucasus* and Lermontov's *Hero of Our Time,* Baron Brambeus is the archetypal jaded Romantic of gentle birth who has grown disillusioned with city life and flees to the Orient in search of excitement. Arriving in Constantinople, the baron immediately has an affair with the erotically hypercharged daughter of a dragoman, "who fell for me with all the passion and sultriness of the Orient." So fiery is their lovemaking that it burns down an entire suburb. Two other voyages lampoon Egyptology and, anticipating Edward Said in a satiric vein, exaggerated notions of the "Other's" alterity in accounts of alien lands. Obscure now, in its day *The Fantastic Journeys* enjoyed tremendous popularity and made the author "one of Russia's first cult heroes" among the reading public.[67]

Senkovskii's literary success spurred him on in his new career. In 1834 he founded the *Biblioteka dlia chteniia* (The Library for Reading), a popular monthly that was the prototype for the "thick journals," encyclopedic monthlies filled with hundreds of pages of news, scholarship, literature and criticism that became a staple of nineteenth-century Russian intellectual life. *Biblioteka dlia chteniia* was a profitable venture for many years, and it published the works of nearly all important writers, from Pushkin to Dostoyevsky. At the same time, its reviews, many of which Senkovskii wrote himself, spared no one from their savage sarcasm. *Biblioteka dlia chteniia*'s overtly commercial aims (and success), not to mention its conservative politics, made its editor one of the intelligentsia's leading bêtes noires. Most would have heartily seconded one author's opinion of him as "the clown of [Russian] letters . . . a fanciful orientologist and linguist, plagiarizing novelist, court jester critic, the most contrary of our literary figures."[68]

Never in the best of health, Senkovskii retired from both his university chair and his journal's editorship in his late forties, and he died a decade later in 1858. A man of contradictory, often paradoxical opinions, he was the Dr. Jekyll and Mr. Hyde of Russian Orientalism. As a scholar, Senkovskii was Russia's leading Arabist during the nineteenth century's first half and, according to Vasilii Barthold, "the founding father of the Petersburg school of Orientology."[69] His most important achievement, however, was to introduce his adoptive compatriots to Near Eastern literature.[70] Despite these accomplishments, the professor also had a strong streak of intellectual nihilism. His vicious assaults on fellow scholars and writers alike were among the less edifying features of Russian culture under Nicholas I.

Despite Senkovskii's gradual abandonment of his teaching in the 1830s, St. Petersburg University continued to offer courses in Arabic, Turkish, and Persian. During his years as education minister from 1833 to 1849, Count Uvarov remained a strong supporter of orientology at the campus. His statute for higher learning of 1835 also provided for Mongolian and Tatar, although these would not be offered for another decade. Meanwhile, because of the difficult campaign to subdue the Caucasus, Armenian, Georgian, and Azeri were also added to the curriculum in 1844.[71]

The university often employed learned native speakers to teach Asian languages. They included Mirza Jafar Topchibaev, who was promoted after Runich's pogrom; Sheikh Muhammad Ayad al-Tantavi, a professor from Cairo's al-Azhar University; and Mirza Kazem-Bek, the Iranian it poached from Kazan in 1849. According to one historian, during its thirty-five-year existence only three out of the eighteen who taught at St. Petersburg University's Department (*razriad*) of Oriental Letters were Russians, compared to seven of Asian origin (the others were mostly Polish, German, and French).[72] It was not unusual that foreigners be so dominant; they were vastly overrepresented in the imperial capital's academic institutions in the early nineteenth century. What *was* unique was that so many of them came from the East rather than the West.

Until midcentury, the razriad's enrollments remained modest, and Kazan overshadowed its place in orientology. All of this changed on October 22, 1854, when Nicholas I signed a decree to promote the St. Petersburg department to a faculty. Kazan's chairs were closed down, and most of its instructors and the more promising students, as well as the bulk of the library's Orientalia, were all transferred to St. Petersburg University. The decision to concentrate orientology in the capital had actually been made three years earlier, but jurisdictional squabbles with the foreign ministry caused considerable delays.

Nicholas's proclamation had not been some autocratic whim. According to his new education minister, Avraam Norov, St. Petersburg was the most suitable location for teaching Asian languages since "it offers more resources to promote orientology."[73] But the real reason had more to do with the autocracy's growing need for expertise about the East, where tsarism continued to pursue an expansionist course. Not only did the empire take up arms against Turkey in 1853, but the Caucasian insurgency also continued to rage. Meanwhile, the Qing dynasty's growing vulnerability opened up new opportunities on the Amur River in the Far East.

The move was justified internally on the grounds that, in 1844 the tsar had commanded that every year five students from Trans-Caucasia be sent to St. Petersburg University to be trained as translators.[74] When enrollments in Kazan's Department of Oriental Letters plummeted around 1850, the education ministry began to consider concentrating all teaching about Asia in a central location to ensure a steady supply of adequately trained officials. St. Petersburg soon emerged as the logical choice.

In its first incarnation, as the Department of Oriental Languages in St. Petersburg University's Faculty of History and Philology, the St. Petersburg school had been Kazan's smaller sibling. The latter, both because of its role then as the autocracy's "window on the East," as well as the enthusiastic support of its leading administrators, had become the leading center for Asian scholarship in Russia if not in Europe during the first half of the nineteenth century. Nevertheless, by 1850, St. Petersburg's professors had established a strong base. Their university was well prepared to assume the mantle of orientological leadership when the tsar took it westward from the Volga to the Neva.

The St. Petersburg school's early decades also left another important legacy. Katya Hokanson has observed that "in Russia, the best-known Orientalists were not necessarily the true scholars, but actually the ones who were intelligent enough to capitalize on the interests in Orientalists and things Oriental that existed in Russia as a result of Western Europe's enthusiasms."[75] Situated in what was the empire's cultural center, the university influenced Russian letters in an age when the East was particularly fashionable. And when its most prominent professor, Osip Senkovskii, turned to more literary endeavors in the 1830s, he did much to stir the interest of writers such as Pushkin and Lermontov in the Orient. Despite his strong streak of nihilism, this was ultimately the most important contribution he made.

8

THE ORIENTAL FACULTY

Nowhere is better suited for fostering Oriental languages than St. Petersburg. . . . Here the passionate poetry of the Arabs, the sumptuous literature of Persia and Turkey, the speculative teachings of the Buddhists, the holy language of the Jews and the hieroglyphs of the Chinese all have their interpreters, their ardent proponents.

—A. V. Popov

A curious structure stands in Staraia Derevnia, at St. Petersburg's northern edge. On 91 Primorskii Prospekt, the busy thoroughfare that stretches along the Bolshaia Nevka River's right bank, a three-story block of roughly faceted grayish violet granite, topped by bands of vivid yellow, blue, and red brick, rises amid the trees of what had once been a quiet neighborhood of dachas. On closer inspection, the edifice displays features startlingly out of place in Russia's most westernized city. The unsuspecting visitor who enters by its southern gate will be puzzled by a massive four-pillar portico entirely unlike the neoclassical variants favored by nineteenth-century Russian architects. Instead of the standard-issue white columns, rectangular pillars and intricate Tibetan capitals support a bright red frieze bearing mirrored discs to ward off evil spirits. Above it rests a gilded eight-spoke dharma wheel flanked by a pair of fallow deer, while two brass cylinders symbolizing Buddhism's victory adorn the roof. With its sternly angular facade, inward sloping lines, flat roof, and exotic details, the building's architecture can best be described as a blend of Petersburg *moderne* and Lhasa traditional.

Consecrated in 1915 by the Buriat Lama Agvan Dorzhiev, the temple in Staraia Derevnia did not enjoy an easy birth. At the turn of the twentieth century, Dorzhiev had served as the Thirteenth Dalai Lama's emissary to the Romanov court, and it was on his initiative that the Buddhist *datsan,* or monastic house of worship, had been built. The temple was meant for St. Petersburg's small community of Buriats and Kalmyks, Asian minorities faithful to the Yellow Hat Buddhism of Tibet, much as a variety of churches, synagogues, and a mosque ministered to the spiritual needs of the other creeds represented in the multiethnic empire's capital.[1]

Nicholas II had approved the datsan in early 1909, in the wake of the 1905 October Manifesto's promise of religious toleration, but it soon roused the ire of some less open-minded Russians. The Orthodox Synod objected that the site's location near the old Blagoveshchensk Church and cemetery might offend its believers, while others worried that the "idolatrous temple" would propagate "paganism" in the heart of Christian Russia. At the same time, reports that the Japanese embassy was subsidizing the Buddhist venture aroused fears of the pan-Mongolist specter. Under strong pressure from the interior ministry's Department of Foreign Creeds, Nicholas II's premier, Petr Stolypin, convinced the tsar to reverse the decision within a few months. Objecting to "the difficulty of placing [the datsan's] Buddhist residents under civilian surveillance because of its distance from the city center," Stolypin arranged to have construction effectively halted.[2]

The temple did have some influential friends. Not long after buying the Staraia Derevnia site, Lama Dorzhiev had astutely invited a number of prominent orientologists to join an advisory committee. Headed by Fedor Shcherbatskoi, a Sanskritist from St. Petersburg University's Faculty of Oriental Languages, the group included two of his colleagues specializing in Mongolian, as well as Academicians Sergei Oldenburg and Vasilii Radlov. Dorzhiev also tapped the artist Nikolai Roerich and a newspaper publisher with a passion for Buddhist art, Prince Esper Ukhtomskii. It was a wise move, for the scholars proved to be the project's most effective advocates. Shcherbatskoi and Oldenburg both appealed to Stolypin to allow work on the temple to proceed. Their pleas initially fell on deaf ears, but by luck Shcherbatskoi's wife happened to be related to the interior minister's deputy, Sergei Kryzhanovskii. When the latter interceded, Stolypin gave way.

The protests quickly resumed with renewed fury. Typical of their vitriol was a pamphlet by Archimandrite Varlaam, who thundered, "The power of darkness and the reign of the Antichrist are upon us, since a temple of idolaters has opened in . . . the capital. . . . This is nothing less than the ancient dragon-serpent's assault on Christ."[3] Meanwhile, the Department of Foreign Creeds spared no effort in trying to sabotage the project, policemen repeatedly warned their superiors of Buddhist subversion, and more malicious individuals sent anonymous death threats to Dorzhiev. By contrast, St. Petersburg's orientologists continued to be enthusiastic supporters of the datsan. When Dorzhiev led a lavish benediction service on August 10, 1915, Oldenburg and Shcherbatskoi, as well as other distinguished scholars, attended the ceremony. Shortly after the October Revolution of 1917, the two academics successfully petitioned the Cheka to spare Dorzhiev's life following the lama's arrest on charges of smuggling valuables across the border. Shcherbatskoi proved unable, however, to prevent the temple, which had been placed in his care, from being pillaged by Red Army troops during the subsequent Civil War.

The role of many of St. Petersburg's leading orientologists in defending the religious rights of the empire's Buddhist minorities during the temple controversy was no aberration. Indeed, as orientology became established as a discipline in the tsarist academy, its practitioners tended to respect the cultures and peoples they studied. There were exceptions, particularly in the Orthodox Church's institutions of higher learning, and many were not entirely free of their prejudices, but on the whole educators in Imperial Russia's university departments of Oriental letters rarely saw Asians as some inferior, contemptuous, or malevolent "other." Nowhere was this truer than at St. Petersburg, whose Faculty of Oriental Languages exercised a virtual monopoly in the field during the nineteenth century's latter half.

St. Petersburg University's Fakul'tet vostochnykh iazykov (Faculty of Oriental Languages) was formally inaugurated at noon on August 27, 1855. (By ironic coincidence, this was the very same hour when Britain and its allies launched their final assault on the Crimean bastion of Sevastopol.)[4] The new faculty boasted fourteen instructors in five sections for the languages of the Islamic Near East, Inner Asia, East Asia, and the Caucasus, as well as Hebrew. Chairs would subsequently be added for Sanskrit, Japanese, Korean, and Tibetan, as well as Asian history and Islamic law. Mirza Kazem-Bek, the first dean, could rightly boast in his opening address that "Nowhere else in Europe have as many orientologists ever gathered in one academic institution as here; nowhere else have all branches of Asia's languages and literatures ever been joined so closely as in our faculty. And, moreover, never have such numbers of native representatives of Eastern learning and Western scholars of the Orient ever been together in a single place as among us."[5]

The overwhelming majority of students entered the Near Eastern departments, whose languages were also in the greatest demand by the foreign ministry, their most likely future employer. Enrollments were often driven by Russian colonial expansion. The tsarist small wars in Turkestan from the 1860s to the 1880s drew even more undergraduates into the Arabic-Persian-Turco-Tatar section, while the drive in East Asia at the turn of the twentieth century encouraged many to sign up for Chinese and Manchu.[6]

Sometimes the curriculum was designed to send a diplomatic message. At the height of the Crimean War, the Asian Museum's director, Bernhard Dorn, offered courses in Afghan to remind London about the vulnerability of British India. He explained to Education Minister Avraam Norov that "The English, who so unjustly began their war against Russia, have long been terrified about Russia's advance in Central Asia. Afghanistan is the barrier between Russia and England's possessions in India. . . . [The English] tremble thinking that Russia might take a step there. . . . England's Parliament will be stunned when it learns that Afghan is being publicly taught in Russia.[7]

Like most of the students, the education ministry saw St. Petersburg's Faculty of Oriental Languages primarily in vocational terms. A letter by the university's rector (a government appointee) in 1888 to the minister was typical of such attitudes: "Our civilizing mission in the East and the political confirmation of our power and influence in all corners of Asia will not succeed unless we carefully prepare for it, unless along with military measures we train men who know these regions, their way of life, beliefs and languages."[8] So important was the imperative to educate officials with knowledge of the East that, when the rest of St. Petersburg University was

shut down during the student disturbances of 1861, the orientology faculty received special dispensation from the tsar to stay open.[9]

Yet if the autocracy considered the faculty to be a tool for imperial ambitions, its professors often saw things differently. While the members of
Kazan University's Oriental Department had tended to regard their principal duty to be training interpreters and other government officials, St.
Petersburg's professors generally favored more scholarly aims. Dean Kazem-
Bek, who had begun his career at Kazan, was an exception. He often spoke
about the need to stress practical training over scholarship. But he was decidedly in the minority. Those who preferred the latter prevailed, and
within three years Kazem-Bek resigned as dean over the question.[10] In
1864 the newly hired historian Vasilii Grigor'ev wrote on behalf of his colleagues: "No matter how important, the Faculty's practical goals are only
part of its duties, and they accompany the most important task—just as in
all other faculties—namely the academic study and dissemination of
knowledge."[11] Even when Alexander III's university statute of 1884 tried
to stress the primacy of the Oriental faculty's vocational mission, its professors successfully parried the move.[12]

This did not mean that St. Petersburg's orientologists refused to serve
the state in more direct ways. Like members of other faculties, some also
held posts in various ministries and commissions.[13] Not surprisingly, Mirza
Kazem-Bek was particularly active in this regard. Beginning in 1850, he
advised the justice ministry on Islamic jurisprudence and even reviewed
individual rulings.[14] During the Crimean War, Kazem-Bek also taught
Turkish to army officers and produced language study aids for the General
Staff Academy.[15] The central Asian historian Vasilii Grigor'ev served the
interior ministry as head of its censorship section for five years, and also sat
on its Jewish commission.[16] Meanwhile, the Indologist Ivan Minaev
briefed the General Staff on affairs in Britain's South Asian colony.[17] But
most St. Petersburg professors preferred to focus on scholarship.

The autocracy's pressure on the faculty to serve its needs more directly
was unrelenting. In 1892 Education Minister Count Ivan Delianov asked
his superintendent of the Kiev district, the Turkologist Vladimir Vel'iaminov-
Zernov, to review the state of orientology at St. Petersburg University.
Vel'iaminov's report was not favorable. Focusing on Near Eastern languages, he found students' knowledge "mediocre at best" and their aca-

demic preparation "rather weak." In his opinion, the main problem was the practice of requiring everyone enrolled in the section to study all three major languages (Arabic, Persian and Turkic-Tatar) rather than fully mastering one of them.[18] Not surprisingly, the faculty vigorously rebutted Vel'iaminov's critique. If its graduates were inadequately prepared, they countered, that was largely due to insufficient resources. As for limiting them to a single language, that was pedagogically unsound because of the historical links between all three.[19]

Frustrated by his inability to bring the Oriental faculty to heel, the minister commissioned inquiry after inquiry, to little effect.[20] The most thoughtful analysis was by a Moscow University emeritus professor of Latin with an interest in Asian languages, Fedor Korsh. In his brief of 1896, Korsh pointed out that the shift away from vocational training was only natural: "Having gradually moved from the practical to the theoretical . . . the Oriental Faculty, which considers itself to be part of an institution of higher learning, has moved in step with Western scholars of the East. In carrying out their academic pursuits, [our orientologists] are paying less attention to practical matters." Castigating its professors for preferring scholarship to practical teaching was basically to say that "the Oriental Faculty is guilty for behaving like a university faculty." Ultimately, Korsh concluded, the minister's desire was unrealistic. If he wanted to train government officials in Asian languages, he should establish a practical institute to that end.[21]

Perhaps one reason St. Petersburg's professors were able to resist the autocracy was that there were alternatives, such as the Lazarev Institute for Oriental Languages in Moscow.[22] Established in 1814 by a prominent Armenian family as a school for fellow nationals, its curriculum featured the languages of the Near East and the Caucasus. Russians were also welcome, and as the state's interest in these regions grew during the nineteenth century, so did its involvement in the establishment. In 1871 Education Minister Count Dmitrii Tolstoi organized a special advanced three-year course at the Lazarev Institute modeled on St. Petersburg University's orientology curriculum, but with a much more practical orientation. Primarily aimed at training dragomans and consular officials, it included instruction in Arabic, Persian, and Turco-Tatar, with optional courses in Armenian and Georgian.

The autocracy's temporary infatuation with the Far East at the turn of the twentieth century inspired a similar initiative in Vladivostok.[23] The Trans-Siberian Railway, as well as equally ambitious plans in northern China in the wake of the 1896 alliance with the Qing dynasty, made the need for officials competent in East Asian languages particularly urgent. In 1899 Finance Minister Sergei Witte, the chief architect of Nicholas II's Pacific adventure, accordingly arranged for an Oriental Institute (*Vostochnyi institut*) to be opened in the port. With a mandate to prepare "individuals for administrative and commercial-economic activities," the school taught Chinese as well as Japanese, Korean, Mongolian, Manchu, and, beginning in 1906, Tibetan. Students flocked to Vladivostok's Oriental Institute, which by 1916 had graduated some three hundred civilians and over two hundred officers.

One of the most distinguished professors in St. Petersburg University's Oriental faculty was Vladimir Petrovich Vasil'ev, who taught Chinese there for nearly half a century. A product of the Kazan school, Vasil'ev continued many of its traditions in the capital, including the emphasis on language training in Asia, a strong reliance on primary sources, and an objective but not unsympathetic attitude toward the East. At the same time, the professor's outlook on the world, which combined scientific materialism, faith in progress, and oppositional political inclinations, were typical of Russia's post-Romantic intelligentsia.

Vasil'ev was born in 1818 in Nizhnyi Novgorod, a Volga market town upriver from Kazan. While his father was a minor functionary in the provincial administration, both parents came from the clerical caste, and the boy was first educated by a deacon in the family. Vasil'ev *père* soon recognized his son's talent for learning, and he began to prepare the boy for university by sending him to the city's gymnasium. Vladimir's ambitions were almost derailed when his father died in 1832, leaving his widow and children in straitened circumstances. As a result, the lad had to work for two years as a tutor both to support his mother and to save up for his studies.

Vasil'ev's early years were not happy. In a brief autobiography written late in life, he devoted three and a half pages to detailing its miseries and only a single paragraph to his professional accomplishments. His first memories were of deaths in the family, his stern father's beatings, and the hardships of poverty. He sardonically recalled that, as a child, "It occurred to me that the entire world had been created solely to torment me; that everything was illusory—thus was I a self-made Buddhist."[24] His mood never lifted. Disappointment, frustration, and sadness are recurring themes in his biographies. Vasil'ev's official portrait, photographed at the height of his scholarly prominence, is suffused with profound melancholy.

In the summer of 1834, at the age of sixteen, Vasil'ev moved to Kazan to write the entrance examination for the university's medical faculty. While he passed, he could not afford the tuition. After relentlessly badgering the rector, the youth was given a scholarship to read Mongolian with Osip Kovalevskii, who had just begun teaching at the Department of Oriental Letters. The better to learn the language, Vasil'ev lodged with a Buriat lama. The rector's confidence was well founded. Vasil'ev's grades won him a silver medal in his second year, and at the end of the third the education ministry awarded him a 300-ruble prize for a Tibetan composition. He also took on Chinese that year when a former member of the Ecclesiastical Mission to Beijing, Archimandrite Daniil (Sivillov), joined the department. Vasil'ev continued to sail through his studies, earning Kazan's first master's degree in Mongolian letters in 1839 with his thesis, "On the Foundations of Buddhist Philosophy."

Even before Vasil'ev had graduated, Kovalevskii saw a future colleague in him. There were plans to set up a chair in Tibetan, and his student seemed to be a good candidate for the post. The respect was mutual. Despite disliking the hostility of his teacher's compatriots toward Russia, Vasil'ev later recalled, "for my development and for my singular views about scholarship and the state, I am nevertheless obliged to the Polish professor (Osip Mikhailovich Kovalevskii)!" He went on to describe Kovalevskii's most important lessons: "Don't bow down before the authorities in your search for the truth. Examine all facts *sine ira et studio* [without malice or favor]. Never consider any question definitively settled."[25]

Kovalevskii proposed a rigorous program to train Vasil'ev for his academic career, to be carried out as a member the Orthodox Church's twelfth mission to Beijing for its full ten-year term. As often happened with promising young Russian scholars sent to foreign lands for further study, there were multiple sets of daunting instructions. His professor wanted him to master Tibetan and the region's other major languages, learn about every surrounding Asian nation, prepare teaching aids, keep a diary, and prepare an extensive list of Chinese and Manchu books. Meanwhile, on behalf of the Academy of Sciences, Isaac Schmidt simply asked that Vasil'ev report on everything "that strikes you of interest to scholarship."[26] Vasil'ev himself had goals too. Not only did he hope to acquire a comprehensive understanding of Buddhism, but he also planned "to add to this a knowledge of China, as well as its history and secular literature, shed light on contested aspects of Central Asia, and acquaint myself with Manchu, Korean and Turkic."[27]

Vasil'ev joined the mission in January 1840 as it stopped in Kazan on its way through Siberia and Mongolia to Beijing. The mission was under the aegis of the Foreign Minister, Count Karl Nesselrode, who thoroughly disliked Education Minister Sergei Uvarov, thereby complicating Vasil'ev's life in the distant Far East. Nor were matters helped by the fact that the mission's domineering head, Archimandrite Polikarp (Turganov) resented a layman's presence among his clerics. Life at the mission itself was lonely and spartan, while the Chinese capital proved to be a tremendous disappointment. Instead of encountering something akin to "the wonders of the Orient one had read about in the *Thousand and One Nights*," as Vasil'ev had anticipated, he found Beijing a vast, arid, and malodorous expanse of entirely uninteresting architecture, where "dirt and unpleasantness" greeted him at every step.[28]

Vasil'ev obeyed his teacher's injunction neither to become a Sinophile nor a Sinophobe during his Beijing sojourn. Over the course of his long career, he would remain a leading authority on the Middle Kingdom's politics. As his articles and commentaries show, he did not allow his own unhappy experience to color his opinions about China.[29] Vasil'ev's first public statement was his inaugural lecture at Kazan in 1850, "On the Meaning of China."[30] After some obligatory grumbling about Russians' ignorance of their eastern neighbor, he went on to debunk various Western stereotypes. For one thing, Asia was hardly uniform, since there were just as many differences between "the Confucian's dry empiricism, the healthy faith of Buddhism and the dreamy legends of the Veda" as between Christianity, Islam, and Judaism in the West.[31]

Anyway, Vasil'ev wondered, "What are East and West?" After all,

Moscow is east of Jerusalem, and the city of Perm, just west of the Ural Mountains (generally considered the boundary between Europe and Asia) lies at the same longitude as the Indus River's mouth.[32] In a later article, he questioned the classical distinction between Orient and Occident in a different way: "The real East includes . . . neither Persia nor Turkey. These countries have long been closely tied to that part of Europe we consider to be the West. Persia and Turkey are nothing more than the southern West, just as Russia and Scandinavia are the northern West. The real East consists of the areas ruled by China, with India to the south and Siberia to the north."[33]

Whatever the East was, Vasil'ev strenuously objected to seeing it as an "other." His guiding principle was that "man, wherever he may live, remains man." While there were some differences, these were largely due to the independent historical development of Eurasia's two halves. As David Wolff has noted, Vasil'ev's views about China resembled those of his teacher, Kovalevskii.[34] Thus Vasil'ev stressed that China was neither immobile nor unchanging. Given sufficient access to European science and technology, its people would recover their former greatness. Indeed, as he cautioned, China might even overtake the West. But the overall tone of his lecture was optimistic: "We are at the dawn of the age when the separation [between East and West] will vanish. One doesn't have to be a seer or a great philosopher to make this prediction. We just have to abandon our common preconceptions."[35]

Despite the tremendous changes the Qing dynasty would see over the next fifty years, Vasil'ev's views remained remarkably consistent. He explained, "My ideas and my opinions were all born in China [at the Beijing mission]."[36] In his editorial of 1884, "On Chinese Progress," the professor vigorously refuted "the false theory that classifies intellectual ability by race."[37] And his earlier article of 1859, "The Discovery of China," had a straightforward explanation for the Middle Kingdom's current weakness: it was all due to the rapacious Qing dynasty.[38] Conquest by the parasitic, alien Manchu nomads in 1644 had sapped the empire of its inherent vitality. As other comments elsewhere would confirm, Vasil'ev had thoroughly assimilated the traditional Chinese prejudice against the nomads of the steppe during his years in Beijing.[39]

Vasil'ev's views about Russia's Asian mission were more ambivalent.

Like many of his compatriots, he was convinced that tsarist rule benefited the Oriental peoples under its sway: "Our *inorodtsy* [Asian minorities] fare better than Russians themselves."[40] The professor also frequently railed against the rapacious colonialism of Britain and other Western powers in the East. At times, he called on his nation to fulfill its Asian manifest destiny: "I love the Orient, which is why I foresee a vast and fruitful enterprise by Russia there, and am convinced that under its aegis, one day we will truthfully be able to say *ex oriente lux* [out of the East is light]."[41] Yet on other occasions Vasil'ev criticized St. Petersburg's territorial grabs in China. Thus, while he originally opposed returning the central Asian Ili Valley to the Qing, by 1876 he was urging a friend at the foreign ministry, Baron Fedor Osten-Sacken, to hand the territory back in the interests of good relations.[42] Some twenty years later, he similarly opposed Russia's occupation of Port Arthur in Manchuria.[43]

Vasil'ev also wrote about domestic matters. In 1875 he compiled his prescriptions for reforms in Russia as a manuscript titled "Contemporary Questions." The first two versions did not pass the censors, but the book finally appeared three years later as *Tri voprosa* (Three Questions). Adopting the French revolutionary motto of *Liberté, égalité, fraternité,* the author called for his country's economic emancipation from Western finance and for all Russians' access to schools, regardless of class. As for the thorny matter of the countryside, he advocated retaining the commune so that the peasantry could decide its fate collectively.[44]

A Soviet biographer hastened to point out that Vasil'ev was hardly a radical himself. However, two of his sons would come under the Third Section's watchful eye for subversive activity during their student days. One of them, Nikolai Vladimirovich, was subsequently exiled to the Arctic port of Archangel in 1878 because of his involvement in worker unrest; he would eventually emigrate to Switzerland. Supported by his father, he remained involved in the labor movement there. Tsarist secret police files include a report that, on May 1, 1892, in Bern, Nikolai "marched at the head of a workers' procession with a red flag, handing out his leaflet."[45]

To Vasil'ev, the long years with the mission in Beijing would be the most difficult of his life. Yet with few distractions and an insatiable appetite for learning, he was able to carry out many of his impossibly extensive instructions. In addition to becoming fluent in Tibetan, Chinese, and Manchu, Vasil'ev compiled a mass of notes during his stay that would nourish much of his scholarship for the rest of his career. The most important of these were for an extensive survey of Buddhism, two volumes of which were eventually published.

He returned to Kazan in September 1850 with a deep knowledge of East Asia's languages, religions, and history. Pleased with his accomplishments, the university made him an associate (*ekstraordinarnyi*) professor. Because its occupant had recently died, however, he was appointed to the chair of Chinese and Manchu letters instead of teaching Tibetan. Not content to rest on his laurels, Vasil'ev quickly published several articles on Chinese finances and geography, which won him election to the Imperial Geographical Society. In 1852 he also found the time to wed the rector's daughter, Sofia Ivanovna Simonova, who would bear him four boys and a girl. Two years later Vasil'ev was promoted to full (*ordinarnyi*) professor.

Vasil'ev was part of the orientological exodus of 1855 from Kazan to St. Petersburg, where he lectured for another forty-five years, until shortly before his death in 1900. Since Mandarin was offered on no other campus in the empire in the nineteenth century's second half, the professor entirely dominated Russian Sinology during his long career there. As its longest-serving dean (from 1878 to 1893), he was also a leading figure in the Faculty of Oriental Letters. While some of his colleagues considered him distinctly old guard, he did much to broaden the curriculum to include more languages, including Hindi, Tibetan, Korean, and Japanese.

The professor largely carried on his alma mater's pedagogical practices at St. Petersburg University. Most important was his disregard of Western orientology. Even more than many of his Kazan colleagues, Vasil'ev based both his scholarship and teaching entirely on Asian texts. While he kept abreast of European trends, he did not consider them significant. As he wrote in one of his studies of Buddhism, "of course, Russian, French, English and German scholars have written a great deal about the subject. I am familiar with most of their works, but they weren't the ones that taught me about Buddhism." Vasil'ev proudly maintained that his decade in Beijing had given him a unique perspective: "I've already often said, I am convinced that I consulted many more sources than the other scholars."[46]

Like Mirza Kazem-Bek and Osip Senkovskii, Vasil'ev strongly advocated teaching the current, living language rather than the classics. In an article of 1886 he remarked that, whereas in academics more generally the trend was away from classicism toward "more realistic learning," the same could not be said about languages. Invoking a Darwinian metaphor, Vasil'ev suggested that "It is as if studying [freshwater] roaches and jellyfish is more elevated and noble than understanding the language, literature and history of a living people." He wondered why his faculty taught Sanskrit ("just as dead as Greek and Latin") rather than modern Hindi.[47]

Two years after St. Petersburg's Oriental faculty was founded, some of its students complained about the lack of proper textbooks.[48] Those who were enrolled in Chinese wrote that the only one they had was Father Hyacinth's "very unsatisfactory" grammar of 1835. Vasil'ev took their concerns to heart. Despite only meager funds, over the next decade the professor compiled readers and dictionaries for both Chinese and Manchu. The system he devised for organizing Chinese characters, which was phonetic in contrast to the Western practice of arranging them by radicals, was still being used in Soviet-era Russian dictionaries. Vasil'ev also differed from other nineteenth-century European Sinologists in his views about Chinese grammar and language. While his colleagues tended to believe that Chinese was much less sophisticated than Indo-European languages, Vasil'ev saw things quite differently: "Man is the same everywhere. If the Chinese brain is structured like the European's, how can we assume that there is no grammar in the former, especially when it has been thinking and expressing thoughts for whole millennia?"[49]

Vasil'ev's life ambition had been to write the first systematic examination of Buddhism in China and Inner Asia. Based on his toils in Beijing, he foresaw a six-volume collection that would examine the religion's dogma, literature, and history, as well as including the seventh-century travel account by the Chinese pilgrim Xuanzang. Vasil'ev's most important innovation was to consider Buddhist beliefs as a whole, rather than focusing on individual texts, as most of his contemporaries did.[50] To him, the faith was a coherent, organic body of thought that was continually evolving. Thus the sutras should not be seen as unchanging, but rather as illustrating "the history of the Buddha's teachings in a specific period."[51]

Vasil'ev never completed his projected study. His teaching, his interest in current events, and possibly bouts of depression as well distracted him from publishing more than two volumes. The first, a general survey, appeared in Russian in 1857 and was subsequently translated into German and French to largely favorable reviews.[52] Likening his achievement in producing the first comprehensive analysis of Buddhism to the periodic table of the elements, Fedor Shcherbatskoi called him "the Mendeleev of our orientology."[53] Twelve years later Vasil'ev managed to complete the second book, a history of Buddhism in India drawn from Tibetan sources.

Despite devoting much of his career to the faith, he was no closet Buddhist. The Soviet Sinologist Vasilii Alekseev was probably right in suggesting that Vasil'ev tended toward atheism.[54] What is certain is that the professor's views were in line with the scientific materialism of the intelligentsia at the time, which did not encourage confessional fervor. Vasil'ev's academic interests also reflected a broader trend in Russian orientology. If philology had dominated the discipline in the nineteenth century's first half, scholars were now tending more toward the study of religion. In his own words, "nothing gives us a greater understanding of a man than his creed."[55]

Given his contributions to scholarship, it took Vasil'ev surprisingly long to be elected to full membership in the Academy of Sciences. He only won the honor in 1886, a year before his university celebrated the fiftieth anniversary of his academic career. According to one scholar, the delay may have been due to the professor's aversion to publishing in any language other than Russian, which made much of his work inaccessible to the West. There was also his propensity to polemicize, which offended some academicians.[56] At the same time, Vasil'ev committed the egregious scholarly sin of being both a generalist and a popularizer, of writing about too many subjects for too broad an audience.

The academy's regulations at the time stated that full members could not continue teaching without a cut in pay. When Vasil'ev accordingly tried to retire from the university, his superiors urged him to stay on with a reduced course load. One of the reasons he faced resistance was the difficulty of finding a proper replacement. Two of his students, Sergei Georgievskii and Aleksei Ivanovskii, were hired with the hope that they might succeed their aging mentor, but premature death claimed the former while the latter succumbed to alcoholism and madness. When Vasil'ev died in April 1900, Sinology at St. Petersburg University was dealt a heavy blow.

On August 20, 1876, the Oriental faculty's dean, Vasilii Grigor'ev, formally opened the Third International Oriental Congress in St. Petersburg University's great hall. After "some fine singing," and accompanied by "representatives of about a dozen different nationalities arrayed in their native garb," he began his remarks in the organization's official language, French: "Consumed by religious and political frenzy, Europe and Asia are in a state of agonizing turmoil. . . . Race arms against race. One faith takes up the banner against another. . . . [Yet] in this ocean of unbridled passions, there is a haven where they do not dare intrude, a sanctuary that gives us a soothing foretaste of happier times to come. That refuge is scholarship." Having stressed science's role as an arena for peaceful cooperation, Grigor'ev went on to proclaim his country's continental identity: "The edifice that shelters you right now is one of the oldest in St. Petersburg; it was built, one could say, by the very hands of Peter the Great, that creator of modern Russia. Here we are all in the shadow of that august monarch who took us into the great family of the nations of the West."[57]

The congress was the brainchild of the French Japanologist Léon de Rosny. To legitimize the discipline's standing within academe, he had first convened an international meeting of orientologists at Paris's Sorbonne in 1873. London hosted a second session the following year, and there would be thirteen more before the First World War. Like the world's fairs, industrial exhibits, and other cross-border gatherings in the age of nationalism, academic conferences provided an opportunity for the host country to show off. The event in St. Petersburg was no exception. When not engaged in their scholarly discussions, the fifty or so delegates who came from abroad were treated to special displays of Islamic art, Oriental manuscripts, and artifacts from the empire's Asian minorities, as well as lavish banquets and an excursion to the imperial palace at Peterhof.

The choice of St. Petersburg as the site for the third congress was a clear indication of Europe's respect for Russia's orientologists. It also heralded a change in the discipline's relationship with the West. When initially established at the Academy of Sciences in the early eighteenth century, foreigners had dominated the study of Asia. During the university's first five decades, the leading scholars had tended to remain largely aloof from their colleagues in the West. As the nineteenth century drew to a close, however, St. Petersburg's orientologists now increasingly began to think of themselves as part of the European scholarly community.

The moving force behind this development was the Arabist Baron Viktor Romanovich Rosen, who succeeded Vasil'ev as the faculty's dean in 1893. As his name suggests, Baron Rosen's background was very different from his predecessors'. Born into a German noble family in the Baltic port of Reval (now Talinn, Estonia), his outlook was Western rather than Eastern.[58] He enrolled at St. Petersburg University in 1866 to read Near Eastern letters, but unlike earlier generations of Russian orientologists, he completed his studies not in Asia but in Europe. After a year with Leipzig's renowned Heinrich Fleischer, he taught Arabic at the faculty from 1872 until his premature death in 1908.

The baron's scholarship focused on medieval Islamic manuscripts at the Asian Museum. While he made important contributions in this respect (Byzantinists still rely on his studies of relations with the Arab world), his most significant achievements were in teaching and administration. Exaggerating only slightly, one student, Ignatii Krachkovskii, claimed that Rosen's "name is tied to our entire new school of orientology."[59] In addition to the former, Rosen trained a number of other prominent early Soviet orientologists, including Vasilii Barthold, Sergei Oldenburg, and Nikolai Marr. Above all, he strove to instill in them his own respect for European scholarship. As Vera Tolz points out, Rosen insisted that everyone preparing for a teaching post at his faculty complete their training in the West to become acquainted with its pedagogy and research, much as he had done himself.[60]

Despite this cosmopolitan outlook, not to mention his German heritage, Rosen was loyal to his empire and he strongly defended Russian as a scholarly language.[61] In this respect, he was not very different from other St. Petersburg orientologists with foreign blood, such as Mirza Kazem-Bek and Osip Senkovskii. Indeed, the baron promoted contacts with the West in part so that the achievements of Russian scholarship might be better known.

Rosen's most important accomplishment was to take the St. Petersburg school well beyond the campus. His first major endeavor was through the

Imperial Russian Archaeological Society's Oriental section, which elected him its president in 1885. Established nearly forty years earlier, the society had long had a strong interest in the antiquities of the empire's Asian cultures; Pavel Savel'ev had been among its founding members. Under Baron Rosen, however, it began to take an active role in promoting Russian orientology more generally through the journal he founded the following year, *Zapiski Vostochnogo otdeleniia Imperatorskago Russkogo arkheologicheskogo obshchestva* (Transactions of the Oriental Section of the Imperial Russian Archaeological Society).

Russia was a latecomer in this respect. Already toward the end of the eighteenth century, William Jones's Asiatic Society in Bengal had begun publishing its *Asiatic Researches,* while the French *Journal asiatique* first appeared in 1823, followed some twenty-five years later by the German Oriental Society's *Zeitschrift* (Journal).[62] This was not for want of trying in St. Petersburg. In 1818 the historian of Siberia, Grigorii Spasskii, had started his *Sibirskii vestnik* (Siberian Herald) there, which, despite its name, focused broadly on the study of the East. Subsequently renamed *Aziatskii vestnik* (Asian Herald) to reflect its interests more accurately, the monthly had a nine-year run.[63] Vladimir Vasil'ev had also attempted to found an *Aziatskoe obozrenie* (Asian Review) in 1865 to be based at the Oriental faculty, but the university's council turned it down for lack of funds.[64]

Rosen had planned to publish the *Zapiski* for a general audience, but it soon became much more academic. While its Russian readership was limited, foreign scholars did pay attention, thanks to the editor's efforts. Through its reviews and articles the *Zapiski* became an important vehicle for promoting the achievements of Russian orientology in the West.[65]

Baron Rosen was also affiliated with the Academy of Sciences, although his relationship with the hallowed institution did not get off on the right foot. When he was first elected in 1879 as a junior (*ad"iunkt*) member at the relatively young age of thirty-three, the study of Asia there had been languishing for some time. Count Uvarov had tried to encourage the discipline by providing for two places for the history of Asian letters (out of a total of twenty-two for full members) in the academy's statute of 1836. Over the years, more positions had been added, so that when Rosen was taken on there were three academicians and one associate. None of them was particularly distinguished, and within three years all had died, save a

Sanskritist who had long ago returned to his native Germany. As a result, by 1881 Rosen was the only orientologist left, and at the lowest rank to boot.

The early 1880s were particularly troubled for the academy. For some time its reputation had been slipping as the empire's universities matured. Moreover, public opinion had grown increasingly resentful of the high numbers of foreigners who held the coveted title of academician. To many Russians, the Academy of Sciences was a "German institution," an eighteenth-century archaism whose sole function was to provide sinecures for mediocre scholars from abroad. Matters came to a head shortly after Rosen was tapped, when in 1880 the renowned chemist Dmitrii Mendeleev was turned down for membership. Already world famous for having drawn up the periodic table of the elements, he seemed highly deserving of the honor, and his rejection unleashed a furor in the press.[66]

Mendeleev's unexpected setback was partly due to a bitter division within the academy. One faction consisted largely of foreign scholars, while the other comprised Russians. Matters were not helped by the often haughty attitude of the former. When a distinguished Russian chemist once complained about their dominance in the institution, a fellow member with Prussian blood snarled, "The Academy is after all not Russian, but rather an Imperial Academy!"[67] Many of the native-born academicians also had ties to the empire's up-and-coming universities, which made them doubly threatening to the "Germans."

Despite his own Teutonic roots, as a patriotic St. Petersburg University professor Rosen was definitely in the Russian camp. When he tried to convince his colleagues to fill the newly vacant chairs for Asian literature and history, his efforts became entirely mired in their fractious politics. As a result, in 1882 Rosen angrily resigned from the academy.[68]

The baron's impetuous move once again earned the institution much public opprobrium. But it had the desired effect, since the Academy of Sciences soon admitted the Turkologist Vasilii Radlov, the Persian specialist Karl Zaleman, and Vladimir Vasil'ev to its membership. Within eight years, Rosen also accepted reelection. Three of the four new academicians taught at the Oriental faculty as well, and all were productive scholars. Before the October Revolution, three more prominent members of the faculty would be invited to join: the Indologist Sergei Oldenburg, the scholar of the Caucasus Nikolai Marr, and the central Asian historian Vasilii Barthold. Most of them would maintain close ties with their university, which considerably lowered the barriers that had previously so separated the two establishments on St. Petersburg's Vasil'evskii Island. Indeed, according to the academy's official history, by the 1880s together they basically constituted a single center for orientology in the Russian capital.[69]

Sergei Fedorovich Oldenburg best exemplified the St. Petersburg school's new course.[70] A specialist in Buddhist folklore and Indian art history, Oldenburg had begun his career at the Oriental faculty but spent most of it with the Academy of Sciences. Like his mentor, Baron Rosen, he saw himself as a member of the European scholarly community rather than a strictly Russian one. And, while he was loyal to his fatherland, Oldenburg strongly championed academic autonomy from the state, although this would prove increasingly difficult after the Romanov dynasty was replaced by a much more ideologically strident regime in 1917.

Sergei Oldenburg traced the beginnings of his interest in orientology to a book about Tibet that had captivated his imagination as a sixth-year secondary school student. But they may well go back much earlier, to his early childhood in the Buriat homeland around eastern Siberia's Lake Baikal, where his father commanded a Cossack regiment. Hailing from the German Baltic region of Mecklenburg, the Oldenburgs were a military family that had entered Russian service under Peter the Great.[71] Sergei's mother, Nadezhda Berg, was half-French and raised her children in the language. Upon retiring from the army, Oldenburg's father moved to western Europe, where he sat in on university lectures and attended to his sons' education. Eventually settling down in Warsaw to send the boys to its gymnasium, the former general died unexpectedly in 1877, when Sergei was only fourteen. Despite the setback, the boy persevered with his schooling, graduating in 1881 with a gold medal. Together with his older brother Fedor, Sergei Oldenburg won admission to St. Petersburg University that year, and he enrolled in the Oriental faculty's Sanskrit-Persian department. Their mother accompanied them to the imperial capital, where she supported herself by teaching French at the posh Smol'ny Institute for women of gentle birth.

At the time when Oldenburg entered the faculty, Russian Indology was a young discipline in relation to scholarship of the Near East and China.[72] The reason was straightforward: Whereas the latter regions bordered on Russia, India did not. As Uvarov's project for an Asian academy had suggested, St. Petersburg was not immune from Europe's fascination with Sanskrit at the turn of the nineteenth century. However, the Oriental faculty only officially added a chair for the subject in 1863. The father of Indology in Russia is generally considered to be Ivan Minaev, who taught at St. Petersburg from 1873 until his death in 1890.

Working under Minaev and Vasil'ev, Oldenburg began his academic career by studying Buddhism. Like his teachers, he was not particularly spiritually inclined. As his colleague Shcherbatskoi explained, Oldenburg, like all Russian Indologists, devoted his attention to the faith since that was the link between the South Asian country and his own: "Through Buddhism India becomes our neighbor along our entire Eastern border, from [Lake] Baikal all the way to the Upper Volga."[73] His research initially focused on the religion's early development. Sergei Fedorovich was particularly intrigued by its popular mythology, and he wrote his master's thesis, "Buddhist Legends," about traditional stories of the Buddha's reincarnation.

This emphasis on folklore may well have reflected Oldenburg's youthful flirtation with populism.[74] As a university student, he became involved in politics. Given the strict restrictions Alexander III had placed on student life in the wake of his father's assassination in 1881, outside of the revolutionary underground such activity was generally limited to informal discussion circles—although these were generally frowned upon as well. Together with his brother and the future geologist Vladimir Vernadskii, among others, he formed a group with vaguely populist and Fabian leanings.[75] Many of its members, including Sergei Fedorovich himself, would later become prominent members of the liberal Constitutional Democratic Party.

Oldenburg also participated in the university's Student Scientific-Literary Association. One of his acquaintances there was a zoology undergraduate from Simbirsk, Aleksandr Ul'ianov. A man of much more radical inclinations, Ul'ianov was hanged for his involvement in a plot to murder the tsar in 1887. Several years later, his younger brother Vladimir, visiting St. Petersburg to write his law school examinations, looked up Oldenburg to ask about Aleksandr. This would not be the last encounter between Sergei Fedorovich and Vladimir, better known by his revolutionary alias, Lenin.

During his graduate years, Oldenburg grew particularly close to his dean, Baron Rosen. Their extensive correspondence betrays Rosen's strong influence on Oldenburg's attitudes toward scholarship, especially when it came to developing links with the West.[76] As one of the faculty's most promising young students, Sergei Fedorovich was sent on a two-year tour of Europe in 1887 (he would never set foot in India, much as Rosen managed to avoid the Near East). Staying in Paris, London, Cambridge, and on various German campuses, he developed a number of lifelong friendships with orientologists abroad. Among the most enduring was with Silvain Lévi, a Parisian Jew who would rise to the summit of his profession as a professor at the Collège de France and the president of the Société Asiatique.[77]

Oldenburg began teaching Sanskrit at St. Petersburg University in 1889. His years at the Oriental faculty were difficult. While he successfully passed his master's examination in 1886, it would take him another nine years to defend it. There were personal tragedies. In 1891 his wife died suddenly from tubercular meningitis, leaving him to care for their young son. Oldenburg's letters to Rosen also allude to his own health problems, which may well have involved depression. At the same time, the young scholar happily took on many extracurricular responsibilities. As a strong supporter of universal education, he became active with the Bestuzhev Higher Women's Courses, an institution that provided university instruction to the sex that had been excluded from Russia's campuses by imperial decree in 1863.

Among the scholars Oldenburg had met during his European tour was the British Indologist Thomas William Rhys Davids. He had been particularly impressed with the Briton's program to publish southern Buddhist texts. Like most Russians who studied the faith, Oldenburg focused on northern Buddhism, that is, the variants that were based on Sanskrit and were dominant around the Himalayas and in Inner and East Asia, as opposed to the Pali-based traditions of Ceylon and southern India that dominated British Indology. In 1897 he began a similar enterprise, the *Bibliotheca Buddhica*, to reproduce important northern Buddhist works. Funded by the Academy of Sciences, the project was a major international venture. Involving Russian and Western scholars such as Lévi, Albert Grün-wedel, Hendrik Kern, and Bunju Nanjio, over the next thirty years some thirty volumes would appear in the series. Oldenburg's own contribution was a collection of Buriat woodblock prints.

Oldenburg did not disdain writing for a more general audience. He translated short stories by Rudyard Kipling and Anatole France into Russian and published a number of popular articles about Buddhism. Their even-handed approach, which often clashed with the more critical accounts by Orthodox missionaries, made him enemies. Some even whispered that the professor had secretly converted to Buddhism. Oldenburg respected the faith's ethical tenets (he became a vegetarian), but his true religion was scholarship. Like his teacher Vasil'ev, he studied Buddhism in a fairly objective light as a cultural phenomenon. Oldenburg also shared the Sinologist's views of the Orient more generally. Thus he saw no great divide between Eurasia's two halves. In a discussion of the relationship between East and West since the days of pharaonic Egypt, he pointed out that modern science had conclusively proven this to be the case: "History examines [the discoveries of nineteenth-century orientologists] more intensively, as if they are entirely new and unusual phenomena, but soon detects analogies, and even sometimes almost complete coincidence [with the West]. It therefore shows convincingly that we all inhabit the same world, with the same events, the same laws of progress. In the Orient man is, above all, just like man everywhere." There were, of course differences. Oldenburg acknowledged that "our schoolchildren know more than even the most sophisticated Eastern minds" about science and technology. But Easterners had a far deeper understanding of humanity. He believed that the Asian, "by the power of his intellect, has penetrated the secrets of life. He has studied and explained that which is closest to all mankind—his very humanity."[78]

In another article, Oldenburg pointed out that the West's temporary military superiority made it unbearably arrogant: "Thus the European is accustomed to see himself as the ruler of the world." But he went on to note: "He is so confident of his superiority that it never even enters his head—unless he happens to be an orientologist or a specialist—that at the time of the Crusades the Europeans were the barbarians in relation to their foes."[79] Oldenburg firmly believed that his profession had an obligation to cure the West of its supercilious attitude. Furthermore, echoing Uva-rov's rationale for his proposed Asian academy a century earlier, he argued that by knowing the East the West would better know itself: "My specialty puts me among the orientologists, who see it as their task to study and understand Asia. We believe that, only by properly comprehending the East with its tremendous cultural achievements can mankind fully under-stand itself."[80]

Oldenburg continued to follow current political developments while teaching at the Oriental faculty. He despaired at the autocracy's seemingly unrelenting interference in academic life as the nineteenth century drew to a close. Responding to an article he read in *The Times* about new regula-tions ordering tsarist university administrators to watch their charges more closely, Oldenburg confessed to Rosen that he yearned for the day "when one can breathe freely in Russia [unlike] now, when all that is honest, that thinks, bows down and is stifled."[81] In the summer of 1899, after another wave of student unrest in St. Petersburg, the university sacked several pro-fessors on suspicion of sympathizing with the protests. Oldenburg was livid. He wrote Rosen, "Obviously when men with whom I am *in full sol-idarity* are expelled from the universities, I cannot stay there anymore, and when I return [from abroad] I will take the appropriate steps."[82]

The professor fully expected that his resignation would kill his academic career. For a time he considered moving to the provinces, to take up a job in the *zemstva*, local agencies of self-government. His colleagues thought otherwise. There happened to be a vacancy in the Sanskrit chair at the Academy of Sciences, where Baron Rosen and two other Oriental faculty professors were members. Most likely on Rosen's initiative, Oldenburg was voted in by a large majority of academicians in February 1900.

Oldenburg was intimately involved with the academy in its various in-carnations for the remaining thirty-four years of his life. At that institution his administrative talents fully blossomed. Promoted to the rank of aca-demician in 1903, he was elected permanent secretary the following year, a post he would hold until he was dismissed in 1929, Oldenburg worked tirelessly to advance the institution's interests. Thus he successfully lobbied the Russian Duma (legislature) to boost the perennially underfunded in-stitution's budget, and he also endeavored to maintain its political inde-pendence.

This did not mean that Oldenburg now stood aloof from contemporary affairs. In January 1905, as the unpopular war with Japan was inciting revolutionary unrest in the empire, he was among the seventeen academicians who signed an open letter "On the Needs of Education (Memorandum of 342 Scholars)." Published in the St. Petersburg daily *Rus'*, it called on the autocracy to halt its interference in the empire's schools and universities. The statement proclaimed that "academic freedom is incompatible with the current political order in Russia," going on to condemn the regime's "police-like policies" in education.[83] Not surprisingly, the move earned a stern rebuke from the academy's president, Grand Duke Konstantin Konstantinovich, who upbraided its members for interfering in politics. Along with his colleagues, Oldenburg stood his ground. He defiantly wrote the grand duke, "I am not only an academician. I am also a citizen, and I am unaware of any law . . . that would forbid me from openly expressing my views about education in Russia."[84] Konstantin Konstantinovich soon relented, and he even issued an apology to the academy's members.

Oldenburg was particularly concerned about the autocracy's intolerant attitude toward minority nationalities. In addition to championing Lama Dorzhiev's temple in the capital, he also participated in the academy's opposition to Russification in Ukraine. The academician expressed his dismay in a letter of 1910 to his son Sergei (whose politics tended more to the right): "It is horrible that this persecution of minorities goes on everywhere—the Caucasus, Poland, the Volga region, Muslims, not to mention the Jews—tens of millions are being tormented."[85] Oldenburg shared the sentiments of many of his colleagues on this issue. Unlike missionaries and some government officials, scholars at the academy and the university tended to oppose Russification and some even encouraged nationalism among the empire's inorodtsy.[86] As Nathaniel Knight points out, sympathy with the objects of their study "was not an uncommon occupational hazard" among Russian orientologists.[87]

One of the most telling expressions of Oldenburg's views about the relationship between learning and society was an essay he contributed, a year before he joined the academy, to an influential collection of essays, *Problems of Idealism*. Published in 1902, the book was the first of several counterattacks on the Russian revolutionary intelligentsia's strident dogmatism by liberals and lapsed Marxists.[88] Oldenburg's contribution, "Renan as Champion of Freedom of Conscience," focused on a nineteenth-century French scholar of religion who had been persecuted by senior Catholic clergy for his objective approach to the life of Jesus.[89]

At first glance, the chapter's robust defense of intellectual freedom could have been seen solely as criticizing the Orthodox Church's obscurantism under its archconservative chief procurator, Konstantin Pobedonostsev. Yet it had another target as well. Citing Ernest Renan, Oldenburg alluded to the intelligentsia's nihilism: "The eighteenth century's skeptics merrily annihilated and saw no need to build a new faith. Their sole concerns were with destruction itself and with being conscious of the living force that animated them."[90]

As the academy's leading orientologist, Oldenburg faithfully carried on Baron Rosen's legacy to promote the discipline both within the institution and beyond. If before his election to membership there had been four chairs for Asian literature and history, by 1914 there were six. Oldenburg's standing was confirmed when in 1916 he became the Asian Museum's director. According to the Sinologist Vasilii Alekseev, who knew him well, it was because of Oldenburg that "despite their small numbers, orientologists have and continue to have such a major role in our scholarship and society."[91]

Four years after being elected permanent secretary, Oldenburg complained to his son that, "other than [my administration at] the Academy, I don't manage to get anything done."[92] He was being a bit hard on himself. The academician did continue to publish, including articles about Buddhist art and Indian literature, as well as the obligatory book reviews. He also led two expeditions in the early 1910s to Turfan, Dunhuang, and other Silk Road sites in Xinjiang. The latter were sponsored by a group Oldenburg had helped to organize over a decade earlier, the Central and East Asian Exploration Fund.[93] This international association had been established in 1898 to coordinate efforts among archaeologists, who had been engaged in an intense rivalry to unearth the region's ancient Buddhist artifacts.[94] Having been launched in the same year as Nicholas II's idealistic peace conference at The Hague, it is perhaps not surprising that European scholars agreed to base the institution in St. Petersburg.

Oldenburg's reaction to the momentous events of 1917 was typical of his caste. Although he favored retaining the monarchy in some limited form, he did not mourn the tsar's abdication in February. Like many fellow scholars, he strongly supported the liberal Kadets (Constitutional Democrats), who formed the coalition Provisional Government along with moderate leftists parties in the wake of the February Revolution.[95] During the summer the academician even served as education minister in one of Aleksandr Kerenskii's short-lived cabinets.

When in October Vladimir Lenin's more militant Bolsheviks seized power in a coup, Oldenburg was horrified. He repeatedly protested the new regime's excesses and was briefly arrested himself as a counterrevolutionary. When his friend the symbolist poet Aleksandr Blok wrote *The Twelve,* a lengthy paean likening the Bolsheviks to Jesus Christ and his apostles, Oldenburg replied with a much gloomier verse, "The Dead." Nevertheless, unlike many others, he did not emigrate. Indeed, by the spring of 1918 the academy's secretary began to seek an accommodation with the new regime, at times meeting directly with Lenin. For the time being, his efforts were successful. Although many of his fellow academicians abhorred the new political order (there were no Communist Party members among their ranks until 1929), this pragmatic approach helped ensure the institution's survival.[96]

Oldenburg even offered the academy's expertise to the Soviet government on occasion. Thus, according to Francine Hirsch, he engineered a "revolutionary alliance" with the Communist Party on policies towards ethnic minorities.[97] Hirsch argues that this partnership was more than a marriage of convenience, since in its early years the party and scholars such as Oldenburg shared similar sentiments about promoting the young Soviet Union's Asian minorities. But as Lenin's successor, Joseph Stalin, readopted a more Russian nationalist line, this arrangement became increasingly tenuous. More important, Stalin's efforts to impose stricter controls on cultural and intellectual life in the late 1920s effectively subordinated the academy to the Communist Party's bidding.[98]

Unlike his earlier efforts to maintain the institution's autonomy, Oldenburg was unable to deflect the Stalinist "cultural revolution."[99] While he was more flexible than some of his colleagues in dealing with the campaign to sovietize what was now the Academy of Sciences of the USSR, his loyalty to the institution's scholarly integrity made him the target of attacks on "bourgeois scientists" and "former persons." In October 1929 Oldenburg was stripped of his post as permanent secretary, and he spent the following nights sleeping fully dressed in anticipation of arrest by the OGPU secret police. Although other academicians did suffer that fate, he never received the dreaded nocturnal summons. Like other leading intellectual lights with an independent streak, such as the poet Anna Akhmatova and his fellow academician Ivan Pavlov, Oldenburg was probably considered too distinguished to be liquidated.

The next year saw the academician's rehabilitation when he was named head of the new Institute of Orientology. Under the academy's aegis, this establishment merged the Asian Museum with several other related organizations. Eventually based in Moscow (although the St. Petersburg branch still flourishes in a formal grand ducal palace on the Neva), it remains Russia's leading institution for the study of the East. In 1933 Oldenburg's colleagues marked the fifty-year jubilee of his scholarly career with a special session at the Academy of Sciences. He died a peaceful death a year later.

From its founding in 1855 through the century's close, St. Petersburg University's Faculty of Oriental Languages was the leading establishment of its kind both in Russia and abroad. There were specialized colleges with a more practical orientation, such as the Moscow's Lazarev Institute and the Ecole spéciale des langues vivantes orientales in Paris. And many of the West's great universities, including Cambridge, Leiden, Göttingen, and Yale, boasted chairs for various Asian languages, some of which dated back centuries earlier. However, no other institution of higher education had an entire faculty devoted to the discipline.

Compared to St. Petersburg University's other sections, such as law and the natural sciences, enrolments at its Oriental faculty were small. If at the turn of the twentieth century there were over 2,000 students in the juridical faculty, only 182, or 5 percent of the total, specialized in Asian languages. Despite the usual complaints to the contrary, the discipline received a disproportionate share of the university's resources. Of St. Petersburg's fifty-eight full professors at the time, nine were affiliated with the Oriental faculty, compared to eighteen in law, which had more than ten times the number of students.[100] These numbers reflected the field's importance as a source both of specialists for the autocracy's Asian ambitions as well as for academic respectability abroad. When in 1916 the prominent classicist Mikhail Rostovtsev surveyed Russian scholarship, he listed orientology as one of his country's most highly esteemed disciplines internationally.[101]

Nicholas I had established the Oriental faculty with utilitarian aims in mind, much like Peter the Great and his Academy of Sciences. The Indologist Ivan Minaev recognized the autocracy's thinking when, in an official address, he proclaimed, "Russia's interests have always been intimately linked to the East, and therefore . . . for our scholars Asia cannot be a lifeless, purely bookish object of academic curiosity."[102] St. Petersburg's professors were government officials and the imperial Table of Ranks carefully delineated their status, as that of any other *chinovnik* (civil servant). A number of them, like Kazem-Bek, Minaev, and Dmitrii Pozdneev, also served the state in more practical ways.

This did not mean that the scholars who studied the East at St. Petersburg University saw themselves as handmaidens of tsarist imperialism. Regardless of their politics, which ranged from conservative in the case of Grigor'ev to the more progressive views of Vasil'ev and Oldenburg, their interests were more esoteric. What impassioned the orientologists on the Neva was not how to conquer or rule the East, but such questions as the origins of Mahayana Buddhism, pre-Islamic Arabic poetry, or Kushite inscriptions on ancient coins. By the same token, their attitudes toward the East tended to be positive. Unlike their colleagues at the Kazan Theological Academy's Missionary Division, the scholars of the St. Petersburg school did not disdain the cultures and peoples they studied. Some might deem the governments that ruled over such antiquated empires as Persia and China as autocratic and decrepit, but they rarely saw Persians and Chinese themselves as inherently inferior.

This phenomenon will be familiar to those acquainted with Sovietology on American campuses during the cold war. At that time, as in Imperial Russia, the state devoted enormous resources to studying a region in which it had a strong strategic stake. Yet even if many scholars in the United States benefited from Washington's largesse during the Cold War, few strongly sympathized with its aims vis-à-vis Moscow.

9

THE EXOTIC SELF

Russia is a Mongol country. We all have Mongolian blood in our veins and [therefore our nation] will not resist the invasion. We are fated to prostrate ourselves before the idol.

—Andrei Bely

No musical composition is more closely associated in the West with the tsarist Orient than Aleksandr Borodin's *In the Steppes of Central Asia*. A track on virtually every bargain-basement recording of Russian classical hits, the orchestral sketch was commissioned to honor the twenty-fifth anniversary of Alexander II's reign in 1880. The celebration's grandiose plans featured a conversation between "the Genius of Russia" and "History," to be illustrated by various orchestral *tableaux vivants* highlighting the monarch's achievements. In addition to Borodin's contribution, other pieces included "Slava" (Glory), a chorus by Nikolai Rimsky-Korsakov, and a march by Modest Mussorgsky commemorating the capture of the Ottoman stronghold of Kars in 1877. While the projected performance never took place (because its promoters mysteriously disappeared), *In the Steppes of Central Asia* quickly acquired great popularity both at home and abroad.[1]

Borodin's sketch combined Russian and Eastern tunes to convey melodically the ethnic harmony of Alexander's newly conquered realms in Turkestan, as the composer explained in his notes to accompany the score: "The unfamiliar strains of a peaceful Russian song first waft over the uniform, sandy Central Asian steppes. We hear the sound of approaching camels' and horses' hooves, we hear the doleful strains of an Oriental tune. A native caravan passes over the boundless desert, guarded by Russian troops. It continues its long journey confidently and without fear under the protection of Russian arms. Farther and farther away the caravan recedes into the distance. The peaceful singing of the Russians and the natives blends into a single harmony, whose refrain is long heard over the steppe until it too vanishes into the distance."[2]

On one level, Borodin's melodic symbiosis of Russian and Asian is typical of European propaganda during the high age of imperialism, which sought to portray colonial subjects as the happy subjects of white rule. The musicologist Richard Taruskin suggests that the composer's opera *Prince Igor* should be heard in the same way: "*Prince Igor* made overt the pervasive subtext to 19th-century Russian essays in orientalism: the racially justified endorsement of Russia's militaristic expansion to the east."[3] But a closer look at Borodin's masterpiece suggests that it does not fit the pattern of other cultural artifacts of European colonialism. Although it was conceived at a time of rapid expansion into central Asia, the opera's portrayal of the Eastern other actually reflects its composer's ambiguous attitude toward his own continental identity. In this way, *Prince Igor* anticipated the fascination with Russia's exotic, Asian self of the Silver Age, tsarism's final cultural flowering.

Much as with painting and poetry, the East entered post-Petrine Russian music by way of the West. The Baroque's taste for the exotic had already made Oriental motifs popular among seventeenth-century European composers such as Jean-Baptiste Lully and Henry Purcell. Turkish motifs were particularly favored, right up to Wolfgang Amadeus Mozart's rococo confection, *The Abduction from the Seraglio* (1782). While direct contact inspired musical *alla turca*—the janissary bands' ominous drums and cacophonous winds during the Ottoman siege of Vienna in 1683 were one notable example—most Orientalist compositions during the Baroque had little grounding in ethnomusicological reality. Instead, they were largely exotic frivolities to amuse periwigged monarchs and other ancien régime patrons. Thus, the four suites of Jean-Philippe Rameau's opéra-ballet *Les Indes galantes* (1735) are incongruously set among Turks, Incans, Persians, and "les sauvages" (indigenous North Americans).[4]

Just as Catherine the Great indulged in architectural chinoiserie for her summer residences, she adopted Orientalisms in some of her theatrical entertainments. *Tsarevich Fevei,* the comic opera scored by the empress's court musician Vasilii Pashkevich about a Siberian prince's travels, includes a "Kalmyk ballet" accompanied by a love song that evokes their customs:

> The people of the Kalmyk
> Eat kaimak,
> Suliak and turmak,
> Smoke tobacco,
> And brew kumys . . .[5]

While the melody was not consciously based on nomadic Mongolian tradition, according to Gerald Abraham its eccentric rhythms and sustained pedal points (a long-held lower note combined with changing harmonies in the higher parts) marked the first effort in Russian opera to evoke the East musically.[6]

The explosion of interest in folklore during the Romantic era encouraged Europeans to study Asian music more closely. One of the pioneers was Félicien David, a young Frenchman active in the utopian socialist Saint-Simonian movement who had fled a government crackdown by traveling to the Near East in 1833. During the two years he spent in the Ottoman Empire, the exile carefully gathered local melodies, which he transcribed for piano and published after his return to France in 1836 as *Mélodies orientales.* While the volume did not fly off the shelves, David's symphonic ode, *Le désert,* proved to be a great hit when it was first performed in 1844. A three-part travelogue combining narrations with orchestral and vocal music, the work also employed material he had gathered during his Levantine sojourn. David went on to a successful career composing operas in exotic settings, including *La perle du Brésil* (The Brazilian Pearl), *Le captive,* and *Lalla-Roukh,* an adaptation of Thomas Moore's Oriental tale.[7]

The closest Russian equivalent to David was a musically inclined veteran of the Napoleonic wars, Aleksandr Aliab'ev (also known as Alabieff and Alyabyev).[8] Friendly with some Decembrists in St. Petersburg, the retired hussar officer preceded the conspirators into Siberian exile when he was falsely accused of murdering a card shark during a game gone sour in

February 1825. In the early 1830s Aliab'ev was permitted to spend a year in Piatigorsk and other Caucasian spas to look after his health. This long respite acquainted him with the region's great variety of melodic riches, which he eagerly set about transcribing. Next transferred to the western Siberian city of Orenburg on the edge of the central Asian steppe, Aliab'ev also copied songs of the local Bashkir and Kirgiz there. He drew on these extensive notes to compose an overture based on Bashkir themes and publish an 1834 collection, *Kavkazskii pevets* (The Caucasian Singer). Eventually allowed to settle in Moscow, he went on to compose an opera based on Bestuzhev-Marlinskii's well-known story, *Ammalat-Bek*. Aliab'ev's name remains obscure in the West—he does not even merit an entry in the massive *Grove Dictionary of Music and Musicians*. He did, however, anticipate the Oriental turn of the next generation.

Much better known was Aliab'ev's approximate contemporary Mikhail Glinka. As the first composer to establish a distinct national idiom, Glinka was to Russian music what Pushkin was to his nation's literature. Active at a time when the autocracy favored Italian opera, Glinka rejected the cosmopolitanism of St. Petersburg's musical establishment to advocate a style based on native themes and motifs. As he supposedly put it, "The common people compose; we only arrange."[9] Glinka took the capital by storm in 1836 with his first opera, *A Life for the Tsar*, a patriotic adventure set in the Polish-Muscovite War during the early seventeenth century's Time of Troubles. His *Ruslan and Ludmilla*, which followed six years later, was less successful but ultimately more influential. Like Pushkin's epic fairy tale of 1820, to which the libretto was set, the opera incorporated Russian folk elements with Orientalisms. The latter included a Persian chorus as well as a set of Turkish, Arabic, and Caucasian dances. But, as Glinka argued, these were not necessarily alien: "There is no doubt that our Russian song is a child of the North, but the people of the East have also given it something."[10]

Some musicologists, suggesting that Russians have exaggerated the originality of Glinka's achievements, point out that he was hardly the first to blend native melodies into his compositions.[11] Furthermore, his folkloric interests were entirely in keeping with European Romanticism. Nevertheless, he did have some influential disciples who carried on his legacy. Among them was a talented young pianist, Mily Balakirev. Like Glinka,

Balakirev hailed from the provinces, and he had similarly been trained out-side of the academy. While his creative achievements were relatively mod-est, he championed Glinka's nationalist orientation to a group of com-posers who in the nineteenth century's second half collectively oversaw the full flowering of what came to be known as the Russian school. Nick-named *Moguchaia kuchka* (The Mighty Handful) or, more simply, the Five, they included some of the greatest names in Russian music: Rimsky-Korsakov, Mussorgsky, and Borodin. (The fifth, and least known today, was César Cui).

Like the painter Vasilii Vereshchagin, the Five subscribed to the realist aesthetics of the 1860s.[12] Balakirev had even contemplated honoring the age's cultural oracle, Nikolai Chernyshevskii, with an opera of his novel-istic manifesto *What Is to Be Done?* In his survey of art during the nine-teenth century's middle decades, the critic Vladimir Stasov, a friend and tireless advocate of the Five, explained the Russian school's approach to music.[13] Most important, its members refused to submit to the dictates of the European tradition. Largely self-taught, Balakirev and his circle op-posed the newly founded St. Petersburg Conservatory, which saw itself as the bearer of Western musical culture. Hand in hand with this aversion to the academy was the Russian school's "aspiration for the national essence" (*stremlenie k national'nosti*). This did not mean strict isolationism; the Five closely followed European developments, traveled abroad, and were friendly with foreign composers. And, of course, nationalism was charac-teristic of Western trends at the time. Meanwhile, in keeping with Cherny-shevskii's teachings, the Five also rejected abstraction in favor of pro-grammatic works, music meant to convey an idea or tell a story.

According to Stasov, another important characteristic of the Russian school was "the Oriental element." Balakirev, who shared Stasov's beliefs about the Asian origins of *byliny,* traveled to the Caucasus several times during the 1860s to collect folk tunes among its diverse peoples.[14] Several of Balakirev's compositions of the time have a distinctly Eastern flavor, in-cluding his Oriental fantasy for piano *Islamey* (1869) and the symphonic poem *Tamara* (1867–82), which was based on Mikhail Lermontov's poem about a legendary Georgian siren.

Rimsky-Korsakov recalled that Balakirev spent many evenings with his fellow kuchkists playing the melodies he had transcribed during his rambles in Russia's Oriental highlands.[15] They likewise developed a fascination for Asian music, reflected in such works as Rimsky-Korsakov's *Scheherazade, Antar,* and *The Golden Cockerel* and Mussorgsky's *Shamil's March,* not to mention Borodin's *In the Steppes of Central Asia.* The musicologist Marina Frolova-Walker suggests that the Five shared Glinka's attitudes about the East: "Balakirev did not see the Oriental style as a means for representing a separate, alien people, and Other, in current parlance, but as an essential component of musical Russianness. The use of the newly constructed Oriental style was thus for Balakirev (and for the rest of the Kuchka in their earlier years) the easiest way to assert a distinct, non-European identity."[16]

Among the kuchkists no one understood this better than Aleksandr Porfir'evich Borodin.[17] Born in 1833 as the illegitimate son of a Georgian prince with Tatar ancestry, Luka Gedeanov, and his much younger Russian mistress, both European and Asian blood coursed through his veins. Stasov, who knew him well, remarked that "all . . . were struck by his characteristically Oriental appearance."[18] In a playful nod to his Eastern roots, Borodin occasionally appeared at costume balls dressed in Chinese robes.

Despite Aleksandr's somewhat bohemian childhood, Prince Gedeanov dutifully carried out his fatherly responsibilities by providing the means for a proper aristocratic upbringing. This allowed Borodin's mother to indulge the boy in his two passions—music and chemistry. He proved unusually gifted in both early on. By the age of nine, Aleksandr had composed his first polka, and four years later he wrote a concerto and a string trio, both of which were subsequently published. Meanwhile, the lad was allowed to concoct dangerous pyrotechnics and carry out chemistry experiments at home, filling the apartment with a variety of noxious odors.

When the time came for Aleksandr to pursue higher education, his mother was reluctant to send him to university. St. Petersburg's campus already had the reputation of being a hotbed of student unrest, and he therefore enrolled in the Military Medical Academy on the advice of a family friend. Borodin excelled in every subject, graduating in 1855 with the highest distinction, *cum eximia laude* (with exceeding praise). He was particularly close to his chemistry professor, who began grooming him as his successor. Although Borodin went on to earn a medical doctorate, his heart was not in being a physician. Instead, he eagerly took up his mentor's advice to join him as an assistant professor at the army's medical school in 1862, after a three-year study trip to Heidelberg and Paris. Respected by his colleagues and well liked by students, in little over two years Borodin won promotion to the chemistry chair, a post he held until his death.[19]

Borodin did not abandon his other love in medical school. The first surviving works, some chamber partitas and songs, date from his undergraduate days. One day during his internship at a military hospital, he met a young subaltern in the elite Preobrazhenskii Guards regiment, Modest Mussorgsky, and the two immediately hit it off as they chatted about music. A few years later, when Borodin again saw the officer, Mussorgsky played some of his own compositions, including an "Oriental" trio. Borodin recalled, "I was flabbergasted by these fantastic musical elements, which were totally new to me. I cannot say that I especially liked them at first; their novelty rather puzzled me. But after listening a little, I began to develop a taste for them."[20]

For the time being, Borodin's musical outlook remained distinctly Occidental. Describing himself as "an avid Mendelssohnian," during his stay in Heidelberg he frequently played chamber works with his friends. It was also in the German university town that he met his future wife, Ekaterina Protopopova, a talented pianist who had traveled there from Moscow in search of a treatment for her consumption. Their romance blossomed quickly as she introduced him to the delights of Frédéric Chopin and Franz Liszt, and they became acquainted with Richard Wagner's operas.

Shortly after taking up his teaching post in St. Petersburg, Borodin fell under the spell of the charismatic musical guru Mily Balakirev, who took him into his circle. His relationship with the domineering Balakirev eventually soured somewhat, but their years together strongly shaped the young professor's tastes. According to Stasov, Borodin "was soon transformed into a composer, whose abilities were most strongly characterized by the Russian, and inseparably linked with it, Oriental element."[21]

Borodin's orchestral debut was his First Symphony, which premiered at the Russian Musical Society in early January 1869 under Balakirev's baton. While there were some negative reviews, the response was generally quite favorable. Emboldened by his success, Borodin told his friends that he now wanted to write an opera, preferably on a Russian subject. One person who was in a good position to provide some ideas was Stasov, who held a post at St. Petersburg's Public Library. In April 1869, after a lengthy conversation, Stasov sent Borodin a detailed plan for an opera based on the twelfth-century *Song of Igor's Campaign*.

The suggestion appealed to Borodin immensely. "I don't know how to thank you," he wrote to Stasov. "*I just adore the subject.* But do I have the strength for it? I don't know. If you are afraid of wolves, do not go into the forest. I will give it a try."[22] With Stasov's help, he devoured almost every relevant work in the public library's holdings, including medieval chronicles, other epics such as the *Zadonshchina*, Nikolai Karamzin and Sergei Solov'ev's histories, and various Turkic songs. Borodin also traveled to Ukraine that summer with his wife to get a better idea of the terrain where Prince Igor's adventures took place, and he learned about the appearance of twelfth-century women by studying the frescoes in Kiev's ancient Saint Sophia cathedral. By September he had begun composing, but it was slow going. Early in 1870 the composer grew discouraged, and he abandoned the new undertaking for four years.

When Borodin took up the project again in 1874, he worked on the second act, which introduces the Polovtsians, Prince Igor's nomadic foe. Curious about their music, he turned to the ethnographer Vladimir Mainov, who wrote to a colleague in Budapest, Pál Hunfalvy. During the Mongol onslaught in the thirteenth century, some Polovtsians had migrated west, and their descendants still lived around northern Hungary's Mátra Mountains. Hunfalvy, who had a strong interest in folklore, had published the words to some of their songs. However, as he pointed out in his reply, by now these erstwhile Polovtsians were almost completely Magyarized. In relaying Hunfalvy's letter, Maikov suggested that Borodin might have more luck by studying the "guttural and jarring sounds" of more pristine, ethnically related Turkic nationalities such as the Chuvash, Bashkirs, and Kirghiz.[23] Nevertheless, Mainov forwarded a list of Hungarian folk songs, which included a "special collection of Polovtsian melodies."[24] Although there is no direct evidence that Borodin used any of the latter for the opera, his most authoritative Soviet biographer makes a convincing case for their influence on the Polovtsian Dances. Other sections of the second act draw on more distant exotic sources, including a French edition of Algerian and Tunisian songs the composer had bought in Paris and even a *chanson nègre* by the American Louis Moreau Gott-schalk.[25]

Borodin's musical depiction of the Polovtsians abounds in Orientalist clichés. Their maidens, who appear as the second act begins, are sultry indeed. The opening solo underscores their strident sexuality with its sinuous melismas (a single syllable sung over several notes), "iconically erotic" syncopation, and descending chromatic line, which, Taruskin suggests, "completes the picture of the seductive East."[26] When the Royal Opera staged *Prince Igor* at London's Covent Garden in 1990, nude bathers gently carried out their ablutions to the melody to further heighten its carnality. As for the men, their vigorous gyrations in the famous Polovtsian Dances and the jarring Polovtsian March that introduces the third act effectively convey their virile savagery. Their leader, Khan Konchak, who is characteristically sung by a bass, lavishes his prisoners with Eastern hospitality.

Yet for all of these genuflections to European conventions about the Asian other, there are also some striking dissonances. While the Polovtsians are clearly a formidable foe, Borodin presents them in a remarkably favorable light. Their warriors cause much misery and grief when they raid the Kievan lands. But war is war. Back in their camp, they are honorable men. The only bad Polovtsian is the secretly baptized Ovlur, who is wicked precisely because he betrays his kinfolk by converting to the enemy's faith.

The contrast with Borodin's portrayal of the Christian Rus is striking. In the prologue, the boyars and people all join in Prince Igor's capital, Putivl, to wish their leader victory as he sets off against the Polovtsians "for the Faith, for Rus', for the People."[27] But their show of unity proves highly deceptive. As soon as Igor has set off, his brother-in-law, Prince Galitskii, tries to usurp power and begins an orgy of drink and rape. Skula and Eroshka, two Russian fiddlers introduced in the opera as comic elements, desert Igor's army in the prologue, and in act 4 hypocritically save their skins by announcing Igor's return from captivity.

One of the opera's most sympathetic characters is the Polovtsian leader, Khan Konchak. Although he is a renowned warrior, the khan is respectful and solicitous of Prince Igor, whom he holds in captivity. When in act 2 Igor rejects Konchak's offer of an alliance, the khan good-naturedly laughs it off, praises his involuntary guest's spirit, and calls in the dancing girls.

In a curious transmutation of stereotypical gender roles, here Konchak the Oriental is the suitor, and Igor the Occidental is the equivalent of a reluctant maiden. Later on, when Igor's son Vladimir tries but fails to escape from Polovtsian captivity, Konchak magnanimously spares his life.

This sympathetic portrayal marked a distinct departure from Stasov's plan, not to mention the original Igor tale.[28] Unusually for a composer, Borodin wrote the opera's libretto himself and, in doing so, made some important changes. If Stasov emphasized the conflict between the Rus and their alien foes, Borodin toned them down. Thus he deleted a violent fit of rage by the khan and instead stressed his chivalry. Stasov's scenario had also included a group of foreign merchants in Putivl who join Prince Galitskii's reign of debauchery after Igor leaves. But in Borodin's libretto the usurpers are all native Russians. And Borodin ends his opera differently. According to Stasov, the formulaic happy-ending nuptials had Prince Igor's son return home with the khan's daughter, where the two would be joined in a Christian ceremony and presumably live happily ever after as Konchakova was fully assimilated into the Rus. By contrast, Borodin's Vladimir Igor'evich does not escape from the Polovtsian camp and instead settles down as Konchak's son-in-law.[29]

Toward the conclusion of their second-act duet, Konchak offers Igor his freedom if the prince pledges never again to take up arms against the Polovtsians. When Igor obstinately refuses, Konchak responds, "I am like that myself!"[30] It is an interesting remark. In a letter to Stasov about the opera, Borodin wrote: "I cannot escape dualism—not in the form of a dualistic theory in chemistry, nor in biology, philosophy and psychology, or in the Austro-Hungarian monarchy!"[31] The composer's motif of the sun offers another example of what the duo has in common. The symbol of regal power for Louis XIV, France's seventeenth-century *Roi Soleil,* is a metaphor in the opera both for the authority of the Christian Prince Igor and the pagan Khan Konchak. The people of Putivl open the prologue by singing to their prince: "All hail the sun in its beauty."[32] Toward the end of act 2, as the Polovtsians dance for Konchak, they salute the khan in a similar vein: "He is like the sun at midday."[33]

The khan's assertion, "I am like that myself!" underscores one of Borodin's central messages. If the twelfth-century Igor tale presented the Polovtsians as the other, in the opera they are binary selves. One Soviet musicologist pointed out that, in *Prince Igor*, Borodin "repeatedly stresses this . . . synthesis of Oriental and Russian."[34] Like its composer, who had both European and Asian blood, *Prince Igor*'s West and East are two sides of the same coin. His Asia is not a Saidian other, but the Christian Rus's alter ego. Together they created Russia; both Prince Igor and Khan Konchak are the empire's ancestors. "Nowhere [in the sources] was there any mention of a decisive victory over the Polovtsians" Borodin reminds us.[35] The composer clearly was no musical Skobelev, wielding bass clef and quarter time instead of *shashka* and knout to subjugate the Orient. As he saw it, Russia did not vanquish the Orient but joined with it, much as the Christian Prince Vladimir Igorevich was united to the pagan khan's daughter Konchakova in marriage.

Borodin did not live to complete his opera. With many distractions, both as professor and as an activist for women's higher education, he could only rarely snatch quiet moments to compose. As he joked in a letter, "In winter I can only write music when sickness keeps me from going to work. For this reason, my musical friends, contrary to general custom, always wish me ill rather than good health."[36] When a heart attack suddenly claimed his life in 1887, eighteen years after he had first begun *Prince Igor*, the opera remained unfinished. Fortunately, Rimsky-Korsakov and a younger composer, Aleksandr Glazunov, recognized its value and picked up where he left off.

Prince Igor's premiere was on October 23, 1890, at St. Petersburg's Marinskii Theater. Reflecting Alexander III's preference for Pyotr Il'ich Tchaikovsky's more Western style, the Marinskii's director had hesitated staging it, and there would be fewer than fifty performances before 1917.[37] At the same time, according to the publisher Aleksei Suvorin, the opera met with an enthusiastic reception from the audience.[38] Although some grumbled that the Polovtsians were portrayed more positively than the Rus, most contemporaries saw *Prince Igor* as a patriotic work that celebrated the Orthodox Slavs' struggle against the heathen foe.[39]

Borodin had remarked about his composition that it was "essentially a national opera," written for Russians who wanted to see "the origins of our nationality brought back to life on stage."[40] His vision of Russia's past, however, was much less hostile to its Asian roots. Albeit with entirely commercial motives, the enterprising impresario Sergei Diaghilev conveyed this well when he began staging some of the more spectacular Polovtsian dances and songs from *Prince Igor* (with choreography by Mikhail Fokine) for Parisian audiences in 1907, thereby launching the fashion abroad for the highly Orientalist *style russe*.

Few who saw *Prince Igor* when it was first performed shared the late composer's ideas about their Asian roots.[41] But during the next decades, which would come to be known as the Silver Age, many more would be receptive to such notions. At the turn of the twentieth century, Russian culture saw both a return to the exotic as well as a retreat from the earnest, civic-minded realism that had dominated it since the 1840s. Emancipating themselves from the obligation to serve social progress, writers and artists in the 1890s let their imaginations wander back to the more ethereal realms they had largely avoided since the days of the Romantics.

The philosopher and poet Dmitrii Merezhkovskii launched the assault on realism in 1892 with his lectures "On the Reasons for the Decline, and the New Currents, in Contemporary Literature."[42] In the guise of a general survey, Merezhkovskii's talks attacked the "fatally stifling positivism" of Russian letters. Instead of slavishly carrying on the realists' strident didacticism and "coarse photographic precision," he urged writers to adopt the "new art" of such artists as Charles Baudelaire and Edgar Allan Poe. This new art, he explained, had three basic elements: "*mystical contents, symbols,* and a broader artistic sensibility."[43] Neither the lectures nor the book that followed the next year attracted much attention. The angry riposte of a leading populist critic, Nikolai Mikhailovskii, however, did much to spread Merezhkovskii's message.[44]

Merezhkovskii was, of course, basically transmitting a literary trend that had first manifested itself in France twenty years earlier in the verse of Paul Verlaine, Arthur Rimbaud, and Stéphane Mallarmé, among others. Labeled symbolism, the movement advocated a poetry that sought to convey the hidden, deeper realities of the cosmos through indirect allusion, analogy, and metaphor. Exoticism and erudition were important features, but the guiding principle was a highly refined aesthetic that sought to appeal to a multitude of senses.[45]

If the realists optimistically believed that they could build a better world by condemning its shortcomings through their art, symbolists tended to

be more pessimistic. Indeed, the literary term *decadence* is virtually synonymous with symbolism. As the nineteenth century drew to a close, the
symbolists looked to the twentieth with grim foreboding. Decades of relative peace and rising prosperity paradoxically bred a sentiment that a cataclysm was inevitable. Resisting the inevitable was pointless, and the only
option was to savor civilization's refined pleasures in its golden twilight.[46]
Verlaine captured the age's spirit with his verse "Languor" (1883):

> I am the Empire at the end of its decadence,
> Watching the blond barbarians pass
> As I compose indolent acrostics
> With golden stylus reflecting the languor of the sun's dance . . .[47]

Merezhkovskii's summons to champion beauty over duty in art found
a ready response among poets like Valerii Briusov and Konstantin Balmont. Both entered the literary scene in 1894. Briusov, an ambitious
young Muscovite, precociously proclaimed himself the head of a new
school that year by producing an anthology of translated French and native verse, *Russian Symbolism*. Meanwhile, the aristocratic polyglot Balmont published his first major volume of poetry, *Under the Northern Sky*
(1894), whose overt eroticism and experimental rhythms were also much
in the style of the French symbolists.

While more traditional readers were shocked by their "decadent"
rhymes, others soon joined Briusov and Balmont in their new course. This
postrealist period in Russian literature, roughly the quarter century before
1917, has been given various labels, including symbolism, decadence, neo-
Romanticism and modernism.[48] But "Silver Age" has emerged as the most
common designation. Popularized by one of its contemporaries, Anna
Akhmatova, in her later *Poem without a Hero* (1940), it is a respectful nod
to the Golden Age of Russian poetry in the time of Pushkin.[49] There is a
classical allusion too, since in Latin literature "Silver Age" refers to the
cosmopolitan flowering during the first century A.D., after the Golden Age
that preceded it. At the same time, as the British Slavist Avril Pyman suggests, by invoking the less radiant precious metal, "the term 'Silver Age,'
with its connotations of art, dusk and the reflected brilliance of the moon
and stars," nicely evokes the spirit of tsarism's crepuscular decades.[50]

As in the Pushkinian Golden Age, the Orient was a favorite theme of

Russia's Silver Age. Balmont, who claimed Mongol heritage on his mother's side of the family, was particularly prolific.[51] Among the most peripatetic poets of his day—Balmont spent over half of his life abroad—he had a great interest in Asian literature, especially that of Egypt, India, and Japan.[52] According to one Russian scholar, *Indian Herbs* (1900), Balmont's cycle of poems inspired by the subcontinent's thought, strongly influenced Silver Age verse.[53] Like the Romantics, the bard also experimented with Eastern forms, and he published verse imitating classical Japanese haiku and tanka after a 1916 trip to the island empire.

Asia's distant past appealed most to Balmont. Sharing his generation's profound distaste for Europe's bourgeois materialism, he hoped to find inspiration for the future on alien shores. The poet wrote his publisher that "Russia is fast approaching a complete transvaluation of all the basic values." He added that neither classical Greece nor Rome could provide any answers, since "the Russian spirit by far does not aspire in tense and hard moments of internal struggle" to their way of thought. Instead, his compatriots should seek new elements through "foreign legends [which] endorsed by the centuries retain light for our days."[54] While these included Maya and Aztec mythology, the poet generally referred to the Orient.

Balmont's ideas about Asia as a source of wisdom echoed those of Count Leo Tolstoy. Having begun his university studies in Kazan with Mirza Kazem-Bek, the novelist had long been interested in the East. Tolstoy's fascination intensified after a profound spiritual crisis in the late 1870s led him to turn to Indian and Chinese thought.[55] Although he did not abandon his Christian faith, the count was particularly taken with Hindu and Buddhist ideas about nonviolence. In his later years, he corresponded with the Indian nationalist Mahatma Gandhi. (It was partly via the Russian writer that Gandhi was inspired by such notions from his own South Asian tradition.)[56] Tolstoy also looked to such Chinese philosophers as Laozi (Laotzu) and Confucius, whose teachings seemed a much better model for Russia than Western rationalism and materialism. Given the author's fetishization of the peasantry, the Middle Kingdom held great appeal. In an unpublished discussion of Confucianism probably written in 1884, he gushed: "The Chinese are the most peaceful people in the world. They seek nothing from others, nor do they engage in war. [This is because] the Chinese are tillers of the soil. Their ruler himself begins the plowing."[57]

Endowed with a remarkable facility for languages, Balmont partly supported himself by translating foreign literature. He focused on European writers, including Shelley, Poe, Shakespeare, Lope de Vega, Ibsen, Maeterlinck, and Julius Słowacki. He also rendered Asian works into Russian, albeit primarily from English and French versions. When in 1911 his friend the Moscow-based publisher Mikhail Sabashnikov asked him to contribute some "ancient texts" to a projected series of "masterpieces of world literature," Balmont agreed to participate, provided that he could go further back than the Greeks and Romans. These, he felt, were nothing more than, "imitators and repeaters . . . of authentic values, such as [those of] Egypt, Chaldea, the Jews and India." The latter were "doubtless much more interesting and worthy of translation than the Greeks and Romans."[58] Balmont therefore offered to provide *The Life of Buddha* by the first-century Indian poet Asvaghosa. After a lengthy journey abroad in 1912, which included South Asia, Balmont enlisted Sergei Oldenburg's help to produce Russian texts of three of the fifth-century Indian dramatist Kalidasa's plays for Sabashnikov's enterprise too.

Balmont and Briusov were of the Silver Age's first generation, which looked to Asia primarily for its exotic aesthetic and alternate spirituality, much as did the symbolists of the West. Rising to prominence in the wake of Russia's disastrous war with Japan of 1904–5, the second generation had a more distinctive perspective. Andrei Bely's remarkable novels capture its essence well.

Bely was the pseudonym of Boris Bugaev, the delicate son of a prominent Moscow University mathematics professor.[59] Born in 1880, the boy did not have an easy childhood; his father, an ungainly academic, and his mother, a high-strung socialite of renowned beauty, were spectacularly mismatched. Their frequent, stormy quarrels, which the author conveyed in his semiautobiographical novellas, *Kotik Letaev* (1917–18) and *The Baptized Chinese* (1927), filled him with a sense of apocalyptic dread from early childhood. One of the author's first memories was a discussion between his parents about whether to divorce. Ultimately they decided against it, since neither dared entrust the other with sole responsibility for their child's upbringing.

Like Borodin, Boris was initially torn between science and art. From his father he absorbed a passion for mathematics and abstract thought, while his mother, an accomplished pianist, instilled in him a love of music. After graduating from Moscow University's Faculty of Mathematics and Physics with first-class standing, the poet decisively opted for the muses. He had become acquainted with literature through the family of a boyhood friend and neighbor, Sergei Solov'ev. In contrast to his own chaotic household, the Solov'evs offered an oasis of domestic tranquility, and the lad visited them daily, if not even more often.

As the brother of the philosopher and poet Vladimir Solov'ev, Sergei's father, Mikhail, closely followed cultural developments. Together with his wife, Olga, an artist and translator, he awoke the latent lyrical talent in young Boris. With Mikhail's strong encouragement and a generous subsidy, in 1902 Boris published his first important work, a highly innovative "symphony" in prose. To avoid scandalizing his father, who now served as his faculty's dean, he adopted the nom de plume of Andrei Bely (Andrew White). A collection of poems, *Gold in Azure,* followed two years later. Given Olga's penchant for Verlaine, Maeterlinck, Wilde, Baudelaire and Balmont, her young protégé not surprisingly adopted their style. Bely did not take his new poetic affiliation lightly. He later reminisced that "at the time I already regarded Symbolism not as a literary school but an original worldview that harmoniously united religion, a way of life, art and speculative thought."[60]

As his recollection suggests, Bely very much shared the era's mystical proclivities. At his gymnasium, whose priest was one of his favorite teachers, he steeped himself in Buddhist and Hindu thought, as well as the Vedic culture of ancient India. Bely also flirted with occultism and Madame Blavatsky's Theosophy, an esoteric belief partly based on Eastern spirituality that stressed direct communion with God (Theos). In his late teens he turned to the ideas of the German philosophers Arthur Schopenhauer and Friedrich Nietzsche. Finally, in 1910 his first wife, Asia Turgeneva, introduced him to the teachings of Rudolf Steiner, an Austrian scientist who had split with the Theosophists to develop Anthroposophy. Similarly aspiring to a more elevated consciousness to reach the spiritual world, the doctrine strongly influenced Bely's writings over the next decade.

It was at his neighbors' flat in the spring of 1900 that Bely had a fateful meeting with Vladimir Solov'ev that profoundly shaped his view of the world. Vladimir was Russia's foremost nineteenth-century philosopher, and in his later years he had increasingly become preoccupied with eschatology, or the study of the end of the world. As Vladimir explained in "Pan-Mongolism," a famous poem composed as Japan's modern military was spectacularly routing the Qing dynasty in 1894, the East was a force of evil that would bring about the final cataclysm:

Pan-Mongolism! Though the word be fierce
It is music to my ear
Like some portent
of God's awesome fate entire . . .

From Malaysian waters to the Altai,
Chieftains from Eastern isles
Gather their hosts
At decadent China's walls.

Like locust swarms uncountable
And insatiable like them too,
By divine strength guarded,
Northwards move the tribes.

O Russia! Forget your former glory:
The double-headed eagle is no more,
And yellow babes play
With the rags remaining from your flags.[61]

Vladimir Solov'ev developed these ideas in his "Short Tale of the Antichrist," which he read at his brother's apartment in Bely's presence. According to this prophecy of the Apocalypse, a Japanese-born emperor would unite the Orient's hordes, as had Genghis Khan eight centuries earlier, and launch a second Asian assault on Europe, whose annihilation would herald the Kingdom of God.[62] The student had a brief conversation with the philosopher, who promised to meet him again that fall. Although Vladimir died a few months later, before he could see Bely again, their brief encounter left its mark. According to the latter, "from that time on, I lived with the feeling of the End."[63]

Despite occasional protestations to the contrary, to the sensitive author the "yellow peril" became more than a poetic metaphor. Sometime after his encounter with Solov'ev, during a summer holiday in the country as he contemplated a network of ravines, he imagined them to be manifestation of the destructive East, "gnawing away the fertile earth, and crawling menacingly toward us." In a Canute-like attempt to stem the corrosive onslaught, Bely frantically took to hurling rocks into the chasm.[64]

Bely was not alone. If the Silver Age's first generation had largely ignored Solov'ev, in his immediate afterlife the gloomy mystic became a dominant influence on a number of Bely's contemporaries, including the poets Aleksandr Blok and Viacheslav Ivanov. Tsarism's stunning defeats in southern Manchuria and the Sea of Japan only five years after the philosopher's death, and the revolutionary violence that convulsed all of Russia in its wake, evidently confirmed Solov'ev's sinister prediction about the yellow peril. In an article appropriately titled "The Apocalypse in Russian Poetry," written shortly after Japanese troops marched into the Manchurian capital of Mukden, Bely announced that "the great mystic was right. . . . The specter of the Mongol assault arose ominously. The vortex flew by, throwing up clouds of dust. And the light turned red, curtained by the dust: Verily, the global conflagration had begun."[65] Yet as Bernice Rosenthal points out, the second generation looked to the coming Armageddon with hope, for it was after all the harbinger the Second Coming.[66]

Although very much of the first generation, the opportunistic Briusov was the first major poet to take up Solov'ev's message about the Oriental threat. He had initially penned patriotic verse when hostilities erupted in early 1904. Writing to a friend, Briusov ironically identified his own compatriots as foes of civilization: "Let Russian shells shatter [Tokyo's] temples, its museums, even its artists. . . . May all Japan turn into a dead Hellas, into ruins of a better and greater past. I am for the barbarians. I am for the Huns. I am for the Russians!"[67] Just for good measure, that fall he even began illustrating issues of his journal, *Vesy* (The Scales), with reproductions of his collection of Japanese woodblock prints. When it became increasingly evident that a Russian victory was not forthcoming, Briusov's mood darkened. By summer 1905, as the tsar's Baltic Fleet lay at the bottom of the Tsushima Strait, the poet now saw the Japanese as culture's nemesis in his "The Coming Huns":

Where are you, coming Huns,
Who weigh on the world like clouds?
I hear your cast-iron tread
From the still hidden Pamir . . .
All that we alone knew
Will perhaps be razed without trace,
But you, who annihilate me,
I greet with welcoming song.

Briusov was clearly echoing Verlaine, who had once joyfully hailed the "blond barbarians" as they might ravage his moribund civilization. Only now, instead of being German, the destructive hordes came from deepest Asia.

Bely's response to war and revolution had a longer gestation period. And when it came, rather than being an alien force, the yellow peril was within Russia itself. In the years after 1905, Bely contemplated writing a trilogy of novels to follow his recent "symphonies." Provisionally titled *East or West,* it was meant to explore Russia's relationship with Eurasia's antipodes. He published the first installment, *The Silver Dove,* in 1909.[68] A meditation on the opposition of East to West, it tells the story of a poet from the city, Petr Darial'skii, who is spending the summer in the country to be near his fiancée, the innocent and lovely Katia. A misunderstanding with Katia's grandmother, Baroness Todrabe-Graaben, leads him to break off the engagement. After a heavy drinking bout in a village tavern, he wanders about aimlessly and eventually finds solace in the arms of Matrena, a coarse peasant woman with "browless and pock-marked face," flaccid breasts, potbelly, and a lascivious smile. Matrena is the "spiritual wife" of the carpenter Kudeiarov, who leads a secret orgiastic sect, the White Doves. Far from intervening, Kudeiarov encourages the liaison with Darial'skii in hopes that Matrena will bear a child who might become the new Messiah. However, she fails to conceive, and when Darial'skii tries to flee Kudeiarov has him brutally murdered.

Set in 1905 against the ominous backdrop of "agrarian disturbances everywhere," *The Silver Dove* contrasts two solitudes that are both malignant in their own way. The West, as suggested by the baroness's macabre German surname, Todrabe-Graaben (dead raven–grave), represents lifeless reason. Personified by the White Doves, the East embodies unbridled, animalistic, destructive irrationality. Like some naive populist intellectuals of the time, Darial'skii had sought true wisdom among the peasantry, only to find "horror; the noose and the pit: not Russia, but some dark abyss of the East presses upon Russia from these bodies wasted by sectarian exultation."[69] But is the Orient truly "not Russia"? Bely is highly ambiguous on this score. The baroness's son, a thoroughly Occidental high state official, tells Darial'skii: "Russia is a Mongol country. We all have Mongolian blood in our veins, and [therefore our nation] will not resist the invasion." He adds, "We are fated to prostrate ourselves before the idol."[70] As for Europe, Darial'skii reflects, "Many are the books in the West; many the unuttered words in Russia. Russia is that against which a book is shattered, knowledge crumbles, and life itself is burnt; the day the West is grafted onto Russia, a universal fire will spread over it."[71]

Two years after *The Silver Dove,* Bely began work on the second novel of his projected trilogy, *Petersburg.*[72] Once again the action takes place during the revolutionary disorders of 1905, but now in the imperial capital during early autumn. The plot, such as it is, revolves around a reactionary senator, Apollon Apollonovich Ableukhov and his student son, Nikolai. Having become involved in a terrorist organization, Ableukhov *fils* is ordered by the conspirator Dudkin to assassinate his father with a bomb, which in the end explodes harmlessly.

While the characters are vividly portrayed, they are purely secondary to the real narrative: the West's desperate struggle to resist destruction by the East. The theme resembles that of *The Silver Dove,* but it plays out on a much larger scale. Instead of depicting an individual caught between a Germanic aristocratic family and a quasi-Oriental peasant sect, the story now involves nothing less than the impending doom of a great metropolis—and, by extension, the Romanov autocracy—as the miasmic yellow peril threatens to engulf it. Written in fragmentary snippets of prose, Bely's novel was described as "a rendition of delirium unprecedented in literature . . . a world of nightmare and horror."[73]

Asia lurks everywhere in the troubled capital. The color yellow is ubiquitous, from the yellow walls of Ableukhov's mansion, his servant Semenich's yellow heels, the "yellow, Mongol mugs" of pedestrians, and the provocateur Lippachenko's vulgar yellow garb, to the yellow-green fog that often envelops the city. Sofia Petrovna Likhutina, Nikolai's paramour, decorates her apartment with Japanese art and wears a kimono. Dudkin consorts with a spectral Persian, Shishnarfne, and sees Tatars and Japanese in his dreams. Meanwhile, the occasional sight of "shaggy Manchurian fur hats"—the *shapkas* of veterans returning from the Far Eastern front—both remind the reader of recent calamities and herald even more momentous ones to come: "Five years have passed [since the Boxer rising]. There has been an uproar of events. Port Arthur has fallen. That region has been inundated by yellow-faced people. The legends about the horsemen of Genghis Khan have come back to life. . . . Listen, listen closely: there is a sound of galloping . . . from the Ural steppes. It is horsemen."[74]

Not unlike a number of prominent real Russian lineages, the fictional Ableukhov family traces its origins to the East, from whence a Kirghiz forefather had entered Russian service in the early eighteenth century. Nevertheless, as Apollon Apollonovich's given name and patronymic suggest, the senator's outlook is entirely Occidental. Devoid of emotion, he has a mania for order; his thoughts are filled with "squares, parallelepipeds, cubes" and other abstract geometric shapes. But if Apollon Apollonovich is the caricature of the West's sterile rationality, his son is regressing to his Asian roots. Having taken to wearing a Bukharan dressing gown, central Asian skullcap, and Tatar slippers, "Nikolai remembered: he was an old Turanian who had been incarnated in the blood, in the flesh of hereditary nobility, in order to carry out a secret mission: to shake everything to its foundation. The Ancient Dragon was to feed on tainted blood, and to consume everything in flame. . . . Nikolai Apollonovich was an old Turanian bomb."[75]

The Slavist Georges Nivat points out that, whereas Dostoyevsky in his novel *The Demons* portrayed revolutionary violence as coming from the West, Bely saw it as Eastern, a manifestation of Solov'ev's pan-Mongolist menace.[76] Yet in contrast to Solov'ev, Bely did not regard the Orient as alien. Just as with Russia's bicontinental geography, Asia and Europe were both inextricable parts of his country's identity. Bely also saw them as constituting his own. He titled a novel based on his childhood, *The Baptized Chinese* (1921), after his father, who assumed various Asian identities throughout the text. In 1915, in a letter about his recent novels to his publisher, the radical literary critic Ivanov-Razumnik, Bely explained, "The soul's *song* is the East; the orchestration and counterpoint are the West," which should join to produce the "symphony" of an ideal Russia. The first parts of his trilogy, *The Silver Dove* and *Petersburg,* explored how the two were discordant, but a third would explain how harmony might be achieved.[77]

Bely never completed his trilogy, since the events of 1917 changed his views of the revolution and the East. Before the collapse of the Romanov dynasty and the Bolshevik takeover, he had portrayed them negatively, emphasizing their violence and destruction. Now he put the accent on their positive aspects. No longer the Apocalypse, in 1918 the revolution assumed the guise of the Second Coming.[78] Like Blok, who hailed the Bolsheviks as latter-day apostles in his celebrated poem of January that year, *The Twelve,* Bely wrote a similarly ecstatic verse a few months later, *Christ Is Risen.* And when he revised *Petersburg* a few years later, he considerably softened his assessment of the political upheavals of the recent past. According to Ivanov-Razumnik, "Between 1913 and 1922 Bely ceased to equate revolution with Mongolism and equated it instead with Scythianism."[79]

By using the term "Scythianism," Ivanov-Razumnik was referring to a literary movement he led in the revolution's immediate aftermath.[80] The group took its name from a nomadic nation of Eastern origin that had roamed the southern Russian steppes in the time of Herodotus, some 2,500 years earlier. Archaeological digs at kurgans (Scythian burial mounds) during the late nineteenth century had done much to raise the profile of this mysterious Inner Asian people with their remarkable gold artifacts. Catherine the Great and Pushkin had already toyed with notions of this savage streak in Russia's ancestry. The latter once proclaimed:

> Temperance suits me not right now,
> I long to drink like a Scythian.[81]

To some Silver Age poets, the Scythians came to represent the untamed vitality of their nation's soul, and verses lauding their putative ancestors proliferated.[82] Among the first was Balmont, who praised the nomads' free spirit and martial prowess in "The Scythians" (1899):

> We blessed hordes of freely roaming Scythians,
> Prize freedom above all else.
> Flying from Olvia's castle with its griffin statues,
> Hidden from the foe, we overtake him everywhere . . . [83]

Russians were not the only or even the first Slavs to identify themselves with Inner Asian nomadic ancestors. The intellectual historian Andrzej Walicki argues that during the seventeenth century the Polish *szlachta* (gentry) proudly proclaimed its affinity with the Sarmatians, an Iranian nation that had supplanted the Scythians in southeastern Europe some two millennia earlier.[84] "Sarmatianism," he argues, was the legacy of Poland's union with Lithuania in 1569, which transformed the Catholic kingdom into the much larger multiconfessional and ethnically diverse Polish Commonwealth. Walicki explains that "the expansion to the East and the Eastern-oriented politics of the Commonwealth weakened the Western character of the Polish national consciousness." The result was "the effective integration of the Polish elite with the recently Polonized elites of Lithuania and Ukraine [which] brought into being a new 'Sarmatian' culture, an original synthesis of East and West, proud of its uniqueness and consciously turning away from Western royalism and moral corruption."[85] Sarmatianism stressed the independent spirit and quasi-anarchic refusal to submit to authority of their imagined nomadic forefathers, which its adherents saw reflected in the commonwealth's own distinct identity. In this way, the seventeenth-century Poles who advocated these ideas prefigured the Russian poets who looked to their Scythian roots at the turn of the twentieth century.

Ivanov-Razumnik, the Scythianists' self-proclaimed leader, enthusiastically accepted the new Bolshevik order. While continuing to associate violent upheaval with the East, he now embodied it in the native Scythians rather than the alien Mongols.[86] For a few years, Bely, Blok, and the other poets associated with Ivanov-Razumnik's literary movement celebrated Russia's barbarous Asian identity in the almanac *Skify* (The Scythians) and other works. Tighter controls on culture and growing disenchantment with Lenin's regime led to the circle's gradual dissolution in the early 1920s.

According to the Italian literary scholar Ettore Lo Gatto, Silver Age authors had adopted an Eastern identity to flout the West: "In Russian poetry, the terms Mongolian, Scythian and Hun are ideological concepts with Slavophile connotations, and they were similarly brandished to proclaim Russia's distinct, so to speak Eurasian, character to the Western world."[87] No one expressed this better than Bely's close friend Blok in

his defiant "The Scythians." Blok wrote the poem in early 1918 as a warning to the West not to interfere in the Bolsheviks' negotiations for a separate peace with the Central Powers at Brest-Litovsk:

> You have your millions. We are hordes, and hordes, and hordes.
> Just try it! Take us on!
> Yes, we are Scythians! Yes, we're Asians too!
> With slanting eyes bespeaking greed! . . .
>
> The day has come. Catastrophe spreads her wings,
> Every day the humiliations mount,
> Until the day dawns
> When your Paestums vanish without trace.
>
> Oh ancient world! While your heart still beats,
> While you languish in sweet torment,
> Stop and think,
> Like Oedipus before the riddling Sphinx.
>
> Russia is the Sphinx. Triumphant yet in sorrow,
> Awash in dark blood,
> She gazes, and gazes, and gazes upon you,
> With hatred and with love! . . .[88]

While some symbolists greeted the revolution with great enthusiasm,
others voted with their feet by going into exile. Rapidly growing disillusioned with the Bolsheviks, Bely joined the expatriates for a time in 1921
when he moved to Berlin. But Mother Russia's pull proved too strong,
and two years later he returned to Moscow. The poet was not greeted
with open arms. Having rebuked Marxism during his stay abroad, he was
lambasted by Lenin's lieutenant Leon Trotsky and now found himself
treated as a "living corpse."[89] Nevertheless, Bely's pen was anything but
moribund. During the next ten years he would publish several novels as
well as a travel account of the Caucasus. In the early 1930s, toward the
end of his life, Bely also wrote three volumes of memoirs that attempted
to reconcile symbolism with revolutionary Marxism. He was at work on a
fourth when he died in January 1934 from natural causes.

Like the early nineteenth-century Russian Romantic fascination with the East, the Silver Age aesthetic was also influenced by tsarist colonialism. If Pushkin and Lermontov were inspired by the "pacification" of the Caucasus, Nicholas II's Far Eastern debacle shaped the outlook of Bely and his generation. On the whole, the literature directly related to the Russo-Japanese War was relatively modest.[90] Combined, however, with the revolutionary upheavals that accompanied the autocracy's defeat on the Pacific, they heightened fin-de-siècle notions of impending cataclysm. The mood was a Western import, which had originated two decades earlier among the French *décadents,* but the upheavals of 1905 made what had been a fashionable literary pose alarmingly tangible. And during the long decade before the Romanov dynasty's collapse, which Georges Florovsky so aptly termed the "spiritual time of troubles," many came to share Solov'ev's pessimistic musings about the Orient's link to Armageddon.[91]

What was unique about the Silver Age was its identification of the coming apocalypse as something internal rather than coming from abroad. In his opera depicting an earlier military adventure in central Asia, Borodin had already alluded to his nation's Oriental origins. But to Bely and his contemporaries, the other, whether as Mongol or Scythian, was even more distinctly part of Russia's exotic self.

CONCLUSION: ASIA IN THE RUSSIAN MIND

The Russian soul undeniably has an "Asian stratification."
—Nikolai Berdiaev

Russians have always known the East. But they only became conscious of Asia as a separate continent when they began to regard themselves as European under Peter the Great. In turning to the West, Peter taught his subjects to think more systematically about the East. Indeed, it was one of the tsar's more learned men, the polymath Vasilii Tatishchev, who definitively set the continental boundary along the Ural Mountains.[1] Peter also launched orientology as an academic discipline in his realm, albeit it partly at Gottfried Leibniz's suggestion.

Educated Russians never identified themselves more closely with the West than during Catherine the Great's reign.[2] Confident of their European identity, they did not necessarily look to Asia with haughty disdain, for their age happened to coincide with the Enlightenment's philo-orientalism. However, toward the end of her rule, even Catherine's enthusiasm for Western ways began to sour when she learned of the Bourbon monarchy's sanguinary end. The revolutionary turmoil that gripped France and Napoleon's invasion in 1812 also led many others to question their ties to Europe. As Nikolai Karamzin put it, "Once upon a time we used to call all other Europeans *infidels;* now we call them brothers. For whom was it easier to conquer Russia—for *infidels* or for *brothers?* That is, who was she likely to resist better?"[3]

The growing influence of German Romanticism in the early decades of the nineteenth century further encouraged speculation about Russia's place in the world. The discussion was spectacularly launched in 1836 by the publication of Petr Chaadaev's "First Philosophical Letter" in the journal *Teleskop* (The Telescope). Written seven years earlier in French and initially privately circulated, the article pessimistically proclaimed that Russia was an orphan among the family of nations, without history or identity: "We are neither of the West nor the East and don't have the traditions of the one or the other. Placed outside of the times, we have been bypassed by mankind's universal education."[4] Chaadaev's "Letter" was a succès de scandale. Aleksandr Herzen later described it as "a shot that rang out in the dark night," while Nicholas I had its author declared insane.[5]

Chaadaev's gloomy assessment initiated the stormy debate between the Westernizers and the Slavophiles in the early nineteenth century. The Westernizers believed that Russia should develop along western European lines toward an order based on rationalism, the rule of law, and the primacy of the individual, while their opponents advocated rejecting Peter the Great's Occidental turn and returning to what they saw as their nation's distinctly spiritual and paternalist course.[6] If the Slavophiles opposed Western modernity, they did not suggest that Russia was Asian. What they championed was Orthodox, Slavic Europe rather than its Romano-German variant.[7]

There was one intriguing partial exception. Much as Friedrich von Schlegel had divided the world between Indo-European Aryans and non-Aryans, Aleksei Khomiakov, the most prominent Slavophile, detected a fundamental dichotomy in humankind. One group, the Kushites, were descended from Noah's disgraced son Ham and had originated in northern Africa. According to Khomiakov, the Kushites embodied submission and nihilism and were in constant struggle with the Iranians, the race that represented freedom and spirituality. As a force of creative vitality, the Iranians had initially established both Greece and Rome. However, Khomiakov argued, successive waves of Kushites had subjected western Europe to their more repressive and heathen order. Only the Slavs had escaped the dominion of the Kushites over the continent.[8] In Khomiakov's conception of history lay the roots of the notion, increasingly popular toward the turn of the twentieth century, that Russians had retained the youthful vigor of their Scythian Oriental ancestors.

Chaadaev, as he subsequently elaborated in his "Apology of a Madman," stood firmly in the Westernizers' camp: "We live in Europe's East, but this fact does not make us Eastern." His aversion for the Orient was clear. "In the East, docile minds that submitted to tradition spent themselves slavishly obeying some sacred principle and in the end . . . fell into a deep slumber, entirely ignorant of their destiny."[9] Chaadaev's negative characterization of Asia as mired in stagnant somnolence reflected a profound transformation from the Enlightenment's Sinophilia to the disparaging European views of China at the turn of the nineteenth century. Beginning with Johann Gottfried Herder's contemptuous dismissal of the empire as "an embalmed mummy, wrapped in silk, and painted with hieroglyphics," Romantic thinkers saw the Middle Kingdom as despotic, and immobile, its people nothing but ants utterly devoid of free will or imagination.[10]

Kitaishchina now acquired a strongly pejorative sense in the Russian vocabulary. If in Catherine's day the noun evoked a playfully exotic China, during the nineteenth century it became associated with antediluvian tyranny, shameless corruption, and utter immobility. *Azia* also began to have negative connotations, much like "Asiatic" in English. Vladimir Dal's dictionary of the Russian language included such definitions as "rude, uneducated person" for the noun *Aziat* (Asian) and "savage, crude" for *aziatskii* (Asian).[11] And *aziatchina* similarly came to signify the continent's defects. In Anton Chekhov's play *The Cherry Orchard*, the haughty student Trofimov dismissed Russia as "nothing but filth, vulgarity, *aziatchina*."[12]

Westernizers often invoked Asia as a warning or even a metaphor for tsarist reaction in their polemics. To the progressive literary critic Vissarion Belinskii, the word *kitaizaism* ("Chinaism") was synonymous with reaction and despotism, and he readily used it as an epithet for Nicholas I's autocracy.[13] Indeed, Belinksii had nothing but contempt for the Orient. He provided a detailed exposition of his views in a lengthy review of some books about Peter the Great and his father, Tsar Alexis; his underlying theme was to praise the former's effort to turn Russia westward. Echoing Hegel's view that China and India lay outside of history, the critic remarked, "Asia was the cradle of the human race and up to now has remained its crib; its offspring grew up, but they are all still there; they acquired strength, but they still have to walk in leading strings."[14]

According to Belinskii, only the Asian's ability to think and talk separated him from animals, and his intellect was primitive at best: "Is something good or is it bad, reasonable or unreasonable—such questions do not enter into his head; they are far too weighty, too indigestible for his brain." Even were he to be endowed with a more sophisticated mind, the Oriental's fatalism rendered him utterly inert: "Why is everything the way it is, and not otherwise, and should it be thus rather than another way,— he has never asked himself such things. Things have been like this for a long time, and they are so with everyone. It is Allah's will!"[15]

Like many of his generation, Belinskii did not trouble himself too much to distinguish between the East's different nations. Even when he did, none were flattered by the comparison. Thus "the Turk is indifferent when his ruler's displeasure causes him to be impaled or hanged." Meanwhile, China's government, "devoid of movement, represents itself as some petrified ancestor." Belinskii never doubted in the West's superiority: "Asia is the land of so-called natural immediacy, Europe is the land of consciousness; Asia—the land of contemplation, Europe—of will and intellect."[16]

Early nineteenth-century poets such as Pushkin and Lermontov did not necessarily share such disdain for the Orient. Influenced by Lord Byron's Romantic verse, their rhymes often portrayed a more colorful and attractive East. While its inhabitants might be violent savages ruled by cruel despots, their archaic culture had the virtue of being as yet uncontaminated by modernity's artifice and mediocrity. Indeed, Pushkin and his contemporaries had a deep respect for Asian civilization. He was hardly disparaging the Islamic world when he penned his *Imitations of the Koran*. Nevertheless, the bard also used Asia metaphorically to comment about affairs closer to home. In "The Giaours [Infidels] Now Praise Istanbul," a poem of 1830 that lampooned those who opposed Western modernity, Pushkin sarcastically praised the Janissaries who had rebelled some twenty years earlier against the Westernizing reforms of the Ottoman Sultan Mahmud II.[17]

If the Slavophiles did not look to Asia as a model to be emulated, there were some Russians who did. According to the Slavist Olga Maiorova, one of the first was a diplomat posted to Istanbul, Vladimir Titov.[18] Like a number of his colleagues at the foreign ministry, Titov was also active in St.

Petersburg's literary life. A member of Prince Vladimir Odoevskii's proto-Slavophile secret society of Liubomudry (the Lovers of Wisdom), he wrote the prince a remarkable letter upon his arrival to the Turkish capital in 1836.[19] "Looking back at Italy and Germany, I became much more of a Turk and an Asian," Titov announced. As he explained, the East had three advantages over the West: its strong religious convictions, its paternal government, and its more sensual pleasures (*kaif*). These were all impossible for Europeans to achieve because of their feudal traditions and the Catholic Church. Fortunately, "in Russia we did not have these two syndromes, nor their . . . consequences; nevertheless, we suffered from another ailment—imitating Europeans." Titov did not want to put the blame for this entirely on Peter the Great's shoulders. "However," he proclaimed, "it is time for us to return to our own ways and those of the East."

While more ambivalent about Asia, Herzen came to share some of Titov's sympathies. As a student at Moscow University in the early 1830s of wealthy albeit illegitimate birth, Herzen initially moved in radical circles that subscribed to the various German philosophies and French utopian socialist ideas then in vogue. Like his Western-oriented contemporaries, the young *intelligent* largely shared Belinskii's negative view of the East as the epitome of stagnation and tyranny. Thus he saw the Orient as a metaphor for Nicholaevan autocracy.

When Herzen inherited a handsome bequest from his father in 1846, he seized the opportunity to leave the repressive political climate at home and resettle in Paris. Firmly committed to his Westernizing, socialist ideals, the émigré greeted the revolution of 1848 with gleeful enthusiasm. When the upheavals failed to sweep away the old order and Europe returned to its traditional ways, however, Herzen broke with the Westernizers and began to look closer to home, to Russia's peasant communes, as his ideal society.[20]

In the context of his evolving political ideas, for Herzen Asia came to acquire both a positive and a negative meaning. If, before his exile, Russian politics had been synonymous with Oriental despotism, he now detected similarities between eastern Europe and East Asia. Chaadaev and Belinskii had always evoked immobile China as Europe's antithesis. But in the wake of the events of 1848, Herzen saw the latter's bourgeois philistinism and passivity as the Occidental incarnation of kitaishchina.[21] Turning the Westernizers on their heads, he invoked a favorite metaphor for the crippling conformity of Confucianism to deride Peter the Great's reforms: "the Chinese shoes of German make, which Russia has been forced to wear for a hundred and fifty years, have inflicted many painful corns." The damage was not permanent, Herzen added, "since whenever [Russia] has had a chance of stretching out its limbs it has exuded a fresh young energy."[22]

This "fresh young energy" came from another Orient. Echoing Khomiakov's division of the world into a repressive and a free component, Herzen also saw the East as the source of rejuvenating vigor; not the stagnant Asia of the Chinese but its nomadic interior, the Turanian Asia of the Scythians and the Mongols. This was the élan vital that kept Russia young. In fact, the Mongol yoke had been a blessing, since it had saved his nation from such invidious Western institutions as feudalism and the Catholic Church.[23] Rather than being offended by traditional European references to his compatriots as barbarians and Tatars, Herzen reveled in such epithets. In a letter to the French anarchist Pierre-Joseph Proudhon, he described himself as "a barbarian . . . [both] by birth and by conviction." "Being a veritable Scythian," he added, "I delight in seeing the old world meet its doom."[24]

Many Russians saw their army's defeat in the Crimea in 1855 against a coalition led by Britain and France as a summons for renewed modernization according to the Western model. Considering their nation to be European, they believed that it had to become more like its Occidental neighbors. The prevailing sentiment that such a course was vital to national survival enabled the new tsar, Alexander II, to introduce sweeping reforms that helped reshape the civic order along more Western lines. But for others, St. Petersburg's steady decline among Europe's great powers during the nineteenth century's second half made Asia all the more appealing. Lieutenant General Ivan Blaramberg spoke for many when he proclaimed, "Russia's future does not lie in Europe: It must look to the East."[25] Some turned to the Orient as an arena for martial glory. Checked in the Near East by the Crimean War and again at the Congress of Berlin two decades later, they saw expansion into central Asia and the Far East as a tonic for their empire's wounded pride. A smaller but nonetheless influential group began to argue that Russia's destiny lay in the East because it was essentially more Asian than European.

Notions of an Oriental manifest destiny were hardly new to Russians. In

his poem of 1848, "Russian Geography," the poet and diplomat Fedor
Tiutchev proclaimed its borders as stretching

> From the Nile to the Neva,
> From the Elbe to China,
> From the Volga to the Euphrates,
> From the Ganges to the Danube . . .[26]

One of the more prominent advocates for a tsarist mission on the continent in the wake of the Crimean debacle was the Moscow University professor Mikhail Pogodin. In addition to occupying the chair in Russian history, Pogodin also published a journal, *Moskvitanin* (The Muscovite),
which he used as a platform for his conservative nationalism. Shortly after
the war, he published a summons to imperial expansion farther east:
"Leaving Europe alone, in expectation of more favorable circumstances,
we must turn our entire attention to Asia, which we have almost entirely
left out of our considerations although it is precisely Asia that is predes-
tined for us." Like Tiutchev, the professor saw few limits for Russia's ambitions on the continent: "to us belongs . . . half of Asia, China, Japan,
Tibet, Bokhara, Khiva, Kokand [and] Persia."[27] Pogodin did not consider
his nation's imperial ambitions to be in a different league from those of the
other European powers. Convinced of the superiority of "Japheth's tribe,"
the white race descended from Noah's son according to biblical tradition,
he believed that its rightful destiny was to rule over "the tribes of Shem
and Ham." Thus he sympathized with the British during the Indian
Mutiny of 1857–58.[28]

St. Petersburg's diplomatic humiliation at the Congress of Berlin in 1878,
after another Turkish war, only reinforced enthusiasm for Asian conquest.
Much like the other colonial powers during the age of high imperialism,
many Russians were convinced of a special mission that justified their territorial expansion. Writing from Xinjiang in 1877, the explorer Nikolai
Przheval'skii reported that "the local population constantly cursed their own
government and expressed their desire to become Russian subjects. Rumors
of how we brought order to Kokand and Ili spread far. The savage Asiatic
clearly understands that Russian power is the guarantee for prosperity."[29]

The most august proponent of such views was Nicholas II. In 1903 his
war minister, General Aleksei Kuropatkin, confided to his diary, "Our sov-

ereign has grandiose plans in his head: to absorb Manchuria into Russia, to begin the annexation of Korea. He also dreams of taking Tibet under his orb. He wants to rule Persia, to seize both the Bosporus and the Dardanelles."[30] These sentiments would become less popular after Japan launched its attack on the tsar's naval base of Port Arthur on the Pacific Ocean a year later.

The nineteenth century saw a growing interest among Russians in their Asian past. Earlier, when Catherine the Great had penned her "Notes about Russian History," she wrote about the Scythians, among the first people known to have lived on Russian territory.[31] Her description was so positive that one scholar has recently suggested the empress might have been the first to claim the nomadic nation's ancestry for her adoptive homeland.[32] From the start, one of the driving forces of the academic discipline of orientology had been studying the Eastern elements of Russian history. At first the scholars who pursued such interests were German— like Catherine herself. However, by the nineteenth century's second half, native Russian orientologists increasingly also became intrigued by the question. They included such prominent scholars as Vasilii Grigor'ev, Nikolai Veselovskii, and Baron Viktor Rosen.[33] Meanwhile, the spectacular finds of intricate gold artifacts, which blended entirely alien Oriental styles with classical Greek motifs, at Scythian kurgans along the empire's southern periphery further encouraged many Russians to think about their Inner Asian ancestry, whether real or imagined.[34]

To be sure, prerevolutionary historians tended not to dwell on Russia's links with the East. There were some exceptions. In the early 1800s Karamzin wrote that "Moscow owes its greatness to the Khans."[35] What he meant was that the Muscovite princes had adopted their autocratic regimentation of society—the strong centralized rule that had enabled Russia to achieve its preeminence—from the political tradition of the Mongols. Nevertheless, most nineteenth-century historians were distinctly uncomfortable with the idea that any good had come from the Mongol yoke. Ideas about the positive influence of these Inner Asian conquerors were very much on the margins of the historiographical mainstream in Moscow and St. Petersburg.

One influential figure who did see significant ties to the East in his nation's heritage was Vladimir Stasov. Historian, archaeologist, librarian, art critic, and tireless champion of the national school of Russian music, Stasov scandalized many of his compatriots when he suggested in a series of articles in 1868 that the beloved *byliny* were nothing more than "emasculated" imitations of tales that had originated in India and Persia. "Our *bogatyrs* merely convey various myths, legends and fairy tales of the ancient East," he concluded.[36] Stasov, as he dutifully acknowledged, derived the basic thesis about the Oriental foundations of European epics from such scholars as the German Sanskritist Theodor Benfey. What distinguished the byliny, however, was that they were much closer to the originals than the *Iliad,* the *Nibelungenlied,* or even the *Kalevala.*

In other works, most notably his *Russian Folk Ornament* of 1872, Stasov likewise stressed the similarities between Russian and Asian cultures.[37] Despite the storm of controversy it initially aroused, "On the Origins of Russian Byliny" earned the author a Demidov Prize and eventually gained many adherents, as did his related ideas.[38] The prominent French architectural historian Eugène-Emmanuel Viollet-le-Duc based his book about Russian art on the notion, as he put it, that "Russia has been one of the laboratories where the arts, having come from throughout all of Asia, have been joined to create an intermediary form between the Oriental and Occidental worlds."[39]

Stasov was a man of relatively progressive views. Although fervently patriotic, his approach to Russia's cultural past tended to be scholarly. But there were others who looked to the East with more partisan motives. Just as Russian liberals saw western Europe's constitutional democracies as their political ideal, some conservatives advocated greater kinship with Asian autocracy. One of the most unusual proponents of the latter group was the mystical reactionary Konstantin Leont'ev. As with Titov some three decades earlier, diplomatic service in the Ottoman Empire awoke in Leont'ev a passion for the Orient. The attraction was primarily aesthetic at first. He explained in a letter to a friend, "Only the life of Constantinople . . . only this multifaceted existence could satisfy my *intolerably* refined tastes."[40] Leont'ev's postings as a consul in various Balkan cities in the 1860s were not overly taxing. Along with the pursuit of earthier pleasures, he devoted his considerable leisure to writing. Typical of his creations at the time was *The Egyptian Dove,* a semiautobiographical novel whose decadent sensibilities recall Joris-Karl Huysmans' *Against Nature.*[41]

A spiritual crisis in the early 1870s led to a profound change of heart. Resigning from the foreign ministry, Leont'ev went on a lengthy retreat at the Orthodox monastic republic of Mt. Athos. Eventually returning to Russia, he lived mostly on his estate until the final years of his life, when he was tonsured as a monk in the venerable Optina Pustina monastery. Leont'ev's credo was straightforward: "More Oriental mysticism and less European enlightened reason."[42] In an age when many Russians subscribed to pan-Slavism, a doctrine that advocated uniting all of eastern Europe's Slavs under the tsar's scepter, he argued for a different course. For one thing, his nation had little in common with its many of its Slavic cousins, who had already been deeply contaminated by Europe's poisonous liberalism: "The very character of the Russian people has very strong and important traits, which are more similar to those of Turks, Tatars and other Asian nations, or perhaps no one at all, than the Southern and Western Slavs. We are more indolent, fatalistic, much more submissive to our ruler, more dissolute, good-natured, insanely brave, unstable, and so much more inclined to religious mysticism than the Serbs, Bulgarians, Czechs and Croats."[43]

Leont'ev believed that, rather than joining with its purported Slavic brethren, Russia's true destiny lay in restoring the Byzantine ideal of an empire that combined East and West, although its firmly autocratic political order would be distinctly more Oriental. After all, he cautioned, "no Polish rising, no Pugachev revolt can bring more harm to Russia than a most orderly and legal democratic constitution."[44] With its capital in Tsargrad (Constantinople) rather than at St. Petersburg, the greater Russia he envisioned "would be more cultured, that is, more true to itself; it would be less rational and less utilitarian, that is, less revolutionary."[45] This new realm might well incorporate the other Slavs, but it would also join with it many Asian peoples including Turks, Indians, and Tibetans, thereby preserving its fundamentally Eastern character.

The turn of the twentieth century was a time of even greater unease among many Russians about their relationship with the West. Outwardly, especially in the great cities, it seemed that the empire was becoming increasingly more European. Railroads, factories, telegraphs, and mass-circulation newspapers all heralded the coming of a new age. This Occidentalization was troubling, not just in the way it challenged the old order, but also because it seemed to emphasize Russia's inferiority to such modern industrial rivals as Great Britain and Germany. Yet if Russia looked to the West from a position of relative weakness, it could still face the East with confidence and strength.

As the nineteenth century drew to a close, Russia's new tsar, Nicholas II, became increasingly preoccupied with his empire's frontier on the Pacific. In the early 1890s his father, Alexander III, had already decreed that a railway be built across Siberia to link St. Petersburg with his distant Far Eastern territories. By the decade's end, Nicholas's diplomats had negotiated a secret treaty of alliance with China, in addition to a leasehold and extensive economic privileges in Manchuria. As the twentieth century dawned, it appeared to many Russians that the empire's destiny lay in Asia. Echoing Leont'ev, some influential political writers known as the *vostochniki* (Asianists) even began to argue that Russia was fundamentally Eastern rather than Western in character.

One of the more prominent advocates of Asianism was Prince Esper Esperovich Ukhtomskii, a newspaper publisher and poet. Close to Nicholas II—the prince had accompanied Nicholas on his 1890–91 Oriental grand tour when he was still the tsarevich—Ukhtomskii exercised considerable influence during the earlier years of the emperor's reign. On the pages of his daily, *Sankt-Peterburskiia Vedomosti* (The Saint-Petersburg Gazette), Ukhtomskii tirelessly advocated the Asianist cause.[46]

Even more than Leont'ev, the prince was convinced about Russia's kinship with Asia: "The West is but dimly reflected in our intellectual life. The depths below the surface have their being in an atmosphere of deeply Oriental views and beliefs."[47] Like Asians, Russians relied more on faith than on reason, Ukhtomskii explained: "We feel our spiritual and political isolation from the Romano-Germanic countries overburdened by a too-exacting civilization. For us . . . [as] for Asia, the basis of life is religious belief."[48] At the same time, both Russians and Asians were repelled by materialism. But above all, the two were bound by a yearning for a ruler's firm, paternal hand: "The East believes no less than we do . . . [in] the most precious of our national traditions—autocracy. Without it, Asia would be incapable of sincere liking for Russia and of painless identification with her."[49]

Asianism lost its appeal among policy makers in St. Petersburg after the catastrophic war with Japan. Meanwhile, Ivanov-Razumnik's Scythians, the Silver Age poets who also detected an affinity with the East, succumbed to tight Bolshevik controls on literature in the early 1920s. In emigration, many of these beliefs were revived by the Eurasianists (Evraziitsi), but with one important difference. Rather than stressing Russia's Oriental nature, the Eurasianists argued that their nation was a world unto itself: neither Asian nor European, but rather combining elements of both. Nevertheless, many of the Eurasianists' core beliefs—such as their rejection of materialism, their advocacy of autocracy, and their stress on spirituality—explicitly rejected the West.[50]

Based in Prague, the Eurasianist movement emerged in 1921 with the publication of a collection of essays, *Exodus to the East*.[51] Among the collaborators were a linguist, Prince Nikolai Trubetskoi; a geographer, Petr Savitskii; a music critic, Petr Suvchinskii; and the theologian Georges Florovsky. A year later, George Vernadsky, a promising young historian who had just landed a job in the Czech capital, joined them. Vernadsky boasted a distinguished academic provenance. His father, Vladimir, had been a leading professor of mineralogy, and Vernadsky *fils* had attended the two leading Russian history departments, at Moscow and St. Petersburg universities, and also studied in Berlin and Freiburg. After five years in Prague, Vernadsky left Europe for America in 1927 to take up a newly established position in Russian history at Yale University.

Vernadsky wrote his most polemical Eurasianist works, *Characteristics of Russian History* and *A Preliminary History of Eurasia,* early in his career.[52] His focus was the great Eurasian steppe, the vast prairie that stretches from Mongolia to Ukraine. As he explained in these books, because of its flat topography, the steppe was repeatedly the meeting place for European and Asian peoples. The nomads who periodically swept westward from the depths of Inner Asia, such as the Scythians, the Huns, and the Mongols, had intermarried with the more sedentary East Slavs. In a subsequent work he explained, "Each of these invasions brought new cultural patterns and each, when it retreated years or centuries later, left its imprint indelibly on the land that was to become Russia."[53]

Muscovite and tsarist conquest completed what Vernadsky called the "millennial historical symbiosis" of the Slavs and the steppe nomads. According to the Eurasianists, together the Russians, Finns, Turks, Mongols, and all the other nations that were spawned from the Inner Asian steppes had blended into a "superethnos," a people they called "Turanian." Eurasia's peoples, the Turanian superethnos, had many characteristics in common, including related blood types and languages, but the most significant was a shared consciousness of the need for strong, autocratic government. All of Eurasia's most successful rulers, from the Scythians to the Romanov tsars, had governed with a firm hand. According to Vernadsky, "The organization of the Eurasian state, because of its enormous size, is very much along military lines."[54] Furthermore, along with an instinctive yearning for strong rule, Eurasia's peoples were also united by a deep spirituality.[55]

In his later New Haven years, Vernadsky moderated some of his Eurasianist ideas. Although he continued to stress the importance of the steppe in Russian history, his biographer Charles Halperin points out that his "immigration to the United States . . . purged [his] Eurasianism of its authoritarian, chauvinist, collectivist, and elitist aspects."[56] For many Russians today, however, it is not the mild-mannered Ivy League incarnation of George Vernadsky that intrigues them, but the youthful firebrand of Prague in the 1920s.

Even at their peak, the Eurasianists never attracted more than a small following among other émigrés. More prominent Russian intellectuals abroad, such as the distinguished liberal historian Pavel Miliukov, strongly disagreed with the movement's anti-Western bias.[57] However, the ideology has enjoyed a renaissance in the years following the collapse of Communist rule. Its resurgence in the 1990s was closely linked to a profound disenchantment with the West among many Russians. The Canadian writer and statesman Michael Ignatieff observed that the dispute over whether Russia is European had once again emerged with a vengeance: "Since Pushkin, Russian intellectuals have argued bitterly about whether Russia is or is not part of European civilization. Slavophiles versus Westernisers, Dostoyevsky versus Tolstoy—the argument goes to the very heart of Russian self-definition. For one side, the Europe of markets, parliamentary democracy, and individual rights represented Russia's only hope of escaping Asiatic backwardness and the madhouse of Slavic nationalism; for the other, Europe's capitalism represented the soulless, gimcrack, heartless individualism that the Russian soul should flee, as from the devil himself."[58] Yet, despite Ignatieff's implication, it was not Slavophilism that had enjoyed a rebirth as much as Eurasianism. Several collections of Eurasianist essays have been issued in large printings. Meanwhile, the works of the Lev Gumilev, a Brezhnev-era dissident with strong Eurasianist leanings, are everywhere, and translations of Vernadsky's *A History of Russia* (first published by Yale University Press in 1929) are also now available in Russian bookshops.[59]

Eurasianism has found a strong following among both friends and opponents of the current regime, including Communists and others who would restore Russia to its former Soviet glory. As John Dunlop, an American scholar who has long studied Russian nationalism, noted: "The resurrection of a formerly obscure émigré ideology in the 1990s should, upon reflection, cause little surprise. With the effective demise of Marxism-Leninism as a 'glue' for holding the Soviet Union together, 'empire savers' were forced to cast about for substitutes."[60]

One well-known cultural figure influenced by Eurasianism is the patriotic film director and sometime presidential candidate, Nikita Mikhailkov. In an interview in December 1991, Mikhailkov thundered against "the [Russian] government's illusory notion that our state is based on the European political model." He went on to proclaim: "We are not Europe's backyard; we are Asia's front door."[61] Mikhailkov's film, *Close to Eden,* shot in 1992, is a clear expression of Eurasianism. It depicts the friendship of a wandering Russian truck driver and a Mongolian nomad who meet on the steppe. The encroaching capitalist materialism of the modern world (here in the guise of an Americanized Chinese city) is portrayed as impure and alien.

On the Russian right, the best-known neo-Eurasianists are Aleksandr Prokhanov and Pavel Dugin, editors, respectively, of the tabloid *Zavtra* (Tomorrow) and the journal *Elementy* (Elements). More curious is the warm response Eurasianism has found among post-Soviet Communists. Gennadii Ziuganov, the chair of the Communist Party of the Russian Federation, speaks and writes glowingly about the movement: "From its beginning, Eurasianism was the creative response of the Russian national consciousness to the Russian Revolution."[62] Yet in the confusing politics of the post-Soviet era, this rehabilitation of an émigré intellectual current from the 1920s by Muscovite Communists seven decades later makes perfect sense. The Russian political scientist Andrei Novikov has observed

238 ASIA IN THE RUSSIAN MIND

that "today people are studying the [Eurasianist geopolitical philosophy] of Lev Gumilev . . . just as diligently as formerly they read Karl Marx's *Das Kapital*. Marxist historical determinism has been transformed into another kind of determinism, the national-geopolitical variant."[63]

In 1997 Ziuganov published his strongest statement on Eurasianist ideas in *The Geography of Victory*. Written in the style of a textbook on geopolitics, the tract predictably attacks American primacy in global affairs. Like Leont'ev and Prince Ukhtomskii, Ziuganov urges his compatriots to reject the Occident in favor of its Oriental nature. "To an important extent, Russia belongs to the East," he proclaims. He also finds much to admire in Confucian values. Echoing a hoary claim of tsarist propaganda, he argues that Russians have traditionally had much more pacific dealings with their neighbors in Asia than with Europeans. In a rare reference to his own party's former leaders, he adds: "In Soviet times the traditional 'turn to the East' . . . received a renewed impulse. It was precisely among the peoples of the Orient that Soviet Russia found allies in its struggle against Western oppression and blackmail." Today, Ziuganov believes, Russians must cement their ties with Asia because "Russia and China are inexorably joined in a single historical destiny."[64]

There is no simple answer to Dostoyevsky's question of what Asia is to Russia. Much more familiar with the East than other Europeans, Russians have invariably seen the Orient in a multiplicity of hues. Whether foe or friend, danger or destiny, other or self, or, as Vladimir Solov'ev put it, "of Xerxes or of Christ,"[65] their perceptions of Asia have defied easy characterization. As in the West, for the Russian imagination the Orient has been the source of both dreams and nightmares, but greater intimacy with its people has fashioned a unique symbiosis of fantasy and reality.

By the same token, Russian orientologists did not reduce the object of their inquiry to some uniform, Saidian other. Their views varied widely, but on the whole, neither fear nor contempt dominated the academy. Some professors were utterly convinced of their cultural superiority and regarded the East with disdain. Many sympathized with tsarist ambitions in Asia. But most respected the nations they studied and even found them appealing. The fact that they were *chinovniki* (government employees) was of little import. Indeed, even more than elsewhere, Russian scholarship about Asia was intimately linked to the state. The continent's languages were taught at universities to train officials who could serve the autocracy in administering its Eastern territories and acquire new ones. Yet, like academics elsewhere, their curiosity was not necessarily motivated by *raison d'état*. Such attitudes were well described by Jean-Jacques Waardenburg in his book about European perceptions of Islam: "Understanding is more than knowing; it is even something else. . . . When [such understanding] involves a foreign, human phenomenon, the summons to knowing can only be answered when the scholar exhibits some esteem for this phenomenon: Perhaps this is because he recognizes that it is human. . . . Understanding something presupposes having an open mind, a mind that can adapt to the question being studied."[66]

The most intriguing element of Russian thinking about Asia is the sense among many of a shared heritage. Not a few noble lineages took pride in their Tartar bloodlines, and the population more generally has been less anxious about intermarriage among races than other Europeans. If there were not many Russians who looked back nostalgically to two and a half centuries of submission to the Golden Horde, the Mongol yoke also left a legacy whose effects still remain a source of lively controversy. Meanwhile, ever since the Cossack Ermak and his heirs conquered Siberia in the late sixteenth century, the bulk of Russia's landmass has lain within the Asian continent. While his outlook was distinctly Occidental, even Lenin understood that "Russia is geographically, economically and historically related both to Europe and Asia."[67]

The advocates of Russia's Oriental character have always been in a minority. However, their ideas have survived, and now, after the fall of the Soviet Union, they can be found among the most prominent political movements in the Russian Federation. Profoundly uneasy about a "new world order" dominated by the West's premier power, it is easy for nationalist Russians to believe that their country shares something with Asia as they reject the intrusive, materialist West, with its World Bank hotshots, fast food, pornography, and unruly parliaments. The "Asian values" of autocracy, order, and paternalism seem much more appealing to those nostalgic for a mighty Russia. Rightist opposition parties—old-line Communists, new-line fascists, and extremist nationalists—often claim a racial affinity to the East. Even senior Kremlin officials occasionally invoke an

Asian identity. One of Boris Yeltsin's foreign ministers, Igor Ivanov, reminded his compatriots: "Russia has been, is, and will be an Asian power."[68] Under Vladimir Putin and Dmitrii Medvedev, the Kremlin is also occasionally given to such posturing while ostentatiously trying to build anti-Western coalitions with Asian powers.

Russian musings about Asia often reflect considerations about national identity. If the nineteenth-century debate between the Slavophiles and the Westernizers received more attention, the East has played a similar role in Russia's ongoing quest to understand its true place in the world. Ultimately these discussions about affinities with the Occident and the Orient are part of the same dialogue. And when the West's allure diminishes, the East often grows more enticing.

NOTES

Introduction

1. For example, in his 1492 edition of Ptolemy's cosmography, the Cracow scholar Janusz Glogowa (Johannes von Glogau) wrote: "haec tabula habet Sarmatiam asiaticam, nunc dictam Moszkowiam" (this table has Sarmatia Asiatica, now called Moscovia). Ekkehart Klug, "Das 'asiatische' Rusland: Über die Entstehung eines europäischen Vorurteils," *Historische Zeitschrift* 245, no. 2 (1987): 273.

2. S. F. Platonov, *Moscow and the West,* trans. Joseph L. Wieczynski (Gulf Breeze, FL: Academic International, 1972), 1–3; Marie-Louise Pelus, "Un des aspects d'une conscience européenne: La Russie vue d'Europe occidentale au XVIᵉ siècle," *La conscience européenne au XVᵉ et XVIᵉ siècles* (Paris: École Normale Supérieure de Jeunes Filles, 1982), 309; Melvyn C. Wren, *The Western Impact upon Tsarist Russia* (Chicago: Holt, Rinehart and Winston, 1971), 1–10.

3. Richard Hakluyt, an English collector of travelers' accounts, credited Chancellor with "the strange and wonderful discovery of Russia." Francesca Wilson, *Muscovy: Russia through Foreign Eyes, 1553–1900* (New York: Praeger, 1970), 19. Two surveys of Western views of Russia at the time are Marshall Poe, *A People Born to Slavery: Russia in Early Modern European Ethonography, 1476–1748* (Ithaca, NY: Cornell University Press, 2000); Stéphane Mund, *Orbis Russiarum: Genèse et développement de la representation du monde "russe" en Occident à la Renaissance* (Geneva: Librarie Droz, 2003).

4. This point is emphatically made in Klug, "Das 'asiatische' Rusland," 265–289.

5. Pelus, "Un des aspects," 317.

6. Pelus, "Un des aspects," 310.

7. In the words of the Elizabethan poet Thomas Lodge. Karl Heinz Ruffmann, *Das Russlandbild im England Shakespeares* (Göttingen: Musterschmidt, 1952), 171.

8. Pellus, "Un des aspects," 119–120.

9. Alstolphe de Custine, *Empire of the Tsar: A Journey through Eternal Russia* (New York: Doubleday, 1989), 214, 230. On French perceptions of Russia more gen-

erally, see Ezequiel Adamovsky, *Euro-Orientalism: Liberal Ideology and the Image of Russia in France (ca. 1740–1880)*, French Studies of the Eighteenth and Nineteenth Centuries 19 (Bern: Peter Lang, 2006).

10. Custine, *Empire of the Tsar*, 229.

11. Karl A. Wittfogel, "Russia and the East: A Comparison and Contrast," *Slavic Review* 22 (1963): 632.

12. In Tibor Szamuely, *The Russian Tradition* (New York: McGraw-Hill, 1974), 19.

13. Wittfogel, "Russia and the East," 627–643.

14. David Aikman, "Russia Could Go the Asiatic Way," *Time,* June 7, 1992, 80.

15. Mikhail Gorbachev, *Perestroika: New Thinking for Our Country and the World* (New York: Harper & Row, 1987), 191.

16. Emanuel Sarkisyanz, *Russland und der Messianismus des Orients* (Tübingen: J. C. B. Mohr, 1955), 203–204; Sarkisyanz, "Russian Attitudes Toward Asia," *Russian Review* 13 (1954): 245; Nicholas V. Riasanovsky, "Asia through Russian Eyes," in Wayne S. Vucinich, ed., *Asia and Russia: Essays on the Influence of Russia on the Asian Peoples* (Stanford, CA: Hoover Institution Press, 1972), 9–10.

17. George Vernadsky, *The Mongols and Russia* (New Haven, CT: Yale University Press, 1953), 333.

18. Aleksandr Blok, "Skify," *Stikhotvoreniia i poemy* (Moscow: Khudozhestvennaia literatura 1968), 231.

19. David Schimmelpenninck van der Oye, *Toward the Rising Sun: Russian Ideologies of Empire and the Path to War with Japan* (DeKalb: Northern Illinois University Press, 2001), 42–60, 203–204.

20. F. M. Dostoevskii, *Pol'noe sobranie sochinenii,* vol. 27 (Leningrad: Nauka, 1984), 32–36.

21. See, among others, Alexandre Koyré, *La philosophie et le problème national en Russie au début du XIXᵉ siècle* (Paris: Honoré Campion, 1929); Alexander von Schelting, *Russland und Europa in Russischen Geschichtsdenken* (Bern: A. Francke, 1948); V. V. Zen'kovskii, *Russkie mysliteli i Evropa* (Paris: YMCA Press, 1955); and Iver B. Neumann, *Russia and the Idea of Europe* (London: Routledge, 1996).

22. Examples include Szamuely, *Russian Tradition,* and Edgar Knobloch, *Russia and Asia: Nomadic and Oriental Traditions in Russian History* (Hong Kong: Odyssey Books, 2007).

23. Mark Bassin, *Imperial Visions: Nationalist Imagination and Geographical Expansion in the Russian Far East, 1840–1865* (Cambridge: Cambridge University Press, 1999); Robert P. Geraci, *Window on the East: National and Imperial Identities in Late Tsarist Russia* (Ithaca, NY: Cornell University Press, 2001). For a Gorbachev-era survey influenced by Halford Mackinder's geopolitical views, see Milan Hauner, *What Is Asia to Us?* (Boston: Unwin Hyman, 1990). There are two recent broader studies in Italian and French, respectively: Aldo Ferrari, *La foresta e la steppa: Il mito dell'Eurasia nella cultura russa* (Milan: Libri Scheinwiller, 2003); Lorraine de Meaux, *L'Orient russe: Représentations de l'Orient et identité russe du début du XIXᵉᵐᵉ siècle à 1917* (Paris: Fayard, 2010).

24. Bernard Lewis, *Islam and the West* (New York: Oxford University Press, 1993), 101.

25. Edward A. Said, "Orientalism Reconsidered," in Francis Barker et al., eds., *Literature, Politics and Theory* (London: Methuen, 1986), 215.

26. Mikhail Pavlovich, "Zadachi Vserossiiskoi nauchnoi assotsiatsii vostokovedeniia," *Novyi vostok* 1 (1922): 5. In an article written some four decades later, the Soviet Japanologist Nikolai Konrad likewise saw orientology as subordinated to colonialist imperatives. N. I. Konrad, *Zapad i Vostok: Statii* (Moscow: Glavnaia redaktsiia vostochnoi literatury, 1972), 9–10.

27. S. Vel'tman, *Vostok v khudozehstvennoi literatura* (Moscow-Leningrad: Gosudarstvennoe Izdatel'stvo, 1928), 42.

28. N. G. Svirin, "Russkaia kolonial'naia literatura," *Literaturnyi kritik* no. 9 (1934): 56. Svirin was arrested in 1937 and died in 1941. Stephanie Sandler, *Distant Pleasures: Alexander Pushkin and the Writing of Exile* (Stanford, CA: Stanford University Press, 1989), 237n24.

29. *Bol'shaia sovetskaia entsiklopediia*, 2nd ed., s.v. "Vostokovedenie."

30. Vera Tolz, "European, National, and (anti-)Imperial: The Formation of Academic Oriental Studies in Later Tsarist and Early Soviet Russia," in Michael David-Fox et al., eds., *Orientalism and Empire in Russia, Kritika* Historical Studies 3 (Bloomington, IN: Slavica, 2006), 132–133.

31. Robert Irwin, *For Lust of Knowing: The Orientalists and Their Enemies* (London: Allen Lane, 2006), 4.

32. Robert D. Kaplan, *The Arabists: The Romance of an Elite* (New York: Free Press, 1993).

33. Henri Baudet, *Het Paradijs op Aarde* (Assen: Van Gorcum, 1959). More recent works of this genre include Maxime Rodinson, *La fascination de l'Islam* (Paris: Librarie François Maspero, 1980); and Peter Rietbergen, *Europa's India: Fascinatie en cultureel imperialisme, circa 1750–circa 2000* (Nijmegen, the Netherlands: Uitgeverij Vantilt, 2007).

34. Raymond Schwab, *La renaissance orientale* (Paris: Payot, 1950). The English-language translation includes a foreword by Edward Said; see Schwab, *The Oriental Renaissance: Europe's Rediscovery of India and the East, 1680–1880*, trans. Gene Patterson-Black and Victor Reinking (New York: Columbia University Press, 1984). See also J. J. Clarke, *The Oriental Enlightenment* (London: Routledge, 1997).

35. Susan Layton, *Russian Literature and Empire: Conquest of the Caucasus from Pushkin to Tolstoy* (Cambridge: Cambridge University Press, 1994); Harsha Ram, *The Imperial Sublime: A Russian Poetics of Empire* (Madison: University of Wisconsin Press, 2003); Ewa M. Thompson, *Imperial Knowledge: Russian Literature and Colonialism* (Westport, CT: Greenwood Press, 2000). See also Katya Hokanson, "Empire of the Imagination: Orientalism and the Construction of Russian National Identity in Pushkin, Marlinskii, Lermontov, and Tolstoi" (PhD diss., Stanford University, 1994). Natan Eidelman's 1990 study of the subject was recently republished to capitalize on

the postcolonialist turn; see Natan Eidelman, *Byt' mozhet za khrebtom Kavkaza* (Moscow: Vagrius, 2006).

36. Kalpana Sahni, *Crucifying the Orient: Russian Orientalism and the Colonization of Caucasus and Central Asia* (Bangkok: White Orchid Press, 1997).

37. Lewis, *Islam and the West,* 108.

38. Nathaniel Knight, "Grigor'ev in Orenburg, 1851–1862: Russian Orientalism in the Service of Empire?" *Slavic Review* 59 (2000): 74–100.

39. Adeeb Khalid, "Russian History and the Debate over Orientalism," *Kritika* 1 (2000): 691–699.

40. Layton, *Russian Literature and Empire,* 191.

41. Knight, "Grigor'ev in Orenburg," 96n80.

42. V. S. Solov'ev, "Ex oriente lux," *Chteniia o Bogochelovechestve: Stat'i, stikhotovreniia i poema. Iz "Trekh razgovorov"* (St. Petersburg: Khudozhestvennaia literatura, 1994), 385.

43. On the links between scholarship and military intelligence in Imperial Russia, see David Schimmelpenninck van der Oye, "Reforming Military Intelligence," in Schimmelpenninck van der Oye and Bruce W. Menning, eds., *Reforming the Tsar's Army* (New York: Cambridge University Press, 2004), 133–150.

44. Barbara Heldt, "'Japanese' in Russian Literature: Transforming Identities," in J. Thomas Rimer, ed., *A Hidden Fire: Russian and Japanese Cultural Encounters* (Stanford, CA: Stanford University Press, 1995), 171.

45. Jonathan D. Spence, *The Chan's Great Continent: China in Western Minds* (New York: W. W. Norton, 1988).

Chapter 1. The Forest and the Steppe

1. Ukraine and Belarus also trace their origins to the East Slavs. Much of the discussion about the Russians before the Mongol invasion of the early thirteenth century applies equally well to the former two nations.

2. P. B. Golden, "The Question of the Rus' Qağanate," *Archivum Eurasiae Medii Aevii,* vol. 2 (Wiesbaden: Otto Harrasowitz, 1982), 81; Simon Franklin and Jonathan Shepard, *The Emergence of Rus, 750–1200* (London: Longman, 1996), 31, 38.

3. V. V. Barthold, *Sochineniia,* vol. 9 (Moscow: Nauka, 1977), 534.

4. *Herodotus,* vol. 2, trans. A. D. Godley (London: William Heinemann, 1921), 198–345.

5. Simon Franklin, "Kievan Rus' (1015–1125)," in Maureen Perrie, ed., *The Cambridge History of Russia,* vol. 1 (Cambridge: Cambridge University Press, 2006), 89–90.

6. P. P. Tolochko, *Kochevye narody stepei i Kievskaia Rus'* (St. Petersburg: Aleteiia, 2003), 45–66, 89–129; Richard Voorheis, "The Perception of Asiatic Nomads in Medieval Russia: Folklore, History and Historiography" (PhD diss., Indiana University, 1982), 10–75; T. S. Noonan, "Rus, Pechenegs and Polovtsy," *Russian History/Histoire Russe* 19 (1992): 300–326; Charles J. Halperin, *Russia and the Golden Horde* (Bloomington: Indiana University Press, 1985), 10–20; Willard Sunderland, *The Taming of*

the Wild Field: Colonization and Empire on the Russian Steppe (Ithaca, NY: Cornell University Press, 2004), 13.

7. Halperin, *Russia and the Golden Horde*, 18.

8. Andreas Kappeler, "Ethnische Abgrenzung: Bemerkungen zur ostslavischen Terminologie des Mittelalters," in Uwe Halbach et al., eds., *Geschichte Altrusslands in der Begriffswelt ihrer Quellen* (Wiesbaden: Franz Steiner, 1986), 128.

9. *Lavrent'evskaia letopis'*, Polnoe sobranie russkikh letopisei, vol. 1 (Moscow: Iazyki slavianskoi kul'tury, 2001), 163, 232.

10. *Lavrent'evskaia letopis'*, 234–236; Leonid S. Chekin, "The Godless Ishmaelites: The Image of the Steppe in Eleventh–Thirteenth Century Rus," *Russian History/Histoire Russe* 19 (1992): 12–17.

11. Alain Ducellier, *Chrétiens d'Orient et Islam au Moyen Age, VIIᵉ–XVᵉ siècle* (Paris: Armand Colin, 1996).

12. Vladimir Nabokov, trans., *The Song of Igor's Campaign* (New York: McGraw-Hill, 1975), 29–31. All other quotations are taken from the original in *Entsiklopediia "Slova o polku Igoreve,"* vol. 1 (St. Petersburg: Dmitrii Bulanin, 1995), 9–14.

13. *Entsiklopediia "Slova o polku Igoreve,"* s.v. "Igor' Sviatoslavich"; Nabokov, *Song*, 111n296.

14. *Ipat'evskaia letopis'*, Polnoe sobranie russkikh letopisei, vol. 2 (Moscow: Iazyki russkoi kul'tury, 1998), 637–644.

15. In George Vernadsky, *Annuaire de l'institut de philologie et d'histoire orientales et slaves* 8 (1845–47), 217.

16. Such speculation has appeared most recently in Edward Keenan, "Josef Dobrovsky and the Origins of the *Igor Tale*," *Jahrbücher für Geschichte Osteuropas* 54 (2006): 556–571. For a defense of the Igor song's authenticity, see D. S. Likhachev, "'Slovo o polku Igoreve' i skeptiki," *Velikoe nasledie* (Moscow: Sovremennik, 1975), 348–363.

17. *Entsiklopediia "Slova o polku Igoreve,"* s.v. "Avtor 'Slova.'"

18. *Novgorodskaia pervaia letopis'* (Moscow: Izd-vo Akademii nauk SSSR, 1950), 62.

19. Ibid., 63.

20. The following discussion is largely based on Halperin, *Russia and the Golden Horde;* Donald Ostrowski, *Muscovy and the Mongols* (Cambridge: Cambridge University Press, 1998); and, to a lesser extent, Vernadsky, *Mongols and Russia;* Bertold Spuler, *Die goldene Horde* (Wiesbaden: Otto Harrassowitz), 1965.

21. Halperin, *Russia and the Golden Horde*, 114.

22. "Povest' o razorenii Riazani Batyem," in V. P. Adrianova-Perets, ed., *Voinskie povesti drevnei Rusi* (Moscow: Izd-vo Akademii nauk SSSR, 1949), 9–19.

23. Ostrowski, *Muscovy and the Mongols*, 109–167.

24. Charles J. Halperin, *The Tatar Yoke* (Columbus, OH: Slavica, 1986), 13.

25. Vernadsky, *Mongols and Russia*, 165; Ostrowski, *Muscovy and the Mongols*, 138. For a more detailed account of Sarai's diplomacy, see Spuler, *Goldene Horde*.

26. Halperin, *Russia and the Golden Horde*, 74.

27. Edward Keenan, "Muscovy and Kazan', 1445–1552: A Study in Steppe Politics" (PhD diss., Harvard University, 1965), 25–51; Halperin, *Tatar Yoke,* 94–136; Ostrowski, *Muscovy and the Mongols,* 164–167.

28. Christopher Atwood, *Encyclopedia of Mongolia and the Mongol Empire* (New York: Facts on File, 2004), s.v. "Tatar"; Denis Sinor, "Le mongol vue par l'Occident," *Studies in Medieval Inner Asia,* vol. 9 (Ashgate, UK: Variorum, 1997), 62.

29. Ostrowski, *Muscovy and the Mongols,* 167.

30. A classic discussion of the joint Byzantine and Tatar impact on Muscovite thinking about statecraft is Michael Cherniavsky, "*Khan* or *Basileus:* An Aspect of Russian Mediaeval Political Theory," *Journal of the History of Ideas* 20 (1959): 459–476.

31. The color white indicated the West in Mongolian geography, and Sarai's chief Russian appointee was therefore known as the "White Prince." When Muscovy's rulers began to view themselves as the khan's equal, they restyled themselves as the "White Tsar." Although Ivan III and his successors simply designated themselves as tsar, the former was still used in dealings with Asian nomads into the nineteenth century. See Keenan, "Muscovy and Kazan'," 385. On diplomacy, see N. Veselovskii, "Tatarskoe vliianie na posol'skii tseremonial v moskovskii period russkoi istorii," *Otchet S. peterburgskogo universiteta za 1910 god* (St. Petersburg, 1911), 1–19; Leonid Iuzefovich, *Put' posla* (St. Petersburg: Izd-vo Ivana Limbakha, 2007).

32. Halperin, *Russia and the Golden Horde,* 90–91. For discussions about the impact of Mongol rule on other aspects of Muscovy, see Gustave Alef, "The Origin and Early Development of the Muscovite Postal Service," *Jahrbücher für Geschichte Osteuropas* 15 (1967): 1–15; Chris Bellamy, "Heirs of Genghis Khan: The Influence of the Tatar-Mongols on the Imperial Russian and Soviet Armies," *RUSI* 128, no. 1 (March 1983): 52–60.

33. Keenan, "Muscovy and Kazan'," 400.

34. Paul Bushkovitch, "Princes Cherkasskii or Circassian Murzas: The Kabardians in the Russian Boyar Elite, 1560–1700," *Cahiers du monde russe* 45 (2004): 28; Janet Martin, "Multiethnicity in Moscow: A Consideration of Christian and Muslim Tatars in the 1550s–1580s," *Journal of Early Modern History* 5 (2001): 1–23; R. G. Landa, *Islam v istorii Rossii* (Moscow: Vostochnaia literatura, 1995), 56–58; Craig Kennedy, "The Jurchids of Muscovy: A Study of Personal Ties between Émigré Tatar Dynasts and the Muscovite Grand Princes in the Fifteenth and Sixteenth Centuries" (PhD diss., Harvard University, 1994), 47–49.

35. Kennedy, "Jurchids of Muscovy," 20.

36. Martin, "Multiethnicity in Moscow," 5. See also Janet Martin, "Tatars in the Muscovite Army during the Livonian War," in Eric Lohr and Marshall Poe, eds., *The Military and Society in Russia, 1450–1917* (Leiden, the Netherlands: Brill, 2002), 365–387.

37. Boris Unbegaun, *Russian Surnames* (Oxford: Oxford University Press, 1972), 23–25; N. A. Baskakov, *Russkie familii tiurkskogo proiskhozheniia* (Moscow: Nauka, 1979).

38. Elaine Feinstein, *Anna of All the Russias* (London: Weindenfeld and Nicholson, 2005), 10.

39. Daniel Clarke Waugh, *The Great Turkes Defiance: On the History of the Apocryphal Correspondence of the Ottoman Sultan in Its Muscovite and Russian Variants* (Columbus, OH: Slavica, 1978), 188.

40. *Russkii khronograf,* Polnoe sobranie russkikh letopisei, vol. 22 (Moscow: Iazyki slavianskoi kul'tury, 2005); I. Iu. Krachkovskii, *Ocherki po istorii russkoi arabistiki* (Moscow: Izd-vo Akademii nauk SSSR), 1950. 20–21; A. A. Zimin, *Russkie letopisi i khronografy kontsa XV–XVI vv* (Moscow: Moskovskii Gos Istoriko-Arkhivnyi Institut, 1960), 8–9.

41. Valerie Kivelson, *Cartographies of Tsardom* (Ithaca, NY: Cornell University Press, 2006), 229n53. Isolde Thyrêt kindly provided a copy of her analysis of the text's reception in Muscovy. See Isolde Thyrêt, "Kosmas Indikopleustes' *Christian Topography* in Sixteenth-Century Russia"(paper presented at the annual conference of the American Association for the Advancement of Slavic Studies, Boca Raton, FL, 1998).

42. B. M. Dantsig, "Iz istorii russkikh puteshestvii i izucheniia Blizhnego Vostoka v dopetrovskoi Rusi," *Ocherki po istorii russkogo vostokovedeniia,* vol. 1 (Moscow: Izd-vo Akademii nauk SSSR, 1953), 209–213. A detailed description of these sources in the seventeenth century is in N. M. Rogozhin, *Posol'skii prikaz* (Moscow: Mezhdunarodnye otnosheniia, 2003).

43. E. I. Maleto, *Antologiia khozhenii russkikh puteshestvennikov, XII–XV veka* (Moscow: Nauka, 2005). See also Klaus-Dieter Seemann, *Die altrussische Wallfahrtsliteratur* (Munich: Wilhelm Fink, 1976); Gail Lenhoff Vroon, "The Making of the Medieval Russian Journey" (PhD diss., University of Michigan, 1978); George P. Majeska, *Russian Travelers to Constantinople in the Fourteenth and Fifteenth Centuries* (Washington, DC: Dumbarton Oaks, 1984).

44. Igumen Daniil, "Khozhenia Daniila, igumena russkoi zemli," in Maleto, *Antologiia,* 163–208.

45. Dantsig, "Iz istorii russkikh," 194.

46. Maleto, *Antologiia,* 134–135.

47. N. S. Trubetskoi, "'Khozhenie za tri moria' Afonasiia Nikitina kak literaturnyi pamiatnik," in Trubetskoi, *Three Philological Studies* (Ann Arbor: Michigan Slavic Materials, 1963), 37–38; Lenhoff Vroon, "Making of the Medieval Russian Journey," 206–214.

48. Afanasii Nikitin, *Khozhenie za tri moria,* ed. V. P. Adrianova-Perets (Moscow-Leningrad: Izd-vo Akademii nauk SSSR), 1958.

49. M. N. Speranskii, "Indiia v staroi russkoi pis'mennosti," in *Sergeiu Fedorovichu Ol'denbergu k piatidesiatiletiiu nauchno-obshchesvennoi deiatel'nosti 1882–1932: Sbornik statei* (Leningrad: Izd-vo Akademii nauk SSSR, 1934), 463–466; Jean-Pierre Sabsoub, *Die Reise des Kaufmanns Nikitin von der Rus' nach Indien, 1466–1472: Ein Beitrag zur Begegnung mit den Anderen,* Mundus Reihe Ethnologie, vol. 20 (Bonn: Holos, 1988), 20–24; R. H. Stacy, *India in Russian Literature* (Delhi: Motilal Banarsidas, 1985), 20–22. On early west European views, see H. G. Rawlinson, "India in European Thought and Literature," in G. T. Garratt, ed., *The Legacy of India* (Oxford: Oxford University Press, 1937), 1–26.

50. "Diuk Stepanovich," in B. N. Putilova, *Byliny* (Leningrad: Sovetskii pisatel', 1957), 354.

51. Nikolai Karamzin (although he did not specify the years) came across a sixteenth-century version of the manuscript in the library of the Holy Trinity Monastery. See N. M. Karamzin, *Istoriia gosudarstva rossiiskago,* book 2 (St. Petersburg: V Tip. Eduarda Pratsa, 1842), 226–227.

52. Nikitin, *Khozhenie,* 11.

53. Ibid., 13.

54. Ibid., 17.

55. Ibid., 21–22. This passage was expurgated from the lavish quadrilingual (Slavonic, Russian, Hindi, and English) presentation edition produced at the height of Soviet-Indian friendship. See Afanasy Nikitin, *Khozhenie za tri moria,* ed. S. N. Kumkes (Moscow: Geografgiz, 1960), 116. On Moscow's efforts to use the tale to promote better ties with New Delhi, see Lowell R. Tillet, "The Soviet Popularization of Afanasii Nikitin's Trip to India: An Example of Planned Publishing," in Balkrishna G. Gokhale, ed., *Images of India* (New York: Humanities Press, 1971), 172–191.

56. Nikitin, *Khozhenie,* 30.

57. Ibid., 26.

58. Gail Lenhoff, "Beyond Three Seas: Afanasij Nikitin's Journey from Orthodoxy to Apostasy," *East European Quarterly* 13 (1979): 431–445; Mark Batunski, "Muscovy and Islam: In a Further Quest of an Empirical and Conceptual Compromise ('The Journey beyond Three Seas' by Afanasy Nikitin)," *Saeculum* 39 (1988): 289–292; Sabsoub, *Reise des Kaufmanns Nikitin,* 161–162; Keenan, "Muscovy and Kazan'," 372–373.

59. Nikitin, *Khozhenie,* 27.

60. *Entsiklopedicheskii slovar'* (St. Petersburg: Brokgauz i Efron, 1899), s.v. "Rossiia."

61. Janet Martin, "Muscovite Travelling Merchants: The Trade with the Muslim East (15th and 16th Centuries)," *Central Asian Survey* 4, no. 3 (1985): 21–22.

62. Paul Bushkovitch, "Orthodoxy and Islam in Russia, 988–1725," *Forschungen zur osteuropäischen Geschichte* (forthcoming).

63. *Lavrent'evskaia letopis',* 86.

64. Bushkovitch, "Orthodoxy and Islam."

65. Abdel-Théodore Khoury, *Les théologiens byzantins et l'Islam* (Leuven, Belgium: Editions Nauwelaerts, 1969), 47–67; John Meyendorff, "Byzantine Views of Islam," *Dumbarton Oaks Papers* 18 (1964): 115–120; Norman Daniel, *Islam and the West: The Making of an Image* (Oxford: Oneworld, 2000), 13–14.

66. Ducellier, *Chrétiens d'Orient,* 19.

67. Wil van den Bercken, *De mythe van het Oosten: Oost en West in de religieuse ideëngeschiedenis* (Zoetermeer, the Netherlands: Uitgeverij Meinema, 1998), 147. Biographies include Elise Denissoff, *Maxime le Grec et l'Occident* (Paris: Desclée, de Brouwer, 1943); Jack Haney, *From Italy to Muscovy: The Life and Works of Maxim the Greek* (Munich: W. Fink, 1973); N. V. Sinitsyna, *Maksim Grek v Rossii* (Leningrad:

Nauka, 1977); A. Langeler, *Maksim Grek: Byzantijn en humanist in Rusland* (Amsterdam: J. Mets, 1986). For a description of Father Maksim's corpus, see A. I. Ivanov, *Literaturnoe nasledie Maksima Greka* (Leningrad: Nauka, 1969).

68. Maksim Grek, *Sochineniia prepodobnogo Maksima Greka,* vol. 1 (Kazan: Tip. Imp. universiteta, 1894), 77–130, 151–168; Krachkovskii, *Ocherki,* 22–23; Bushkovitch, "Orthodoxy and Islam."

69. Buskovitch, "Orthodoxy and Islam."

70. Daniel, *Islam and the West,* 76–88; John V. Tolan, *Saracens: Islam in the Medieval European Imagination* (New York: Columbia University Press, 2002), 251–254. For a recent study of the missionary's works, see Rita George Tvrtkovic, "The Ambivalence of Interreligious Experience: Riccoldo da Monte Croce's Theology of Islam" (PhD diss., University of Notre Dame, 2007).

71. Surveys of medieval European attitudes toward Islam include Daniel, *Islam and the West;* Tolan, *Saracens;* and Richard Southern, *Western Views of Islam in the Middle Ages* (Cambridge, MA: Harvard University Press, 1962).

72. Putilova, *Byliny;* James Bailey and Tatyana Ivanova, trans., *An Anthology of Russian Folk Epics* (Armonk, NY: M. E. Sharpe, 1998); Alex E. Alexander, *Bylina and Fairy Tale* (The Hague: Mouton, 1973); A. N. Afana'sev, ed., *Narodnye russkie skazki,* 3 vols. (Moscow: Gosudarstvennoe izd-vo Khudozhestvennoi literatury, 1953).

73. I am grateful to Natalia Kononeko for this observation. Putilova, *Byliny,* 104; Tolochko, *Kochevye,* 118.

74. Roman Jakobson, "On Russian Fairy Tales," in *Russian Fairy Tales,* trans. Norbert Gutman (New York: Pantheon, 1973), 649–650.

75. The Tatars, in turn, had adopted it from the Persian noun *bagadur,* or athlete. Jakobson, "On Russian Fairy Tales," 646; V. V. Stasov, "Proiskhozhdenie russkikh bylin," *Vestnik Evropy* 4 (1868), 309.

76. Jeffrey Brooks, *When Russia Learned to Read* (Princeton, NJ: Princeton University Press, 1985), 214–245.

77. In ibid., 228.

78. For a discussion of Muscovy's relationship with the steppe, see Willard Sunderland, *Taming the Wild Field: Colonization and Empire on the Russian Steppe* (Ithaca, NY: Cornell University Press, 2004), 15–34. Another recent work stresses the hostility between Russians and their Islamic neighbors. See Michael Khodarkovsky, *Russia's Steppe Frontier: The Making of a Colonial Empire, 1500–1800* (Bloomington: Indiana University Press, 2002).

79. Landa, *Islam v istorii Rossii,* 74–85. See also Albert Seaton, *The Horsemen of the Steppes* (New York: Hippocrene Books, 1985). A more focused study of one Cossack host's intimacy with adjacent Muslim communities, albeit during the imperial era, is Thomas M. Barrett, *At the Edge of Empire: The Terek Cossacks and the North Caucasus Frontier, 1700–1860* (Boulder, CO: Westview Press, 1999).

80. V. Dal', *Poslovitsy russkogo naroda* (Moscow: Gosudarstvennoe izd-vo Khudozhestvennoi literatury, 1957), 348.

Chapter 2. The Petrine Dawn

1. V. V. Bartol'd, *Sochineniia,* vol. 9 (Moscow: Nauka, 1977), 391.

2. O. Franke, "Leibniz und China," *Zeitschrift der Deutschen Morgenländischen Gesellschaft* 82 (1928): 155–178; Olivier Roy, *Leibniz et la Chine* (Paris: J. Vrin, 1972); Donald E. Lach, "Leibniz and China," in Julia Ching and Willard G. Oxtoby, eds., *Discovering China: European Interpretations in the Enlightenment* (Rochester, NY: University of Rochester Press, 1992), 97–116.

3. Gottfried Wilhelm Leibniz, "Preface to the Novissima Sinica," in *Writings on China,* trans. Daniel J. Cook and Henry Rosemont Jr. (Chicago: Open Court, 1994), 45.

4. Ibid., 47.

5. Spence, *The Chan's Great Continent,* 83.

6. Upon learning of Peter's victory over Sweden at the Battle of Poltava in 1709, Leibniz had, however, called him "a sort of Turk of the North." See Lindsey Hughes, *Russia in the Age of Peter the Great* (New Haven, CT: Yale University Press, 1998),

7. Leibniz, "Preface," 45.

8. Vladimir Ger'e, *Otnosheniia Leibnitsa k Rossii i Petru Velikomu* (St. Petersburg: Pechatni V. O. Golovinam, 1871), 124.

9. Ibid., 2.

10. Franke, "Leibniz und China," 160.

11. Ger'e, *Otnosheniia,* 11–18.

12. Ibid., 119; Petr Pekarskii, *Istoriia imperatorskoi Akademii nauk v Peterburge,* vol. 1 (St. Petersburg: Tip. Imp. Akademii nauk, 1870), xxi–xxii.

13. Ger'e, *Otnosheniia,* 133–200; P. Pekarskii, *Nauka i literatura v Rossii pri Petre Velikom,* vol. 1. *Vvedenie v istoriiu prosveshcheniia v Rossii XVIII stoletiia* (St. Petersburg: V tip. tov. Obshchestvennaia Pol'za, 1862), 25–33. Patriotically minded Russians who have found the influence of Germans on their academic institutions distasteful occasionally have downplayed Leibniz's role. See, for example, Pekarskii, *Istoriia imperatorskoi Akademii nauk,* 32–33.

14. Alexander Vucinich, *Science in Russian Culture: A History to 1860* (Stanford, CA: Stanford University Press, 1963), 65–66; K. V. Ostrovitianov et al., eds., *Istoriia Akademii nauk SSSR,* vol. 1 (Moscow-Leningrad: Izd-vo Akademii nauk SSSR, 1958), 30; Hughes, *Russia in the Age of Peter the Great,* 307.

15. Vucinich, *Science in Russian Culture,* 46–47.

16. Ostrovitianov, *Istoriia Akademii nauk,* 32–33.

17. Bartol'd, *Sochineniia,* vol. 9, 31; Vucinich, *Science in Russian Culture,* 78–80.

18. Franke, "Leibniz und China," 174–174.

19. Ger'e, *Otnosheniia,* 133.

20. Bartol'd, *Sochineniia,* vol. 9, 31–32.

21. Franz Babinger, *Gottlieb Siegfried Bayer (1694–1738): Ein Beitrag zur Geschichte der morgenländischen Studien im 18. Jahrhundert* (Leipzig: Otto Harrasowitz, 1916); Pekarskii, *Istoriia imperatorskoi Akademii nauk,* 180–196; P. E. Skachkov, *Ocherki istorii russkogo kitaevedeniia* (Moscow: Nauka, 1977), 52–54; A. N. Kononov, *Istoriia*

izucheniia tiurkskikh iazykov v Rossii: Dooktiabr'skii period (Leningrad: Nauka, 1972), 31–33.

22. Bartol'd, *Sochineniia,* vol. 9, 32. See also Tuska Benes, "Comparative Linguistics as Ethnology: In Search of Indo-Germans in Central Asia, 1770–1830," *Comparative Studies of South Asia, Africa and the Middle East* 24, no. 2 (2004): 117.

23. Bartol'd, *Sochineniia,* vol. 9, 32. On the German fascination with central Asia more generally, see Benes, "Comparative Linguistics," 117–129.

24. It was never, however, quite as acrimonious a debate as the Normanist one.

25. Krachkovskii, *Ocherki,* 45. Nevertheless, Bayer's translations made an important impact on early Russian historiography. See J. L. Black, *G.-F. Müller and the Imperial Russian Academy* (Kingston, ON: McGill-Queen's University Press, 1986), 39–40.

26. M. Shuvalov, "Kritiko-biograficheskii ocherk zhizni i deatel'nosti Orientalista Kera," *Sbornik moskovskago glavnago arkhiva Ministerstva inostrannykh del* 5 (1893): 91–110; Kononov, *Istoriia izucheniia tiurkskikh iazykov,* 33–45; B. M. Dantsig, "Iz istorii izucheniia Blizhnego Vostoka v Rossii (vtoraia chetvert' XVIII v.)," *Ocherki po istorii russkogo vostokovedeniia,* vol. 5 (Moscow: Izd-vo vostochnoi literatury, 1959), 7–11.

27. Hughes, *Russia in the Age of Peter the Great,* 315.

28. Pekarskii, *Nauka i literatura,* vol. 1, 558–561; Jozien Driessen, *Tsaar Peter en zijn Amsterdamse vrienden* (Utrecht/Antwerp: Kosmos—Z & K Uitgevers, 1996), 55–56.

29. Bartol'd, *Sochineniia,* vol. 9, 391.

30. Shuvalov, "Kritiko-biograficheskii ocherk," 91.

31. Bartol'd, *Sochineniia,* vol. 9, 34.

32. Skachkov, *Ocherki,* 54.

33. For the first four years, its minutes adhered to the Gregorian calendar, rather than the Julian. See Black, *G.-F. Müller,* 12.

34. Kononov, *Istoriia izucheniia tiurkskikh iazykov,* 25.

35. N. N. Ogloblin, "Pervyi Iaponets v Rossii, 1701–1705 gg.," *Russkaia Starina* 72 (October 1891): 11–24; K. E. Cherevko, *Zarozhdenie russko-iaponskikh otnoshenii XVII–XIX veka* (Moscow: Nauka, 1999), 43–55; George Alexander Lensen, *The Russian Push toward Japan: Russo-Japanese Relations, 1697–1875* (Princeton, NJ: Princeton University Press, 1959), 26–30.

36. Cherevko, *Zarozhdenie,* 78–82; Lensen, *Russian Push,* 41–42; Bartol'd, *Sochineniia,* vol. 9, 26–29.

37. There would be a Japanese language school in Irkutsk from 1753 to 1816, but according to historian Vladimir Bartol'd, "during its entire existence [the school] did not manage to prepare anyone to be competent in Japanese nor did it leave any traces in the history of Russian orientology." Bartol'd, *Sochineniia,* vol. 9, 390.

38. Eric Widmer, *The Russian Ecclesiastical Mission in Peking during the Eighteenth Century* (Cambridge, MA: Harvard University Press, 1976), 159–160.

39. Pekarskii, *Nauka i literatura,* vol. 1, 187; Bartol'd, *Sochineniia,* vol. 9, 29.

40. Among the studies of his musical contributions is Eugenia Popescu-Judet, *Prince Dimitrie Cantemir: Theorist and Composer of Turkish Music* (Istanbul: Pan

Yayıncılık, 1999). A recent audio compact disc features both some of his own music as well as several modern Turkish compositions in his honor: *Cantemir: Music in Istanbul and Ottoman Europe around 1700*, with Linda Burman-Hall, İhsan Özgen, and Lux Musica (Golden Horn Records CD GHP-0192).

41. In Jonathan D. Spence, *The Search for Modern China* (New York: W. W. Norton, 1999), 101.

42. Hughes, *Russia in the Age of Peter the Great*, 47–48.

43. Werner Bahner, "Ein bedeutender Gelehrter an der Schwelle zur Frühauflärung: Dimitrie Cantemir (1673–1723)," *Sitzungsberichte der Akademie der Wissenschaften der DDR* 13 (1973): 7–9; P. Panaitescu, "Le prince Démètre Cantemir et le mouvement intellectuel russe sous Pierre le Grand," *Revue des études slaves* 6, nos. 3–4 (1926): 253–256.

44. Vasilii Nikitich Ermuratskii, *Dmitrii Kantemir: Myslitel' i gosudarstvennyi deiatel'* (Kishinev: Kartia Moldoveniaske, 1973), 36.

45. N. A. Smirnov, *Ocherki istorii izucheniia Islama v SSSR* (Moscow: Izd-vo Akademii nauk SSSR, 1954), 27; Popescu-Judet, *Prince Dimitrie Cantemir*, 35–36; Ermuratskii, *Dmitrii Kantemir*, 108.

46. In Ermuratskii, *Dmitrii Kantemir*, 94; Christina Bîrsan, *Dimitrie Cantemir and the Islamic World*, trans. Scott Tinney (Istanbul: Isis Press, 2004), 40–43.

47. Pekarskii, *Nauka i literatura*, vol. 1, 567–570; Panaitescu, "Le prince," 252. A Soviet scholar suggests that the synod saw in Cantemir's critique of Islam an aesopian attack on Christianity; see Ermuratskii, *Dmitrii Kantemir*, 100–103.

48. Demetrius Cantemir, *The History of the Growth and Decay of the Othman Empire*, trans. N. Tindal, 2 vols. (London: A. Millar, 1756).

49. Joseph von Hammer, "Sur l'histoire du prince Cantemir," *Journal asiatique* 4 (1824): 23–45. Robert Irwin suggests that this was a case of the pot calling the kettle black, as Hammer's own book "is not much more than an uncritical compilation of Turkish and Greek source material gutted and ordered approximately according to chronology." Irwin, *For Lust of Knowing*, 151.

50. Alexandru Duţu and Paul Cernovodeanu, eds., *Dimitrie Cantemir: Historian of South East European and Oriental Civilizations* (Bucharest: Association internationale d'études du Sud-Est européen, 1973), 319–329; Edward Gibbon, *The History of the Decline and Fall of the Roman Empire*, vol. 8 (London: Folio Society, 1990), 85n; Voltaire, *Essai sur les moeurs et l'esprit des nations*, vol. 1 (Paris: Editions Garnier Frères, 1963), 805; George Gordon, Lord Byron, *Don Juan* (Boston: Houghton Mifflin, 1958), 194, 206.

51. In fact, one German encyclopedia mistakenly identified Cantimir as holding the post. M. I. Radovskii, *Antiokh Kantemir i Peterburgskaia Akademii nauk* (Moscow: Izd-vo Akademii nauk SSSR, 1959), 7; Ostrovitianov, *Istoriia Akademii nauk SSSR*, vol. 1, 36.

52. "The Life of Prince Cantemir," in Cantemir, *History of the Othman Empire*, vol. 2, 458.

53. Kononov, *Istoriia izucheniia tiurkskikh iazykov*, 30.

54. Sergei Vladimirovich Fomin, *Kantemiry v izobratel'nykh materialakh* (Kishinev: Shtinitsa, 1988), 8–9, 75.

55. Popescu-Judet, *Prince Dimitrie Cantemir,* 33.

56. In fact, the surname was adopted by Dimitrie's father, who came from a modest Moldavian family. Ermuratskii, *Dmitrii Kantemir,* 20; Radovskii, *Antiokh Kantemir,* 3. With the notable exception of Voltaire, earlier biographers tended to accept this fabricated lineage. See, for example, V. G. Belinskii, "Kantemir," in *Sobranie sochinenii v trekh tomakh,* vol. 2 (Moscow: OGIZ, 1948), 734; Kononov, *Istoriia izucheniia tiurkskikh iazykov,* 28. On the philosophe's scepticism, see Voltaire, "Histoire de Charles XII," *The Complete Works of Voltaire,* vol. 4 (Oxford: Voltaire Foundation, 1996), 404.

57. Bartol'd, *Sochineniia,* vol. 9, 537.

58. A. P. Baziants et al., eds., *Aziatskii muzei—Leningradskoe otdelenie Instituta vostokovedeniia AN SSSR* (Moscow: Nauka, 1972), 7; Kononov, *Istoriia izucheniia tiurkskikh iazykov,* 27; A. L. Gal'perin, "Russkaia istoricheskaia nauka o zarubezhnom Dal'nem Vostoke v XVII v.—Seredine XIX v.," *Ocherki po istorii russkogo vostokovedeniei,* vol. 2 (Moscow: Izd-vo Akademii nauk SSSR, 1956), 11.

59. Yuri Slezkine, "Naturalists Versus Nations: Eighteenth-Century Russian Scholars Confront Ethnic Diversity," *Representations* 47 (1994): 170–171. According to Lindsey Hughes, "The received opinion that Peter's concept of science and learning was 'narrowly utilitarian' has been rightly challenged." Hughes, *Russia in the Age of Peter the Great,* 308.

60. Bartol'd, *Sochineniia,* vol. 9, 29–30.

Chapter 3. Catherinian Chinoiserie

1. The most thorough study is A. G. Brikner, "Puteshestvie Ekateriny II v Krim," *Istoricheskii vestnik* 21 (1885), no. 7: 5–23; 8: 242–264; 9: 444–509. Among primary accounts are Louis-Philippe, comte de Ségur, *Memoirs and Recollections,* vol. 3 (London: Henry Colburn, 1827), 1–190; Charles-Joseph, prince de Ligne, *Lettres à Marquise de Coigny* (Paris: Librairie ancienne Honoré Champion, 1914); Catherine II, "Pis'ma imperatritsy Ekateriny II k Grimmu (1774–1796)," *Sbornik imperatorskogo russkogo istoricheskogo obshchestva* 23 (1878): 392–412. See also Simon Sebag Montefiore, *Prince of Princes: The Life of Potemkin* (London: Weidenfield & Nicolson, 2000), 351–379. On Catherine's tours of her realm more generally, see Nina Viacheslavovna Bessarabova, *Puteshestviia Ekateriny II po Rossii* (Moscow: Moskovskii gumanitarnyi institut, 2005).

2. Ségur, *Memoirs,* vol. 3, 45.

3. Ibid., 62.

4. Henri Troyat, *Catherine la Grande* (Paris: Flammarion, 1977), 392.

5. Larry Wolff, *Inventing Eastern Europe: The Map of Civilization on the Mind of the Enlightenment* (Stanford, CA: Stanford University Press, 1994), 129; Troyat, *Catherine,* 394. At one point Ligne joked to Ségur about the impression that would be made on Europe "if these twelve hundred Tartars who now surround us, should

take it into their heads to conduct us to some little neighbouring port, there to embark the august Catherine, together with the powerful Emperor of the Romans, Joseph II, and thence to steer them to Constantinople, for the amusement of his Highness Abdul-Hamet, sovereign lord of the faithful?" Ségur, *Memoirs,* 139–140.

6. Ségur, *Memoirs,* vol. 3, 130–131.

7. For a study of the eighteenth-century Russian drive to the Black Sea, including the annexation of the Crimea, from the perspective of a former tsarist diplomat, see Boris Nolde, *La formation de l'Empire russe,* vol. 2 (Paris: Institut d'études slaves, 1953), 5–195. A somewhat more recent account, based also on Turkish sources, is Alan W. Fisher, *The Russian Annexation of the Crimea, 1772–1783* (Cambridge: Cambridge University Press, 1970).

8. Potemkin entirely ignored all traces of Crimea's Hellenic past, to the point of using the stones of Greek ruins when building fortifications. See Andreas Schönle, "Garden of the Empire: Catherine's Appropriation of the Crimea," *Slavic Review* 60 (2001): 11.

9. Catherine, who by her own admission was no great poet, probably had the verse substantially polished by her secretary, Aleksandr Khrapovitskii. See Douglas Smith, *Love and Conquest: Personal Correspondence of Catherine the Great and Prince Grigory Potemkin* (DeKalb: Northern Illinois University Press, 2004), 179.

10. In Brikner, "Puteshestvie," 490.

11. Ségur, *Memoirs,* vol. 2, 142, 144–145.

12. Andrei Zorin, *Kormia dvuglavogo orla* . . . (Moscow: Novoe literaturnoe obozrenie, 2001), 100.

13. Schönle, "Garden," 2; Zorin, *Kormia,* 114–116.

14. On Hellenism in Russian letters, see Harold B. Segel, "Classicism and Classical Antiquity in Eighteenth- and Early-Nineteenth-Century Russian Literature," in J. G. Garrard, ed., *The Eighteenth Century in Russia* (Oxford: Oxford University Press, 1973), 48–71.

15. Richard Wortman, *Scenarios of Power: Myth and Ceremony in Russian Monarchy,* vol. 1 (Princeton: Princeton University Press, 1995), 138; Sara Dickinson, "Russia's First 'Orient': Characterizing the Crimea in 1787," *Kritika* 3, no. 1 (Winter 2002): 12.

16. Charles-Joseph, prince de Ligne, *Mémoires du prince de Ligne* (Brussels: Emile Flatau, 1860), 98; Ligne, *Lettres,* 21; Ségur, *Memoirs,* vol. 3, 2.

17. Isabel de Madariaga, *Russia in the Age of Catherine the Great* (New Haven, CT: Yale University Press, 1981), 394.

18. Apparently, in 1783 Catherine's new ally, Emperor Joseph II, ordered Christoph Willibald Gluck's opera *Iphigénie en Tauride* performed in Vienna to honour her annexation of the Crimea. Zorin, *Kormia,* 112

19. Dickinson, "Russia's First 'Orient,'" 9–10.

20. In a slightly different but related context, Marc Raeff detected in Potemkin's grand projects for his viceroyalty "an unmistakable element of 'play,' in the Huizinga sense, of course." Marc Raeff, "In the Imperial Manner," in *Catherine the Great: A Profile* (New York: Hill and Wang, 1972), 228. Leiden's historian suggested that eighteenth-century European culture saw the Orient as a source of aristocratic diversion,

when he referred to the rococo's "naive exoticism, which plays with erotic or sentimental images of Turks, Chinese and Indians." J. Huizinga, *Homo Ludens: Proeve eener bepaling van het spel-element der cultuur* (Groningen, the Netherlands: H. D. Tjeenk Willink, 1974), 182.

21. In Wolff, *Inventing Eastern Europe,* 127.

22. In W. F. Reddaway, ed., *Documents of Catherine the Great: The Correspondence with Voltaire and the Instruction of 1767* (Cambridge: Cambridge University Press, 1931), 216.

23. Ségur, *Memoirs,* vol. 2, 122, 182.

24. V. N. Tatishchev, "Vvedenie k gistoricheskomu i geograficheskomu opisaniiu velikorossiiskoi imperii," in *Izbrannye trudy po geografii Rossii,* ed. A. I. Andreev (Moscow: Gosudarstvennoe izd-vo geograficheskoi literatury, 1950), 156; Mark Bassin, "Russia between Europe and Asia: The Ideological Construction of Geographical Space," *Slavic Review* 50 (1991): 2–7; Wolff, *Inventing Eastern Europe,* 149–154.

25. In Pierre Martino, *L'Orient dans la littérature française au XVIIᵉ et au XVIIIᵉ siècle* (Paris: Hachette, 1906), 22.

26. Vasilii Osipovich Kliuchevskii, "Aforizmy i mysli ob istorii," in *Sochineniia v deviati tomakh,* vol. 9, *Materialy raznykh let* (Moscow: Mysl', 1990), 414.

27. Madariaga, *Russia in the Age of Catherine the Great,* 327, 532.

28. In Reddaway, *Documents of Catherine the Great,* xxvi.

29. Catherine II, *The Memoirs of Catherine the Great,* trans. Mark Cruse and Hilde Hoogenboom (New York: Modern Library, 2005), passim.

30. Catherine II, *Sochineniia Imperatritsy Ekateriny II,* 11 vols., ed. A. N. Pypin (St. Petersburg: Tip. Imp. Akademii nauk, 1901–7).

31. Michael von Herzen, "Catherine II—Editor of *Vsiakaia Vsiachina*? A Reappraisal," *Russian Review* 38 (1979): 296–297. The Soviet literary scholar Grigorii Gukovskii's dismissal of Catherine's literary talents is typical of such disdain. See G. A. Gukovskii, "Ekaterina II," in *Literatura XVIII veka: Istoriia russkoi literatury,* eds. G. A. Gukovskii and V. A. Desnitskii, vol. 4, pt. 2 (Moscow: Akademii nauk SSSR, 1947), 364–380. On popular views of the empress's amatory exploits, see John T. Alexander, *Catherine the Great: Life and Legend* (Oxford: Oxford University Press, 1989), 329–341.

32. In A. Lentin, ed., *Voltaire and Catherine the Great: Selected Correspondence* (Cambridge: Oriental Research Partners, 1974), 29.

33. Barbara Widenor Maggs, *Russia and 'le rêve chinois': China in Eighteenth-Century Russian Literature* (Oxford: Voltaire Foundation, 1984), 127–128.

34. Petr Romanovich Zaborov, *Russkaia literatura i Vol'ter: XVIII-pervaia tret' XIX veka* (Moscow: Nauka, 1978), 7–78.

35. Giovanni Giacomo Casanova, *Mémoires,* ed. Robert Abirached, vol. 3 *(1763–1774)* (Paris: Librairie Gallimard, 1960), 460. Marc Raeff begs to differ; see his "The Enlightenment in Russia," in Garrard, *Eighteenth Century,* 38.

36. Catherine II, *Memoirs,* 48. Among published collections of the letters she exchanged with Voltaire, see Reddaway, *Documents of Catherine the Great.*

37. Madariaga, *Russia in the Age of Catherine the Great,* 215–218.

38. Among good surveys of the philosophe's views of China, see Shun-Ching Song, *Voltaire et la Chine* (Aix-en-Provence: Université de Provence, 1989); Walter Engemann, *Voltaire und China* (Leipzig, 1932). The former includes a thorough bibliography of Voltaire's writings about the topic, on pp. 235–243.

39. François Arouet Voltaire, *The Works of Voltaire,* trans. William F. Fleming, vol. 30 (Paris: E. R. Dumont, 1901), 119.

40. In Song, *Voltaire et la Chine,* 304.

41. Voltaire, *Works,* vol. 24, 29.

42. In Maggs, *Russia and 'le rêve chinois,'* 137–138.

43. According to Barbara Maggs, very few of Catherine's contemporaries questioned Voltaire with respect to the Middle Kingdom. See Maggs, *Russia and 'le rêve chinois,'* 112. One was the diplomat, Vasilli Bratishchev, who in 1757 during a brief stay in Beijing compiled a "Verification of Voltaire's remarks about China." See Barbara Widenor Maggs, "Answers from Eighteenth-Century China to Certain Questions on Voltaire's Sinology," *Studies on Voltaire and the Eighteenth Century* 120 (1974): 179–198.

44. V. S. Miasnikov, *Dogovornymi statiami utverdili: Diplomaticheskaia istoriia russko-kitaiskoi granitsy XVII–XX vv.* (Khabarovsk: Priamurskoe geograficheskoe obshchestvo, 1997), 260–265; Madariaga, *Russia in the Age of Catherine the Great,* 474; Michael Khodarkovsky, *Where Two Worlds Met: The Russian State and the Kalmyk Nomads, 1600–1771* (Ithaca, NY: Cornell University Press, 1992), 224–235; John LeDonne, "Proconsular Ambitions on the Chinese Border: Governor General Iakobi's Proposal of War on China," *Cahiers du monde russe* 45, nos. 1–2 (2004): 31–60.

45. In Reddaway, *Documents of Catherine the Great,* 101.

46. Ibid., 91.

47. Catherine II, *Les lettres de Catherine II au prince de Ligne (1780–1796),* ed. Princess Charles de Ligne (Brussels: Librairie nationale d'art et d'histoire, 1924), 38

48. Catherine II, *Sochineniia,* vol. 2, 332–363; Lurana Daniels O'Malley, *The Dramatic Works of Catherine the Great* (Aldershot, UK: Ashgate, 2006), 170–174.

49. This fairy tale was made into a comic opera, *Khlor-Tsarevich, or the Rose without Thorns,* by D. I. Khvostov in 1786. See P. I. Berkov, *Istoriia russkoi komedii XVIII v.* (Leningrad: Nauka, 1977), 265.

50. Catherine II, *Sochineniia,* vol. 1, 347–406. For a translation of the play, see Lurana Daniels O'Malley, *Two Comedies by Catherine the Great, Empress of Russia* (Amsterdam: Harwood Academic Publishers, 1998).

51. For a brief survey of Eastern themes in eighteenth-century Russian literature, see Berkov, *Istoriia russkoi komedii XVIII v.,* 262–266. A more extensive review of Chinese motifs is in Maggs, *Russia and 'le rêve chinois,'* 81–112.

52. In Maggs, *Russia and 'le rêve chinois,'* 91.

53. N. I. Novikov, "Zaveshchanie Iundzhena, kitaiskogo khana, k ego synu," in *Satiricheskie zhurnaly N. I. Novikova,* ed. P. N. Berkov (Moscow: Izd-vo Akademii nauk SSSR, 1951), 267–268.

54. G. Makogonenko, *Nikolai Novikov i russkoe prosveshchenie XVIII veka* (Moscow: Gosudarstvennoe izd-vo Khudozhestvennoi literatury, 1952), 167–170.

55. D. I. Fonvizin, "Ta-Gio, ili velikaia nauka zakliuchaiushchaia v sebe vysokuiu kitaiskuiu filosofiiu," in *Sobranie sochinenii,* vol. 2. (Moscow: Gosudarstvennoe izd-vo Khudozhestvennoi literatury, 1959), 231–253.

56. Walter Gleason, *Moral Idealists, Bureaucracy, and Catherine the Great* (New Brunswick, NJ: Rutgers University Press, 1981), 189–190.

57. Hugh Honour, *Chinoiserie: The Vision of Cathay* (New York: Harper & Row, 1961), 125. On the journal's influence in Russia, see G. Gareth Jones, "Novikov's Naturalised *Spectator,*" in Garrard, *Eighteenth Century,* 149–165.

58. Charles de Secondat, baron de Montesquieu, *Lettres persanes* (Paris: Garnier, 1963).

59. Honour, *Chinoiserie,* 117; N. A. Samoilov, "Rossiia i Kitai," in S. M. Ivanova and B. N. Mel'nichenko, *Rossiia i Vostok* (St. Petersburg: Izd-vo S. Peterburgskogo universiteta, 2000), 241; O. L. Fishman, *Kitai v Evrope: Mif i real'nost' XIII–XVIII vv.* (St. Petersburg: Peterburgskoe Vostokovedenie, 2003), 400–404.

60. Skachkov, *Ocherki,* 67.

61. Dimitri Shvidkovsky, *The Empress and the Architect: British Architecture and Gardens at the Court of Catherine the Great* (New Haven, CT: Yale University Press, 1996), 168.

62. Galina Agarkova and Nataliia Petrova, *250 let Lomonosovskomu farforovomu zavodu v Sankt-Peterburge 1744–1994* (St. Petersburg: LFZ, 1994), 5–13; T. I. Dul'kina and N. A. Asharina, *Russkaia keramika i steklo 18–19 vekov* (Moscow: Izobrazitel'noe iskusstvo, 1978), 106; Heikki Hyvönen, *Russian Porcelain* (Helsinki: Vera Saarela Foundation, 1982), 14–19.

63. V. A. Popov, *Russkii farfor: Chastnye zavody* (Leningrad: Khodozhnik SSSR, 1980), 5–15.

64. Maria Menshikova, "Oriental Rooms and Catherine's Chinese Collections," in Mikhail B. Piotrovski, ed., *Treasures of Catherine the Great* (New York: Harry N. Abrams, 2000), 207.

65. Aleksandr Benois, "Kitaiskii dvorets v Oranienbaume," *Khudozhestvennyia sokrovishchia Rossii,* 1, no. 10 (1910): 196–201; V. G. Klement'ev, *Kitaiskii dvorets v Oranienbaume* (St. Petersburg: BLITs, 1998); Will Black, *The Chinese Palace at Oranienbaum* (Boston: Bunker Hill, 2003); Dawn Jacobson, *Chinoiserie* (London: Phaidon, 1993), 107–110.

66. Klement'ev, *Kitaiskii,* 74.

67. Igor Grabar, *Peterburgskaia arkhitektura v XVIII i XIX v.* (St. Petersburg: Lenizdat, 1994), 244–248; Shvidkovsky, *Empress and the Architect,* 171–180; Jacobson, *Chinoiserie,* 171.

68. In Shvidkovsky, *Empress and the Architect,* 179.

69. Alain Grosrichard, *Structure du serial: La fiction du despotisme asiatique dans l'Occident classique* (Paris: Editions du Seuil, 1979), 34–67; Asli Çirakman, *From the "Terror of the World" to the "Sick Man of Europe": European Images of the Ottoman*

Empire and Society from the Sixteenth Century to the Nineteenth (New York: Peter Lang, 2002), 105–110; Baudet, *Paradijs*.

70. M. A. Batunskii, *Rossiia i Islam*, vol. 2 (Moscow: Progress-Traditsiia, 2003), 66n54.

71. Madariaga, *Russia in the Age of Catherine the Great*, 336.

72. Bartol'd, *Sochineniia*, vol. 9, 411.

73. Daniel, *Islam and the West*, 310–313; Reddaway, *Documents of Catherine the Great*, 20, 24–5.

74. In Reddaway, *Documents of Catherine the Great*, 33–34.

75. Rodinson, *Europe and the Mystique of Islam*, 44.

76. In Novikov, *Satiricheskie*, 262–263, 277–278.

77. Berkov, *Istoriia russkoi komedii XVIII v.*, 262–266.

78. G. R. Derzhavin, "Felitsa," in *Stikhotvoreniia* (Moscow: Khudozhestvennaia literatura, 1958), 18–25.

79. William Edward Brown, *A History of 18th-Century Russian Literature* (Ann Arbor, MI: Ardis, 1980), 382; Harold B. Segel, *The Literature of Eighteenth-Century Russia*, vol. 2 (New York: E. P. Dutton, 1967), 264.

80. I. A. Krylov, "Kaib: Vostochnaia povest'," in *Sochineniia*, vol. 1 (Moscow: Khudozhestvennaia literatura, 1969), 377–406.

81. In Nikolai Stepanov, *Ivan Krylov* (New York: Twayne, 1973), 54.

82. Krylov, "Kaib," 384.

83. Maggs, "Answers from Eighteenth-Century China."

84. Maggs, *Russia and 'le rêve chinois,'* 146.

85. Widmer, *Russian Ecclesiastical Mission*, 166–167.

86. Madariaga, *Russia in the Age of Catherine the Great*, 588.

Chapter 4. The Oriental Muse

1. Henri Laurens, "Les Lumières et l'Egypte," in *Orientales I: Autour de l'expédition d'Egypte* (Paris: CNRS Editions, 2004), 49–54; Marie-Noëlle Bourguet, "Des savants à la conquête de l'Egypte? Science, voyage et politique au temps de l'expédition française," in Patrice Bret, ed., *L'expédition d'Egypte, une enterprise des Lumières, 1798–1801* (Paris: Technique et Documentation, 1999), 21–36; Juan Cole, *Napoleon's Egypt: The Invention of the Middle East* (New York: Palgrave Macmillan, 2007); Geoffrey Symcox, "The Geopolitics of the Egyptian Expedition, 1797–1798," in Irene A. Bierman, ed., *Napoleon in Egypt* (London: Ithaca Press, 2003), 13–14.

2. Edward W. Said, *Orientalism* (New York: Pantheon, 1978), 80.

3. Todd Porterfield, *The Allure of Empire: Art in the Service of French Imperialism, 1798–1836* (Princeton, NJ: Princeton University Press, 1998), 43–79; Gérard-Georges Lemaire, *The Orient in Western Art* (Paris: Könemann, 2001), 105–109.

4. Jean Alazard, *L'Orient et la peinture française au XIXe siècle* (Paris: Librairie Plon, 1930), 35–36; Philippe Julian, *The Orientalists* (Oxford: Phaidon, 1977), 122–125.

5. Claudine Grossir, *L'Islam des Romantiques,* vol. 1, *Du refus à la tentation* (Paris: Editions Maisonneuve et Larose, 1984), 69–78.

6. Victor Hugo, *Les Orientales,* vol. 1, ed. Elisabeth Barineau (Paris: Librairie Marcel Didier, 1968), 11–12.

7. Maurice Cranston, *The Romantic Movement* (Oxford: Blackwell, 1994), 1–48.

8. Friedrich Schlegel, "Gesprach über die Poesie," in *Charakteristiken und Kritiken I,* ed. H. Eichner, Kritische-Friedrich-Schlegel-Ausgabe 2 (Munich: Ferdinand Schöningh; Zürich: Thomas-Verlag, 1967), 320.

9. S. Kaganovich, "Romantizm i Vostok," *Voprosy literatury* 2 (February 1979): 169; D. I. Belkin, "Pushkinskie stroki o Persii," in E. P. Chelyshev, ed., *Pushkin i mir Vostoka* (Moscow: Nauka, 1999), 99.

10. Orest Somov, "O romaticheskoi poezii," in *Selected Prose in Russian,* eds. John Merserau Jr. and George Harjan (Ann Arbor: Department of Slavic Languages and Literatures, University of Michigan, 1974), 174–175.

11. V. G. Belinskii, *Pol'noe sobranie sochinenii,* vol. 7 (Moscow: Izd-vo Akademii nauk SSSR, 1955), 372.

12. V. M. Zhirmunskii, *Bairon i Pushkin* (1924; repr., Munich: Wilhelm Fink, 1972), vi–vii. For a recent discussion by an American scholar, see Monica Greenleaf, "Pushkin's Byronic Apprenticeship: A Problem in Cultural Syncretism," *Russian Review* 53 (1994): 382–398.

13. This biographical sketch is largely based on B. V. Tomashevskii, *Pushkin,* 2 vols. (Moscow: Izd-vo Akademii nauk SSSR), 1956–1961; P. V. Annenkov, *Materialy dlia biografiia A. S. Pushkina* (Moscow: Sovremennik, 1984); Iu. M. Lotman, *Aleksandr Sergeevich Pushkin* (Leningrad: Prosveshchenie, 1982); T. J. Binyon, *Pushkin: A Biography* (London: HarperCollins, 2002); and Ernest J. Simmons, *Pushkin* (New York: Vintage Books, 1964).

14. Aleksandr Puskhin, *Pol'noe sobranie sochinenii,* vol. 3 (Moscow: Izd-vo Akademii nauk SSSR, 1963), 208.

15. Although initially thought to be Ethiopian, according to a Beninese scholar, Abraham was born near Lake Chad in what is now the city of Logone in Cameroon. See Dieudonné Gnammankou, *Abraham Hanibal: L'aïeul noir de Pouchkine* (Paris: Présence Africaine, 1996), 19–24. A more recent British writer believes that "the dispute is unresolved." See Hugh Barnes, *The Stolen Prince* (New York: HaperCollins, 2006), 49.

16. Pushkin, *Sochinenii,* vol. 8, 76–77. The official Russian genealogy corroborates this. See *Obshchii gerbovnik dvorianskikh rodov Vserossiiskoi imperii,* s.v. "Pushkin."

17. Italics mine. Simmons, *Pushkin,* 7.

18. Pushkin, *Sochinenii,* vol. 2, 44; David M. Bethea, "How Black Was Pushkin? Otherness and Self-Creation," in Catharine Theimer Nepomnyashchy et al., eds., *Under the Sky of My Africa* (Evanston, IL: Northwestern University Press, 2006), 122–123.

19. Catherine O'Neil, "Pushkin and *Othello*," in Nepomnyashchy, *Under the Sky,* 197.

20. A historian of German Arabism points out that "the Orient, which concerns the Orientalist, does not lie to the East, geographically speaking, but rather to the South East." Rudi Paret, *The Study of Arab and Islam at German Universities* (Wiesbaden, Germany: Franz Steiner, 1968), 3–4.

21. Hugo, *Orientales*, vol. 1, 11.

22. Pushkin, *Sochinenii*, vol. 3, 210.

23. Binyon, *Pushkin*, 19.

24. Ibid., 63.

25. Belkin, "Pushkinskie," 104.

26. Paul Austin, "The Exotic Prisoner in Russian Romanticism," *Russian Literature* 16 (1984): 219.

27. A. S. Pushkin, *The Captive of the Caucasus,* trans. Katya Hokanson, in Hokanson, "Empire of the Imagination," 263–285.

28. For example, see Alexander Etkind, "Orientalism Reversed: Russian Literature in the Time of Empires," *Modern Intellectual History* 4 (2007): 620.

29. In Eidelman, *Byt' mozhet.*

30. Pushkin, *Sochinenii*, vol. 10, 17–18.

31. Pushkin, *Sochinenii,* vol. 9, 48–54, 422–437; Belkin, "Pushkinskie," 134–141.

32. Tomashevskii, *Pushkin*, vol. 1, 407–408; Ram, *Imperial Sublime,* 130–132.

33. Layton, *Russian Literature and Empire,* 87.

34. Hokanson, "Empire of the Imagination," 53–54.

35. Laurence Kelly, *Lermontov* (London: Constable, 1977), 192. The phrase tellingly originated in Pushkin's *Eugene Onegin.* See Pushkin, *Sochinenii,* vol. 5, 150.

36. Layton, *Russian Literature and Empire,* 156–174.

37. Ibid., 17–30, 103.

38. Belinksii, *Sochinenii,* vol. 7, 372.

39. Pushkin, *Sochinenii,* vol. 4, 175–195. On the poem's origins, see L. P. Grossman, "U istokov 'Bakhchisaraisaia Fontana,'" *Pushkin: Issledovaniia i materialy,* vol. 3 (Moscow: Izd-vo Akademii nauk SSSR, 1960), 49–100.

40. N. M. Lobikova, *Pushkin i Vostok* (Moscow: Nauka, 1974), 57–62; Belkin, "Pushkinskie," 100–101, Hokanson, "Empire of the Imagination," 135–136.

41. Belinskii, *Pol'noe sobranie sochinenii,* vol. 7, 379–380.

42. Lobikova, *Pushkin i Vostok,* 52–55.

43. Pushkin, *Sochinenii,* vol. 10, 135.

44. Lobikova, *Pushkin i Vostok,* 65–68.

45. I. S. Braginskii, "Zametki o zapadno-vostochnom sinteze v lirike Pushkina," *Narody Azii i Afriki* (1965): no. 4, 123–125; Tomashevskii, *Pushkin,* vol. 2, 21–22, 31–35.

46. Pushkin, *Sochinenii,* vol. 6, 637–701.

47. Ibid., vol. 10, 92.

48. D. S. Mirsky, *A History of Russian Literature* (New York: Vintage, 1958), 86.

49. Iurii Slezkine, *Arctic Mirrors* (Itahaca, NY: Cornell University Press, 1994), 75; Etkind, "Orientalism Reversed," 626.

50. Lemaire, *Orient in Western Art,* 20–57.

51. Julian, *Orientalists,* 28; Michelle Verrier, *Les peintres orientalistes* (Paris: Flammarion, 1979), 1–2.

52. Jean Alazard, *L'Orient et la peinture française au XIXe siècle* (Paris: Librarie Plon, 1930), 42–44.

53. Porterfield, *Allure of Empire,* 117–121; Julian, *Orientalists,* 47–50.

54. Julian, *Orientalists,* 28.

55. The following four paragraphs draw on my article, "Orientalizm delo tonkoe," *Ab Imperio* 1 (2002): 249–261.

56. Steven Vincent, "Must We Burn the Orientalists?" *Art & Auction* 20, no. 3 (November 1997): 128.

57. Said, *Orientalism.*

58. But by no means did all art historians follow suit. See, for example, Donald Rosenthal, *Orientalism: The Near East in French Painting, 1800–1880* (Rochester, NY: Memorial Art Gallery of the University of Rochester, 1982); MaryAnne Stevens, "Western Art and Its Encounter with the Islamic World, 1798–1914," in *The Orientalists: Delacroix to Matisse* (London: Royal Academy of Arts, 1984), 15–23; Vincent, "Must We Burn the Orientalists?"; Lemaire, *Orient in Western Art;* Kristian Davies, *The Orientalists: Western Artists in Arabia, the Sahara, Persia and India* (New York: Laynfaroh, 2005). For surveys of the debate, see John M. MacKenzie, *Orientalism: History, Theory and the Arts* (Manchester, UK: Manchester University Press, 1995), 43–71; Louise Jacqueline Shalev, "Vasilii Vereshchagin (1842–1904): Orientalism and Colonialism in the Work of a 19th Century Russian Artist" (master's thesis, San Jose State University, 1993), 61–76.

59. Linda Nochlin, "The Imaginary Orient," *Art in America,* May 1983, 119–131, 186–191.

60. Ibid., 123.

61. Ibid., 122.

62. The most thorough biography is A. K. Lebedev, *V. V. Vereshchagin* (Moscow: Iskusstvo, 1972). Among others, an account written by a friend shortly after his death stands out: F. I. Bulgakov, *Vasilii Vasil'evich Vereshchagin i ego proizvedeniia* (St. Petersburg: A. S. Suvorina, 1896). A more recent work focuses on the artist's many travels: Lev Demin, *S mol'bertom po zemnomu sharu: Mir glazami V. V. Vereshchagina* (Moscow: Mysl', 1991). Aside from a spate of articles written at the turn of the twentieth century, the only English-language biography is Vahan D. Barooshian, *V. V. Vereshchagin: Artist at War* (Gainesville: University Press of Florida, 1993). There are also many details in the painter's own published autobiographical writings, such as V. V. Vereshchagin, *Detstvo i otrochestvo khudozhnika,* vol. 1 (Moscow: Tip. T-va. I. N. Kushnerev, 1895); and V. V. Vereshchagin, *Na voine v Azii i Evrope* (Moscow: Tip. T-va. I. N. Kushnerev, 1898).

63. Lev Demin, "Vereshchagin i Vostok," *Afrika i Aziia segodnia,* August 1992, 61.

64. Vladimir Vasil'evich Stasov, "Vasilii Vasil'evich Vereshchagin," in *Izbrannye sochineniia,* vol. 2 (Moscow: Iskusstvo, 1952), 215.

65. Elizabeth Valkenier, *Russian Realist Art* (New York: Columbia University Press, 1989), 11; Richard Stites, *Serfdom, Society, and the Arts in Imperial Russia: The Pleasure and the Power* (New Haven, CT: Yale University Press, 2005), 343.

66. Vereshchagin, *Detstvo,* 56.

67. Valkenier, *Russian Realist Art,* 3–7; David Jackson, *The Wanderers and Critical Realism in Nineteenth-Century Russian Painting* (Manchester, UK: Manchester University Press, 2006), 9–13.

68. N. G. Chernyshevskii, "Esteticheskie otnosheniia iskusstva k deistvitel'nosti," in *Sobranie sochinenii v piati tomakh,* vol. 4 (Moscow: Pravda, 1974), 5–117.

69. Ibid., 115.

70. Valkenier, *Russian Realist Art,* 33–40; Stites, *Serfdom,* 413–418; Jackson, *Wanderers,* 27–33. Although less objective, a good overview of the general trends of Russian art at the time by a champion of the Society is V. V. Stasov, "Dvadtsat'-piat' let russkogo iskusstva," in *Izbrannye sochineniia,* vol. 2, 391–472.

71. V. V. Vereshchagin, *Listki iz zapisnoi knizhki khudozhnika* (Moscow: Tip. T-va. I. N. Kushnerev, 1898), 70.

72. Bulgakov, *Vereshchagin,* 28.

73. Ibid., 29.

74. The latter is argued convincingly in Gerald Ackerman, "Gérôme's Oriental Paintings and the Western Genre Tradition," *Arts Magazine,* March 1986, 75–80.

75. Largely neglected after his death at the turn of the twentieth century, the artist was rehabilitated in the 1980s by the American art historian Gerald M. Ackerman, whose biography remains the definitive study: Ackerman, *The Life and Work of Jean-Léon Gérôme* (London: Sotheby's Publications, 1986). See also Hélène Lafont-Couturier, *Gérôme* (Paris: Herscher, 1998; and Lemaire, *Orient in Western Art,* 238–242.

76. Basile Vereschaguine [Vasilii Vereshchagin], "Voyage dans les provinces du Caucase," trans. Ernest le Barbier, *Le tour du monde* 17 (1868): 162–208; 19 (1869): 241–336.

77. Ibid., 196.

78. Ibid., 200.

79. Italics in the original. In Lebedev, *Vereshchagin,* 54.

80. The journey is described in Basile Vereschaguine, "Voyage dans l'Asie centrale: D'Orembourg à Samarcande," *Le tour du monde* 25 (1873): 193–272.

81. E. Blanc, "Notes de voyages en Asie centrale: A travers la Transoxiane," *Revue des deux mondes* 129 (1895): 904, cited in Irina Kanterbaeva-Bill, "Vasilij Vereščagin (1842–1904): Une vision de l'Orient lors de la conquête russe de l'Asie centrale" (master's thesis, Université de Toulouse-Le-Mirail, 2005), 31.

82. Vereshchagin, " Voyage dans l'Asie," 211.

83. Ibid., 263.

84. Ibid., 248.

85. Vereshchagin, *Na voine,* 1–60. See also A. I. Maksheev, *Istoricheskii obzor Turkestana i nastupatel'nago dvizheniia v nego russkikh* (St. Petersburg: Voennaia ti-

pografiia, 1890), 268–273; M. A. Terent'ev, *Istoriia zavoevaniia Srednei Azii,* vol. 1 (St. Petersburg: Tipo-litrografiia V. V. Komarova, 1906), 453–471.

86. V. V. Vereshchagin to V. V. Stasov, 20 September 1882, in A. K. Lebedev, ed., *Perepiska V. V. Vereshchagina i V. V. Stasova,* vol. 2 (Moscow: Iskusstvo, 1951), 134.

87. Vereshchagin's public refusal of the appointment generated a lively controversy. See Lebedev, *Perepiska,* vol. 1, 20–25, 30–31. He also turned down the Order of Saint Stanislaus; see ibid., vol. 2, 320n6.

88. Lebedev, *Vereshchagin,* 76.

89. Stasov, "Vereshchagin," 235; Bulgakov, *Vereshchagin,* 54.

90. The scene was based on personal observation. See Vereshchagin, "Voyage dans l'Asie," 224.

91. On "the pleasures of the pipe" in Orientalist art, see Davies, *Orientalists,* 121–143.

92. Kistin [Andrei Ivanovich Somov], "Zametki o khudozhnikakh," *Sankt-Peterburskie Vedomosti,* March 16, 1869. Affiliated with the Imperial Academy of Art, the critic was the father of the *Mir iskusstva* painter Konstantin Andreevich Somov.

93. Vereshchagin, "Voyage dans l'Asie," 224.

94. Barooshian, *Vereshchagin,* 32–33.

95. Nor, for that matter, did women appear in many of his other paintings. Stasov, "Dvadtsat'-piat'," 445–6.

96. Vereshchagin, "Voyage dans l'Asie," 227.

97. Bulgakov, *Vereshchagin,* 64.

98. Ibid., 139.

99. Vereshchagin, *Na voine,* 16.

100. Ibid., 12.

101. Vladislav Artemov, *Voiny, srazheniia, polkovodtsy v proizvedeniiakh klassicheskoi zhivopisi* (Moscow: Olma-Press, 2002), 206.

102. "Sketches of Central Asia," *Pall Mall Gazette,* April 9, 1873, 11; "Khiva on Canvas," *The Spectator,* April 12, 1873, 470.

103. A. M. Gorchakov, memorandum, November 21, 1864, in D. C. B. Lieven, ed., *British Documents on Foreign Affairs: Reports and Papers from the Foreign Office Confidential Print* (Frederick, MD: University Publications of America, 1983–1989), part I, series A, vol. 1, 287.

104. Retranslated from the Russian in Lebedev, *Vereshchagin,* 119.

105. In "Sketches of Central Asia," 11.

106. A. V. Nikitenko, *Zapiski i dnevnik* (Moscow: Zakharov, 2005), vol. 3, 426.

107. Some conservative papers, however. criticized it for being "antipatriotic." See Solomon Volkov, *St. Petersburg: A Cultural History* (New York: Free Press, 1995), 104.

108. In Bulgakov, *Vereshchagin,* 12; Volkov, *St. Petersburg,* 105–106.

109. Italics in the original. Vereshchagin to Stasov, mid-March 1874, in Lebedev, *Perepiska,* vol. 1, 13.

110. Bulgakov, *Vereshchagin,* 139.

111. Vereshchagin to Stasov, mid-March 1874, *Perepiska,* vol. 1, 15.

112. Vereshchagin, "Voyage dans l'Asie," 222.

113. In Lebedev, *Vereshchagin,* 57.

114. Vereshchagin to Stasov, 4 October 1877, in Lebedev, *Perepiska,* vol. 1, 192.

115. Vereshchagin to Nicholas II, 18 February 1904, *Krasnyi Arkhiv* 2 (1931): 169.

116. Vereshchagin, *Listki,* 146.

117. Vereshchagin, Ibid., 82.

118. A. A. Bestuzhev-Marlinskii, *Sochinenii v dvukh tomakh,* vol. 2 (Moscow: Gosudarstvennoe izd-vo Khudozhestvennoi literatury, 1958), 599.

Chapter 5. The Kazan School

1. A. V. Martynov, *Zhivopisnoe puteshestvie ot Moskvy do kitaiskoi granitsy* (St. Petersburg: Tipografiia Aleksandra pliushara, 1819), 28.

2. In A. N. Khokhlov, "Mirza Kazem-Bek i V.P. Vasil'ev v Kazani i Peterburge (kharakter nauchnykh kontaktov vostokovedov)," in M. Z. Zakiev and R. M Valeev, eds., *Mirza Kazem-Bek i otechestvennoe vostokovedenie* (Kazan: Izd-vo Kazanskogo universiteta, 2001), 189–190.

3. The definitive account of tsarist nationalities policy in the region is Andreas Kappeler, *Russlands erste Nationalitäten: Das Zarenreich und die Völker der Mittleren Wolga vom 16. bis 19. Jahrhundert* (Cologne: Böhlau, 1982).

4. Geraci, *Window on the East.*

5. G. F. Shamov, "Nauchnaia deiatel'nost O. M. Kovalevskogo v Kazanskom universitete," *Ocherki po istorii russkogo vostokovedeniia* 2 (1956): 118–119.

6. M. K. Korbut, *Kazanskii gosudarstvennyi universitet imeni V. I. Ul'ianova-Lenina za 125 let,* vol. 1 (Kazan: Izd-vo Kazanskogo universiteta, 1930), 133.

7. V. Vladimirtsov, ed., *Istoricheskaia Zapiska o 1-i Kazanskoi gimnazii: XVIII stoletie,* part 1 (Kazan: Universitetskaia tipografiia, 1867), 45–48; N. P. Zagoskin, *Istoriia imperatorskago Kazanskogo universiteta za pervye sto let ego sushchestvovaniia, 1804–1904,* vol. 1 (Kazan: Tip. Imp. Kazanskogo universiteta, 1902), 220; Ramil M. Valeev, *Kazanskoe vostokovedenie: Istoki i razvitie (XIX v.–20 GG. XX v.)* (Kazan: Izd-vo Kazanskogo universiteta, 1998), 74.

8. Alexander I also confirmed the status of universities already existing at Helsinki and Dorpat, and fifteen years later he elevated the status of St. Petersburg's pedagogical institute, thereby bringing the total number of universities in his empire to seven.

9. Vucinich, *Science in Russian Culture,* 191–193; James T. Flynn, *The University Reform of Tsar Alexander I, 1802–1835* (Washington, DC: Catholic University of America Press, 1988).

10. S. V. Rozhdestvenskii, *Istoricheskii obzor' deiatel'nosti Ministerstva Narodnago Prosveshcheniia, 1802–1902* (St. Peterburg: Ministerstva Narodnago Prosveshcheniia, 1902), 54; Aleksandr Aleksandrovich Kizevetter, "Iz istorii borby s prosveshcheniem," in *Istoricheskie ocherki* (Moscow: Izd-vo Okto, 1912), 157.

11. N. I. Veselovskii, "Svedeniia ob offitsial'nom prepodavanii vostochnykh iazykov v Rossii," in V. V. Grigor'ev, *Trudy tret'iago mezdhunarodnago s"ezda or'entalistov v*

S. Peterburge (St. Petersburg: Tip. Brat'ev Panteleevikh, 1876), 109; Bartol'd, *Sochineniia,* vol. 9, 232.

12. Bartol'd, *Sochineniia,* vol. 9, 43; G. F. Kim and P. M. Shastitko, *Istoriia otechestvennogo vostokovedeniia do serediny XIX veka* (Moscow: Nauka, 1990), 111–114.

13. As censor, Boldyrev permitted the Russian translation of Petr Chaadaev's highly critical "First Philosophical Letter" to be published. See Alla Mikhailovna Kulikova, *Vostokovedenie v rossiiskikh zakonodatel'nykh aktakh (konets XVII v. — 1917 g.)* (St. Petersburg: Institut vostokovedenie, 1994); Kim and Shastitko, *Istoriia otechestvennogo,* 98–99.

14. P. Savel'ev, *O zhizn' i uchenykh trudakh Frena* (St. Petersburg: Tipografiia Ekspeditsii zagotovleniia bumag, 1855), 13–23.

15. N. A. Mazitova, *Izuchenie blizhnego i srednego vostoka v kazanskom universitete (pervaia polovina XIX veka)* (Kazan: Izd-vo Kazanskogo universiteta, 1972), 34.

16. There are no comprehensive surveys of German orientology. However, the following provide useful details about the development of the discipline: Rudi Paret, *The Study of Arabic and Islam at German Universities: German Orientalists since Theodor Nöldeke* (Wiesbaden, Germany: Franz Steiner, 1968), 2–15; Johann Fück, *Die arabischen Studien in Europa* (Leipzig: Otto Harrasowitz, 1955), esp. 158–194; Kaushik Bagchi, "Orientalism without Colonialism? Three Nineteenth-Century German Indologists and India" (PhD diss., Ohio State University, 1996), 92–129.

17. Suzanne Marchand, "To Be a German Orientalist (1830–1930)" (paper presented at National Humanities Center, Research Triangle Park, NC, November 2002).

18. Sergei Timofeevich Aksakov, *A Russian Schoolboy,* trans. J. D. Duff (Oxford: Oxford University Press, 1978), 147.

19. Kizevetter, "Iz istorii," 155.

20. Zagoskin, *Istoriia imperatorskago Kazanskogo universiteta,* vol. 1, 375; Korbut, *Kazanskii gosudarstvennyi universitet,* 13–18; Pavel Nikolaevich Miliukov, *Ocherki po istorii russkoi kul'tury,* vol. 2 (Paris: Sovremennyia zapiski, 1930), 780; Edward Tracy Turnerelli, *Russia on the Borders of Asia: Kazan, the Ancient Capital of the Tatar Khans,* vol. 1 (London: R. Bentley, 1854), 290–291.

21. S. V. Rozhdestvenskii, *Istoricheskii obzor',* 106.

22. Kizevetter, "Iz istorii,"171–174.

23. N. P. Zagoskin, *Iz vremen Magnitskogo: Stranichka iz istorii Kazanskogo universiteta 20-kh godov* (Kazan: Tip. Tov. Pechenkina i K., 1894), 8; Valeev, *Kazanskoe vostokovedenie,* 97.

24. Mazitova, *Izuchenie blizhnego,* 100.

25. William H. E. Johnson, *Russia's Educational Heritage* (Pittsburgh: Carnegie Press, 1950), 79–80.

26. Korbut, *Kazanskii gosudarstvennyi universitet,* 19; Johnson, *Heritage,* 80–81.

27. Although the government's Siberian Committee approved the initiative, the project was deferred. Rozhdestvenskii, *Istoricheskii obzor',* 158–159.

28. A. K. Kazem-Bek, "Avtobiograficheskaia zapiska," *Russkii Arkhiv,* October 1893, 220.

29. Krachkovskii, *Ocherki*, 126.

30. A. K. Rzaev, *Mukhammad Ali Kazem-Bek* (Moscow: Nauka, 1989), 23.

31. Kazem-Bek, "Avtobiograficheskaia," 222–223.

32. Along with Kazem-Bek's own recollections, there are also some English-language accounts of his conversion. As the first and most distinguished Muslim that the Presbyterian "Tatar Mission" to Astrakhan managed to baptize, Kazem-Bek inspired several devotional tracts, including Rev. Dr. Ross, "The Persian Convert," in Rev. William Ellis, ed., *The Christian Keepsake and Missionary Annual* (London: Fisher, Son & Co., 1836), 155–168; *A Brief Memoir on the Life and Coversion of Mohammed Ali Bey, A Learned Persian, of Derbent* (New York: Carlton and Porter, ca. 1830). See also Rev. William Brown, *History of the Propagation of Christianity among the Heathen since the Reformation*, vol. 3 (Edinburgh: William Blackwood & Sons, 1854), 425–428.

33. In Rzaev, *Kazem-Bek*, 25.

34. Kazem-Bek's noble status was only formally registered in 1840, when he successfully petitioned the government of Kazan to have him inscribed in the *rodoslovnaia kniga* (family register). Kazem-Bek was listed in the third section, for those who were eligible by virtue of state service. As a professor at the time, he held the seventh chin in the Table of Ranks, thereby being entitled to this estate. See Il'ia Nikolaevich Berezin, "Aleksandr Kasimovich Kazem-Bek," *Protokoly zasedanii soveta Imperatorskago S.-Peterburgskago universiteta* no. 4 (1872): 110. Nevertheless, Ermolov was not being untruthful, since it was common practice in Russia to recognize foreign nobility.

35. E. Kozubskii, "A. P. Ermolov i A. K. Kazem-Bek: Po povodu biograficheskikh svedenii o Kazembeke," *Russkii Arkhiv*, December 1893, 556–560. "Eshche k biografii A. K. Kazem-Beka," *Russkii Arkhiv*, June 1894, 165–174; Rzaev, *Kazem-Bek*, 26.

36. Berezin, "Kazem-Bek" 103.

37. Rozhdestvenskii, *Istoricheskii obzor'*, 358; Valeev, *Kazanskoe vostokovedenie*, 97–99; Shamov, "Nauchnaia," 122–123; Korbut, *Kazanskii gosudarstvennyi universitet*, 114.

38. Barthol'd, *Obzor*, 83.

39. Sergei Semenovich Uvarov, "Project d'une académie asiatique," *Etudes de philologie et de critique* (St. Petersburg: L'imprimerie de l'académie impériale des sciences, 1843), 3–65; P. S. Savelev, "Predpolozheniia ob uchrezhdenii vostochnoi akademii v S. Peterburge, 1733 i 1810 gg.," *Zhurnal Ministerstvo Narodnago Prosveshcheniia* 89 (1855): 27–36; Cynthia Whittaker, "The Impact of the Oriental Renaissance in Russia: The Case of Sergej Uvarov," *Jahrbücher für Geschichte Osteuropas* 26 (1978): 503–524.

40. Shamov, "Nauchnaia," 120–122.

41. Mazitova, *Izuchenie blizhnego*, 70.

42. Geraci, *Window on the East*, 309–341.

43. The most complete bibliography of the scholar's published and unpublished works is in Rzaev, *Kazem-Bek*, 191–193.

44. B. Dorn, "Razbor sochineniia Ordinarnago Professora Mirzy Aleksandra

Kazem-Beka: Grammatika Turetsko-Tatarskago Iazyka," *Desiatoe prisuzhdnie uchrezh-dennykh P. N. Demidovym nagrad* (St. Petersburg: Tip. Imp. Akademii nauk, 1841).

45. A. K. Kazem-Bek, *Allgemeine Grammatik der türkisch-tatarischen Sprache,* trans. Julius Theodor Zenker (Leipzig: W. Engelmann, 1848).

46. A. K. Kazem-Bek, "Notice sur la marche et du progrès de la jurisprudence parmi les sects orthodoxies musulamanes," *Journal asiatique* ser. 4, vol. 15 (1850): 158–214; Rzaev, *Kazem-Bek,* 177.

47. Berezin, "Kazem-Bek," 116–118.

48. Thus one columnist for the pro-government *Severnaia Pchela* roundly condemned Kazem-Bek's "Muslim articles" for *Russkoe Slovo*. M. Kazem-Bek, *Izbrannye proizvedeniia* (Baku: ELM, 1985), 378; Berezin, "Kazem-Bek," 113, Mazitova, *Izuchenie blizhnego,* 159.

49. Rzaev, *Kazem-Bek,* 54.

50. A. K.Kazem-Bek, "Muridizm i Shamil'," *Russkoe Slovo,* December 1859, 182–242; A. K. Kazem-Bek, "Bab et les Babis, ou le soulèvement politique et réligieux en Perse de 1845 à 1853," *Journal asiatique,* April–May 1866, 329–384; August–September 1866, 196–252; October–November 1866, 357–400; December 1866, 473–507.

51. Rzaev, *Kazem-Bek,* 28–29.

52. P. Znamenskii, *Na pamiat' Nikolae Ivanovich Il'minskom* (Kazan: Tip. N. A. Il'iashenko, 1892), 15.

53. V. B. Shklovskii, *Lev Nikolaevich Tolstoi* (Moscow: Molodaia Gvardiia, 1967), 49–54. V. M. Dantsig, *Izuchenie Blizhnego Vostoka v Rossii* (XIX–nachalo XX v.) (Moscow: Nauka, 1968), 43.

54. August Freiherr von Haxthausen, *The Russian Empire: Its People, Institutions and Resources,* trans. Robert Faire (London: Frank Cass, 1968), vol. 1, 325–326; Rzaev, *Kazem-Bek,* 30.

55. Berezin, "Kazem-Bek," 105.

56. Turnerelli, *Russia on the Borders of Asia,* vol. 1, 178.

57. These children were in addition to two legitimate sons and a daughter by his wife, Praskovia Aleksandrovna, née Kostlivtseva. See Mireille Massip, *La Vérité est fille du temps: Alexandre Kasem-Beg et l'émigration russe en Occident, 1902–1977* (Geneva: Georg Editeur, 1999), 19. This work is a biography of the Mirza's great-grandson, Aleksandr-Lvovich, the leader of the émigré monarchist movement Mladorossii. Another work about the latter is Nicholas Hayes, "Kazem-Bek and the Young Russians' Revolution," *Slavic Review* 39 (1970): 255–268.

58. A. K. Kazem-Bek, "Istoriia Islama," *Russkoe Slovo* (1860): no. 2, 119–152; no. 3, 267–306; no. 8, 129–162; no. 10, 270–302.

59. Ibid., no. 10, 280.

60. Ibid., no. 10, 281.

61. Ibid., no. 10, 283–284.

62. Ibid., no. 10, 290–291.

63. Italics in the original. Ibid., no. 8, 162.

64. Ibid., no. 2, 151.

65. Kazem-Bek, "Muridizm i Shamil," 187.

66. The American scholar Paul Werth suggests that the European notion of Islam as fanatical arose with the difficult French effort to subdue Algeria beginning in the 1830s. Paul Werth, *At the Margins of Orthodoxy: Mission, Governance, and Confessional Politics in Russia's Volga-Kama Region, 1827–1905* (Itahaca, NY: Cornell University Press, 2002), 181n13.

67. Kazem-Bek, "Muridizm i Shamil," 183.

68. Ibid.

69. Kazem-Bek, "O poiavlenii i uspekhkakh slovesnosti v Evrope i upadke ee v Azii," in *Izbrannye proizvedeniia* (Baku, Azerbaijan: Elm, 1985), 339.

70. Ibid., 338.

71. Kazem-Bek, "Bab et les Babis," 66.

72. Ibid., 67.

73. Ibid.

74. Berezin, "Kazem-Bek," 124.

75. Kazem-Bek was named acting state councillor (*deistvitel'nyi statnyi sovetnik*) in 1852 and made confidential councillor (*tainyi sovetnik*) eleven years later. His decorations included the Order of Saint Anne, first class with an Imperial Crown (1860); Order of Saint Stanislas, first class (1855); and the Order of Saint Vladimir, third class (1851). Meanwhile, the Persian shah also bestowed upon him his Order of the Lion and the Sun. See Berezin, "Kazem-Bek," 117–119; Rzaev, *Kazem-Bek,* 73.

76. Cynthia H. Whittaker, *The Origins of Modern Russian Education: An Intellectual Biography of Count Sergei Uvarov, 1786–1855* (DeKalb: Northern Illinois University Press, 1984), 160–161.

77. Veselovskii, "Svedeniia," 180–184.

78. In Korbut, *Kazanskii gosudarstvennyi universitet,* 116.

79. Shirap Bodievich Chimitdorzhiev, ed., *Rossiiskie Mongolovedy (XVIII–nachalo XX vv.)* (Ulan-Ude, Buriat Republic: Izd-vo BNTs, 1997), 19–23; C. R. Bawden, *Shamans, Lamas and Evangelicals: The English Missionaries in Mongolia* (London: Routledge & Kegan Paul, 1985), 30–34.

80. G. F. Shamov, "Mongolskaia kafedra Kazanskogo universiteta (Istoriia otkrytiia)," *Uchenye zapiski Kazanskogo Gosudarstvennogo universiteta* 114, no. 9 (1954): 173.

81. Norman Davies, *God's Playground: A History of Poland,* vol. 2 (New York: Columbia University Press, 1982), 313.

82. Ibid., 314.

83. G. F. Shamov, *Professor O. M. Kovalevskii: Ocherk zhizni i nauchnoi deiatel'nosti* (Kazan: Izd-vo Kazanskogo universiteta, 1983), 13–15; Władysław Kotwicz, *Józef Kowalewski Orientalista (1801–1878)* (Wroclaw: Nakladem wroclawskiego towarzystwa naukowego, 1948), 27.

84. Shamov, *Professor O. M. Kovalevskii,* 22.

85. Ibid., 25–28.

86. Ibid., 26.

87. Kim and Shastitko, *Istoriia otechestvennogo,* 125–127; A. N. Khokhlov, "Poezdka

O. M. Kovalevskogo v Pekine (1830–1831 gg.) i ego sviazi s rossiiskimi kitaevedami," *Voprosy istorii* 5 (2003): 150–159.

88. A. S. Shofman and G. F. Shamov, "Vostochnyi razriad Kazanskogo universiteta," *Ocherki po istorii russkogo vostokovedeniia,* vol. 2 (Moscow: Izd-vo Akademii nauk SSSR, 1956), 427–430; Kim and Shastitko, *Istoriia otechestvennogo,* 427–430.

89. Bawden, *Shamans,* 32; Shamov, *Professor O. M. Kovalevskii,* 76–78.

90. R. M. Valeev, *Osip Mikhailovich Kovalevskii* (Kazan: Izd-vo Kazanskogo universiteta, 2002), 12.

91. The most complete bibliography is in Kotwicz, *Kowalewski,* 145–155.

92. O. M. Kovalevskii, "O znakomstve evropeitsev s Aziei," *Obozrenie prepodavaniia nauk v Imperatorskom Kazanskom universitete na 1837–1838 uchebnyi god* (Kazan: Universitetskaia tipografiia, 1857), 22–36.

93. Shamov, *Professor O. M. Kovalevskii,* 52–53.

94. Spence, *The Chan's Great Continent,* 99.

95. Shamov, *Professor O. M. Kovalevskii,* 52.

96. Ibid., 58.

97. Kovalevskii, "O znakomstve," 22–36.

98. Kotwicz, *Kowalewski,* 134–135.

99. Dorzhi Banzarov, *Chernaia vera ili shamanstvo u mongolov* (St. Petersburg: Tip. Imp. Akademii nauk, 1891).

100. Khokhlov, "Poezdka," 150.

101. Karl Voigt, *Obozrenie khoda i uspekhov prepodavaniia aziatskikh iazykov v Imperatorskom Kazanskom Universitete* (Kazan: V universitetskom tipografii, 1852).

102. Freiherr August von Haxthausen, *Studien über die inneren Zustände, das Volksleben und insbesondere die ländlichen Einrichtungen Russlands,* vol. 1 (Hildesheim, Germany: Georg Olms, 1973), 469.

103. Turnerelli, *Russia on the Borders of Asia,* vol. 1, 277–278.

104. Zagoskin, *Istoriia imperatorskago Kazanskogo universiteta,* vol. 2, 333–335; Chantal Lemercier-Quelquejay, "Les missions orthodoxes en pays musulmans de moyenne-et bas-Volga, 1552–1865," *Cahiers du monde russe et soviétique* 8 (1967): 394–395; Werth, *At the Margins,* 193–194.

105. *Materialy dlia istorii Fakul'tet vostochnykh iazykov,* vol. 1 (St. Petersburg: Tip. M. M. Stasiulevich, 1905), 7.

106. Ibid., 12.

107. Ibid., 29.

108. Ibid., 4–5.

109. Ibid., 14.

110. Ibid., 143–145.

111. Berezin, "Kazem-Bek," 125–126.

112. Bartol'd, *Sochineniia,* vol. 9, 46–47; Rzaev, *Kazem-Bek,* 15; R. M. Valeev, "Mirza A. Kazem-Bek i vostokovedenie v Rossii v XIX v.," in M. Z. Zakiev and R. M. Valeev, eds., *Mirza Kazem-Bek i otechestvennoe vostokovedenie* (Kazan: Izdatel'stvo Kazanskogo universiteta, 2001), 58.

113. A good indication of his pedagogy is given in the curriculum he developed for

the First Kazan Gymnasium: A. K. Kazem-Bek, *Raspredelenie prepodavaniia arabskago, persidskago i turetsko-tatarskago iazykov v Pervoi Kazanskoi Gimnazii* (Kazan: V universitetskoi tipografii, 1836). The itinerary for two of his students was also published: A. K. Kazem-Bek, *Plan uchenago puteshestviia po Vostoky magistrov kazanskago universiteta Dittelia i Berezina* (Kazan: V universitetskoi tipografii, 1841).

114. Rzaev, *Kazem-Bek*, 8–9.

115. Berezin, who opposed his former teacher on this point, cattily speculated that Kazem-Bek's poor knowledge of German may have been one reason for his practical orientation. Berezin, "Kazem-Bek," 126. See also Krachkovskii, *Ocherki*, 126–127.

116. In Rzaev, *Kazem-Bek*, 7.

117. Korbut, *Kazanskii gosudarstvennyi universitet*, 116; Shofman and Shamov, *Vostochnyi razriad*, 424.

118. Shamov, "Nauchnaia," 118; Bartol'd, *Sochineniia*, vol. 9, 83–84; Berezin, "Kazem-Bek," 121–122.

119. Veselovskii, "Svedeniia," 14; Bartol'd, *Sochineniia*, vol. 9, 467.

Chapter 6. Missionary Orientology

1. Veselovskii, "Svedeniia," 113–114.

2. Epiphanus the Wise, *Zhitie Sv. Stefana episkopa Permskogo*, ed. V. Druzhinin (1897; repr., The Hague: Mouton, 1959).

3. Nolde, *La formation de l'Empire russe*, vol. 1, 35–36; Jaroslav Pelenski, *Russia and Kazan: Conquest and Imperial Ideology (1438–1560s)* (The Hague: Mouton, 1974), 251. According to the American historian Michael Khodarkovsky, "These conquests were first and foremost a manifestation of the political and ideological supremacy of Orthodox Muscovy over its former Muslim overlords." Michael Khodarkovsky, "The Conversion of Christians in Early Modern Russia," in Robert P. Geraci and Michael Khodarkovsky, eds., *Of Religion and Empire: Missions, Conversion, and Tolerance in Tsarist Russia* (Ithaca, NY: Cornell University Press, 2001), 120.

4. Kappeler, *Russlands erste Nationalitäten.*

5. Nolde, *La formation de l'Empire russe*, vol. 1, 36–41.

6. A. Mozharovskago, "Izlozhenie khoda missionerskago dela po prosveshcheniiu kazanskikh inorodtsev s 1552 po 1867 goda," *Chteniia v Imperatorskom Obshestv istorii i drevnostei pri Moskovskom universitete* no. 1 (1880): 2.

7. Isabelle Teitz Kreindler, "Educational Policies towards the Eastern Nationalities in Tsarist Russia: A Study of the Il'minskii System" (PhD diss., Columbia University, 1969), 25.

8. Josef Glazik, *Die Islammission der russisch-orthodoxen Kirche* (Münster, Germany: Aschendorff, 1959), 50.

9. Lemercier-Quelquejay, "Les missions orthodoxes," 371.

10. Matthew P. Romaniello, "Mission Delayed: The Russian Orthodox Church after the Conquest of Kazan," *Church History* 73 (2007): 513.

11. Bushkovitch, "Orthodoxy and Islam in Russia."

12. Nancy Shields Kollman, *Cartographies of Tsardom* (Ithaca, NY: Cornell University Press, 2006), 165.

13. Before the Stalin era, the only analogous example in Russia was in the 1850s, toward the end of the Caucasus war, when several hundreds of thousands of Muslims left the empire. See Robert Crews, *For Prophet and Tsar: Islam and Empire in Russia and Central Asia* (Cambridge, MA: Harvard University Press, 2006), 15.

14. Eugene Smirnoff, *A Short Account of the Historical Development and Present Position of Russian Orthodox Missions* (London: Rivingtons, 1903), 73.

15. Orlando Figes, "Islam: The Russian Solution," *New York Review of Books,* December 12, 2006, 74.

16. Kappeler, *Russlands erste Nationalitäten,* 270–287; Glazik, *Islammission,* 68; Yuri Slezkine, *Arctic Mirrors: Russia and the Small Peoples of the North* (Ithaca, NY: Cornell University Press, 1994), 47–53.

17. Paul W. Werth, "Coercion and Conversion: Violence and the Mass Baptism of the Volga Peoples, 1740–55," *Kritika* 4 (2003): 543.

18. Ibid., 545–546.

19. Crews, *For Prophet and Tsar,* 32–34.

20. Glazik, *Islammission,* 112.

21. Nikolai Il'minskii, "Izvlechenie iz proekta 1849 o tatarskoi missii," in P. Znamenskii, *Na pamiat',* 328–330.

22. Geraci, *Window on the East,* 39.

23. Werth, *At the Margins,* 180–183.

24. P. Znamenskii, *Istoriia Kazanskoi dukhovnoi akademii za pervyi (doreformennnoi) period eia sushchestvovaniia (1842–1870 gody),* vol. 1 (Kazan: Tip. Imp. universiteta, 1891–1892), 1–5.

25. Elena Vladimorovna Kolesova, "Vostokovedenie v sinodal'nykh uchebnykh zavedeniiakh Kazani (seredina XIX–nachalo XX vekov)" (diss., Kazan State University, 2000).

26. Glazik, *Islammission,* 116; V. L. Uspenskii, "Kazanskaia dukhovnaia akademiia—odin iz tsentrov otechstvennogo mongolovedeniia," *Pravoslavie na Dal'nem Vostoke* 2 (1996): 118.

27. Znamenskii, *Istoriia Kazanskoi,* vol. 1, 21.

28. Ibid., 1–7; Veselovskii, "Svedeniia," 140–141; Kolesova, "Vostokovedenie," 46–47.

29. Znamenskii, *Na pamiat',* 18–19.

30. Ibid., 29.

31. Geraci, *Window on the East,* 52.

32. Znamenskii, *Istoriia Kazanskoi,* 360–362

33. Igor Smolitsch, *Geschichte der russischen Kirche,* vol. 2, ed. Gregory L. Freeze, Forschungen zur osteuropäischen Geschichte 45 (Leiden, the Netherlands: E. J. Brill, 1991), 287. For similar opinions, see Glazik, *Islammission,* 133, and Lemercier-Quelquejay, "Les missions orthodoxes," 403–403, as well as Kreindler, "Educational Policies," and, more recently, Wayne Dowler, *Classroom and Empire: The Politics of Schooling Russia's Eastern Nationalities, 1860–1917* (Montreal: McGill-Queen's University Press, 2001). Robert Geraci has a distinctly less positive view; see Geraci, *Window on the East.*

34. B. V. Lunin, *Sredniaia Aziia v dorevoliutsionnom i sovetskom vostokovedenii*

(Tashkent, Uzbekistan: Nauka, 1965), 57. The chapter about "The Study of Islam in the Capitalist Period (1860s–1890s)," in the Stalin-era history of Russian Islamology ignores Il'minskii altogether. See Smirnov, *Ocherki istorii izucheniia Islama*, 58–83.

35. Isabelle Kreindler, "A Neglected Source of Lenin's Nationality Policy," *Slavic Review* 36 (1977): 86–100.

36. Kreindler, "Educational Policies," 114.

37. Znamenskii, *Na pamiat'*, 7.

38. Il'minskii, "Izvlechenie," 323–337.

39. Ibid., 337.

40. N. I. Il'minskii, "Oproverzhenie islamizma, kak neobkhodimoe uslovie k tverdomu priniatiiu tatarami khristianskoi very," in Znamenskii, *Na pamiat'*, 388.

41. Znamenskii, *Na pamiat'*, 82–84.

42. Krachkovskii, *Ocherki*, 180.

43. N. I. Il'minskii, "Otchet bakkalavra Kazanskoi Dukhovnooi Akademii N. I. Il'minskago za pervyi god prebyvaniia ego na Vostoke," in Znamenskii, *Na pamiat'*, 338–356.

44. N. I. Il'minksii, "Obshchii otchet bakkalavra N. I. Il'minskago ob ego zaniatiakh vo vse vremie prebyvaniia na Vostoke," in Znamenskii, *Na pamiat'*, 357–386.

45. Ibid., 361.

46. Ibid., 367.

47. Ibid., 379.

48. Znamenskii, *Na pamiat'*, 107.

49. Glazik, *Islammission*, 134.

50. Znamenskii, *Na pamiat'*, 262.

51. Ill'minskii, "Oproverzhenie islamizma," 401.

52. Znamenskii, *Istoriia Kazanskoi*, 375–376.

53. Geraci, *Window on the East*, 55.

54. Glazik, *Islammission*, 140.

55. Znamenskii, *Na pamiat'*, 95–102.

56. Dowler, *Classroom and Empire*, 57.

57. Znamenskii, *Na pamiat'*, 107–111.

58. Smirnoff, *A Short Account*, 52.

59. Geraci, *Window on the East*, 77.

60. Ibid., 109.

61. The feeling appears to have been mutual. According to one liberal author, "Mention [Il'minskii's] name in front of even a partially educated Russian Muslim and you will see that he will either turn pale or make a face as if seeing the devil in person." In Kreindler, "Educational Policies," 113.

62. N. I. Il'minskii to K. P. Pobedonostsev, February 2, 1887, in *Pis'ma Nikolaia Ivanovicha Il'minskago* (Kazan: Tipografiia Imperatorskago universiteta, 1895), 215.

63. In Mark Batunsky, "Russian Clerical Islamic Studies in the Late 19th and Early 20th Centuries," *Central Asian Survey* 13 (1994): 218.

64. Znamenskii, *Istoriia Kazanskoi*, 405.

65. In Kolesova, "Vostokovedenie," 139.

66. Ibid., 64–65; Werth, *At the Margins,* 192.

67. A. V. Talanov and N. I. Romanova, *Drug Chzhungo* (Moscow: Molodaia gvardiia, 1955); V. Krivtsov, *Otets Iakinf* (Leningrad: Lenizdat, 1984); V. P. Romanov, *Vol'n-odumets v riase* (Cheboksary, Chuvash Republic: Chuvhashskoe knizhnoe izd-vo, 1987).

68. Ieromonakh Nikolai (Adoratskii), *Istoriia Pekinskoi Dukhovnoi Missii v pervyi period ee deiatel'nosti (1685–1745)* (Kazan: Tipografiia Imperatorskago universiteta, 1887); B. G. Aleksandrov, ed., *Bei-guan': Kratkaia istoriia Rossiiskoi dukhovnoi missii v Kitae* (Moscow: Alians-Arkheo, 2006); Widmer, *Russian Ecclesiastical Mission.*

69. Mark Mancall, *Russia and China: Their Diplomatic Relations to 1728* (Cambridge, MA: Harvard University Press, 1971); Gaston Cahen, *Histoire des relations de la Russie avec la Chine sous Pierre le Grand* (Paris: F. Alcan, 1912); "O nachale torgovykh i Gosudarstvennykh snoshenii Rossii s Kitaem i o zavedenii v Pekine Rossiiskoi tserkvi i Dukhovnoi Missii," *Sibirskii vestnik* 18 (1822): 95–196; V. A. Aleksandrov, *Rossiia na dalnevostochnykh rubezhakh (vtoraia polovina XVII v.)* (Moscow: Nauka, 1969); V. S Miasnikov, *Imperiia Tsin i Russkoe gosudarstvo v XVII veke* (Khabarovsk, Russia: Khabarovskoe knizhnoe izd-vo), 1987; Peter Perdue, *China Marches West: The Qing Conquest of Central Eurasia* (Cambridge, MA: Harvard University Press, 2005), 161–173.

70. V. S. Miasnikov, *Russko-kitaiskie dogovorno-pravovye akty (1689–1916)* (Moscow: Pamiatniki istoricheskoi mysli, 2004), 27–29.

71. E. F. Timkovskii, *Puteshestvie v Kitai cherez Mongoliiu v 1820 i 1821 godakh,* vol. 2. (St. Petersburg: V Tip. Meditsinskago departamenta Ministerstva vnutrennykh del, 1824), 181.

72. Miasnikov, *Russko-kitaiskie,* 44.

73. Nikolai, *Istoriia Pekinskoi,* 17–18.

74. Adoratskii's claim that Russians were less driven by commercial greed than their Western rivals in China was disingenuous. Leading Russians from Peter the Great to the late-nineteenth-century finance minister Sergei Witte held great hopes for developing the China trade. However, Russians were never capable of competing effectively with more adept mercantile powers like the British. See Schimmelpenninck van der Oye, *Toward the Rising Sun,* 79–80.

75. P. M. Ivanov, "Pravoslavnye missionerskie stany v Kitae v nachale XX veka," in S. L. Tikhvinskii et al., eds., *Istoriia rossiiskoi dukhovnoi misii v Kitae* (Moscow: Izd-vo Sviato-Vladimirskogo Bratstva, 1997), 253.

76. The most complete biography of Father Hyacinth is P. V. Denisov, *Zhizn' monakha Iakinfa Bichurina* (Cheboksary, Chuvash Republic: Chuvashskoe knizhnoe izd-vo, 1997). See also I. N. A. [Ieromonakh Nikolai Adoratskii], "Otets Iakinf Bichurin: Istoricheskii etiud," *Pravoslavnyi sobesednik* (1886): no. 1, 164–80, 245–278; no. 2, 53–80, 271–316; Skachkov, *Ocherki,* 89–120; Edward J. Kasinec, "A Secular Religieux of Late Imperial Russia: The Sinologist Father Iakinf" (master's thesis, Columbia University, 1968).

77. In Skachkov, *Ocherki,* 92.

78. Iakinf Bichurin, "Opisanie bunta, byvshego v Kitae v 1813 g.," *Dukh zhurnalov* (1819): no. 10, 527–558, in Kim and Shastitko, *Istoriia otechestvennogo,* 290.

79. Nikitenko, *Dnevnik,* vol. 3, 43.

80. In Denisov, *Zhizn' monakha,* 65.

81. Nikitenko, *Dnevnik,* vol. 3, 43. Timkovskii's own extensive travel account, which was also published in French, German, and English, was another important early contribution to early Russian Sinology. Timkovskii, *Puteshestvie v Kitai.*

82. For a list of Father Hyacinth's publications, see Hertmut Walraven, *Iakinf Bičhurin: Russischer Mönch und Sinologe, Eine Bibliographie* (Berlin: C. Bell, 1988).

83. O. I. Senkovskii, *Sobranie sochinenii Senkovskago* (St. Petersburg: Tip. Imp. Akademii nauk, 1858), vol. 5, 380–407.

84. D. I. Belkin, "Russkie literatory 20-kh—nachala 40-kh godov XIX v. i kitaeved N. Ia. Bichurin," *Formirovanie gumanisticheskikh traditsii otechestvennogo vostokovedeniia (do 1917 goda)* (Moscow: Nauka, 1984), 53–99.

85. In Denisov, *Zhizn' monakha,* 104.

86. M. P. Alekseev, "Pushkin i Kitai," in Chelyshev, *Pushkin i mir Vostoka,* 65–73; D. I. Belkin, "Pushkin i kitaeved o. Iakinf," *Narody Azii i Afriki* (1974): no. 6, 126–134; L. A. Cherevskii, *Pushkin i ego okruzhenie* (Leningrad: Nauka, 1975), 37–38; Binyon, *Pushkin,* 310–311.

87. Pushkin, *Sochinenii,* vol. 8, 293n8.

88. Binyon, *Pushkin,* 311.

89. Iakinf Bichurin, "Otrivok liubopytnago pis'ma . . . iz Kiakhty," *Moskovskii Telegraf* (1841): no. 42, 142.

90. Kim and Shastitko, *Istoriia otechestvennogo,* 186–194.

91. Senkovskii, *Sochinenii,* vol. 6, 406.

92. V. G. Belinskii, *Sobranie sochinenii* (Moscow: Khudozhestvennaia literatura, 1982), vol. 8, 598.

93. A. N. Khokhlov, "N. Ia. Bichurin i ego trudy o Mongolii i Kitae," *Voprosii istorii* (1978): no. 1, 71; V. G. Rodionov, "Po puti v khrame," in Iakinf Bichurin, *Radi vechnoi pamiati* (Cheboksary, Chuvash Republic: Chuvashkoe knizhnoe izd-vo, 1991), 13–14.

94. Iakinf Bichurin, *Kitai v grazhdanskom i nravstvennom sostoianii,* vol. 4 (St. Petersburg: V tipografii voenno-uchebnykh zavedenii, 1848), 173.

95. Ibid., vol. 1, 299.

96. Senkovskii, *Sochinenii,* vol. 6, 27.

97. Bichurin, *Radi vechnoi,* 19.

98. Ibid., 175.

99. A. N. Bernshtam, "N. Ia. Bichurin (Iakinf) i ego trud," in Iakinf Bichurin, *Sobranie svedenii o narodakh, obitavshikh v Srednei Azii v drevnie vremena,* vol. 1 (Moscow: Izd-vo Akademii nauk SSSR, 1950), xxvi.

100. A. K. Kazem-Bek, review of *Sobranie svedenii o narodakh, obitavshchikh v Srednei Azii v drevnie vremena,* by Iakinf Bichurin, *Otechestvennye zapiski* 84 (1852): pt. 5, 1–34.

101. Iakinf, *Radi vechnoi,* 20.

102. Senkovskii, *Sochinenii*, vol. 6, 28.

103. The assessment of the University of St. Petersburg's Professor Nikolai Veselovskii is fairly typical; see *Russkii biograficheskii slovar'*, s.v. "Iakinf." See also Bernshtam, "Bichurin," xxv–xlvii.

104. In Kim and Shastitko, *Istoriia otechestvennogo*, 305.

105. From the start Russia's theological academies did teach Hebrew, which is technically an Asian language. See Krachkovskii, *Ocherki*, 178.

106. A notable exception is Kolesova, "Vostokovedenie."

107. Mark Batunsky, "Russian Missionary Literature on Islam," *Zeitschrift für Religions- und Geistesgeschichte* 39 (1987): 261.

Chapter 7. The Rise of the St. Petersburg School

1. Vucinich, *Science in Russian Culture* 222. See also F. A. Petrov, *Formirovania sistemy universitetskogo obrazovaniia v Rossii v pervye desiatiletiia XIX veka*, vol. 1 (Moscow: Izd-vo Moskovskogo universiteta, 2002–3), 1.

2. Walter Rüegg, "Themes," in *A History of the University in Europe*, vol. 3, *Universities in the Nineteenth and Early Twentieth Centuries (1800–1945)* (Cambridge: Cambridge University Press, 2004), 4–6; A. Iu. Andreev, "'Gumbol'dt v Rossii': Ministerstvo narodnogo prosveshcheniia i nemetskie universitety v pervoi polovine XIX veka," *Otechestvennaia istoriia* no. 2 (2004): 37–55.

3. Petrov, *Formirovanie*, vol. 1, 12. For a discussion of the reasons behind this decision, see Andreev, "Gumbol'dt," 37–54.

4. Nicholas I awarded him the title in 1849.

5. Particularly scathing about Uvarov's politics is S. Durylin, "Drug Gete," *Literaturnoe nasledstvo* 4–6 (1932): 186–217. See also Ostrovitianov, *Istoriia Akademiia nauk SSSR*, vol. 2, 20; Nicholas V. Riasanovsky, *Nicholas I and Official Nationality in Russia, 1825–1855* (Berkeley: University of California Press, 1959), 46, 70–72.

6. The best description of his political views is in Cynthia H. Whittaker, "The Ideology of Sergei Uvarov: An Interpretive Essay," *Russian Review* 37 (1978): 158–176. See also Whittaker, *Origins of Modern Russian Education*; and M. M. Shevchenko, *Konets odnogo Velichiia: Vlast', obrazovanie i pechatnoe slove v Imperatorskoi Rossii na poroge Osvoboditel'nykh reform* (Moscow: Tri Kvadrata, 2003), esp. 57–86.

7. Sergei Mikhailovich Solov'ev, "Moi zapiski dlia detei moikh, a esli mozhno, i dlia drugikh," in *Sochineniia*, vol. 18 (Moscow: Mysl', 1995), 571.

8. *Obshchii gerbovnik dvorianskikh rodov Vserossiiskoi imperii*, s. v. "Uvarov."

9. Friedrich von Schlegel, "Über die Sprache und Weisheit der Indier," in *Studien zur Philosophie und Theologie*, ed. Ernst Behler and Ursula Struc-Oppenberg, Kritische-Friedrich-Schlegel-Ausgabe 8 (Munich: Ferdinand Schöningh; Zürich: Thomas-Verlag, 1975), 111.

10. Schwab, *La renaissance orientale*, 79–86.

11. S. S. Uvarov, "Projet d'une académie asiatique," in *Etudes de philologie et de critique* (St. Petersburg: Académie impériale des sciences, 1843), 3–49.

12. Ibid., 12.

13. Ibid., 22–23.

14. Ibid., 8.

15. Ibid., 9.

16. Mention of the interpreters, however, was only made in a footnote. Ibid., 9.

17. Ibid., 28.

18. Ibid., 26.

19. P. S. Savel'ev, "Predpolozheniia ob uchrezhdenii vostochnoi akademii v S. Peterburge, 1733 i 1810 gg.," *Zhurnal Ministerstvo Narodnago Prosveshcheniia* 89 (1855): pt. 3, 27–36; A. P. Baziants and I. M. Grinkrug, "Tri proekta organizatsii izucheniia vostochnykh iazykov i Vostoka v Rossii v XVIII–XIX stoletiiakh," in *Formirovanie gumanisticheskikh traditsii otechestvennogo vostokovedeniia (do 1917 goda)* (Moscow: Nauka, 1984), 33–52; A. M. Kulikovo, "Proekty vostokovednogo obrazovaniia v Rossii (XVIII-1-ia pol XIX v.), *Narody Azii i Afriki* (1970): no. 4, 133–139.

20. N. V. Tairova, "Proekt I. O. Pototskogo otnositel'no sozdaniia Aziatskoi Akademii v Rossii," *Narody Azii i Afriki* (1973): no. 2, 202–207.

21. Krachkovskii, *Ocherki*, 97.

22. Whittaker, "Impact of the Oriental Renaissance," 517; Georg Schmid, ed., "Goethe und Uwarow und ihr Briefwechsel," *Russische Revue* 28 (1888): 139–143.

23. V. V. Grigor'ev, *Imperatorskii S. Peterburgskii universitet* (St. Petersburg: Tip. Bezobrazova i komp., 1870), 6.

24. A. M. Kulikova, *Stanovlenie universitetskogo vostokovedeniia v Peterburge* (Moscow: Nauka, 1982), 28–31. A. N. Kononov, "Vostochnyi fakul'tet Leningradskogo universiteta (1855–1955)," *Vestnik Leningradskogo universiteta, Seriia istorii iazyka i literatury* 8, no. 2 (1957): 3–4.

25. Sergei Uvarov, *Rech' prezidenta Imp. Akademii nauk, popechitelia Sanktpeterburgskogo uchebnogo okruga v torzhestvennom sobranii Glavnogo pedagogicheskogo instituta 22 marta 1818 goda* (St. Petersburg, 1818), 3. For a partial translation of the speech's second half, which outlines Uvarov's Burkean vision of the Russian empire's gradual evolution toward constitutionalism, see Cynthia Whittaker, ed. and trans., "On the Use of History: A Lesson in Patience: A Speech by Sergei Uvarov," *Slavic and European Education Review* 2 (1978): no. 2, 29–38.

26. Kulikova, *Stanovlenie*, 38; Barthold, *Obzor*, 52.

27. Baziants et al., *Aziatskii muzei* 5–29; S. F. Ol'denburg, *Aziatskii Muzei Rossiiskoi Akademii nauk, 1818–1918* (Petrograd: Rossiiskaia Gosudarstvennaia Akedemicheskaia Tipografiia, 1919). For an exhaustive chronicle of the institution's acquisitions under its first director, see his predecessor's work, Bernhard Dorn, *Das Asiatische Museum der kaiserlichen Akademie der Wissenschaften zu St. Petersburg* (St. Petersburg: Kaiserliche Akademie der Wissenschaften, 1846), 2 vols. He provides a brief description in B. Dorn, "Aziiatskii Muzei," *Zapiski Imp. Akademii nauk* 5 (1864): 163–174.

28. Whittaker, *Origins of Modern Russian Education*, 74.

29. S. V. Rozhdestvenskii, *"Pervonachal'noe obrazovanie": S.-Peterburgskogo universiteta 8 fevralia 1819 goda i ego blizhaishaia sud'ba* (Petrograd: 2-ia Gosudarstvannaia tipografiia, 1919), 32–62; Grigor'ev, *Imperatorskii*, 33–38.

30. Kulikova, *Stanovlenie*, 44–45, 58.

31. P. S. Savel'ev, "O zhizni i trudakh O. I. Senkovskago," in O. I. Senkovskii, *Sobranie sochinenii Senkovskago* (St. Petersburg: Tip. Imp. Akademii nauk, 1858), vol. 1, xciv. Two other biographies are Louis Pedrotti, *Józef-Julian Sękowski: The Genesis of a Literary Alien* (Berkeley: University of California Press, 1965), and Veniamin Aleksandrovich Kaverin, *Baron Brambeus* (Moscow: Nauka, 1966). On Senkovskii and the Orient, see L. G. Alieva, "O. I. Senkovskii—Puteshestvennik i vostokoved" (candidate's diss., Tadzhikskii gosudarstvennoe universitet, 1977), and the relevant chapter in John Hope, "Manifestations of Russian Literary Orientalism" (PhD diss., University of Michigan, 2001), 48–102. A more recent American monograph examines Senkovskii's career as a literary entrepreneur: Melissa Frazier, *Romantic Encounters: Writers, Readers, and the "Library for Reading"* (Stanford, CA: Stanford University Press, 2007).

32. Pedrotti, *Sękowski*, 11–15; Kaverin, *Baron Brambeus*, 24–29.

33. A. I. Gertsen, *Sobranie sochinenii*, vol. 7 (Moscow: Izd-vo Akademi nauk SSSR, 1956), 89.

34. Jan Reychman, *Podróżnicy polscy na bliskim wschozie w XIX w* (Warsaw: Wydawnictwo Wiedza Powszechna, 1971), 23; D. A. Korsakov, *O. I. Senkovskij i M. P. Pogodin kak zhurnalisti* (Kazan: Tip. Imperatorskogo universiteta, 1902), 3–5.

35. Krachkovskii, *Ocherki*, 86–87; Izabela Kalinowska, *Between East and West: Polish and Russian Nineteenth-Century Travel to the Orient* (Rochester, NY: University of Rochester Press, 2004), 62–63.

36. In Savel'ev, "O zhizni," 19.

37. The details of his trip are difficult to reconstruct, in part because the various travelogues he published were embellished. See Senkovskii, *Sobranie sochinenii*, vol. 1, 3–218. The most detailed and reliable account is in Alieva, "Senkovskii," 62–93. Senkovskii's letters are also helpful: O. I. Senkovskii, *Senkovskii v svoei perepiske s I. Lelevelem* (Warsaw: Tip. A Paevskogo, 1878), 9–29. If Senkovskii kept a diary of his journey (he had promised to send one to his Polish sponsors), it does not appear to have been preserved. However, the central archive in Lithuania does hold extensive notes and transcriptions he made during his Near Eastern travels in Polish, French, Greek, Turkish, Arabic, and Hebrew: O. I. Senkovskii, "Notaty Jozefa Sękowskiego dotycace jego podrozy na Wschod, 1819–21," Tsentr. gosudarstvennoe istoricheskii arkhiv MVD Lit. SSR, fond 56, opis' 5, ed. khr. 91. I am very grateful to Jurga Miknyte-Vigotiene for helping me with this source.

38. On Arida, see the entry Senkovskii wrote in the *Entsiklopedicheskii leksikon*, vol. 3 (St. Petersburg: Tip. A. Pliushara, 1835), 295–296.

39. Senkovskii, *Sobranie sochineniia*, vol. 1, 191–192.

40. Ibid., 8–23.

41. Ibid., 59–104.

42. In Alieva, "Senkovskii," 67.

43. In Pedrotti, *Sękowski*, 48.

44. Ibid., 61–62.

45. Ibid., 31.

46. Kulikova, *Stanovlenie,* 46–49; Alieva, "Senkovskii," 96–97.

47. Senkovskii, *Sobranie sochinenii,* vol. 7, 149–164.

48. Savel'ev, "O zhizni," 42; I. Iu. Krachkovskii, "Vostokovedenie v pismakh P. Ia. Petrov k V. G. Belinskomu," in *Ocherki po istorii russkogo vostokovedeniia,* vol. 1 (Moscow: Izd-vo vostochnoi literatury, 1953), 12.

49. Antoine Isaac Sylvestre de Sacy, review of *Supplément à l'histoire générale des Huns, des Turks et des Mogols,* by M. Joseph Senkowski [O. I. Senkovskii], *Journal des savants,* July 1825, 387–395.

50. [O. I. Senkovskii], *Lettre de Tutundju-Oglou-Moustafa-Aga* (St. Petersburg: Imprimerie de N. Gretsch, 1828). This is a more extensive version of the original, which was published in Russian the previous year. It also appears in Senkovskii, *Sobranie sochinenii,* vol. 5, 335–379.

51. Savel'ev, "O zhizni," 55–56. For a rebuttal, see "M. von Hammer's Reply to M. Senkowski," *Asiatic Journal and Monthly Miscellany* 26 (September 1828): 271–277. The Austrian's reputation has not improved with time. The British Arabist Robert Irwin judges "many [of his ideas and insights] not only wrong but also slightly mad." See Irwin, *For Lust of Knowing,* 150–151.

52. Senkovskii, *Sobranie sochinenii,* vol. 6, 17.

53. Hope, "Manifestations," 64–65.

54. Senkovskii, *Sobranie sochinenii,* vol. 6, 74–75; vol. 7, 41.

55. Ibid., vol. 6, 379, 384.

56. [Senkovskii], "Vostochnye iazyki," *Entsiklopedicheskii leksikon,* vol. 12, 110.

57. Senkovskii, *Sobranie sochinenii,* vol. 7, 171; "Aziia," *Entsiklopedicheskii leksikon,* vol. 1, 271.

58. Ibid., vol. 6, 92, 112–113.

59. Ibid., vol. 8, 111.

60. Mirsky, *History of Russian Literature,* 125. See also Sidney Monas, *The Third Section: Police and Society in Russia under Nicholas I* (Cambridge, MA: Harvard University Press, 1961), 117–122.

61. As early as 1825, he wrote Lelewel that his erstwhile mentor "seems to be going mad." See Senkovskii, *Senkovskii v svoei perepiske,* 76. Two decades later, he confided to a friend that he found Bulgarin "a man without character or scruples, the unhappy slave of his own whims." See E. N. Akhmatova, "Osip Ivanovich Senkovskii (Baron Brambeus)," *Russkaia starina* 20 (May 1889): 296.

62. Alieva, "Senkovskii," 15–16.

63. In Pedrotti, *Sękowski,* 56.

64. For an interesting comparison of Senkovskii's and Pushkin's literary Orientalism, see Rachel Polonsky, "Hajji Baba in St. Petersburg: James Morier, Osip Senkovskii and Pushkin's Literary Diplomacy between East and West," *Journal of European Studies* 35 (2005): 253–270.

65. Senkovskii, *Sobranie sochinenii,* vol. 2, 1–278. For a recent reading by a Slavist, see Andreas Schönle, *Authenticity and Fiction in the Russian Literary Journey, 1790–1840* (Cambridge, MA: Harvard University Press, 2007), 169–181.

66. V. Zilber, "Senkovsky (Baron Brambeus)," in B. M. Eikhenbaum and Yuri Tynyanov, eds., *Russian Prose* (Ann Arbor, MI: Ardis, 1985), 133.

67. Timothy Kiely, "The Professionalization of Russian Literature: A Case Study of Vladimir Odoevsky and Osip Senkovsky" (PhD diss., University of Michigan, 1998), 141–142.

68. In Pedrotti, *Sękowski,* 4. Senkovskii is still generally regarded as a second-rate writer, although there are periodic efforts in Russia to rehabilitate him. See Kaverin, *Baron Brambeus;* A. E. Novikov, "Tvorchestvo O. I. Senkovskogo v kontekste razvitiia russkoi literatury kontsa XVIII–pervoi poloviny XIX v" (Avtoreferat disertatsii na soiskanie uchenoi stepeni kandidata filologicheskikh nauk) (St. Petersburg: Institut russkoi literatury, 1995).

69. Bartol'd, *Sochineniia,* vol. 9, 620.

70. Krachkovskii, *Ocherki,* 107.

71. Kim and Shastitko, *Istoriia otechestvennogo,* 147–148; Bartol'd, *Sochineniia,* vol. 9, 67–71; Whittaker, *Origins of Modern Russian Education,* 209–211.

72. Kulikova, *Stanovlenie,* 158.

73. *Materialy dlia istorii,* vol. 1, 141. This collection is the basic resource for the faculty's organizational history. See also Bartol'd, *Sochinenii,* vol. 9, 85–106; Grigor'ev, *Imperatorskii,* 123–125; A. A. Vigasin, A. N. Khokhlov, and P. M. Shastitko, *Istoriia otechestvennogo vostokovedeniia s serediny XIX veka do 1917 goda* (Moscow: Vostochnaia literatura, 1997), 7–18.

74. *Materialy dlia istorii,* vol. 1, 7.

75. Katya Hokanson, "Russian Orientalism" (MA thesis, Stanford University, 1987), 28.

Chapter 8. The Oriental Faculty

1. The story of this remarkable house of worship is told in Aleksandr Ivanovich Andreev, *Khram Buddy v Severnoi stolitse* (St. Petersburg: Nartang, 2004). See also John Snelling, *Buddhism in Russia: The Story of Agvan Dorzhiev, Lhasa's Emissary to the Tsar* (Shaftesbury, Dorset: Element, 1993), 129–141, 157–162.

2. In Andreev, *Khram Buddy,* 54.

3. In ibid., 65.

4. Krachkovskii, *Ocherki,* 123.

5. A. K. Kazem-Bek, "Rech' po sluchaiu otkrytiia v S. Peterburgskom universitete fakul'teta Vostochnyk iazykov," *Zhurnal ministerstva narodnago prosveshcheniia* 88 (1855): 19–20.

6. Bartol'd, *Sochineniia,* vol. 9, 169–172; V. M. Alekseev, *Nauka o Vostoke* (Moscow: Nauka, 1982), 7n1.

7. *Materialy dlia istorii,* vol. 1, 188–189.

8. Ibid., vol. 2, 185.

9. Ibid., vol. 1, 366–375.

10. Bartol'd, *Sochineniia,* vol. 9, 118–119.

11. *Materialy dlia istorii,* vol. 1, 507.

12. Ibid., vol. 2, 140.

13. Petrov, *Formirovanie,* vol. 2, 447.

14. Crews, *For Prophet and Tsar,* 178–189; Berezin, "Kazem-Bek," 116–118.

15. Ol'ga Boratynskaia, "Trudy Aleksandra Kasimovicha Kazembeka," *Russkii Arkhiv* no. 2 (1894): 282.

16. N. I. Veselovskii, *Vasilii Vasil'evich Grigor'ev po ego pis'mam i trudam, 1816–1881* (St. Petersburg: Tip. A. Transhelia, 1887), 244–249.

17. A. A. Vigasin, "I. P. Minaev, i russkaia politika na Vostoke v 80–e gody XIX v.," *Vostok* (1993): no. 3, 109.

18. *Materialy dlia istorii,* vol. 2, 200–205.

19. Ibid., 207–218.

20. Ibid., 218–278. See also the scathing critique by the Sinologist Dmitrii Pozdneev in response to yet another inquiry ordered by the education minister: D. M. Pozdneev, *K voprosu ob organizatsii izucheniia Vostoka v russkikh uchebnyh zavedeniiakh* (St. Petersburg: Tip. B. M. Volf'fa, 1904).

21. *Materialy dlia istorii,* vol. 2, 260–278.

22. A. P. Baziants, *Lazarevskii institut v istorii otechestvennogo vostokovedeniia* (Moscow: Nauka, 1973); Vigasin, Khokhlov, and Shastitko, *Istoriia otechestve,* 27–35.

23. Vigasin, Khokhlov, and Shastitko, *Istoriia otechestve,* 48–75; Skachkov, *Ocherki,* 27–35; David Wolff, *To the Harbin Station: The Liberal Alternative in Russian Manchuria, 1898–1914* (Stanford, CA: Stanford University Press, 1999), 187–190.

24. V. P. Vasil'ev, "Vasil'ev, Vladimir Petrovich," in S. A. Vengerov, *Kritiko-biograficheskii slovar' russkikh pisatelei i ucheenykh.*

25. Ibid., 154.

26. A. N. Khoklov, "V. P. Vasil'ev v Nizhnem Novgorode i Kazani," in L. S. Vasil'ev, ed., *Istoriia i kul'tura Kitaia* (Moscow: Nauka, 1974), 41.

27. Z. L. Gorbacheva et al., "Russkii kitaeved akademik Vasilii Pavlovich Vasil'ev (1818–1900)," in *Ocherki po istorii russkogo vostokovedeniia,* vol. 2 (Moscow: Izd-vo Akademii nauk SSSR, 1956), 239.

28. V. P. Vasil'ev, "Vospominanii o starom Pekine," in *Otkritye Kitaia i drugie stat'ia Akademika V. P. Vasil'eva* (St. Petersburg: Vestnik vsemirnoi istorii, 1900), 34–62.

29. The most extensive bibliography is in Gorbacheva et al., "Russkii kitaeved akademik," 329–338.

30. V. P. Vasil'ev, "O znachenii Kitaia," manuscript, 1850, S. P. B. Filial Arkhiva Rossiiskii Akademii nauk, fond 775, opis' 1, delo 32.

31. Ibid., list 6.

32. Ibid., list 5.

33. Vasil'ev, "Otkrytie Kitaia," in *Otkrytie Kitaia,* 1.

34. Wolff, *To the Harbin Station,* 185.

35. Vasil'ev, "O znachenii," list 8.

36. Vasil'ev, "Vasil'ev," 153.

37. V. P. Vasil'ev, "Kitaiskii progress," *Vostochnoe obozrenie* (1884), no. 4, 8.

38. Vasil'ev, "Otkrytie," 1–33.

39. K. Sh. Khafizova, "Rossiia, Kitai i narody Turkestana v publitsistike V. P. Vasil'eva," Vasil'ev, *Istoriia i kul'tura Kitaia,* 116–117.

40. Vasil'ev, "O znachenii," list 32.

41. In Gorbacheva et al., "Russkii kitaeved akademik," 258.

42. Skachkov, *Ocherki,* 227–228.

43. V. P. Vasil'ev, "Vei-kha-veiskii vopros," *Sankt-Peterburgskie vedomosti,* April 10, 1898, 1–2.

44. V. P. Vasil'ev, *Tri voprosa: Uluchshenie ustroistvo sel'skoi obshchiny. Assignatsii-den'gi. Chemu i kak uchitsia* (St. Petersburg: Tip. G. E. Blagosietova, 1878).

45. Gorbacheva et al., "Russkii kitaeved akademik," 248–250.

46. W. Wassiljew [V. P. Vasil'ev], *Der Buddhismus, seine Dogmen, Geschichte und Literatur,* vol. 1 (St. Petersburg: Kaiserliche Akademie der Wissenschaften, 1860), v–vi.

47. N. A. Petrov, "Akademik V. P. Vasil'ev i vostochnyi fakul'tet," *Vestnik Leningradskogo universiteta* (1856): no. 8, 87.

48. Skachkov, *Ocherki,* 210–211; Petrov, "Akademik V. P. Vasil'ev," 89–91.

49. In Gorbacheva et al., "Russkii kitaeved akademik," 270–272.

50. Victoria Lysenko, "La philosophie bouddhique en Russie: Brève histoire de l'approche et des methods d'étude de la fin du XIX siècle aux années 1940," *Slavica occitania* 21 (2005): 93–95.

51. Wassiljew, *Buddhismus,* 25.

52. Wassiliew, *Buddhismus.* One German called it "epochal," while another confessed that, until he had read the book, his publications about the subject were like those "of a blind man writing about colors." See S. F. Ol'denburg, "Pamiati Vasiliia Pavlovicha Vasil'eva i o ego trudakh po buddizmu," *Izvestiia Rossiiskoi Akademii nauk* 12 (1918): 545 n9.

53. In Ia. V. Vasil'kov, "Vstrecha Vostoka i Zapada v nauchnoi deiatel'nosti F. I. Shcherbatskogo," *Vostok-Zapad,* vol. 4 (Moscow: Nauka, 1989), 185.

54. V. M. Alekseev, "Akademik V. P. Vasil'ev: Zamechaniia po povodu nauchnogo tvorchestva i naslediia," in *Nauka o Vostoke,* 67.

55. V. P. Vasil'ev, "Religii Vostoka: Konfutsianstvo, Buddizm i Daotsism," *Zhurnal ministerstva narodnago prosveshcheniia,* April 1873, 239.

56. Alekseev, "Akademik V. P. Vasil'ev," 66.

57. *Bulletin de la 3ème session du congrès internationale des orientalistes* no. 4 (1876): 25–26; "The Oriental Congress," *Times* (London), August 6, 1876, 8.

58. The family is best known today for the Decembrist Baron Andrei Evgenevich Rozen. Victor's brother, Roman, also made a career of the East, as minister to the Russian mission in Tokyo at the turn of the twentieth century.

59. Krachkovskii, *Ocherki,* 139. Baron Rosen was the only prerevolutionary Russian to merit a separate entry in an important German history of the field: Fück, *Arabischen Studien,* 222–223.

60. Tolz, "European, National, and (anti-)Imperial," 118.

61. Krachkovskii, *Ocherki,* 143; Tolz, "European, National, and (anti-)Imperial," 120.

62. Irwin, *For Lust of Knowing,* 146–147.

63. Kim and Shastitko, *Istoriia otechestvennogo,* 209–210.

64. *Materialy dlia istorii,* vol. 2, 1–7.

65. D. E. Mishin and M. A. Sidorov, eds., "Perepiska V. R. Rozena i S. F. Ol'denburga," *Neizvestnye stranitsy otechestvennogo vostokovedeniia* 2 (2004): 202; Bartol'd, *Sochineniia,* vol. 9, 590–593; Tolz, "European, National, and (anti-)Imperial," 115, 118–119.

66. Michael D. Gordin, *"A Well-Ordered Thing": Dmitrii Mendeleev and the Shadow of the Periodic Table* (New York: Basic Books, 2004), 113–138; K. V. Ostrovit'ianov, ed., *Istoriia Akademii nauk SSSR,* vol. 2 (Moscow: Nauka, 1964), 272–275; Alexander Vucinich, *Science in Russian Culture, 1861–1917* (Stanford, CA: Stanford University Press, 1970), 66–68.

67. In Gordin, *Well-Ordered Thing,* 124.

68. Rosen explained his reasons for the move in a letter to a sympathetic academician. See I. Iu. Krachkovskii, ed., *Pamiati Akademika V. R. Rozena* (Moscow: Izd-vo Akademii nauk SSSR, 1947), 119–123; Ostrovit'ianov, *Istoriia Akademii nauk,* vol. 2, 622–623; Tolz, "European, National, and (anti-)Imperial," 113–114.

69. Ostrovit'ianov, *Istoriia Akademii nauk,* vol. 2, 622.

70. The definitive biography was recently published: B. S. Kaganovich, *Sergei Fedorovich Ol'denburg: Opyt biografii* (St. Petersburg: Fenix, 2006). See also Oldenburg's brief autobiographical entry in *Materialy dlia biograficheskago slovaria deistvitel'nykh chlenov Imperatorskoi Akademii Nauk,* vol. 2 (Petrograd: Imp. Akademii nauk, 1917), 54–62; G. K. Skriabin et al., eds., *Sergei Fedorovich Ol'denburg* (Moscow: Nauka, 1986); I. Iu. Krachkovskii, ed., *Akademik S. F. Ol'denburg: K piatidesiatiletiiu nauchno-obshestvennoi deiatel'nosti* (Leningrad: Izd-vo Akademii nauk SSSR), 1934.

71. They should not be confused with the princely Ol'denburgskii line.

72. Bartol'd, *Sochineniia,* vol. 9, 463–464.

73. Krachkovskii, *Akademik S. F. Ol'denburg,* 18.

74. Kaganovich, *Ol'denburg,* 22.

75. G. V. Vernadskii, "Bratstvo 'Priiutino'," *Novyi zhurnal* 27, no. 93 (1968): 147–170; E. V. Anichkov, "Ustav 1884-go goda i studenchestvo na pereput'i," *Pamiati russkogo studenchestva kontsa XIX, nachala XX vekov* (Paris: Izd-vo Svecha, 1934), 50–55.

76. Mishin and Sidorov, "Perepiska V. R. Rozena i S. F. Ol'denburga," 201–399.

77. Lévi's letters to his Russian friend were recently published in Grigorij M. Bongard-Levin et al., eds., *Correspondances orientalistes entre Paris et Saint-Pétersbourg (1887–1935)* (Paris: Boccard, 2002).

78. S. F. Ol'denburg, [editorial], *Vostok* (1922): no. 1, 4, 5.

79. S. F. Ol'denburg, *Kultura Indii* (Moscow: Nauka, 1991), 48.

80. Ol'denburg, [editorial], 5.

81. Mishin and Sidorov, "Perepiska," 216.

82. Italics in the original. Mishin, "Perepiska," 314.

83. In V. S. Sobolev, *Avgusteishii president: Velikii kniaz' Konstantin Konstantinovich vo glave Imperatorskoi Akademii nauk* (St. Petersburg: Iskusstvo-SPB, 1993), 46.

84. Kaganovich, *Ol'denburg*, 48.

85. Ibid., 42.

86. Vera Tolz, "Orientalism, Nationalism, and Ethnic Diversity in Late Imperial Russia," *Historical Journal* 48 (2005): 135–145.

87. Nathaniel Knight, "Grigor'ev in Orenburg," *Slavic Review* 59 (2000): 97n84.

88. For a good analysis, see Randall Poole's introduction to his translation of the volume, in Poole, ed., *Problems of Idealism* (New Haven, CT: Yale University Press, 2003), 1–78.

89. S. F. Ol'denburg, "Renan, kak pobornik svobody mysli," in *Problemy idealizma* (1902; repr., ed. Modest Kolerov, Moscow: Tri Kvadrata, 2002), 795–808.

90. Ibid., 805.

91. Alekseev, *Nauka o Vostoke*, 26.

92. In Kaganovich, *Ol'denburg*, 53.

93. On the Exploration Fund's Russian branch, see N. N. Nazirova, *Tsentral'naia Aziia v dorevoliutsionnom otechestevennom vostokovedenii* (Moscow: Nauka, 1992).

94. The classic account is Peter Hopkirk, *Foreign Devils on the Silk Road* (London: John Murray, 1980).

95. William G. Rosenberg, *Liberals in the Russian Revolution* (Princeton, NJ: Princeton University Press, 1974), 53, 209, 230.

96. Vera Tolz, *Russian Academicians and the Revolution* (Houndmills, Basingstoke, UK: Macmillan, 1997), 111–115.

97. Francine Hirsch, *Empire of Nations* (Ithaca, NY: Cornell University Press, 2005), 58–61.

98. Loren Graham, *The Soviet Academy of Sciences and the Communist Party, 1927–1932* (Princeton, NJ: Princeton University Press, 1967), 120–153; Tolz, *Russian Academicians*, 39–67; Hirsch, *Empire of Nations*, 138–143.

99. B. S. Kaganovich, "Nachalo Tragedii," *Zvezda* (1994): no. 12, 136–144; V. M. Alpatov and M. A. Sidorov, "Dirizher akademicheskogo orkestra," *Vestnik Rossiiskoi Akademii nauk* 67 (1997): 169–172; Tolz, *Russian Academicians*, 115–122.

100. *Entsiklopedicheskii slovar*, s.v. "Sankt-Peterburgskii universitet"; *Materialy dlia biograficheskago*, vol. 2, 216.

101. Tolz, "European, National, and (anti-)Imperial," 108.

102. Ivan Minaev, "Ob izuchenii Indii v russkikh universitetakh," *Otchet o sostoianii Imp. S.-Peterburgskago universiteta* (St. Petersburg: Tip. Shakht, 1884), 89.

Chapter 9. The Exotic Self

1. Nikolai Rimsky-Korsakoff, *My Musical Life*, trans. Judah A. Joffe (New York: Tudor Publishing, 1935), 181–182.

2. A. Borodin, *"V Srednei Azii": Muzikal'naia kartinka dlia orkestra* (Leipzig: M. P. Beliaev, 1890), 3.

3. *The New Grove Dictionary of Opera,* s.v. "Prince Igor."

4. Miriam K. Whaples, "Early Exoticism Revisited," and Mary Hunter, "The *Alla Turca* Style in the Late Eighteenth Century: Race and Gender in the Symphony and the Seraglio," both in Jonathan Bellman, ed., *The Exotic in Western Music* (Boston: Northeastern University Press, 1998), 3–25 and 43–72, respectively.

5. Catherine II, *Sochineniia,* vol. 2, 355.

6. Gerald Abraham, "The National Element in Early Russian Opera, 1799–1800," *Music & Letters* 42, no. 3 (July 1961): 261. See also L. A. Rapatskaia, "Problema orientalizma v russkoi muzykal'noi kul'ture XVIII–XIX vv.," in B. D. Pak, ed., *Vzaimootnosheniia narodov Rossii, Sibiri i stran Vostoka: Istorii i sovremennost'* (Irkutsk, Siberia: Irkutsk State Pedagogical Institute, 1995), 31–35. According to one Stalin-era musicologist, the opera's libretto "set something of a record in feebleness and tastelessness," while the score "did not succeed in achieving a musical whole." Political considerations may have played a role in this negative assessment. See A. S. Rabinovich, *Russkaia opera do Glinki* (Moscow: Muzgiz, 1948), 73.

7. Ralph Locke, "Cutthroats and Casbah Dancers, Muezzins and Timeless Sands: Musical Images of the Middle East," in Bellman, *Exotic in Western Music,* 110–114.

8. B. Dobrokhotov, *Aleksandr Aliab'ev: Tvorcheskii put'* (Moscow: Izdatel'stvo Muzyka, 1966); Thomas P. Hodge, *A Double Garland: Poetry and Art-Song in Early Nineteenth-Century Russia* (Evanston, IL: Northwestern University Press, 2000), 102–103; Adalyat Issiyeva, "Nationalism, Decembrism and Aliab'ev: Reconsidering Russian Orientalism in Song" (paper presented at the annual conference of the Canadian University Music Society, Vancouver, 2008). I am grateful to Ms. Issiyeva for giving me a copy of her work.

9. In Edgar Istel and Theodore Baker, "Rimsky-Korsakov, the Oriental Wizard," *Musical Quarterly* 15 (1929): 393.

10. Stasov, "Dvadtsat'-piat'," 528.

11. Richard Taruskin, *Defining Russia Musically* (Princeton, NJ: Princeton University Press, 1997), 38–44.

12. Francis Maes, *Geschiedenis van de Russische muziek* (Nijmegen, the Netherlands: Uitgevery SUN, 1996), 67–68; Taruskin, *Defining Russia,* 145–146.

13. Stasov, "Dvadtsat'-piat'," 523–528.

14. Marina Frolova-Walker, *Russian Music and Nationalism* (New Haven, CT: Yale University Press, 2007), 151–152.

15. Rimsky-Korsakoff, *Musical Life,* , 58.

16. Frolova-Walker, *Russian Music,* 153.

17. The definitive biography, written by his adopted daughter's son, is S. A. Dianin, *Borodin* (Moscow: Gosudarstvennoe muzykal'noe izd-vo, 1955). See also V. A. Stasov, "Aleksandr Porfir'evich Borodin," in *Izbrannye sochineniia,* vol. 3 (Moscow: Iskusstvo, 1952), 329–365; André Lischke, *Alexandre Borodine* (Paris: Bleu nuit, 2004). A more impressionistic account is Nina Berberova, *Alexandre Borodin, 1834–1887: Biographie,* trans. Luba Jurgenson (Arles, France: Actes sud, 1989).

18. Stasov, "Borodin," 329.

19. On Borodin's scientific career, see N. A. Figurovskii and Yu. I. Solov'ev, *Aleksandr Porfir'evich Borodin: A Chemist's Biography,* trans. Charlene Steinberg and Georgre B. Kauffman (Heidelberg, Germany: Springer, 1988).

20. Dianin, *Borodin,* 38–39.

21. Stasov, "Borodin," 347.

22. Italics in the original. A. P. Borodin, *Pis'ma A. P. Borodina,* vol. 1 (Moscow: Gosudarstvennoe Izd-vo Muzykal'nyi sektor, 1927–28), 142.

23. Dianin, *Borodin,* 194–195.

24. Ibid., 329.

25. Serge Dianin, *Borodin,* trans. Robert Lord (London: Oxford University Press, 1963), 305–321. This English edition includes an extensive analysis of the composer's principal works. For a more recent discussion of the second act's sources, see Marek Bobéth, *Borodin* (Munich: Musikverlag Emil Katzbichler, 1982), 47–51.

26. Taruskin, *Defining Russia,* 165.

27. A. P. Borodin, *Kniaz' Igor* (Leipzig: M. P. Belaieff, n.d.), 11.

28. The text of Stasov's scenario is reproduced in Dianin, *Borodin,* 70–75.

29. Firoozeh Kharzai, "Orientalism in Borodin's *Prince Igor*" (unpublished paper, August 1997, http://www.anotherbirth.net/orientalism.htm).

30. Borodin, *Knaz' Igor,* 195.

31. Borodin, *Pis'ma,* vol. 3, 69.

32. Borodin, *Knaz' Igor,* 2.

33. Borodin, *Knaz' Igor,* 203.

34. G. N. Khubov, *A. P. Borodin* (Moscow: Gosudarstvennoe muzykal'noe izd-vo, 1933), 73.

35. Dianin, *Borodin,* trans. Lord, 325n1.

36. Borodin, *Pis'ma,* vol. 2, 108.

37. Harlow Robinson, "'If You're Afraid of Wolves, Don't Go into the Forest': On the History of Borodin's *Prince Igor,*" *Opera Quarterly* 7, no. 4 (Winter 1990–91): 9–11.

38. A. S. Suvorin, "'Igor' Opera Borodina," *Novoe vremia,* October 24, 1890, 2.

39. A. S. Suvorin, "Malenkiia Pis'ma," *Novoe vremia,* October 30, 1890, 2.

40. In Alfred Habets, *Alexandre Borodine* (Paris: Librarie Fischbacher, 1893), 63.

41. I am grateful for the help of my research assistant, Denis Kozlov, with this section.

42. D. S. Merezhkovskii, *Pol'noe sobranie sochinenii,* vol. 18 (St. Petersburg: Tip. T-va. I. D. Sytina, 1914), 173–275; B. G. Rosenthal, *D. S. Merezhkovskii and the Silver Age: The Development of a Revolutionary Mentality* (The Hague: Martinus Nijhoff, 1975), 43–56.

43. Italics in the original. Merezhkovskii, *Sochinenii,* vol. 18, 215–218.

44. Avril Pyman, *A History of Russian Symbolism* (Cambridge: Cambridge University Press, 1994), 9.

45. The classic study remains Arthur Symons, *The Symbolist Movement in Literature* (New York: E. P. Dutton, 1919).

46. George C. Schoolfield, *A Baedeker of Decadence: Charting a Literary Fashion,*

1884–1927 (New Haven, CT: Yale University Press, 2003), 1–15; Brian Stableford, ed., *The Dedalus Book of Decadence (Moral Ruins)* (Sawtry, UK: Dedalus, 1990), 1–83.

47. Paul Verlaine, *Jadis et naguère chair* (Paris: Rombaldi, 1936), 94.

48. Roger Keys, *The Reluctant Modernist: Andrei Bely and the Development of Russian Fiction, 1902–1914* (Oxford: Clarendon Press, 1996), 3–18.

49. The relevant stanzas were included as an appendix to an important American anthology, Carl Proffer and Elendea Proffer, eds., *The Silver Age of Russian Culture* (Ann Arbor, MI: Ardis, 1971–75), 447–452.

50. Pyman, *Russian Symbolism,* 2.

51. Referring to his prolific romantic entanglements, the poet once remarked, "I have many wives, after all on my mother's side I am by blood the Mongol Prince White Swan of the Golden Horde." In *The Dictionary of Literary Biography*, s.v. "Konstantin Dmitrievich Balmont." According to the Slavist Robert Bird, the poet's Asian genealogy is probably spurious. Robert Bird, e-mail message to author, August 3, 2008.

52. K. M. Azadovskii and E.M. D'iakonova, *Balmont i Iaponiia* (Moscow: Nauka, 1991), 4–35.

53. G. M. Bongard-Levin, ed., *Ashvaghosha. Zhizn' Buddy. Kalidasa. Dramy* (Moscow: Khudozhestvennaia literatura, 1990), 10.

54. In ibid., 15.

55. The classic study is A. I. Shifman, *Lev Tolstoi i Vostok* (Moscow: Nauka, 1971). See also Paul Birukoff, *Tolstoi und der Orient* (Zürich: Rotapfel-verlag, 1925); Derk Bodde, *Tolstoy and China* (Princeton, NJ: Princeton University Press, 1950); Dmitrii Burba, *Tolstoi i Indiia: Prikosnovenie k sokrovennomu* (St. Petersburg: Izd-vo "Fen-shui tsentr," 2000).

56. Schwab, *Oriental Renaissance,* 451–452.

57. In Bodde, *Tolstoy and China,* 37.

58. In Susmita Sundaram, "*The Land of Thought:* India as Ideal and Image in Konstantin Balmont's Oeuvre" (PhD diss., Ohio State University, 2004), 36.

59. Konstantin Mochulsky, *Andrei Bely: His Life and Works* (Ann Arbor, MI: Ardis, 1977); J. D. Elsworth, *Andrei Bely* (Letchworth, UK: Bradda Books, 1972). See also Andrei Bely, *Vospominaniia ob Aleksandre Aleksandroviche Bloke* (Letchworth, UK: Bradda Books, 1964) and the brief autobiography he submitted to a literary encyclopedia: Andrei Bely, "Avtobiograficheskaia spravka," in S. A. Vengerov, ed., *Russkaia literatura XX veka,* vol. 2, pt. 3 (Moscow: Tovarishchesta Mir, 1916), 9–12. The memoir trilogy Bely wrote in later life is overly subjective: Andrei Bely, *Nachalo veka* (Moscow: Gosudarstvennoe izd-vo Khudozhestvennoi literatury, 1933); Bely, *Na rubezhe dvukh stoletii* (Moscow: Khudozhestvennaia literatura, 1989); Bely, *Mezhdu dvukh revoliutsii* (Leningrad: Izd-vo pisatelei v Leningrade, 1934).

60. Bely, "Avtobiograficheskaia spravka," 11.

61. V. S. Solov'ev, "Panmongolism," in Solov'ev, *Cheteniia o bogochelovechestve* (St. Petersburg: Khudozhestvennaia literatura, 1994), 392–393. For a more extensive discussion of Asia's place in Solov'ev's eschatology, see Schimmelpenninck van der Oye, *Toward the Rising Sun,* 82–86.

62. V. S. Solov'ev, "Kratkaia povest' ob Antikhriste," in *Chteniia*, 459–486.

63. Bely, *Vospominaniia*, 17.

64. In Vladimir Alexandrov, *Andrei Bely: The Major Symbolist Fiction* (Cambridge, MA: Harvard University Press, 1985), 72.

65. Andrei Bely, "Apokalipsis v russkoi poezii," *Vesy* (1905): no. 4, 12.

66. Bernice Glatzer Rosenthal, "Eschatology and the Appeal of Revolution: Merezhkovsky, Bely, Blok," *California Slavic Studies* 11 (1980): 110.

67. In I. V. Koretskaia, "K istorii 'griadushchikh gunnov' Briusova," in Z. S. Papernyi and E. A. Polotskaia, eds., *Dinamicheskaia poetika* (Moscow: Nauka, 1990), 182. Another study of the poet's attitudes to the war is Dany Savelli, "L'appel à la violence de Valerij Brjusov en 1904 et 1905," in Savelli, ed., *Faits et imaginaires de la guerre russo-japonaise*, Carnets de l'exotisme 5 (Paris: Kailash, 2005), 129–150.

68. Andrei Bely, *The Silver Dove*, trans. George Reavy (New York: Grove Press, 1974).

69. Ibid., 342; Pyman, *Russian Symbolism*, 256.

70. Bely, *Silver Dove*, 307–308.

71. Ibid., 303.

72. Andrei Bely, *Petersburg*, trans. Robert A. Maguire and John E. Malmsted (Bloomington: Indiana University Press, 1978).

73. Mochulsky, *Bely*, 147–148.

74. Bely, *Petersburg*, 238–239.

75. Ibid., 166.

76. Georges Nivat, "Du 'panmongolisme' au 'mouvement eurasien,'" in *Vers la fin du mythe russe* (Lausanne, Switzerland: L'Age d'homme, 1988), 131.

77. Italics in the original. A. V. Lavrov and John E. Malmsted, eds., *Andrei Belyi i Ivanov-Razumnik: Perepiska* (St. Petersburg: Atheneum-Feniks, 1998), 57.

78. Rosenthal, "Eschatology," 107.

79. In Mochulsky, *Bely*, 150.

80. The most detailed study in English is Stefani Hope Hoffman, "Scythianism: A Cultural Vision in Revolutionary Russia" (PhD thesis, Columbia University, 1957). See also Stefani Hoffman, "Scythian Theory and Literature," in Nils Åke Nilsson, ed., *Art, Society, Revolution: Russia, 1917–1921* (Stockholm: Almqvist & Wiksell International, 1979), 138–164, as well as N. V. Kuzina, "Ideologiia skifstva v russkoi obshchestvennoi mysli i literatury," in *Gosudarstvenno-patrioticheskaia ideologiia i problemy ee formirovaniia* (Smolensk, Russia: Izd-vo Voennoi akademii, 1997), 95–97.

81. Pushkin, *Sochinenii*, vol. 3, 390.

82. The most important works are listed in Koretskaia, "K istorii," 181.

83. K. D. Bal'mont, *Stikhotvoreniia* (Leningrad: Sovetskii pisatel', 1969), 150.

84. Andrzej Walicki, *Poland between East and West* (Cambridge, MA: Harvard Ukrainian Research Institute, 1994), 9–15. See also Kalinowska, *Between East and West*, 3.

85. Walicki, *Poland*, 11.

86. Nivat, "Panmongolisme," 135–136; Irene Masing-Delic, "Who Are the Tatars in Aleksandr Blok's *The Homeland*?" *Poetica* 35 (2003): 131–132.

87. Ettore Lo Gatto, "*Panmongolismo* di V. Solovëv, *I venienti unni* di V. Brjusov e *Gli Sciti* di A. Blok," in Morris Halle et al., eds., *For Roman Jakobson* (The Hague: Mouton, 1956), 300.

88. Alexandre Blok, *Selected Poems* (Oxford: Pergamon Press, 1972), 183.

89. In Alexandrov, *Bely,* 3.

90. Barry Scherr, "The Russo-Japanese War and the Russian Literary Imagination," in John W. Steinberg et al., eds., *The Russo-Japanese War in Global Perspective,* vol. 1 (Leiden, the Netherlands: Brill, 2005), 426.

91. In Rosenthal, "Eschatology," 106.

Conclusion

1. Mark Bassin, "Russia between Europe and Asia: The Ideological Construction of Geographical Space," *Slavic Review* 50 (1991): 6–7. See also W. H. Parker, "Europe: How Far?" *Geographical Journal* 126 (1960): 278–297.

2. Madariaga, *Russia in the Age of Catherine the Great,* 588.

3. Nikolai Karamzin, *Karamzin's Memoir on Ancient and Modern Russia,* ed. Richard Pipes (New York: Atheneum, 1974), 123–124.

4. P. Ia. Chaadaev, *Pol'noe sobranie sochinenii i izbrannye pis'ma* (Moscow: Nauka, 1991), vol. 1, 89.

5. Aleksandr Herzen, *My Past and Thoughts,* trans. Constance Garnett (London: Chatto & Windus, 1968), vol. 2, 516.

6. Andrzej Walicki, *The Slavophile Controversy,* trans. Hilda Andrews-Rusiecka (Notre Dame, IN: University of Notre Dame Press, 1989), 445–455.

7. Riasanovsky, "Asia through Russian Eyes," 9–10.

8. Nicholas Riasanovsky, *Russia and the West in the Teaching of the Slavophiles* (Cambridge, MA: Harvard University Press, 1952), 66–83, 215–218.

9. Chaadaev, *Sobranie sochinenii,* vol. 1, 531.

10. Spence, *The Chan's Great Continent,* 99–100. Ernst Rose, "China as a Symbol of Reaction in Germany," *Comparative Literature* 3 (1951): 57–65.

11. *Tol'kovyi slovar' russkogo iazyka,* 3rd ed., s.v. "Aziat," "azitatskii."

12. In Dany Savelli, "L'asiatisme dans la literature et la pensée russe de la fin du XIXème siècle au début du XXème siècle" (PhD thesis, Université de Lille III, 1994), 9.

13. Belinskii, *Sobranie sochinenii,* vol. 8, 660n19.

14. V. G. Belinskii, *Pol'noe sobranii sochinenii* (Moscow: Izd-vo Akademii nauk SSSR, 1954), vol. 5, 98.

15. Ibid., vol. 5, 99.

16. Ibid., vol. 5, 92–99.

17. V. A. Koshelov, "Istoriosofskaia oppozitsiia 'Zapad-Vostok' v tvorcheskom soznanii Pushkina," in Chelyshev, *Pushkin i mir Vostoka,* 157–170.

18. Olga Maiorova, "Intelligentsia Views of Asia in the 19th Century" (paper presented at the annual meeting of the American Association for the Advancement of Slavic Studies, Philadelphia, 2008).

19. V. I. Sakharov, ed., "Rossiia—zveno Vostoka s Zapadom," *Mezhdunarodnaia zhizn'* (1998), no. 4, http://www.ln.mid.ru/mg.nsf/ab07679503c75b73c325747f004 dodc2/4c09412e9f344444c32565e5002b7f52.

20. Emmanuel Sarkisyanz, "Russian Attitudes toward Asia," *Russian Review* 13 (1954): 246–247.

21. Susanna Soojung Lim, "Chinese Europe: Alexander Herzen and the Russian Image of China," *Intertexts* 10 (2006): 56–59.

22. In ibid., 58.

23. Sarkisyanz, "Russian Attitudes," 246–247.

24. Gertsen, *Sobranie sochinenii,* vol. 23, 175. Herzen's geography is not always consistent. On another occasion, he likened Russians to a more Occidental destructive force: "Our relations with the Europeans . . . bear some resemblance to those of the Germans and the Romans." Ibid., vol. 16, 169.

25. In P. M. Shastitko et al., eds., *Russko-indiiskie otnosheniia v XIX v.: Sbornik arkhivnykh dokumentov i materialov* (Moscow: Vostochnaia literatura, 1997), 8.

26. In Roger Conant, *The Political Poetry and Ideology of F. I. Tiutchev* (Ann Arbor, MI: Ardis, 1983), 34.

27. In Nicholas Riasanovsky, "Russia and Asia: Two Russian Views," *California Slavic Studies* 1 (1960): 179–180.

28. Ibid., 178–179.

29. N. M. Przheval'skii, "On the Current Situation in Eastern Turkestan," memorandum, June 6, 1877, Archive of the Russian Geographical Society, fund 13, inventory 1, file 26, 2.

30. A. N. Kuropatkin, "Dnevnik A. N. Kuropatkina," *Krasnyi Arkhiv* 2 (1922): 31.

31. Catherine II, *Sochineniia,* vol. 8, 17–20.

32. Zorin, *Kormia,* 110n1.

33. Kononov, *Istoriia izucheniia tiurkskikh iazykov,* 39n82.

34. I. Tolstoi and N. Kondakov, *Russkiia drevnosti v pamiatnikakh iskusstva,* vol. 2 (St. Petersburg: A. Benke, 1889); Véronique Schiltz, *La redécouverte de l'or des Scythes* (Paris: Gallimard, 1991), 56–99.

35. Karamzin, *Istoriia gosudarstva rossiiskago,* vol. 5, 223.

36. V. V. Stasov, "Proiskhozhdenie russkikh bylin," *Vestnik Evropy* 3 (1868): 597.

37. V. V. Stasov, *Sobranie sochinenii,* vol. 1 (St. Petersburg: Tipografiia M. M. Stasiulevicha, 1894), 197–212. See also V. Stasov, *Slavianskii i vostochnyi ornament po rukopisiam drevniago i novago vremeni* (St. Petersburg: Kartograficheskoe zavedenie A. A. Il'ina, 1887).

38. Vladimir Karenin, *Vladimir Stasov: Ocherk ego zhizni i deiatel'nosti* (Leningrad: Mysl', 1927), 315–318. One notable exception was in Alfred Rambaud, *Russie épique: Etude sur les chansons héroïques de la Russie* (Paris: Maisonneuve, 1876), 163–193.

39. E. Viollet-le-Duc, *L'art russe: Ses origins, ses éléments constitutifs, son apogée, son avenir* (Paris: A. Morel, 1877), 58.

40. Nicolas Berdiaev, *Constantin Leont'ev,* trans. Hélène Iswolski (Paris: Berg International, 1993), 49.

41. Konstantin Leontiev, *The Egyptian Dove*, trans. George Reavy (New York: Weybright and Talley, 1969).

42. In Savelli, "L'asiatisme," 46.

43. K. Leont'ev, *Vostok, Rossiia i Slavianstvo* (Moscow: Eksmo, 2007), 606–607.

44. Ibid., 147.

45. Ibid., 636.

46. For more details about Prince Ukhtomskii, see the relevant chapter in Schimmelpenninck van der Oye, *Toward the Rising Sun*, 42–60.

47. Prince Hesper Ookhtomsky [Ukhtomskii], *Travels in the East of Nicholas II, Emperor of Russia, When Cesarewitch*, vol. 2 (Westminster, England: A. Constable, 1900), 287.

48. vol. Ibid., 32.

49. vol. Ibid., 446.

50. Until recently, the most thorough study of the Eurasian movement was Otto Böss, *Die Lehre der Eurasier: Ein Beitrag zur russischen Ideengeschichte des 20. Jahrhunderts* (Wiesbaden, Germany: Otto Harrassowitz, 1961). In recent years, however, there has been a renewed interest in the movement, especially in Russia. Two useful monographs are Margarita Georgievna Vandalovskaia, *Istoricheskaia nauka rossiiskoi emigratsii: "Evraziiskii soblazn"* (Moscow: Pamiatniki istoricheskii mysli, 1997), and O. D. Volkogonova, *Obraz Rossii v filosofii Russkogo zarubezhia* (Moscow: ROSSPEN, 1998). For an account that takes the story up to the present, see Marlène Laruelle, *Russian Eurasianism: An Ideology of Empire*, trans. Mischa Gabowitsch (Baltimore: Johns Hopkins University Press, 2008).

51. P. N. Savitskii et al., eds., *Exodus to the East: Foreboding and Events, an Affirmation of the Eurasians*, trans. Ilya Vinkovetsky (Idylwild, CA: Charles Schlacks Jr., 1996).

52. G. V. Vernadsky, *Nachertanie russkoi istorii: Chast' pervaia* (Prague: Evraziiskoe knigoizdatelstvo, 1927), and *Opyt istorii Evrazii s poloviny VI veka do nastoiashchego vremeni* (Berlin: Izdania evraziitsev, 1934).

53. Vernadsky, *A History of Russia* (New Haven, CT: Yale University Press, 1961), 10.

54. Vernadsky, *Nachertanie*, 12–13, 18.

55. Ryszard Paradowski, "The Eurasian Idea and Leo Gumilëv's Scientific Ideology," *Canadian Slavonic Papers* 41 (1999): 3.

56. Charles J. Halperin, "Russia and the Steppe: George Vernadsky and Eurasianism," *Forschungen zur osteuropäischen Geschichte* 36 (1985): 185.

57. See his spirited critique of Eurasianism in Paul Miliukov, "Eurasianism and Europeanism in Russian history," *Festschrift Th. G. Masaryk zum 80. Geburtstag*, vol. 1 (Bonn: Friedrich Cohen, 1930), 225–36.

58. Michael Ignatieff, "Can Russia Return to Europe?" *Harper's Magazine*, April 1992, 15.

59. Among such anthologies are L. N. Novikova and I. N. Sizemskaia, eds., *Rossiia mezhdu Evropoi i Aziei: Evraziiskii soblazn* (Moscow: Nauka, 1993); I. A. Isaev, ed., *Puti Evrazii: Russkaia intelligentsiia i sudby Rossii* (Moscow: Russkaia kniga, 1992);

N. N. Tolstoi, ed., *Russkii uzel evraziistva: Vostok v russkoi mysli* (Moscow: Belovode, 1997).

60. John B. Dunlop, *The Rise of Russia and the Fall of the Soviet Empire* (Princeton, NJ: Princeton University Press, 1993), 292.

61. Interview with Nikita Mikhailkov, *Rossiiskaia gazeta,* December 14, 1991.

62. Gennady Zyuganov, *My Russia: The Political Autobiography of Gennady Zyuganov* (Armonk, NY: M. E. Sharpe, 1997), 71–72.

63. Andrei Vladimirovich Novikov, "Brak v kommunalke: Zametki o sovremennom evraziistve," *Zvezda* (1998): no. 2, 230.

64. G. A. Ziuganov, *Geografiia pobedy: Osnovy rossiiskoi geopolitiki* (Moscow: n.p., 1997), 182–183.

65. Solov'ev, *Chteniia,* 385.

66. Jean-Jacques Waardenburg, *L'Islam dans le mirroir de l'Occident* (Paris: Mouton, 1963), 315.

67. V. I. Lenin, *Pol'noe sobranie sochinenii* (Moscow: Gosudarstvennoe izd-vo politicheskoi literatury, 1962), 196.

68. Igor Ivanov, "Dipkurer," *Nezavisimaia gazeta,* January 2000, 1.

INDEX

Academy of Arts, Russian, 77, 78, 82
Academy of Sciences, Russian, 33, 35–
36, 37, 38, 42, 97, 105, 110, 113, 114,
137, 139, 145, 149, 150, 151, 153, 157,
158, 159, 179, 184, 185, 187, 188, 189,
191, 193, 195, 196, 197, 198
Africa, 6, 39, 64, 65, 225
Agafangel (Solov'ev), Archimandrite,
135
Alexander I, Emperor, 65, 95, 99, 102,
111, 121, 153, 154, 155, 156, 157, 159
Alexander III, Emperor, 104, 175, 190,
209, 234
Aliab'ev, Aleksandr, 201–202
Arabic (language), 25, 34, 38, 39, 42,
57, 66, 71, 96, 98, 100, 101, 102, 104,
105, 112, 114, 117, 118, 120, 121, 122,
128, 130, 131, 132, 136, 138, 157, 158,
159, 160, 161, 162, 164, 168, 174, 176,
186, 198, 202
Armenian (language), 104, 117, 168, 176
Asian Department of the Russian Foreign Ministry, 98, 144, 145
Asian Museum, 159, 174, 186, 195, 197
Asianism, 234
aziatchina, 226

Balakirev, Mily, 202, 203, 204, 205
Balmont, Konstantin, 211, 212–213, 214,
220

Banzarov, Dorzhi, 9, 117
Bärendt, Johann-Gottfried, 97
Barthold, Vasilii, 13, 34, 43, 150, 168,
186, 189
Batu Khan, 18, 20, 94
Bayer, Gottlieb-Siegfried, 34, 35, 49
Belinskii, Vissarion, 58, 63, 70, 71, 146,
148, 226–227, 228
Bely, Andrei, 213–223
  Petersburg, 218–219, 220
  Silver Dove, The, 217–218, 220
Berezin, Il'ia, 106, 113, 118, 119
Bestuzhev, Aleksandr, 8, 70, 91, 146,
191, 202
Bichurin, Nikita. *See* Iakinf, Father
Blaramberg, Lieutenant General Ivan,
229
Blok, Aleksandr, 4, 196, 216, 220, 221–
222
Bobrovnikov, Aleksei, 117, 128
Boldyrev, Aleksei, 97
Borodin, Aleksandr, 199–200, 203,
204–209, 213, 223
  In the Steppes of Central Asia, 199–
  200
  Prince Igor, 200, 205–210
Brambeus, Baron. *See* Senkovskii, Osip
Bratishchev, Vasilii, 58–59
Briusov, Valerii, 211, 213, 216–217
Buddhism, 49, 51, 113, 135, 139, 140, 151,